Informatik – Fachberichte

Band 11: Methoden der Informatik für Rechnerunterstütztes Entwerfen und Konstruieren, GI-Fachtagung, München, 1977. Herausgegeben von R. Gnatz und K. Samelson. VIII, 327 Seiten. 1977.

Band 12: Programmiersprachen. 5. Fachtagung der GI, Braunschweig, 1978. Herausgegeben von Klaus Alber. VI, 179 Seiten. 1978.

Band 13: W. Steinmüller, L. Ermer, W. Schimmel: Datenschutz bei riskanten Systemen. X, 244 Seiten. 1978.

Band 14: Datenbanken in Rechnernetzen mit Kleinrechnern. Fachtagung der GI, Karlsruhe, 1978. Herausgegeben von W. Stucky und E. Holler. X, 198 Seiten. 1978.

Band 15: Organisation von Rechenzentren. Workshop der Gesellschaft für Informatik, Göttingen, 1977. Herausgegeben von D. Wall. X, 310 Seiten. 1978.

Band 16: GI-8. Jahrestagung, Proceedings 1978. Herausgegeben von S. Schindler und W. K. Giloi. VI, 394 Seiten. 1978.

Band 17: Bildverarbeitung und Mustererkennung. DAGM Symposium, Oberpfaffenhofen, 1978. Herausgegeben von E. Triendl. XIII, 385 Seiten. 1978.

Band 18: Virtuelle Maschinen. Nachbildung und Vervielfachung maschinenorientierter Schnittstellen. GI-Arbeitsseminar, München 1979. Herausgegeben von H. J. Siegert. X, 231 Seiten. 1979.

Band 19: GI - 9. Jahrestagung. Herausgegeben von K. H. Böhling und P. P. Spies. XIII, 690 Seiten. 1979.

Band 20: Angewandte Szenenanalyse. DAGM Symposium, Karlsruhe 1979. Herausgegeben von J. Foith. XIII, 362 Seiten. 1979.

Band 21: Formale Modelle für Informationssysteme. Fachtagung der GI, Tutzing 1979. Herausgegeben von H. C. Mayr und B. E. Meyer. VI, 265 Seiten. 1979.

Band 22: Kommunikation in verteilten Systemen. Workshop der Gesellschaft für Informatik e. V.. Herausgegeben von S. Schindler und J. Schröder. VIII, 338 Seiten. 1979.

Band 23: K.-H. Hauer, Portable Methodenmonitoren. XI, 209 Seiten. 1980.

Band 24: N. Ryska, S. Herda: Technischer Datenschutz. Kryptographische Verfahren in der Datenverarbeitung. V, 401 Seiten. 1980.

Band 25: Programmiersprachen und Programmierentwicklung. 6. Fachtagung, Darmstadt, 1980. Herausgegeben von H.-J. Hoffmann. IV, 236 Seiten. 1980.

Band 26: F. Gaffal, Datenverarbeitung im Hochschulbereich der USA. Stand und Entwicklungstendenzen. IX, 199 Seiten. 1980.

Band 27: GI-NTG Fachtagung, Struktur und Betrieb von Rechensystemen. Kiel, März 1980. Herausgegeben von G. Zimmermann. IX, 286 Seiten. 1980.

Band 28: Online-Systeme im Finanz- und Rechnungswesen. Anwendergespräch, Berlin, April 1980. Herausgegeben von P. Stahlknecht. X, 547 Seiten. 1980.

Band 29: Erzeugung und Analyse von Bildern und Strukturen. DGaO – DAGM Tagung, Essen, Mai 1980. Herausgegeben von S. J. Pöppl und H. Platzer. VII, 215 Seiten. 1980.

Informatik-Fachberichte

Herausgegeben von W. Brauer
im Auftrag der Gesellschaft für Informatik (GI)

29

Erzeugung und Analyse von Bildern und Strukturen

DGaO – DAGM Tagung
Essen, 27. – 31. Mai 1980

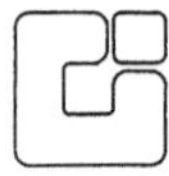

Herausgegeben von S. J. Pöppl und H. Platzer

Springer-Verlag
Berlin Heidelberg New York 1980

Herausgeber

Dr.-Ing. S. J. Pöppl
Institut für Medizinische Informatik und
Systemforschung (MEDIS) der
Gesellschaft für Strahlen- und Umweltforschung m.b.H.
Arabellastraße 4/III
8000 München 81

Dipl.-Ing. H. Platzer
Institut für Informationstechnik der TU München,
Lehrstuhl für Nachrichtentechnik
Arcisstraße 21
8000 München 2

AMS Subject Classifications (1979): 68-00, 68-02,
CR Subject Classifications (1974): 3.63

ISBN-13: 978-3-540-10130-7   e-ISBN-13: 978-3-642-67687-1
DOI: 10.1007/978-3-642-67687-1

<u>Vorwort</u>

Der vorliegende Tagungsband enthält die meisten Vorträge der gemeinsamen Tagung
der Deutschen Gesellschaft für Angewandte Optik (DGaO) und der Deutschen Arbeits-
gemeinschaft für Musterkennung (DAGM).

Die Beziehungen der beiden Organisationen sind folgendermaßen:
Während die DGaO eine traditionsreiche wissenschaftliche Gesellschaft ist, stellt
die DAGM einen problemorientierten Dachverband folgender wissenschaftlicher
Gesellschaften dar:
- Deutsche Gesellschaft für angewandte Optik (DGaO)
- Deutsche Gesellschaft für Nuklearmedizin (DGNM)
- Deutsche Gesellschaft für Ortung und Navigation (DGON)
- Deutsche Gesellschaft für Medizinische Dokumentation,
  Informatik und Statistik (GMDS)
- Deutsche Gesellschaft für Angewandte Datenverarbeitung und Automation
  in der Medizin (GADAM)
- Gesellschaft für Informatik (GI)
- Nachrichtentechnische Gesellschaft (NTG).

Die DAGM fördert den Erfahrungsaustausch auf dem Gebiet der Mustererkennung und
ist Mitglied der International Association for Pattern Recognition (IAPR).

Die verantwortungsvolle Arbeit des Programmausschusses wurde unter Vorsitz von
Prof. Hertel, Berlin, von folgenden Herren geleistet:
Dr. Dreher, Bonn; Prof. Fercher, Essen; Dr. Kossel, Wetzlar; Prof. Lanzl,
Oberpfaffenhofen; Dipl.Ing. Platzer, München; Dr.-Ing. Pöppl, München;
Dr. Pretschner, Hannover; Prof. Schmidt, Oberkochen; Dr. Triendl, Oberpfaffenhofen;
Dr. Walter, München; Prof. Winkler, Berlin.

Unser ganz besonderer Dank gilt dem Schriftführer der Deutschen Gesellschaft für
Angewandte Optik, Herrn Preuß, Wetzlar, insbesondere für seine Mitarbeit im
Programmausschuß und für die Drucklegung des gemeinsamen Tagungsprogramms.

Wir wünschen allen Teilnehmern, daß diese gemeinsame Tagung für sie ein
interessanter und fruchtbarer Erfahrungsaustausch wird.

A.F. Fercher   S.J. Pöppl
                                H. Platzer

Tagungsleiter   Die Herausgeber

INHALTSVERZEICHNIS

BILDVERARBEITUNG

POSTER - SESSION

LASER SPECKLE AND RELATED PHENOMENA
CURRENT DEVELOPMENTS

G Parry
Royal Signals and Radar Establishment
Malvern, Worcs
England

SUMMARY

Although the intense activity and revival of interest in speckle phenomena which
occurred in the late sixties and early seventies has to some extent subsided, there
are still a substantial number of papers appearing in the main optics journals. A
large number of these have been concerned with further developments of existing or
proposed applications of speckle to problems in engineering and astronomy. But papers
have also been published reporting new experimental results and new theories.

One new theory (which will be discussed in detail) is concerned with the statistics
of a particular class of non-Gaussian speckle patterns which have been found to arise
when laser light is scattered from refractive index variations in turbulent fluids
[1,2]. This theory is important because it is based on a reconsideration of the simple
random walk model frequently used to derive statistical properties of intensity variations in speckle patterns. According to the random walk model the field at a point
in a speckle pattern is considered to be the sum of a number of randomly phased contributions from the random medium or surface. It is usually stated that when a large
number of scatterers contribute, the central limit theorem leads to a prediction of
negative exponentially distributed intensity variations. Jakeman and Pusey have
pointed out [2] that this need not always be true. If the number of scatterers fluc-
tuates in a particular way then in the limit of a large mean number of scatterers the
intensity should be a K-distribution. This distribution has been observed in a number
of experiments [2].

Other non-Gaussian speckle patterns - those produced by a small number of scatterers
or from polychromatic light sources have also been studied extensively recently in
order to determine the feasibility of deducing surface roughness parameters from the
speckle statistics (see for example [3-6]). Experiments have established that in both
cases the statistical properties of the intensity are sensitive to surface parameters,
but unfortunately, all the methods proposed appear to be rather complicated and depen-
dent on the surface model used. So it is not yet clear whether these techniques will
be of use to engineers.

Somewhat in contrast to this the technique of stellar speckle interferometry has
already become well accepted in astronomy. A large number of measurements have been

made successfully determining binary star separations and extensive developments of
on-line processing systems have been carried out. Many of these are reported in
reference [7].

References

1.   G. Parry, P. N. Pusey, E. Jakeman and J. G. McWhirter, Opt.Commun. $\underline{22}$, 195(1977).

2.   E. Jakeman and P. N. Pusey, Phys.Rev.Lett. $\underline{40}$, 546 (1978).

3.   J. Ohtsubo, and T. Asakura, Opt.Commun. $\underline{25}$, 315 (1978).

4.   P. J. Chandley and H. M. Escamilla, Opt.Commun. $\underline{29}$, 151 (1979).

5.   K. Nakagawa and T. Asakura, Appl.Opt. $\underline{18}$, 3725 (1979).

6.   M. Giglio, S Musazzi and U. Perini, Opt.Commun. $\underline{28}$, 166 (1979).

7.   J. Davis and W. J. Tango, E. "High Angular Resolution Stellar Interferometry"
      I.A.U Colloquium No.50). (Published by Chatterton Astronomy Dept., School of
      Physics, University of Sydney, NSW 2006, Australia).

PHOTOACOUSTIC AND PHOTOTHERMAL SPECTROSCOPY
FOR SURFACE AND POWDER ANALYSIS

Per-Erik Nordal and Svein Otto Kanstad
Central Institute for Industrial Research
P.O.Box 350 Blindern, Oslo 3 - Norway

A specimen subjected to pulsewise illumination, may experience pulsating temperature
excursions in its surface layers. The amplitude of those temperature fluctuations
depends on the absorption spectrum of the sample, and may be measured <u>photoacoustically</u>
through pressure waves (sound) created in a chamber enclosing the specimen, or <u>photo-
thermally</u> by observing similar pulsations in the thermal reradiation. Those techniques
offer new and highly sensitive means for the analysis of condensed media.

1. Introduction

The last decade has seen a considerable expansion of analytical tools available for
characterization of solids and liquids. While reflecting a general trend towards
higher degrees of technological sophistication, this development is also propelled by
the potential for scientific and technical impact in widely diverse fields of study,
e.g.: the relationship between surface microstructure and mechanical or electrical
properties, heterogeneous catalysis, corrosion, protective coatings on metallic and
non-metallic surfaces, photo-induced processes, annealing, etc.

Photoacoustic and photothermal methods, to be reviewed below, are still in a state
of rapid development, but appear to provide entirely new analytic possibilities,
particularly relating to relaxed requirements on sample preparation. Most signifi-
cantly, studies can be performed on realistic samples under conditions that closely
approximate those of practical interest. For instance, powdered material and rough
surfaces, which often pose problems in optical spectroscopy by traditional reflection
and transmission techniques, generally lend themselves well to photoacoustic and
photothermal studies.

2. Photoacoustic spectroscopy

2.1 Basic principles

When light impinges on a solid or liquid sample, some of the radiation is reflected
or scattered, the remainder bieng absorbed on penetration into the solid or liquid
medium. The absorbed radiation may be reradiated (fluorescence), or dissipated to

heat. If the incident radiation is made to oscillate periodically, e.g., by means of a rotating chopper wheel, the heat deposition will be periodic, and the temperature in the illuminated portion of the sample will oscillate at the chopping frequency. Temperature excursions in the sample depend in a complicated manner[1] upon power and chopping frequency f of the incident radiation, on material properties such as specific heat c, thermal conductivity k, density ρ and optical absorption coefficient $\alpha(\lambda)$, and on macro- and micro-geometry of the sample. Theory[1] shows that, for a broad class of experimental conditions, the amplitude of the temperature oscillations will be approximately given by

$$\delta T = \frac{\mu^2 I_o}{4\,k}\,\alpha(\lambda), \tag{1}$$

where I_o is the radiation intensity at wavelength λ and $\mu = (k/\pi f\rho c)^{\frac{1}{2}}$ is the thermal diffusion length of the sample material. Detection of such oscillating temperature components, which may typically be in the range 10^{-6} to 10^{-1} K, can be made in several ways: Most commonly, a device of the type shown in Fig. 1 is used, where the sample is enclosed in a small chamber, being illuminated through a window. Temperature oscillations at the sample surface cause periodic heating of the adjoining air layer, and pressure oscillations in the chamber gas volume result. If the incident radiation is chopped at an audio frequency, the sound thus generated can be simply detected by means of a microphone. Similarly, the phase lag between the illumination pulses and the sound waves depend on the mode, strength and place of absorption within the cell, and can be used to discriminate against spurious absorption in windows, walls etc.

Alternatively, an experimental set-up as shown in Fig. 2 can be used. Absorption of radiation causes heating and distortion of the sample, and the distortion is sensed by a piezoelectric transducer directly or indirectly contacting the specimen. PZT detection has been demonstrated both with a continuous, periodically chopped beam of radiation, and with short, intense laser pulses. In the latter case, using time-delayed gated detection[2], interesting possibilities arise for discrimination against

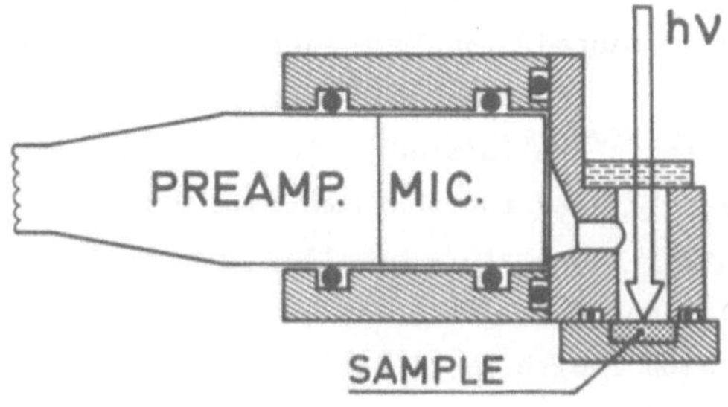

Fig. 1 Spectrophone chamber with microphone.

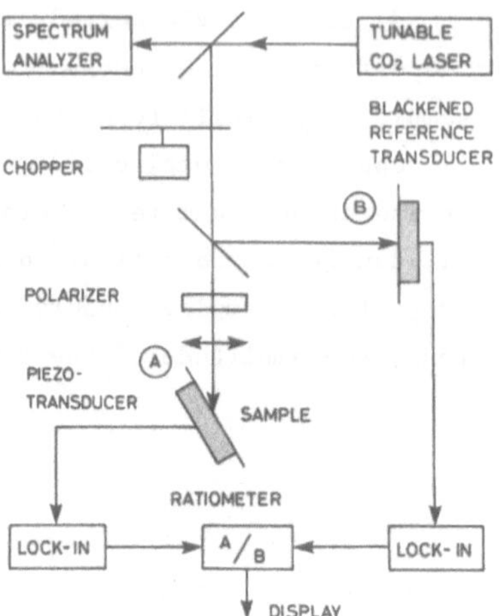

Fig. 2 Experimental arrangement in photoacoustic spectroscopy, with piezoelectric detection and real-time compensation for source variations.

scattered radiation, for specific localization of the volume being probed, and for detection in liquid media.

2.2 Surface and subsurface structure (non-spectral studies)

Consider a situation where the incident radiation, which may be spectrally broad, is focused to a narrow region on a surface. If the (chopped) beam is scanned across the sample, the presence of voids, inclusions or cracks manifest themselves as changes in photoacoustic signal amplitude and phase when the beam strikes the defect. This may be ascribed to scattering and/or light trapping effects that change the heat deposition, or to changes in local thermal transport properties within the sample. By scanning a focused laser beam across the surface of a silicon-nitride ceramic material inside a photoacoustic cell, Wong et al.[3] obtained the results shown in Fig. 3, where the presence of cracks gives rise to sharply increased photoacoustic signals. These data correlated with defects visible under the microscope, but in addition exhibited structure that could not be detected visually. Indeed, subsurface defects may be revealed photoacoustically, even in cases where the incident radiation does not penetrate to the depth where defects are located. Theory[1] shows that, for an opaque homogeneous material where $\mu \gg \alpha(\lambda)$, the photoacoustic signal will be proportional to $Q \sim (k\rho c)^{-\frac{1}{2}} f^{-1}$. Consequently, temperature oscillations at the sample surface are influenced by the thermal properties of the medium inside, to a depth approximately equal to the thermal diffusion length μ. Clearly, μ may vary widely for different materials, and can be adjusted within certain limits by proper choice of chopping frequency f. Typically, f is in the range 20-10000 Hz. At f = 100 Hz, μ = 50 μm for a poor thermal conductor such as glass, while $\mu \simeq 0.6$ mm for aluminium. Recent work[4,5]

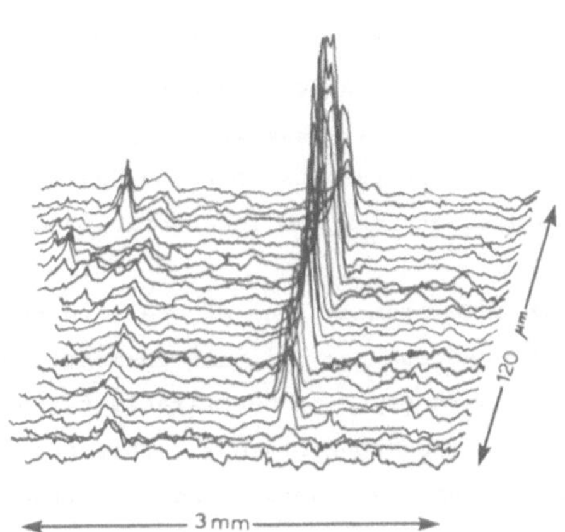

Fig. 3   Photoacoustic X-Y scan of silicon-nitride ceramic surface with cracks, using
a focused laser beam and a spectrophone (Wong et al., Appl. Phys. Lett. 32
538 (1978), courtesy R.L. Thomas, Wayne State University, Mich., USA).

has shown that probing depths of 1.5-2 times the thermal diffusion length can be
obtained by measuring the photoacoustic phase rather than amplitude.

An obvious limitation to the lateral resolution obtainable by such probing methods,
is the minimum spot size attainable for the illuminating radiation. Depending on
optical wavelength and beam quality, typical practical limits lie in the region from
below 1 μm to $\simeq$ 20 μm diameter when laser sources are used. Scanning techniques of
the type described here, termed SPAM (scanning photoacoustic microscopy) or PAM (photoacoustic microscopy), have been applied to ceramic materials[3,6,7], metals[4,5], semiconductors[8,9], and integrated circuits[10]. Rosencwaig[11] has recently discussed the
subject in some detail, with particular attention to possibilities that can be envis-
aged using piezoelectric detection instead of air microphones. A technique has also
been demonstrated[12], whereby a mode locked Nd:YAG laser was used to generate high
frequency acoustic waves from an illuminated spot on the sample. The acoustic waves
at 810 MHz were coupled to a transducer via an index matching fluid, and photoacoustic
images were formed by mechanically scanning the sample in a raster pattern.

2.3 Photoacoustic spectroscopy

When the wavelength of the incident radiation is made to vary through a certain spectral region, the temperature oscillations at the specimen's surface are given by
Eq. (1) (assuming that $\mu \ll \alpha(\lambda)$). Hence the photoacoustic signal $Q \sim \delta T/f^{\frac{1}{2}}$ depends
linearly on the absorption coefficient $\alpha(\lambda)$. A photoacoustic spectrum therefore will
be identical to the true absorption spectrum of the material[13,14] as recorded by conventional means. In practice, it is necessary to compensate for temporal and spectral
intensity variations of the incident radiation. Efficient suppression of noise in the

microphone signal is essential, too. Lock-in amplifiers are commonly used, as indicated in Fig. 2, to detect only those signal components that are coherent with the chopped illuminating radiation. - In Fig. 4 are shown spectra of lobster shell, recorded by Mackenthun et al.[15]. Their results serve in several manners to illustrate how photoacoustic spectroscopy presents new and interesting analytic possibilities:

i) The spectra were recorded *in situ* from a piece of shell in its natural state, without prior preparation that might destroy the original chemical composition. Those clearly defined spectra contrast strongly with the largely featureless ones that can be obtained by conventional reflectance spectroscopy. This stems in large measure from the fact that only radiation that is absorbed and converted to heat contributes to the photoacoustic signal; masking and distortions by scattered light is avoided.

ii) Selective probing of layers at different depths below the surface is possible, by proper choice of chopping frequency and lock-in detector phase setting: Through the diffusion length μ, phase lags associated with thermal transport from deeper layers can be used for discrimination against contributions from surface absorption, and *vice versa*. Clearly, the lobster shell pigments absorbing in the blue are near the surface, while those absorbing in the red are located in deeper layers.

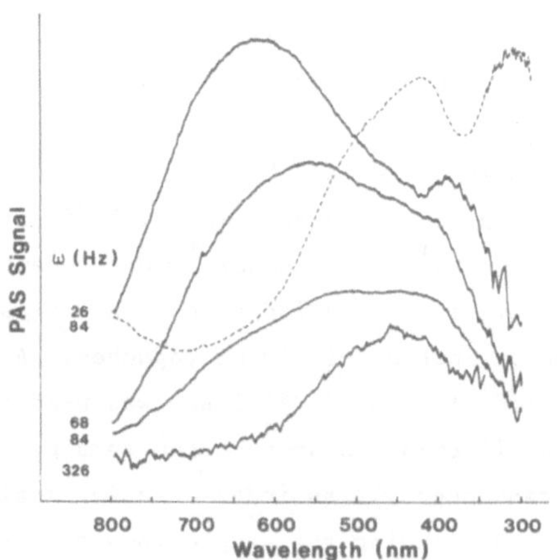

Fig. 4   Photoacoustic absorption spectra of native lobster shell as a function of modulation frequency ω (indicated with each spectrum) and phase φ. The interior spectra (———) were recorded with φ selected for maximum discrimination against the surface signal. In this case, decreasing ω allows response from deeper within the sample. The surface region spectra (————) were recorded with φ selected for maximum response from the surface. This selection of phase angle restricts the response to the surface-region and results in a spectrum which is essentially independent of ω. (Mackenthun et al., Nature <u>279</u> 265 (1979), courtesy T.A. Moore, Arizona State University, USA).

Absorbed energy that is reradiated as fluorescence or is consumed in photochemical processes does not heat the sample surface, and little or no photoacoustic signal results. Comparison with observations by traditional spectroscopic techniques that do not discriminate between loss mechanisms, thereby yields insight into decay pathways and energy conversion following optical excitation. Investigations of this general type have already been made on many different systems, and include non-radiative decay in solids[16-18], photochemical processes[13,19,20], fluorescence quantum yields in liquid media[21-23] and photovoltaic energy conversion efficiency[24]. Another remarkable attribute of photoacoustic techniques is the high sensitivity that can be attained, even with comparatively simple apparatus. Rosencwaig & Hall[25] have recorded ultraviolet spectra of adsorbed material on thin layer chromatography plates, demonstrating that material can be identified directly on the plates in quantities down to monolayer thickness. Using a CO_2 laser, we have recorded infrared spectra of nanogram to microgram amounts of particulate samples. Low intensities of conventional IR sources have limited work in this spectral region. However, at the relatively low resolutions typically required for solid and liquid phase spectroscopy, it seems possible to cover the important 2-20 μm region with sources based on special thermal radiator/monochromator combinations, as has recently been partially demonstrated[26].

For sensitive detection of material adsorbed on metal surfaces in particular, photoacoustic reflection-absorption spectroscopy (PARAS) has been developed[27]. Obliquely incident radiation polarized in the plane of incidence may be absorbed in a surface film; flipping of polarization discriminates against spurious absorption. Signals are recorded with samples either in a spectrophone or bonded to a piezoelectric transducer (Fig.2). A spectrum of aluminium oxide on aluminium as recorded by the latter method is shown in Fig. 5. Estimates show that sensitivities attainable by PARAS are

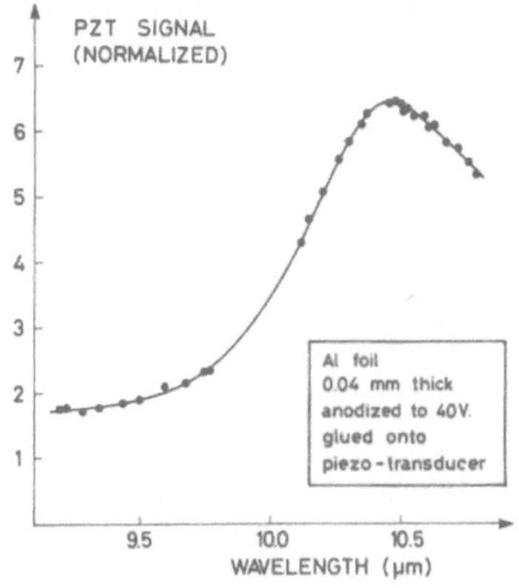

Fig. 5   Spectrum of a 580 Å thick aluminium oxide film on a polished aluminium foil, recorded by means of the piezoelectric PARAS scheme of Fig. 2, using a $^{12}CO_2$ laser.   Pulsing frequency f = 39 Hz.

very high and should extend to coverages of 1/100 monolayer or below, but experimental verification of this must await careful studies under vacuum. PARAS techniques circumvent requirements on sample polishing etc. set by current multireflection techniques; the use of a single reflection simplifies experimental design and gives spectra that are less prone to systematic distortions.

3. Photothermal radiometry

Related means of recording small temperature rises in samples illuminated for spectroscopy include, among others, the superconducting transition in a lead film[28], cryogenic germanium thermometers[29], thermistors[30] and the "mirage" effect[31]. Alternatively, consider Stefan-Boltzmann's law, $W = \sigma T^4$. The incremental radiant emittance δW caused by a temperature difference δT of a blackbody is

$$\delta W = 4\sigma T^3 \delta T, \tag{2}$$

$\sigma = 5.67 \cdot 10^{-12} \mathrm{Wcm}^{-2} \mathrm{K}^{-4}$ is the Stefan-Boltzmann constant. By including a spectrally varying emission coefficient $\varepsilon(\lambda) < 1$, a similar expression is obtained that is approximately valid for bodies that are not ideally black. If for δT we substitute Eq. (1), δW is seen to vary linearly with the absorption coefficient $\alpha(\lambda)$ when the body is heated by pulsewise irradiation. By recording δW vs. λ with a thermal (usually infrared) detector, contact-free spectroscopy can be performed, as shown in Fig. 6. The technique, which we have termed photothermal radiometry (PTR)[32], shares many advantages with the photoacoustic techniques described above, such as making possible direct spectroscopic analysis of opaque or strongly scattering objects, or studies of properties that affect thermal transport in given samples, including surface and subsurface defects. Important attributes of PTR are the absence of physical contact with

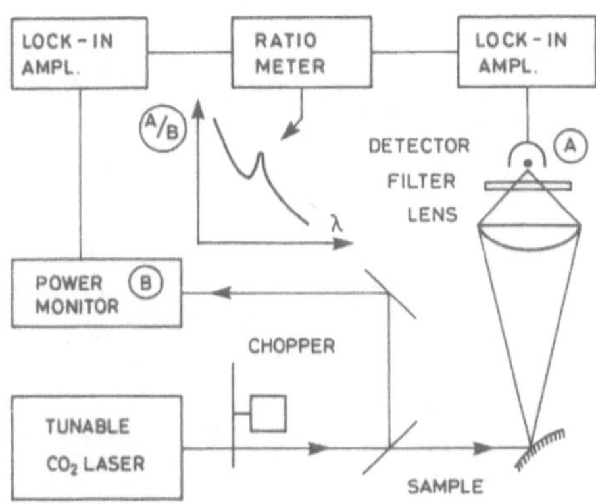

Fig. 6 Experimental arrangement in photothermal radiometry.

the sample, and the ability of the emitted radiation to penetrate suitably chosen optical materials. Samples in hostile environments or in inaccessible locations may be studied, an example being objects at high temperatures. For instance, spectra of powdered K_2SO_4 at temperatures from 295 K to 942 K are shown in Fig. 7, as obtained using a $\sim$ 100 mW CO_2 laser source. Recent work[33], however, has shown that high-quality spectra in the visible region can be recorded with a conventional Xe lamp/ monochromator combination of $\sim$ 1 mW power. Interesting possibilities for technical improvement exist in combining pulsed, tunable sources with gating techniques[32].

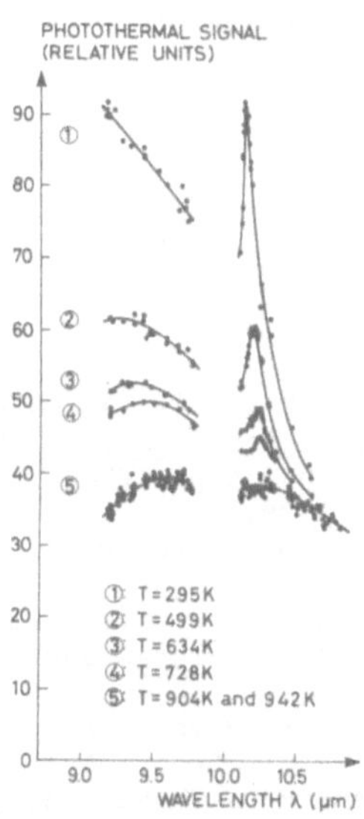

Fig. 7 PTR spectra of powdered K_2SO_4. Pulsing frequency f = 77 Hz.

4. Discussion

Despite their novelty, photoacoustic techniques have already reached a high level of diversification and sophistication. Photothermal radiometry, on the other hand, is still in need of conceptual and technical developments. Some interesting applications deserve particular emphasis: Photoacoustic methods employing piezoelectric detection have proven quite successful in measurements of (bulk and surface) absorption in optical components[34,35] and pure liquids[36]; this may otherwise be exceedingly difficult. In stimulated Raman scattering, the vibrational energy deposition in a medium is encouraged by another collinear laser beam tuned to the Raman line. The enhanced excitation can be detected photoacoustically, and has led to sensitive spectral measurements in gases[37] and liquids[38]. Multiplex techniques such as Fourier transform spectroscopy have been shown to improve the signal-to-noise ratios in PAS[39]. Moreover, spectral patterns of a surface showing the distribution of various molecular species might be recorded by photoacoustic or photothermal microscopy, using specifically chosen wavelengths for illumination.

5. Conclusion

By their simplicity, robustness and high sensitivity, photoacoustic and photothermal techniques appear to transcend the traditional confines of optical spectroscopy, with implicit opportunities for radically new applications in the study of condensed matter. Our current presentation can only offer a glimpse of this largely uncharted new territory, which ought to attract pioneering spirits from widely diverse fields of science and industry.

References

1. A. Rosencwaig and A. Gersho, J. Appl. Phys. 47 64 (1976).
2. A.C. Tam and C.K.N. Patel, Appl. Phys. Lett. 35 843 (1979).
3. Y.H. Wong, R.L. Thomas and G.F. Hawkins, Appl. Phys. Lett 32 538 (1978).
4. G. Busse, Appl. Phys. Lett. 35 759 (1979).
5. R.L. Thomas, J.J. Pouch, Y.H. Wong, L.D. Favro, P.K. Kuo and A. Rosencwaig, J. Appl. Phys. (in press).
6. Y.H. Wong, R.L. Thomas and J.J. Pouch, Appl. Phys. Lett. 35 368 (1979).
7. J.J. Pouch, R.L. Thomas, Y.H. Wong, J. Schuldies and J. Srinivasan, J. Opt.Soc.Am. (in press).
8. J.F. McClelland and R.N. Kniseley, Appl. Phys. Lett. 35 585 (1979).
9. R.A. McFarlane and L.D. Hess, Appl. Phys. Lett. 36 137 (1980).
10. L.D. Favro, P.K. Kuo, J.J. Pouch, and R.L. Thomas, Appl. Phys. Lett. (in press).
11. A. Rosencwaig, Internat. Laboratory 9 Sept./Oct. 1979, p. 37.
12. H.K. Wickramasinghe, R.C. Bray, V. Jipson, C.F. Quate and J.R. Salcedo, Appl. Phys. Lett. 33 923 (1978).
13. A. Rosencwaig, Anal. Chemistry 47 592A (1975).
14. A.A. King and G.F. Kirkbright, Lab. Practice 25 377 (1976).
15. M.L. Mackenthun, R.D. Tom and T.A. Moore, Nature 279 265 (1979).
16. J.C. Murphy and L.C. Aamodt, J. Appl. Phys. 48 3502 (1977).
17. L.D. Merkle and R.C. Powell, Chem. Phys. Lett. 46 303 (1977).
18. R.G. Peterson and R.C. Powell, Chem. Phys. Lett. 53 366 (1978).
19. K. Kaya, W.R. Harshbarger and M.B. Robin, J. Chem. Phys. 60 4231 (1974).
20. R.C. Gray and A.J. Bard, Anal. Chemistry 50 1262 (1978).
21. M.J. Adams, J.G. Highfield and G.F. Kirkbright, Anal. Chemistry 49 1850 (1977).
22. W. Lahmann and H.J. Ludewig, Chem. Phys. Lett. 45 177 (1977).
23. M.G. Rockley and K.M. Waugh, Chem. Phys. Lett. 54 597 (1978).
24. D. Cahen, Appl. Phys. Lett. 33 810 (1978).
25. A. Rosencwaig and S.S. Hall, Anal. Chemistry 47 548 (1975).
26. M.J.D. Low and G.A. Parodi, Applied Spectroscopy 34 76 (1980).
27. S.O. Kanstad and P.-E. Nordal, Appl. Surface Sci. (in press).
28. M.B. Robin, J. Luminesc. 12/13 131 (1976).
29. R.B. Bailey and P.L. Richards, Proc. Second Internat. Conf. on Infrared Phys., ETH Zurich, Switzerland, March 5-9, 1979 (E. Affolter and F. Kneubühl, Ed.).
30. G.H. Brilmyer, A. Fujishima, K.S.V. Santhanam and A.J. Bard, Anal. Chemistry 49 2057 (1977).
31. A.C. Boccara, D. Fournier and J. Badoz, Appl. Phys. Lett. 36 130 (1980).

32. P.-E. Nordal and S.O. Kanstad, Physica Scripta $\underline{20}$ 659 (1979).
33. P.-E. Nordal and S.O. Kanstad, (to be published).
34. A. Hordvik and H. Schlossberg, Appl. Opt. $\underline{16}$ 101 (1977).
35. M.J. Adams, B.C. Beadle, G.F. Kirkbright and K.R. Menon, Appl. Spectroscopy $\underline{32}$ 430 (1978).
36. C.K.N. Patel and A.C. Tam, Appl. Phys. Lett. $\underline{34}$ 467 (1979).
37. J.J. Barrett and M.J. Berry, Appl. Phys. Lett. $\underline{34}$ 144 (1979).
38. C.K.N. Patel and A.C. Tam, Appl. Phys. Lett. $\underline{34}$ 760 (1979).
39. M.M. Farrow, R.K. Burnham and E.M. Eyring, Appl. Phys. Lett. $\underline{33}$ 735 (1978).

- o -

<u>OPTOAKUSTISCHE BILDABTASTUNG</u>

G. Busse
Zentrale Wissenschaftliche Einrichtung Physik
Hochschule der Bundeswehr München
8014 Neubiberg, Germany F.R.

<u>Zusammenfassung:</u> Optoakustische Bilder zeigen optische oder thermische Strukturen von Festkörpern. Die Besonderheit dieser Methode liegt darin, daß mit optischer Strahlung die lokalen thermischen Eigenschaften undurchsichtiger Proben in variablen Tiefen gemessen werden können.

Der optoakustische Effekt - die Erzeugung von Schall durch intensitätsmodulierte Strahlung - ist insbesondere in seinen Festkörperanwendungen erst seit wenigen Jahren wieder populär, aber der Effekt als solcher wurde vor viel längerer Zeit entdeckt: Als A.G. Bell 1880 Untersuchungen zur Nachrichtenübertragung mit Licht durchführte (ein Thema, das ebenfalls wieder modern ist), fand er, daß die Modulation des Lichtes direkt als Schall hörbar wurde, wenn es auf absorbierende Festkörper fiel /1/.

Das Prinzip des optoakustischen Effekts am Festkörper soll Abb. 1 erläutern. Die zu untersuchende Probe befindet sich in einer abgeschlossenen Zelle, die mit einem möglichst transparenten Gas gefüllt ist. Durch ein Fenster fällt intensitätsmoduliertes Licht auf die absorbierende Probe, die dabei periodisch erwärmt wird. Die Temperatur an der Probenoberfläche ändert

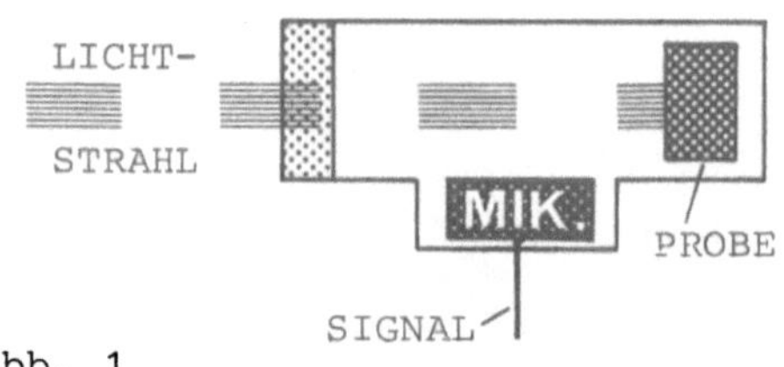

Abb. 1

sich mit der Modulationsfrequenz des Lichts und führt zu einer Druckmodulation des eingeschlossenen Gases. Dieser Schall wird als optoakustisches Signal z.B. mit einem Mikrofon nachgewiesen. Das Signal ist proportional zu der Leistung des einfallenden Lichtes. Beispielsweise ist die als breitbandiger thermischer Strahlungsdetektor gebräuchliche Golayzelle eine optoakustische Zelle mit nahezu schwarzem Absorber, bei der die Druckmodulation optisch (und nicht mit einem Mikrofon) gemessen wird.

Das Signal hängt weiterhin ab von den optischen und thermischen Eigenschaften der Probe (Wärmeleitfähigkeit, spezifische Wärme, thermische Ankopplung an das Gas). Die Zusammenhänge wurden erstmals von Rosencwaig und Gersho /2/ dargelegt.

Schon Bell untersuchte an Festkörpern, Flüssigkeiten und Gasen, wie die Lautstärke des erzeugten Schalls von der Farbe des Lichts abhängt. Im Unterschied zu optischer Absorptionsspektroskopie, bei der man die noch hinter der Probe vorhandenen Photonen nachweist, hat diese optoakustische Spektroskopie den Vorteil, daß nur die in der Probe absorbierten und schließlich in Wärme umgesetzten Photonen ein Signal ergeben. Der Vorteil ist besonders deutlich bei Proben mit sehr großen oder sehr kleinen Absorptionskoeffizienten und bei pulverförmigen oder stark streuenden Substanzen.

Nach Bells erfolgreichen Versuchen folgte aber eine heute unverständliche Unterbrechung von 6 Jahrzehnten, dann wurden praktisch nur Gase untersucht, und erst 1973 wurden die Arbeiten an Festkörpern von Rosencwaig fortgesetzt /3,4/, der die mittlerweile parallel verwendete Bezeichnung "photoakustisch" einführte, um die ansonsten naheliegende Verwechslung mit "akusto-optisch" auszuschließen.

1. Eindringtiefe bei optoakustischen Untersuchungen

Eine Besonderheit des optoakustischen Effekts an Festkörpern liegt darin, daß man mit der Modulationsfrequenz die Schichtdicke der Probenoberfläche vorgeben kann, die zum Signal beiträgt. Damit wird tiefenaufgelöste Spektroskopie ermöglicht /4/. Bei optoakustischer Bildabtastung wird ein enges Lichtbündel, z.B. ein fokussierter Laserstrahl, über die Probe bewegt und das ortsabhängige Signal als Bild dargestellt. Die Tiefe, bis zu der man hierbei in die Probe "hineinsehen" kann, ist variabel; es lassen sich also Bilder verschiedener Tiefenschichten aufnehmen. Im folgenden werden theoretische Grundlagen kurz zusammengestellt, bevor in den nächsten beiden Kapiteln Bilderzeugung und Anwendungsbeispiele beschrieben werden.

1.1. Bedeutung der thermischen Eindringtiefe.

Am einfachsten läßt sich dieser Begriff an einem bekannten makroskopischen System beschreiben: Die auf die Erde einwirkende Strahlung der Sonne ist durch die Erdrotation mit der Frequenz ω moduliert. An der Erdoberfläche ist das Zeitverhalten der Temperatur T näherungsweise darstellbar durch

$$T(t) = T_o + T_1 \sin\omega t$$

wobei T_o den zeitlichen Mittelwert und T_1 die Amplitude bezeichnen. Das Temperaturverhalten unter der Oberfläche wird durch die Wärmeleitungsgleichung beschrieben, die eine Diffusionsgleichung ist. Die Strahlungs-

modulation bewirkt also einen periodischen Wärmetransport, und die
Temperatur in der Tiefe x ist /5/

$$T(x,t) = T_o + T_1\, e^{-x/\mu}\, \sin\,(\omega t - \tfrac{x}{\mu}),$$

wobei μ die durch die Gleichung

$$\mu = \sqrt{\frac{2k}{\omega C}}$$

gegebene thermische Eindringtiefe ist (k = Wärmeleitfähigkeit, c = Wär-
mekapazität pro Volumen).

Die Temperaturmodulation setzt sich also von der Oberfläche aus
als thermische Welle nach innen fort, die aber so stark gedämpft ist,
daß die Eindringtiefe μ nur etwa 16% der Wellenlänge beträgt. Für die
Tageswelle in der Erdoberfläche ist μ = 16 cm /5/. Entsprechend folgt
für Aluminium und 20 Hz Modulationsfrequenz eine thermische Eindringtiefe von μ = 1,2 mm.

Das optoakustische Signal entsteht im wesentlichen in der Schichtdicke μ der Probe /2/. Beim optoakustischen Bildabtasten wird das lokale Signal als Funktion des Probenortes dargestellt. Strukturen innerhalb der Probe können abgebildet werden, wenn sie in dieser Schichtdicke liegen. Mit optischer Strahlung kann man also Bilder aus Tiefen
bekommen, die im Fall undurchsichtiger Proben weit jenseits der optischen Eindringtiefe liegen.

1.2. Phasen- und Betragsabbildung

Das optoakustische Signal als thermisches Antwortverhalten des Fest-
körpers auf eine einwirkende modulierte Strahlung läßt sich als Vek-
tor in der komplexen Ebene darstellen, also durch den Betrag der
Wechselspannung am Mikrofonausgang und durch die Phasenverschiebung
zwischen diesem optoakustischen Signal und der Intensität des modulierten Lichtes. Zum Abbilden läßt sich jede der beiden Größen verwenden; im allgemeinen ist jedoch das "Phasenwinkelbild" der Probe vom
"Betragsbild" verschieden, wie man anschaulich einsehen kann: Wird die
Leistung der verwendeten Strahlungsquelle verändert, so ändert sich
zwar der Betrag des Signals, nicht aber die Phase. Wenn eine lokale
Veränderung der optischen Eigenschaften der Probe eine Signalverän-
derung bewirkt, die auch durch Änderung der Laserleistung entstanden
sein kann, dann ist diese optische Struktur nur im Betragsbild zu erkennen. Der Phasenwinkel, den man ja als wärmeleitungsabhängigen Lauf-
zeiteffekt verstehen kann, hängt hingegen mehr von den thermischen
Eigenschaften der Probe ab. Kürzlich wurde demonstriert, daß das Phasenwinkelbild auch in Gegenwart optischer Strukturen nur die thermischen Strukturen aufweist /6/.

Aber auch bei Proben ohne optische Struktur liefern Phasenwinkel

und Betrag des Signals unterschiedliche Informationen. Das soll am
Beispiel eines keilförmigen homogenen Metallstücks diskutiert werden,
über das der abtastende Lichtstrahl bewegt wird. In dem dickeren Pro-
benteil wird die Wärme, die mit der modulierten optischen Einstrahlung
in der Oberfläche erzeugt wird, auf ein größeres Volumen verteilt. Darum ist dort das Signal kleiner. Die Umverteilung der Wärme erfordert
eine umso längere Zeit, je dicker die Probe ist, deswegen ist bei großen Schichtdicken die benötigte Zeit länger als die Modulationsdauer,
die Amplitude verringert sich dann mit wachsender Probendicke nicht
mehr. Dieser Zusammenhang wurde nach der Rosencwaig-Gersho Theorie /2/
berechnet. Das Ergebnis /7/ ist in Abb. 2 dargestellt: Die Kurve A
zeigt den Betrag des Signals als Funktion der Schichtdicke von Alumi-

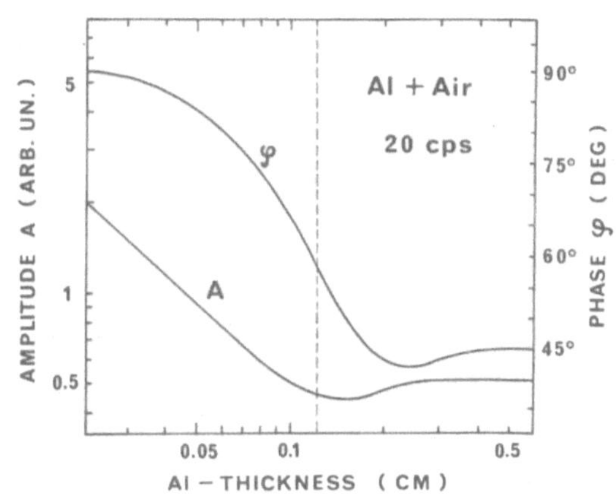

Abb. 2 /7/

nium, wenn die einfallende optische Strahlung mit 20 Hz moduliert wird. Das Minimum vor dem
Erreichen des waagerechten
Teils kommt davon, daß die Wär-
meausbreitung wellenartig erfolgt und daß schwache gegen-
phasige Anteile zum Signal bei-
tragen. Ein eindeutiger Zusammenhang mit der Schichtdicke
ist in dem Bereich der Kurve
gegeben, der oberhalb des waag-
rechten Teils liegt. Für Anwendungen ist interessant, daß
sich dieser Bereich bei der
Kurve, die den Verlauf des Phasenwinkels φ zeigt, bis zu einer
Schichtdicke erstreckt, die beinahe um den Faktor 2 größer ist. Die
Tiefenreichweiten sind also beim optoakustischen Abbilden davon abhängig, ob man den Betrag oder den Phasenwinkel des Signals benutzt.
Zwischen beiden Reichweiten (ca. 1 mm und 2 mm bei 20 Hz) liegt die
durch die gestrichelte vertikale Linie angedeutete thermische Eindringtiefe µ.

2. Optoakustische Bildabtastung

Das Prinzip ist einfach: Statt wie bei üblicher optoakustischer Spektroskopie das Signal einer Probe als Funktion der Lichtwellenlänge
oder der Modulationsfrequenz zu untersuchen, wird bei der optoakustischen Abbildung die Probe mit einem gebündelten intensitätsmodulierten
Lichtstrahl abgetastet, das Signal (Phase oder Betrag) wird als Funk-

tion der Probenkoordinaten x und y geeignet dargestellt.

In Abb. 3 ist ein entsprechender apparativer Aufbau gezeigt.
Als Strahlungsquelle wird ein modulierter Dauerstrichlaser verwendet
mit Emission im sichtbaren oder infraroten Spektralbereich. Der Strahl
wird zeilenweise über die Probe geführt ähnlich der Bildabtastbewegung
beim Fernsehgerät, nur ist die Bewegung hier so langsam, daß mechanisch drehbare spannungsgesteuerte Spiegel ("Scanner" SCX und SCY)
eingesetzt werden können, jeweils einer für die beiden Koordinaten
x und y der Probe.

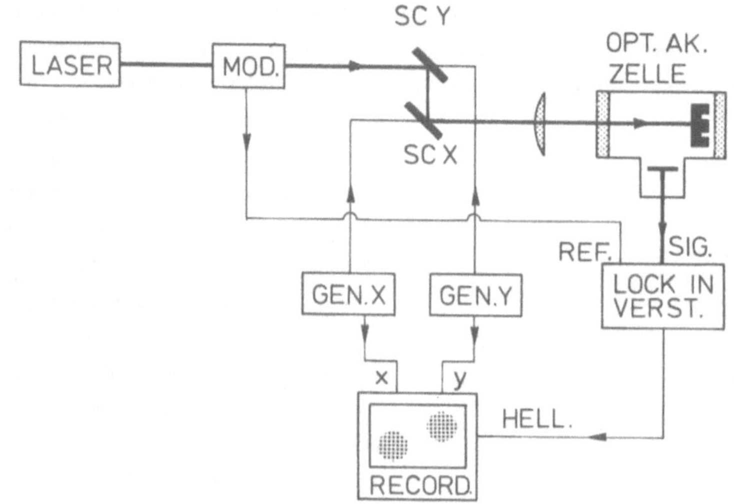

Abb. 3

Der Laserstrahl wird dann auf die Probe in der optoakustischen Zelle
fokussiert. Das Mikrofonsignal wird nach phasenempfindlicher Gleich-
richtung und Verstärkung zur Helligkeitssteuerung eines Schreibers
(RECORD.) oder Oszillographen verwendet, dessen Auslenkung synchron
zur Spiegelbewegung von Sägezahngeneratoren (GEN X und GEN Y) gesteuert wird. So wird das optoakustische Signal (Betrag oder Phasenwinkel)
ortsabhängig z.B. als Halbtonbild dargestellt. Für eine mehr quantitative Auswertung des Signals ist eine reliefartige Darstellung geeigneter.

Statt das optoakustische Signal über die Erwärmung und Druckerhö-
hung des Zellengases zu registrieren, wurde bei einem Teil der Experimente durch mechanische Ankopplung der Probe an eine Piezokeramik ein
direkter und störschallunempfindlicher Signalnachweis ermöglicht /8,9/.
Die Zeitdauer für die Aufnahme eines Bildes hängt von der Laserleistung
und der Probe ab, typischerweise beträgt sie einige Minuten.

3. Beispiele optoakustischer Bilder

Optoakustische Abbildungen können die lokalen optischen und thermischen Eigenschaften einer Probe darstellen, wobei letztere die Wärmeleitung von der Probe zum Gas einschließen.

Die Vielzahl möglicher Beispiele muß zunächst reduziert werden. Wenn die Probe nur bezüglich ihrer optischen Eigenschaften eine Struktur aufweist, ist das optoakustische Bild gleich dem optischen, die neue Abbildungsart liefert dann keine neue Information. Entsprechende Beispiele brauchen also nicht gezeigt zu werden.

Interessanter sind Proben, deren optische und thermische Eigenschaften nicht ortsabhängig sind, die aber geometrische Oberflächenstrukturen haben, z.B. Risse oder Stufen. Der Wärmekontakt zum Gas ist an solchen Stellen wegen der größeren Oberfläche verbessert (wie bei den Kühlrippen eines Motors). Optoakustische Bildabtastung wurde verwendet zum Nachweis von Rissen in Keramikmaterial /10/ und von Stufen auf Aluminium /11/. Aber auch hier ließe sich dieselbe Information mit konventionellen optischen Methoden gewinnen.

3.1. Strukturen in undurchsichtigem Material.

Die zusätzliche Information durch optoakustische Abbildungen ist am besten an solchen Proben zu demonstrieren, die unergiebig sind für optische Untersuchungen, z.B. Proben mit einer ebenen und für die Laserstrahlung praktisch undurchlässigen Oberfläche, die im Bereich der optischen Eindringtiefe homogen ist und unter der Strukturen verborgen sind. In diesem Fall ist die optoakustische Abbildung praktisch eine lokale dynamische Messung der Wärmeableitung in das Probeninnere, und hierbei ist - wie oben beschrieben - die Tiefenreichweite etwa durch die thermische Eindringtiefe μ gegeben.

Eine solche Probe ist in Abb. 4 gezeigt: Unter einer undurchsichtigen Graphitschicht, die auf Metall aufgetragen ist, ist stellenweise Material mit schlechter Wärmeleitung versteckt. Die Abbildung mit dem Betrag des Signals zeigt in Reliefdarstellung diese Stellen deutlich

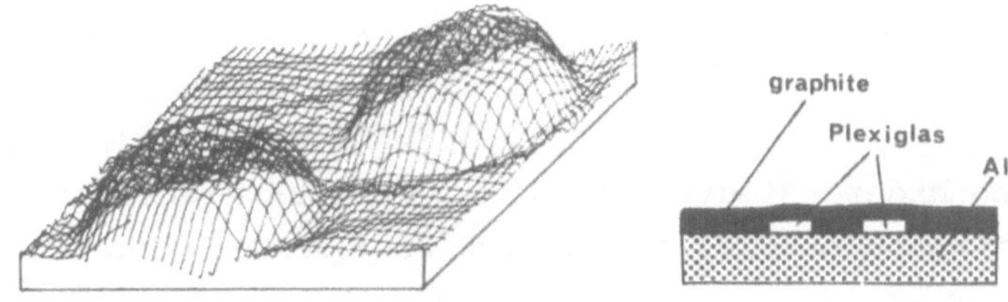

Abb. 4   /11/

als Erhöhung, weil die Wärmeableitung in das darunterliegende Metall
gestört ist bzw. weil die thermische Eindringtiefe bei 37 Hz durch die
Plexiglasscheibchen stellenweise reduziert wird /11/. Ein solches Bild
hätte man auch erhalten, wenn die Graphitschicht an diesen Stellen
schlechten mechanischen Kontakt zur metallischen Unterlage gehabt hätte; die optoakustische Abbildung eignet sich also zur Untersuchung der
Oberflächenhaftung von aufgetragenen Materialschichten, z.B. Farben,
oder auch zur Abbildung von Schichtdickenänderungen.

In ähnlicher Weise wurden auch Strukturen im Inneren von Keramik-
proben untersucht /12/.

Der Vorteil gegenüber optischen Abbildungen ist umso größer, je
größer die thermische Eindringtiefe im Vergleich zur optischen Eindringtiefe ist. Metalle sind also besonders gut geeignet. In eine Alu-
miniumprobe wurden senkrecht zur Oberfläche von der nicht beleuchteten
Seite her 2 Löcher von 3 mm Durchmesser und 4 mm Abstand gebohrt; das
eine Loch endete 0,2 mm unter der vom Laserstrahl abgetasteten Oberfläche, das andere 0,4 mm. Nach dem Bohren wurde die Oberfläche nochmals
geschliffen und poliert, so daß die Löcher optisch nicht mehr zu lo-
kalisieren waren. Bei zwei Frequenzen (18 Hz und 180 Hz) wurde dann
die Probe optoakustisch abgebildet, und zwar jeweils mit Betrag A und
Phase φ des optoakustischen Signals, das in diesem Fall mit Piezokeramik nachgewiesen wurde /9/. Das Ergebnis ist in Abb. 5 als Halbtonbild
gezeigt. Bei 18 Hz liegen beide Bohrungen innerhalb der Tiefenreichweite beider Abbildungsverfahren. Für die Betragsabbildung ist die-
se Reichweite aber geringer (s. Abb. 2), darum ist bei 180 Hz auf dem Betragsbild das tiefer liegende Loch kaum noch zu sehen, während das mit dem Phasenwinkel erhaltene Bild noch beide Löcher zeigt (der Streifen am linken Bildrand ist ein elektronischer Effekt). Die Möglichkeiten tie-fenaufgelöster Abbildung in Me-tallen durch Bildsubtraktion wer-den hier besonders deutlich.

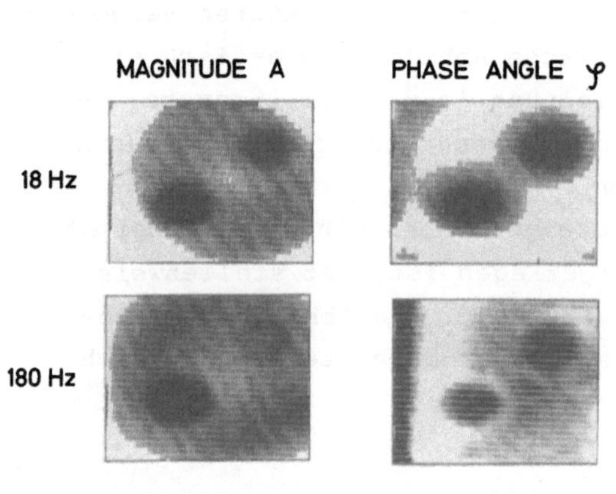

Abb. 5

Durch eine andere Bildverarbeitung, nämlich Signalgradientenabbil-
dung durch Ortsmodulation, lassen sich bestimmte Strukturrichtungen
im optoakustischen Bild unterdrücken /11/.

3.2. Auflösungsvermögen

Bei der Erzeugung optischer Bilder mit einem abtastenden Laserstrahl
ist das Auflösungsvermögen bestimmt durch die Fokusgröße: Die Bild-
struktur ist die Faltung der wirklichen optischen Struktur mit der Intensitätsverteilung im Fokus, das Bild eines kleinen Punktes hat daher
den Brennfleckdurchmesser.

Bei optoakustischen Bildern thermischer Strukturen muß zusätzlich
berücksichtigt werden, daß die thermische Eindringtiefe μ etwa den
Probenbereich angibt, der zum Signal beiträgt. Wäre der Fokus punktför-
mig, so würde beim Abtasten mit dem Laserstrahl auf der "Innenseite"
einer homogenen Probe eine Halbkugel mitgeführt, die die Auflösung bestimmt. Bei nichtpunktförmigem Fokus müßte man entsprechend ähnlich
dem Huygensschen Prinzip eine Faltung der Intensitätsfunktion mit solchen Halbkugeln durchführen, deren Radius etwa die thermische Eindringtiefe ist. Sind Fokusdurchmesser und thermische Eindringtiefe sehr
verschieden, so bestimmt der größere Wert die Auflösung.

Die bisher gezeigten Beispiele wurden mit 10,6 µm Wellenlänge erhalten, die Fokusgröße war 0,3 mm, während die Eindringtiefe in Aluminium bei 20 Hz 1,2 mm beträgt (s. Fig. 2). Eine Auflösungsverbesse-
rung ist in dieser Situation nicht durch Verkleinerung des Brennflecks,
sondern durch eine Erhöhung der Modulationsfrequenz zu erreichen, weil
sich die thermische Eindringtiefe mit $f^{-1/2}$ ändert. Das ist in Abb. 6
an dem Phasenwinkelbild von 2 Löchern mit 1 mm Durchmesser gezeigt,

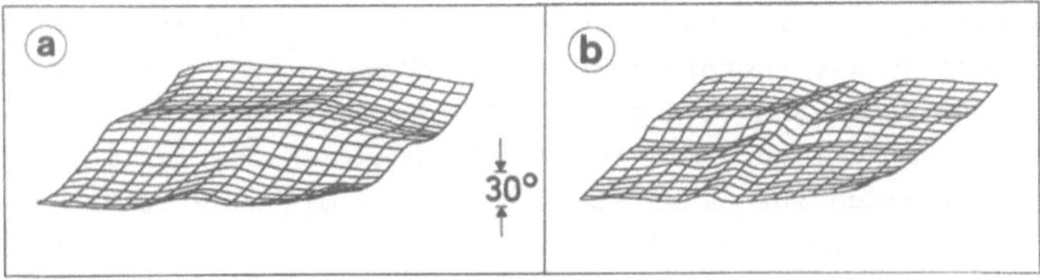

Abb. 6

die in Tiefen von ca. 0,8 mm und 0,3 mm unterhalb der Metalloberfläche
und senkrecht zueinander verlaufen. In dieser Reliefdarstellung ist
gut zu sehen, wie die Erhöhung der Modulationsfrequenz von 36 Hz (a)
auf 288 Hz (b) das Auflösungsvermögen erhöht /9/.

3.3. Optoakustische Mikroskopie.

Dieses Beispiel beweist, daß man optoakustische Mikroskopie - die Abbildung von Strukturen der thermischen Probeneigenschaften im µm Bereich - nicht einfach mit einem entsprechend verkleinerten Brennfleck durchführen kann, sondern nur bei gleichzeitiger Verringerung der thermischen Eindringtiefe bzw. der Erhöhung der Modulationsfrequenz /8/. Zur Verbesserung des Signal-Rausch-Verhältnisses bei höheren Frequenzen war der differentielle Helmholtz-Resonator vorgeschlagen worden, der eine Signalerhöhung und Rauschverminderung erlaubt /13/; die mit Mikrofonen erreichbaren Frequenzen sind aber trotzdem zu tief für optoakustische Mikroskopie. Dieses Problem kann durch die oben erwähnte Ankopplung der Probe an Piezokeramik verringert werden. Bei ersten optoakustischen thermischen Abbildungen mikroskopischer Strukturen wurde ein Auflösungsvermögen von etwa 8 µm erreicht/6/. In Abb. 7 ist das Phasenwinkelbild einer integrierten Schaltung gezeigt. Es handelt sich um eine Übersichtsaufnahme, die Rasterung ist für die Auflösung zu grob. Der Probenbereich ist 300 µm x 250 µm groß.

Abb. 7

4. Ausblick

Bei Verwendung des optoakustischen Effekts können nicht nur optische, sondern auch lokale thermische Eigenschaften in bzw. unter der Oberfläche einer Probe als Bild dargestellt werden, wobei Tiefenreichweite und thermische Auflösung mit der Modulationsfrequenz variiert werden können. Zusätzlich zur akustischen Abbildung mit elastischen hochfrequenten Wellen, die in den letzten Jahren bis zur akustischen Mikroskopie entwickelt wurde /13,14/, gibt es damit eine weitere nicht-optische Abbildungsart. Die physikalischen Eigenschaften der Probe, die den beiden Verfahren zugrunde liegen, sind verschieden und damit auch die beim Abbilden erhaltene Information. Ein Vergleich wird dadurch erschwert, daß beide Methoden noch neu sind; die optoakustische Abbildungstechnik scheint derzeit noch fast am Anfang zu stehen.
Es ist aber schon jetzt klar zu erkennen, daß beide Methoden Informationen liefern, die jenseits der Möglichkeiten optischer Abbildungstechnik liegen.

Literatur

/1/   A.G. Bell: Proc. Am. Assoc. Adv. Sci. $\underline{29}$, 115 (1880)

/2/   A. Rosencwaig, A. Gersho: J. Appl. Phys. $\underline{47}$, 64 (1976)

/3/   A. Rosencwaig: Opt. Comm. $\underline{7}$, 305 (1973)

/4/   A. Rosencwaig: Adv. in Electronics and Electron Physics $\underline{46}$, 207 (1978)

/5/   S. Flügge: Lehrbuch der theoret. Physik, Bd. I (Springer-Verlag 1961)

/6/   A. Rosencwaig, G. Busse: Appl. Phys. Lett. (im Druck)

/7/   G. Busse: Appl. Phys. Lett. $\underline{35}$, 759 (1979)

/8/   A. Rosencwaig: Am. Lab. $\underline{11}$, 39 (1979)

/9/   G. Busse, A. Rosencwaig: Appl. Phys. Lett. (im Druck)

/10/   Y.H. Wong, R.L. Thomas, G.F. Hawkins: Appl. Phys. Lett. $\underline{32}$, 538 (1978)

/11/   G. Busse: Proc. Topical Meeting on Photoacoustic Spectroscopy, Ames/Iowa, USA (1979)

       G. Busse, A. Ograbeck: J. Appl. Phys. (im Druck)

/12/   Y.H. Wong, R.L. Thomas, J.J. Pouch: Appl. Phys. Lett. $\underline{35}$, 368 (1979)

/13/   G. Busse, D. Herböck: Appl. Opt. $\underline{18}$, 3959 (1979)

<u>THE EXPANSION OF AN OPTICAL SIGNAL</u>

<u>INTO A DISCRETE SET OF GAUSSIAN BEAMS</u>

Martin J. Bastiaans

Technische Hogeschool Eindhoven, Afdeling der Elektrotechniek,
Postbus 513, 5600 MB Eindhoven, The Netherlands

<u>Abstract</u>

It is shown how an optical signal can be expanded in Gaussian beams.
The expansion is essentially the one suggested by Gabor in 1946, when
he proposed to expand a signal into a discrete set of properly shifted
and modulated Gaussian elementary signals; determining the expansion
coefficients, however, seemed difficult, since the set of Gaussian elementary signals is not orthogonal. A set of functions is described,
wnich is bi-orthonormal to the set of Gaussian elementary signals; this
bi-orthonormality property allows an easy determination of the expansion
coefficients.

1. Introduction

In 1946 Dennis Gabor suggested the expansion of a signal into a discrete set of Gaussian elementary signals[1]. In the case of Fourier optics,
where the signals are functions of two space variables, Gabor's sugges-
tion results in the expansion of the signal into a discrete set of
Gaussian beams. Since the Gaussian elementary signals that Gabor used
are not orthogonal, there seemed to be no direct way to determine the
expansion coefficients[1,2]. In this paper we shall show, however, that
such a way does exist and that the expansion coefficients can be expressed as integral transforms of the signal.

We present the entire analysis for one-dimensional time signals only;
the extension to two-dimensional optical signals is straightforward.
For time signals Gabor's expansion can be considered as a signal representation in terms of musical notes that appear at discrete moments and
that have discrete pitches. Such a representation resembles the musical
score of the time signal, or, to put it in more general terms, it is
something like the discrete version of what might be called the momen-
tary frequency spectrum of the signal.

The mathematics of Gabor's signal expansion is outlined in Section 2.
The main results of this paper will be derived in Section 3, in which
we show a way to determine the expansion coefficients. Finally, in Section 4, we shall represent some simple signals by means of their Gabor
expansions.

2. Gabor's signal expansion

We shall define the Gaussian elementary signal by

$$g(t) = \left(\frac{\sqrt{2}}{T}\right)^{\frac{1}{2}} \exp\left[-\pi\left(\frac{t}{T}\right)^2\right] ; \tag{1}$$

the constant $(\sqrt{2}/T)^{\frac{1}{2}}$ has been included in order to have

$$\int |g(t)|^2 dt = 1 . \tag{2}$$

(Unless otherwise stated, all integrations and summations in this paper extend from $-\infty$ to $+\infty$). With this Gaussian elementary signal Gabor's expansion of the signal $\phi(t)$ reads[1]

$$\phi(t) = \sum_{mn} a_{mn} g(t-mT) \exp[in\Omega t] , \tag{3}$$

where Ω and T satisfy the relation

$$\Omega T = 2\pi . \tag{4}$$

Eq. (3) represents the signal as a superposition of a set of Gaussian elementary signals that are shifted over discrete distances mT and that are modulated with discrete angular frequencies $n\Omega$.

The extension to two-dimensional optical signals in the plane $z=0$, say, is evident: the cross section of a Gaussian beam in the plane $z=0$ will be defined by

$$g(x,y) = \left(\frac{\sqrt{2}}{X}\right)^{\frac{1}{2}} \left(\frac{\sqrt{2}}{Y}\right)^{\frac{1}{2}} \exp\left[-\pi\left\{\left(\frac{x}{X}\right)^2 + \left(\frac{y}{Y}\right)^2\right\}\right] , \tag{5}$$

and Gabor's signal expansion takes the form

$$\phi(x,y) = \sum_{mnpq} a_{mnpq} g(x-mX, y-pY) \exp[i(nUx+qVy)] . \tag{6}$$

Eq. (6) represents an optical signal in the plane $z=0$ as a superposition of a set of Gaussian beams that pass through the points $(x=mX, y=pY, z=0)$ and have directions that are determined by the direction cosines $(nU/k, qV/k, \sqrt{\{k^2 - (nU)^2 - (qV)^2\}}/k)$, where $k=2\pi/\lambda$ is the usual wave number. For the sake of convenience we shall restrict ourselves in this paper to the one-dimensional case; the extension to two (or more) dimensions is straightforward throughout.

The shifted and modulated Gaussian elementary signals are not ortho-normal, i.e., they do <u>not</u> satisfy the relation

$$\int g(t)g^*(t-mT)\exp[-in\Omega t] = \delta_m\delta_n \ , \tag{7}$$

where δ_m is the Kronecker delta ($\delta_0=1$, $\delta_m=0$ for $m\neq0$) and the asterisk * denotes complex conjugation. For this reason it seemes difficult[1,2] to find the coefficients a_{mn} of Gabor's signal expansion directly. We shall show, however, that a formula does exist which expresses these expansion coefficients explicitly as integral transforms of the signal.

3. <u>Determination of the expansion coefficients</u>

With the help of the discrete Fourier transforms

$$\tilde{\phi}(\tau,\omega) = \sum_m \phi(\tau+mT)\exp[-im\omega T] \ , \tag{8a}$$

$$\tilde{g}(\tau,\omega) = \sum_m g(\tau+mT)\exp[-im\omega T] \tag{8b}$$

and

$$\tilde{a}(\tau,\omega) = \sum_m\sum_n a_{mn}\exp[-i(m\omega T-n\Omega\tau)] \ , \tag{9}$$

Gabor's signal expansion (3) can be transformed into

$$\tilde{\phi}(\tau,\omega) = \tilde{a}(\tau,\omega)\tilde{g}(\tau,\omega) \ . \tag{10}$$

Note that the function $\tilde{a}(\tau,\omega)$ is periodic in ω and τ (with periods Ω and T, respectively), and that the functions $\tilde{\phi}(\tau,\omega)$ and $\tilde{g}(\tau,\omega)$ are periodic in ω (with period Ω) and quasi-periodic in τ (with quasi-period T).

We can now determine the expansion coefficients a_{mn} as follows. Under the assumption that division by $\tilde{g}(\tau,\omega)$ is allowed, the function $\tilde{a}(\tau,\omega)$ can be found via Eq. (10). The expansion coefficients can then be determined through the relation

$$a_{mn} = \frac{1}{2\pi} \iint_{T\Omega} \tilde{a}(\tau,\omega)\exp[i(m\omega T-n\Omega\tau)]d\tau d\omega \ , \tag{11}$$

which is, in fact, the inverse of the discrete Fourier transformation (9); the integrations in Eq. (11) extend over one period T and one period Ω, respectively.

The function $\tilde{\phi}(\tau,\omega)$ is completely determined by the signal $\phi(t)$, while $\tilde{g}(\tau,\omega)$ follows from the Gaussian elementary signal $g(t)$. Since $g(t)$ has the form (1), the function $\tilde{g}(\tau,\omega)$ reads

$$\tilde{g}(\tau,\omega) = \left(\frac{\sqrt{2}}{T}\right)^{\frac{1}{2}}\exp[-\pi\left(\frac{\tau}{T}\right)^2]\theta_4\left(\frac{\pi}{2} + \pi\frac{\omega}{\Omega} + i\pi\frac{\tau}{T}\right) \ , \tag{12}$$

where $\theta_4(.)$ is a theta function[3,4] with nome $\exp[-\pi]$.

In the previous paragraphs we showed how the coefficients a_{mn} of the Gabor expansion (3) could be determined when the signal $\phi(t)$ and the

Gaussian elementary signal g(t) are known. There is, however, a simpler way to find these expansion coefficients. Under the assumption, again, that division by $\tilde{g}(\tau,\omega)$ is allowed, we define the function $\tilde{\gamma}(\tau,\omega)$ by

$$\tilde{\gamma}(\tau,\omega)\tilde{g}^*(\tau,\omega) = \frac{1}{T} \ . \tag{13}$$

Substitution of this relation into Eq. (10) yields

$$\frac{1}{T}\tilde{a}(\tau,\omega) = \tilde{\phi}(\tau,\omega)\tilde{\gamma}^*(\tau,\omega) \ . \tag{14}$$

With the relationship

$$\gamma(\tau+mT) = \frac{1}{\Omega}\int_{\Omega}\tilde{\gamma}(\tau,\omega)\exp[im\omega T]d\omega \ , \tag{15}$$

which is, in fact, the inverse of a discrete Fourier transformation similar to Eq. (8), Eq. (14) can be transformed into

$$a_{mn} = \int\phi(t)\gamma^*(t-mT)\exp[-in\Omega t]dt \ . \tag{16}$$

We conclude that, when the signal $\phi(t)$ and the function $\gamma(t)$ are known, the expansion coefficients can be determined immediately by means of Eq. (16).

From Eq. (13) we see that the functions g(t) and $\gamma(t)$ are bi-orthonormal in a certain sense. Indeed, Eq. (13) is equivalent to

$$\int\gamma(t)g^*(t-mT)\exp[-in\Omega t]dt = \delta_m\delta_n \ . \tag{17}$$

In the case of the Gaussian elementary signal (1), the function $\tilde{\gamma}(\tau,\omega)$ takes the form

$$\tilde{\gamma}(\tau,\omega) = \left(\frac{1}{T\sqrt{2}}\right)^{\frac{1}{2}}\exp\left[\pi\left(\frac{\tau}{T}\right)^2\right]\frac{1}{\theta_4^*\left(\frac{\pi}{2}+\pi\frac{\omega}{\Omega}+i\pi\frac{\tau}{T}\right)} \ . \tag{18}$$

Eq. (18) can be expressed as

$$\tilde{\gamma}(\tau,\omega) = \left(\frac{1}{T\sqrt{2}}\right)^{\frac{1}{2}}\exp\left[\pi\left(\frac{\tau}{T}\right)^2\right]\left(\frac{K_0}{\pi}\right)^{-\frac{3}{2}}\left[\tfrac{1}{2}c_0+\sum_{m\geq 1}c_m\cos\left\{2m\left(\frac{\pi}{2}+\pi\frac{\omega}{\Omega}+i\pi\frac{\tau}{T}\right)\right\}\right]^* , \tag{19a}$$

where

$$c_m = 2\sum_{n\geq 0}(-1)^n\exp[-\pi(n+\tfrac{1}{2})(2m+n+\tfrac{1}{2})] \tag{19b}$$

(see, for instance, Ref. 3, p. 489, example 14); the constant
$K_0 = 1.85407468$ is the complete elliptic integral for the modulus $\tfrac{1}{2}\sqrt{2}$
(see, for instance, Ref. 3, p. 524). It is now easy to determine $\gamma(t)$
via Eq. (15), yielding

$$\gamma(\tau+mT) = \left(\frac{1}{T\sqrt{2}}\right)^{\frac{1}{2}} \exp\left[\pi\left(\frac{\tau}{T}\right)^2\right] \left(\frac{K_0}{\pi}\right)^{-\frac{3}{2}} (-1)^m \exp\left[2\pi m\frac{\tau}{T}\right] \cdot$$

$$\cdot \sum_{n\geq 0} (-1)^n \exp\left[-\pi(n+\tfrac{1}{2})(2m+n+\tfrac{1}{2})\right] , \qquad (20a)$$

or

$$\gamma(t) = \left(\frac{1}{T\sqrt{2}}\right)^{\frac{1}{2}} \left(\frac{K_0}{\pi}\right)^{-\frac{3}{2}} \exp\left[\pi\left(\frac{t}{T}\right)^2\right] \sum_{n+\frac{1}{2}\geq\frac{t}{T}} (-1)^n \exp\left[-\pi(n+\tfrac{1}{2})^2\right] . \qquad (20b)$$

The function $\gamma(t)$ is plotted in Figure 1.

Without proof we mention some properties of the function $\gamma(t)$. As is
also the case for the Gaussian elementary signal $g(t)$, the Fourier
transform of $\gamma(t)$ has the same form as $\gamma(t)$ itself. Moreover, the function $\gamma(t)$ satisfies the differential equation

$$\frac{d\gamma(t)}{dt} = \frac{2\pi}{T} \frac{t}{T} \gamma(t) - \left(\frac{1}{T\sqrt{2}}\right)^{\frac{1}{2}} \left(\frac{K_0}{\pi}\right)^{-\frac{3}{2}} \sum_m (-1)^m \delta(t-\{m+\tfrac{1}{2}\}T) , \qquad (21)$$

where $\delta(.)$ represents the Dirac function; note that all other solutions
of this differential equation become infinite for $|t|\to\infty$.

<u>Note</u>. It will be clear that the theory outlined in this paper is not
restricted to the case of the Gaussian elementary signal (1). The entire
analysis holds, in principle, when $g(t)$ is an arbitrary function of t;
for any function $g(t)$ a function $\gamma(t)$ can be found[5,6], which is bi-
orthonormal to $g(t)$ in the sense of Eq. (17). Some other functions $g(t)$
and their corresponding functions $\gamma(t)$ can be found in Ref. 6.

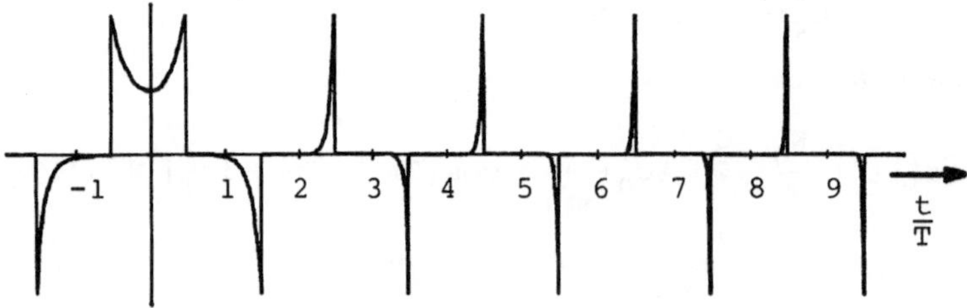

Fig. 1. The function $\gamma(t)$.

4. Examples

As a first example we shall represent the Dirac function

$$\phi(t) = T\delta(t) \tag{22}$$

by its Gabor expansion. With the help of Eq. (16) it can readily be derived that the expansion coefficients read

$$a_{mn} = \left(\frac{T}{\sqrt{2}}\right)^{\frac{1}{2}} \left(\frac{K_0}{\pi}\right)^{-\frac{3}{2}} \exp[\pi m^2] \sum_{k \geq m} (-1)^k \exp[-\pi(k+\tfrac{1}{2})^2] \; . \tag{23}$$

In Figure 2 we have sketched the array of expansion coefficients for the Dirac function (22); the area of a dot is proportional to the absolute value of the corresponding expansion coefficient. We see that for t=0 all frequencies are present, while there is almost no contribution from Gaussian elementary signals that are not located around t=0.

In the second example we consider the function

$$\phi(t) = 1 \; , \tag{24}$$

which is merely a constant. We remark that the constant function (24) and the Dirac function (22) are each other's duals, i.e., the Fourier transform of one function has the same form as the other function. Since the function $\gamma(t)$ is its own dual, we can easily obtain the Gabor coefficients of the constant $\phi(t)=1$, by simply rotating the result of the previous example over 90°. The array of expansion coefficients for a constant has been sketched in Figure 3. We see that $\omega=0$ is present at all moments, while there is almost no contribution from other frequencies.

Fig. 2. The expansion coefficients for a Dirac function.

Fig. 3. The expansion coefficients for a constant.

Finally, we determine the Gabor coefficients of the step function

$$\phi(t) = \begin{cases} 1 & \text{for } t<0 \\ 0 & \text{for } t>0 \ . \end{cases} \tag{25}$$

The array of expansion coefficients has been sketched in Figure 4. Note that for $m\to-\infty$ all the coefficients become zero, while for $m\to+\infty$ the array of coefficients equals the one derived in example 2.

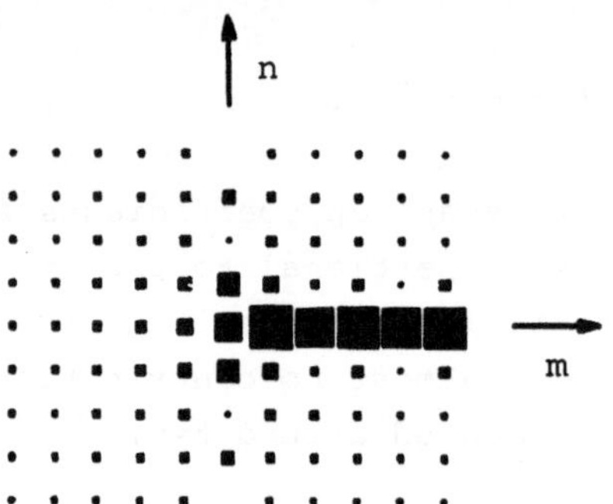

Fig. 4. The expansion coefficients for a step function.

References

1. D. Gabor, "Theory of communication", J. IEE (London) $\underline{93\ (III)}$ (1946) 429-457.
2. C.W. Helstrom, "An expansion of a signal in Gaussian elementary signals", IEEE Trans. Inf. Theory $\underline{IT-12}$ (1970) 81-82.
3. E.T. Whittaker, and G.N. Watson, A course of modern analysis. Cambridge University Press (1927).
4. M. Abramowitz, and I.A. Stegun, Handbook of mathematical functions. Dover Publications (1965).
5. M.J. Bastiaans, "Gabor's expansion of a signal into Gaussian elementary signals", Proc. IEEE $\underline{68}$ (1980) in press.
6. M.J. Bastiaans, "A sampling theorem for the complex spectrogram, and Gabor's expansion of a signal in Gaussian elementary signals", to be published in the Proceedings of the International Optical Computing Conference, Washington, D.C., 8-11 April, 1980.

GESCHWINDIGKEITSMESSUNG MIT HILFE ZEITDIFFERENZIERTER LASER SPECKLES[+]

A.F. Fercher

Fachbereich Physik, Universität Essen

Zusammenfassung

Mit Hilfe statistischer Methoden erster Ordnung läßt sich ein sehr effektives Verfahren zur Messung der Geschwindigkeit von lichtstreuenden Objekten realisieren. Im folgenden werden der quantitative Zusammenhang zwischen Geschwindigkeit und Varianz des zeitlichen Differentialquotienten der Intensität im Streufeld sowie erste Meßergebnisse präsentiert.

1. Einleitung

Geschwindigkeitsmessungen mit Hilfe von Lichtstreumethoden sind wegen deren berührungsfreier Arbeitsweise sehr vorteilhaft. Da die Geschwindigkeit ein zeitlicher Differentialquotient ist, gilt es, das dynamische Verhalten der Laser Speckles zu analysieren. Hierzu gibt es mehrere grundsätzliche Möglichkeiten. Beispielsweise kann man die Bewegung der Speckles im Streufeld analysieren /1/ oder man kann versuchen, die Geschwindigkeit der strukturellen Veränderung des Speckle Felds zu erfassen /2/. Ferner können diese Analysen am reinen Speckle Feld erfolgen oder es kann den Speckles ein kohärenter Untergrund beigefügt werden. Im letzteren Falle ergibt sich eine erhebliche Steigerung der Empfindlichkeit durch die nun erfaßbare Dopplerverschiebung in den Laser Speckles.

Die mathematische Analyse der resultierenden Streufeldintensität kann mit Hilfe statistischer Methoden erster oder zweiter Ordnung erfolgen. Darüber hinaus kann die Streufeldintensität vorher zeitlich integriert oder zeitlich differenziert werden. Die bereits bekannten Laser-Velocimeter /3/ und Laser-Doppler-Spektroskopiegeräte /4/ analysieren die Streufeldintensität mit Hilfe statistischer Methoden zweiter Ordnung. Die Anwendung statistischer Methoden erster Ordnung auf zeitlich integrierte Laser Speckles ist in den Arbeiten von Ohtsubo und Asakura /5,6/ sehr ausführlich beschrieben. Geschwindigkeitsmessungen mit Hilfe statistischer Methoden zweiter Ordnung und zeitlich differenzierten Laser Speckles wurden kürzlich von Takai et al. /7/ beschrieben. In der vorliegenden Arbeit wird die Anwendung statistischer Methoden erster Ordnung auf zeitdifferenzierte Laser Speckles zur Geschwindigkeitsmessung beschrieben.

Wir beschreiben die Intensität $I(t)$ im Streufeld als stochastischen Prozeß $I(t)$ und betrachten zunächst einige statistische Eigenschaften des zeitlichen Differentialquotienten $\dot{I}(t)$. Ist die Speckle Intensität stationär, dann muß offenbar der Mittelwert von $\dot{I}(t)$ verschwinden:

$$\langle \dot{I}(t) \rangle = 0 \tag{1}$$

Hier bedeutet $\langle \cdots \rangle$ Ensemblemittelung. Wir nehmen im folgenden für alle in Frage kommenden stochastischen Prozesse Ergodizität an und können damit die Ensemblemittelung durch eine Zeitmittelung von der Art

$$\lim_{T \to \infty} \frac{1}{2T} \int_{-T}^{T} \cdots \, dt$$

ersetzen. Bewegt sich der Streuer mit der Geschwindigkeit v so erzeugt er ein zweites Moment $\langle \dot{I}^2 \rangle \neq 0$. Eine Beschleunigung des Streuers auf eine Geschwindigkeit $\alpha \cdot v$ läßt sich auch durch eine Zeittransformation $t' = t/\alpha$ beschreiben. Wir erhalten für das zweite Moment von $I' = \frac{d}{dt'} I(t)$ das Ergebnis $\langle I'^2 \rangle = \alpha^2 \langle \dot{I}^2 \rangle$. Es ist daher nahelie-

---

[+] Von der Deutschen Forschungsgemeinschaft unterstützt

gend, die Varianz des zeitlichen Differentialquotienten der Speckle Intensität zu untersuchen. Die Autokovarianz ist wegen Gl.(1)

$$R_{\dot{I}}(\tau) = \langle \dot{I}(t)\,\dot{I}(t+\tau) \rangle \qquad (2)$$

2. Die Varianz der zeitdifferenzierten Speckle Intensität

Wir betrachten den allgemeinen Fall des Speckle Felds mit kohärentem Untergrund. Abb.1 zeigt den grundsätzlichen Strahlengang. Der sich bewegende Streuer befindet sich in einem Arm eines Twyman Interferometers. Der zweite Arm des Interferometers liefert den kohärenten Untergrund.

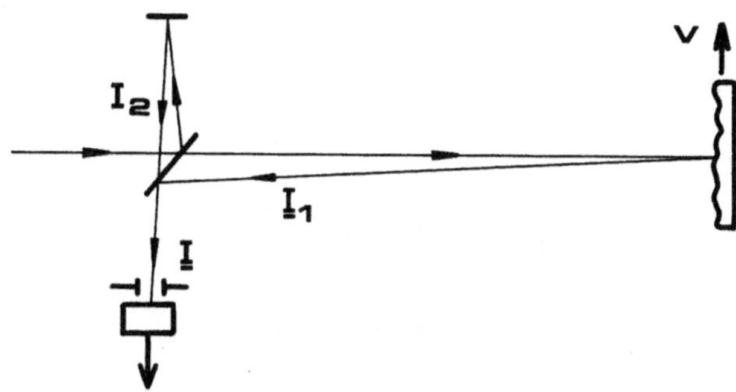

Abb.1: Twyman Interferometer zur Überlagerung des Speckle Felds mit einem kohärenten Untergrund

Die Speckle Feld Intensität sei $\underline{I_1}$ und die Intensität des Untergrunds sei $\underline{I_2}$. Die zugehörigen Lichtfelder sind:

$$\underline{V_1}(t) = \underline{A_1}(t)\,exp\left[-2\pi i\nu_1 t - i\phi_1(t)\right]$$

$$\underline{V_2}(t) = A_2\,exp\left[-2\pi i\nu_2 t - i\phi_2(t)\right] \qquad (3)$$

$\underline{A_1}(t)$ ist die fluktuierende Laser Speckle Amplitude. Wenn der Laser wie üblich oberhalb seiner Schwelle betrieben wird, ist die Amplitude des Untergrunds konstant.

ν_2 ist die Frequenz der Laseremission und ν_1 ist die Frequenz des Streulichts mit der Dopplerverschiebung $\Delta\nu = \nu_1 - \nu_2$. ϕ_1 und ϕ_2 sind die entsprechenden Phasenfluktuationen. $\phi_1 = \phi_1 + \Delta\phi$, wobei $\Delta\phi$ gleich $2\pi/\lambda$ mal der optischen Wegdifferenz ist. Eine einfache Rechnung (analog der von Jakeman in /4/ Seite 75 ff angegebenen) ergibt für die Autokorrelation der resultierenden Gesamtintensität

$$G_I(\tau) = \langle I(t)\,I(t+\tau) \rangle$$

$$= G_{I_1}(\tau) + 2I_2\langle \underline{I_1} \rangle + I_2^2 +$$

$$+ 2I_2\,|G_{A_1}(\tau)|\,cos\,2\pi\left[\Delta\nu\,\tau + \psi_1(\tau)\right] \qquad (4)$$

$\psi_{1}(\tau)$ ist die Phase der Kohärenzfunktion $G_{A_{1}}(\tau)$ im Speckle Feld. Unter sehr allgemeinen Voraussetzungen (z.B. /8/ Seite 12 ff) können wir für die Speckle Feld Amplitude eine zirkular symmetrische Gaußverteilung mit verschwindendem Mittelwert annehmen. Dann ist $\psi_{1}(\tau)=0$ für alle τ.

Die Autokovarianz der Gesamtintensität wird damit:

$$R_{I}(\tau) = G_{I_{1}}(\tau) - \langle I_{1}^{2} \rangle + 2 I_{2} |G_{A_{1}}(\tau)| \cos(2\pi \Delta \nu \tau) \tag{5}$$

und für die Varianz des zeitlichen Differentialquotienten erhalten wir (siehe /9/):

$$R_{\dot{I}}(o) = -\frac{d^{2}}{d\tau^{2}} R_{I}(\tau)\Big|_{\tau=0}$$

$$= -\frac{d^{2}}{d\tau^{2}} G_{I_{1}}(\tau) +$$

$$- 2 I_{2} \frac{d^{2}}{d\tau^{2}} |G_{A_{1}}(\tau)| \Big|_{\tau=0} + \tag{6}$$

$$+ 2 I_{2} (2\pi \Delta \nu)^{2} |G_{A_{1}}(o)|$$

Der erste Summand auf der rechten Seite ist die Varianz $R_{\dot{I}_{1}}(o)$ des zeitlichen Differentialquotienten der Speckle Intensität. Der zweite Summand ist bis auf den Faktor $2 I_{2}$ gleich der Varianz des Differentialquotienten der Speckle Amplitude $A_{1}(t)$ und der dritte Summand enthält die Doppler Frequenz.

3. Zusammenhang zwischen Geschwindigkeit und Varianz des zeitlichen Differentialquotienten der Speckle Intensität. Experimentelle Ergebnisse.

Entsprechend Gl.(6) benötigen wir nun die Autokovarianzen von Amplitude und Intensität im Speckle Feld. Deren quantitative Berechnung ist für das Fernfeld ohne großen Aufwand möglich, wenn für die Kohärenzfunktion des Streuers physikalisch sinnvolle Annahmen getroffen werden können (näheres hierzu in /1o/). Für einen sich in ξ-Richtung mit der Geschwindigkeit v bewegenden Streuer , der von einem Laserstrahl konstanter Intensität und einem Querschnitt von d (in ξ-Richtung) mal L (senkrecht zur ξ-Richtung) beleuchtet wird, ist die Varianz der Gesamtintensität im Fernfeld /1o/:

$$R_{\dot{I}}(o) = 8 \langle I_{1} \rangle^{2} \frac{v^{2}}{d\lambda} + 8 I_{2} \langle I_{1} \rangle \frac{v^{2}}{d\lambda} + \tag{7}$$

$$+ 2 I_{2} \langle I_{1} \rangle (2\pi \Delta \nu)^{2}$$

Die v^{2}-Terme rühren von den Fluktuationen der Speckle Intensität und Speckle Amplitude her; der $(\Delta \nu)^{2}$-Term wird durch die Dopplerverschiebung des Streulichts erzeugt. Das relative Gewicht des Dopplerterms kann durch die Wahl des Streuwinkels verändert werden. Für $I_2 = 0$ ergibt sich der Fall des reinen Speckle Felds.

Bei einer ersten experimentelle Erprobung dieses Geschwindigkeitsmeßverfahrens wurden zunächst reine Laser Speckles benutzt. Eine mit bekannter Geschwindigkeit v bewegte Mattscheibe wurde von einem He-Ne-Laser Strahl von 2 mm Durchmesser in den $1/e^2$ Punkten beleuchtet. Das Gaußsche Intensitätsprofil führt natürlich zu etwas anderen Proportionalitätskonstanten, als in Gl.(7) angegeben. Die Speckle Intensität wurde mit einem SEV mit davorgesetzter Lochblende von 3o µm Durchmesser im Abstand von etwa 5o cm vom Streuer registriert. Die Berechnung der Varianz erfolgte on line in einem hp 9825 A Tischrechner.

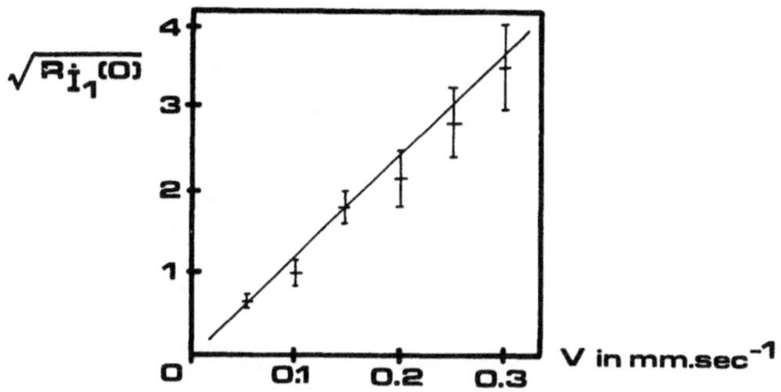

Abb.2: Quadratwurzel aus Varianz der Speckle Intensität versus Geschwindigkeit. Abszisseneinheiten willkürlich.

Die relativen Fehler der obigen Meßergebnisse sind von der Größe des Kehrwerts der Quadratwurzel aus der Anzahl der auf der Meßblende auftretenden Laser Speckles. Hinreichend große Meßstrecken erlauben diesen Fehler deutlich zu reduzieren.

In Abb.3 sind die Ergebnisse einer Geschwindigkeitsmessung mit kohärentem Untergrund dargestellt. Die übrigen Parameter entsprechen jenen der Messung zu Abb.2.

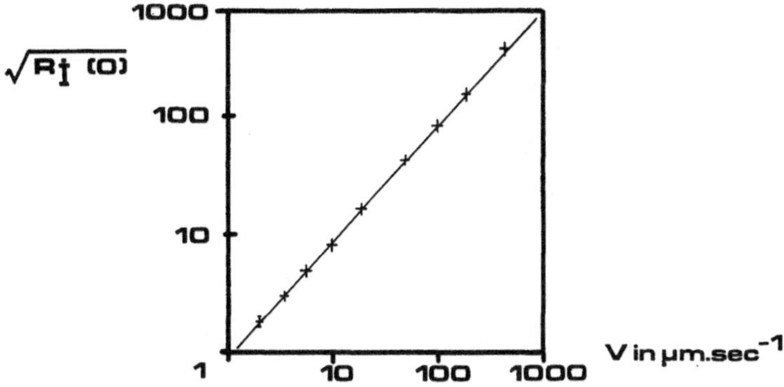

Abb.3: Quadratwurzel aus Varianz der Gesamtintensität versus Geschwindigkeit. Abszisseneinheiten willkürlich.

Die Standardabweichung dieser Meßergebnisse liegt bei 1 % und ist daher in der Abb. nicht mehr zu erkennen.

<u>Literatur</u>

/1/   G. Stavis, Instrum. Control Syst. 39 (1969) 99

/2/   S. Komatsu, I. Yamaguchi and H. Saito, Opt. Commun. 18 (1976) 314

/3/   F. Durst, A. Melling and J.H. Whitelaw, Principles and Practice of Laser-Doppler Anemometry, Academic Press 1976

/4/   H.Z. Cummins and E.R. Pike (Editors), Photon Correlation and Light Beating Spectroscopy, Plenum Press 1974

/5/   J. Ohtsubo and T. Asakura, Opt. Quant. El. 8 (1976) 523

/6/   J. Ohtsubo and T. Asakura, Optik 52 (1979) 413

/7/   N. Takai, T. Iwai, T. Ushizaka and T. Asakura, Opt. Commun. 3o (1979) 287

/8/   J.C. Dainty (Editor), Laser Speckle and Related Phenomena, Springer Verlag 1975

/9/   E. Parzen, Stochastic Processes, Holden-Day Inc., 1962

/1o/   A.F. Fercher, Opt. Commun., zur Veröffentlichung angenommen

<u>AUTOMATISIERTE DIGITALE VERARBEITUNG HOLOGRAFISCHER</u>
<u>INTERFERENZMUSTER</u>

Th. Kreis, H. Kreitlow, W. Jüptner[*]

Institut für Meßtechnik im Maschinenbau der Universität Hannover,
[*] Bremer Institut für Angewandte Strahltechnik(BIAS)

<u>Zusammenfassung</u>

Ein umfassender Einsatz der holografischen Interferometrie als Meßmethode im μm-Bereich erfordert eine weitgehende Automatisierung der quantitativen Auswertung der Interferenzmuster. Im folgenden wird über einige Aspekte bei der Lösung dieses Problems mit Hilfe eines Mikroprozessorsystems berichtet. Dabei steht die Verbesserung der im allgemeinen mehr oder weniger stark gestörten Interferenzmuster mit Hilfe von digitalen Bildverarbeitungsmethoden im Vordergrund.

1. Einleitung

Die holografische Interferometrie ist ein Verfahren zur berührungslosen Messung von Objektbewegungen oder Schwingungsamplituden an rauhen technischen oder biologischen Oberflächen mit interferometrischer Genauigkeit. Im Gegensatz zur qualitativen Interpretation erfordert jedoch eine quantitative Auswertung einen immensen Arbeits- und Zeitaufwand, so daß erst eine weitgehende Automatisierung der quantitativen Auswertung einen wirtschaftlichen Einsatz der holografischen Interferometrie ermöglicht. Mit Hilfe eines Mikroprozessorsystems läßt sich ein Großteil der Auswertung steuern und durchführen. Ein wesentlicher Schritt dabei ist die Verbesserung der gestörten Interferenzmuster, um eine zuverlässige Auswertung zu gewährleisten. Im folgenden werden einige Möglichkeiten zur Verbesserung der Muster

durch einen geeigneten holografischen Aufbau und die Anwendung digitaler Filtermethoden aufgezeigt.

2.Holografisch interferometrische Verfahren

Um aus dem holografischen Interferenzmuster, welches nach einem der
bekannten Verfahren - Doppelbelichtungs-, Echtzeit- oder strobosko-
pischem Verfahren, um nur einige zu nennen - aufgenommen wurde, die
Veränderungsvektoren zu bestimmen, werden im wesentlichen zwei
Methoden benutzt: die statische und die dynamische Auswertemethode
der holografischen Interferometrie /1/. Die Datenerfassung aus dem
holografischen Interferenzmuster ist auf folgende Arten möglich:
- Das virtuelle Bild der Objektoberfläche zusammen mit dem Interferenzmuster wird mit einer Video-Kamera aufgenommen. Die Auswertung
  geschieht dann nach der statischen Methode.
- Mit Hilfe einer Linse großer Apertur oder durch eine zur Aufnahmereferenzwelle konjugierten Rekonstruktionswelle wird ein reelles
  Bild erzeugt. Bei Beobachtung durch eine kleine Apertur im reellen
  Bild erscheinen Interferenzstreifen auf die Hologrammplatte proji-
  ziert. Da sich dieses Interferenzmuster auf einen Objektpunkt und
  eine Gesamtheit von Punkten der Hologrammplatte bezieht, muß nach
  den Gleichungen der dynamischen Methode ausgewertet werden, obwohl
  ein feststehendes Muster erfasst worden ist.
- Beim sogenannten Referenzstrahl-Scan-Verfahren wird das reelle Bild
  erzeugt, indem mit einem unaufgeweiteten Laserstrahl, welcher einem
  Teil der zur Aufnahmereferenzwelle konjugierten Welle entspricht,
  rekonstruiert wird, siehe Bild 1. Während der Rekonstruktionsstrahl
  die gesamte Hologrammplatte abscant, wird die im reellen Bild an
  einem Punkt entstehende Intensitätsverteilung mit einem Photodetek-
  tor aufgezeichnet und entsprechend dem durchstrahlten Punkt der
  Hologrammplatte abgespeichert. Das entstehende Muster wird wieder
  nach den Gleichungen der dynamischen Methode ausgewertet /2,3/.

In allen diesen Fällen bleibt das Problem, eine nichtmonotone Änderung der Interferenzstreifenordnung festzustellen. Andernfalls würden Interferenzstreifen gleicher Ordnung mehrfach gezählt, obwohl sich ihre Beiträge zur Interferenzstreifenzahl gegenseitig aufheben /4/. Um diesen Fall zu erkennen, werden die zwei Belichtungen des Hologramms mit verschiedenen Referenzwellen gemacht, siehe Bild 2. Bei der Rekonstruktion mit beiden Referenzwellen wird die eine um eine feste Phasen differenz, z. B. $\pi/2$ verschoben. Falls im Interferenzmuster eine maximale Streifenordnung auftrat, werden sich dabei die Streifen zu beiden Seiten des Maximums in verschiedene Richtungen bewegen. Der holografische Aufbau mit zwei Referenzwellen kann darüber hinaus die für ein besonderes Verfahren zur Bildverbesserung benötigten Muster liefern, siehe Kap.4.

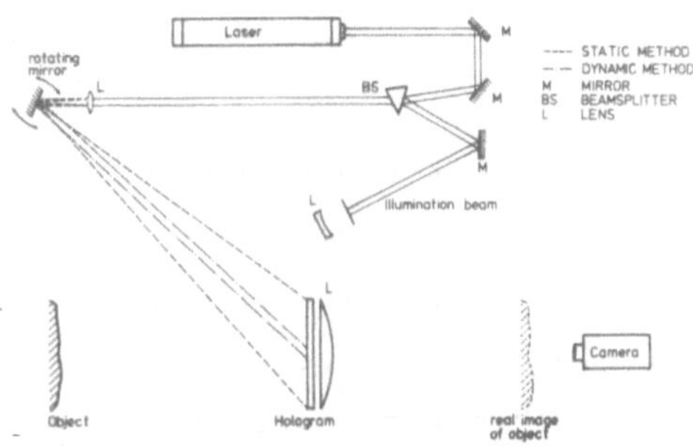

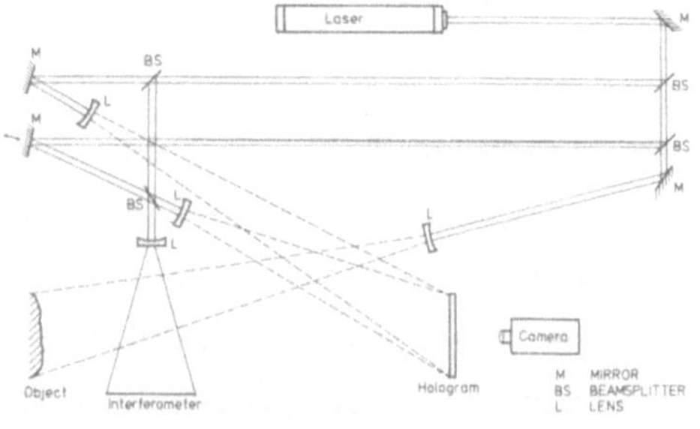

Bild 1. Referenzstrahl-Scan-Verfahren

Bild 2. Holografischer Aufbau mit zwei Referenzwellen

3. Störungen der holografischen Interferenzmuster

Holografische Interferenzmuster sind grundsätzlich mehr oder weniger stark gestört. Die hauptsächlichen Störquellen sind die im folgenden beschriebenen:

- Da mit kohärentem Licht gearbeitet werden muß, entsteht das Specklerauschen. Dabei erscheinen die Speckles um so größer, je kleiner die Beobachtungsapertur wird. Eine kleine Beobachtungsapertur wird jedoch angestrebt, um die im allgemeinen im Raum lokalisierten Interferenzstreifen auf die Objektoberfläche oder die Hologrammplatte zu projizieren.

- Da sowohl das Objekt wie das Hologramm von einem aufgeweiteten Laserstrahl beleuchtet werden, variiert der Hintergrund des Interferenzmusters entsprechend einer zweidimensionalen Gaußverteilung.
- Durch Staubteilchen auf den Oberflächen der optischen Komponenten des holografischen Aufbaus entstehen Beugungsmuster, die dem Interferenzmuster überlagert sind.

Um diese Störungen zu unterdrücken, konnten die im folgenden beschriebenen Bildverarbeitungsmethoden mit Erfolg angewandt werden /5,6,7/.

4. Digitale Bildverarbeitungsmethoden angewandt auf holografische Interferenzmuster

Im vorliegenden Fall wird das Interferenzmuster mit einer Video-Kamera aufgenommen und deren Bild in ein 256x256 Bildpunkte umfassendes Raster eingeteilt. Der Grauwert jedes Bildpunkts wird in diskrete Werte von 0 bis 255 quantisiert. Die Wahl dieser Parameter folgte in erster Linie aus der Verwendung eines 8-bit-Mikroprozessors. Eine Quantisierung in 256 Graustufen ist darüber hinaus voll ausreichend sowohl für eine visuelle Beurteilung wie für eine automatisierte Auswertung.

Nach der Wahl der 256x256-Abtastmatrix ist die Klasse der Interferenzmuster, die verarbeitet werden können, allerdings eingeschränkt durch das Whittaker-Shannon-Theorem. Bild 3. zeigt ein Balkenmuster mit höheren Ortsfrequenzen, als nach diesem Theorem zulässig sind. Das aus den abgetasteten Werten rekonstruierte Bild 4. zeigt ein für diesen Fall typisches Moire-Muster /8,9/.

Auf das digitalisierte Interferenzmuster können nun die folgenden Bildverarbeitungsverfahren angewandt werden, die keine oder nur wenig Information über Lage und Intensität der einzelnenStörungen benutzen.

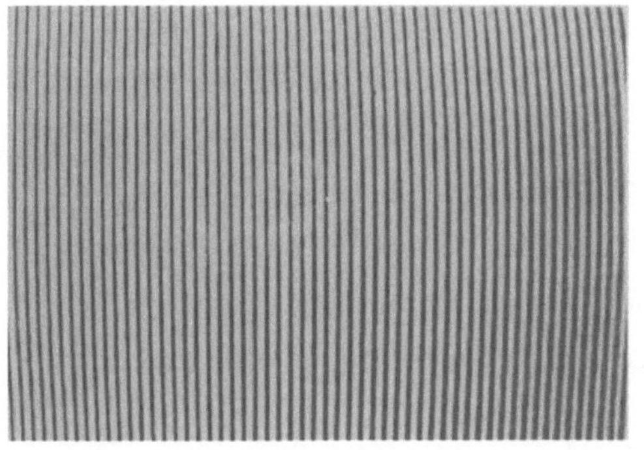

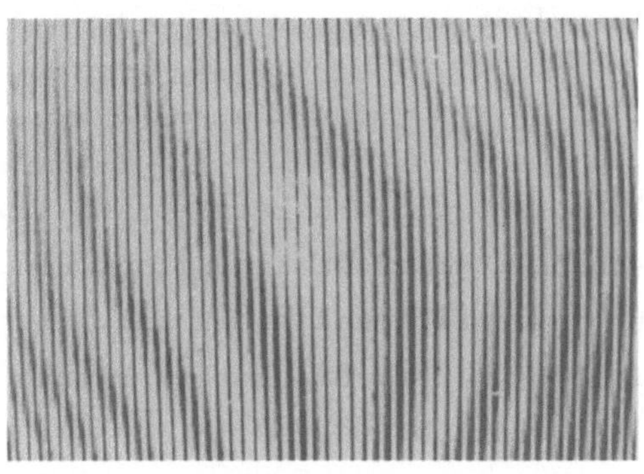

Bild 3. Balkenmuster,kontinuier-
       lich

Bild 4. Balkenmuster,digitali-
       siert

4.1 Modifikation der Grauskala

Zur Verbesserung von Interferenzmustern mit schwachem Kontrast eignet
sich eine Transformation der Grauwerte: Liegt der überwiegende Anteil
der Grauwerte im Bereich $[a,b]$, kann die Transformation

$$I' = \begin{cases} \dfrac{255}{b-a}\,(I-a) & \text{für } a \leqq I \leqq b \\[2mm] 0 & I < a \\[2mm] 255 & I > b \end{cases}$$

benutzt werden. Dabei ist I' der transformierte Grauwert I. Grauwerte
unter a werden auf schwarz (0), Grauwerte über b werden auf weiß (255)
transformiert, der Bereich zwischen a und b wird auf die gesamte
Grauskala abgebildet.

4.2 Bildglättung

Das im Interferenzmuster vorhandene Specklerauschen erfordert eine
Methode zur Glättung des Bildes. Da im Normalfall das Specklerauschen
höhere Ortsfrequenzanteile als das Interferenzmuster hat, bringt
schon eine einfache räumliche Tiefpassfilterung eine Verbesserung.
Jede solche Filterung besteht aus der diskreten Faltung der Bildmatrix mit einer Matrix H. Eine Matrix H für eine Tiefpassfilterung,
welche sich besonders einfach mit einem 8-bit-Mikroprozessor verar-

beiten läßt, ist

$$H = \frac{1}{16}\begin{pmatrix} 1 & 2 & 1 \\ 2 & 4 & 2 \\ 1 & 2 & 1 \end{pmatrix}$$

Bild 6. zeigt das Ergebnis nach einer Tiefpassfilterung des holografischen Interferenzmusters aus Bild 5. Hierbei wurde eine 3x3-Umgebung jedes Bildpunkts benutzt, um seinen gefilterten Grauwert zu bestimmen. Größere Umgebungen können durch mehrfache Anwendung solcher Filter erreicht werden.

Eine weitere Bildverarbeitungsmethode, die sich zur Unterdrückung des Specklerauschens eignet, ist die Medianfilterung. Dabei wird der Grauwert jedes Bildpunkts durch den Median der Grauwerte einer Umgebung ersetzt. Das Medianfilter glättet im Gegensatz zum oben beschriebenen Tiefpassfilter Stufen und Rampen in der Grauwertverteilung nicht, so daß Unstetigkeiten im holografischen Interferenzmuster, die von Inhomogenitäten des Objekts, wie z. B. Rissen, herrühren,erhalten bleiben. Ein Ergebnis einer Medianfilterung zeigt Bild 7.

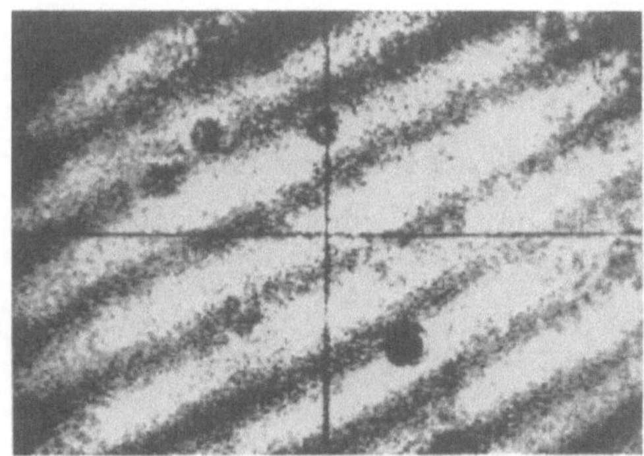

Bild 5. Digitalisiertes Interferenzmuster

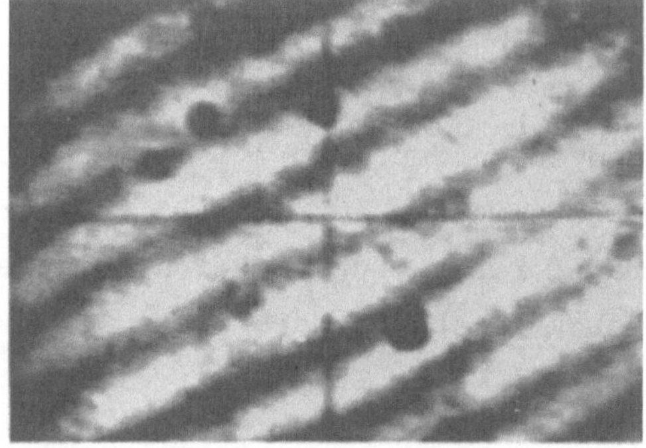

Bild 6. Tiefpassgefiltertes Muster aus Bild 5.

4.3 Hintergrundkorrektur

Da die Variation des Hintergrunds im allgemeinen von wesentlich niedrigerer Ortsfrequenz als das Interferenzmuster ist, kann diese Variation mit Hilfe eines digitalen Hochpass-Filters unterdrückt werden. Dies geschieht durch Subtraktion des Ergebnisses einer Tief-

pass-Filterung vom Originalbild und Addition eines konstanten Grauwert
zur Vermeidung negativer Grauwerte.

4.4 Bildverbesserung durch phasenverschobene Interferenzmuster

Die in 4.2 und 4.3 beschriebenen Filtermethoden eignen sich nicht zur
Unterdrückung der Beugungsmuster von Staubteilchen, da die Ortsfrequenzen dieser Muster im Bereich der Ortsfrequenzen des Interferenz-
mustersliegen. Die Beugungsmuster, wie auch die Hintergrundvariation,
lassen sich jedoch weitgehend eliminieren, wenn statt eines Interferenzmusters zwei Rekonstruktionen desselben herangezogen werden,
wobei bei einer dieser Rekonstruktionen die zweite Referenzwelle
gegenüber der anderen Rekonstruktion um π verschoben wurde. Dies ist
mit dem in Kapitel 2. beschriebenen holografischen Aufbau möglich.
Wird aus den beiden Rekonstruktionen für jeden Bildpunkt das arithmetische Mittel der Grauwerte gebildet, so löschen sich die beiden
Interferenzmuster gegenseitig aus, während die Beugungsmuster, Störungen und Hintergrundvariation erhalten bleiben, da sie nicht mit-
geschoben wurden. In Bild 8. ist das gegenüber Bild 5. um π verscho-
bene Interferenzmuster zu sehen. Bild 9. zeigt das arithmetische
Mittel aus den Bildern 5. und 8. Eines der beiden gestörten Interferenzmuster kann nun durch das Störmuster dividiert werden und nur die
Interferenzinformation bleibt erhalten, während die Störungen unterdrückt wurden. Bild 10. zeigt das Ergebnis nach der Division von Bild
5. durch Bild 9.

4.5 Geometrische Korrektur

Um alle drei Komponenten des Veränderungsvektors zu bestimmen, braucht
man Interferenzmuster aus verschiedenen Beobachtungsrichtungen /10/.
Dies kann mit mehreren Hologrammen oder durch Beobachtung über geeignet angebrachte Spiegel geschehen. In beiden Fällen wird die Objektoberfläche unter einem Winkel aufgenommen, so daß eine Methode benö-

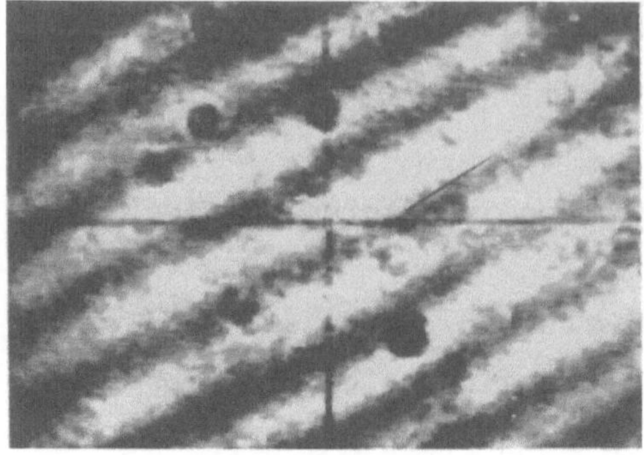

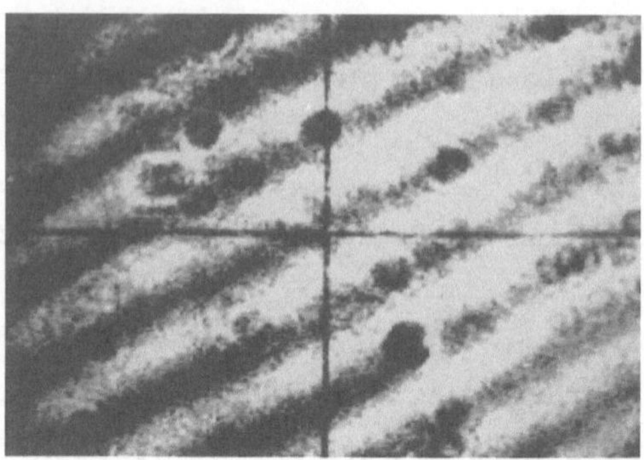

Bild 7. Mediangefiltertes Muster
aus Bild 5.

Bild 8. Gegenüber Bild 5. phasen-
verschobenes Muster

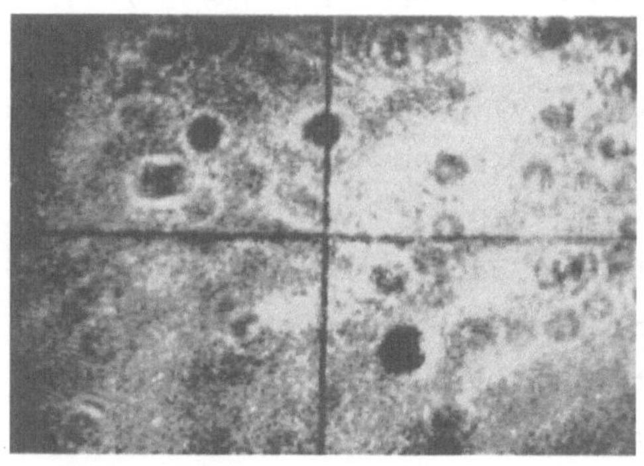

Bild 9. Arithmetisches Mittel
der Bilder 5. und 8.

Bild 10. Division von Bild 5.
durch Bild 9.

tigt wird, die geometrische perspektivische Verzeichnung zu korri-
gieren. Eine beliebige geometrische Verzeichnung wird durch die
Gleichungen

$$x' = h_1(x,y) \qquad y' = h_2(x,y)$$

beschrieben. Die geometrischen Verzeichnungen können nun korrigiert
werden, indem man eine diskrete Approximation der inversen Transformation anwendet. Nach einer Korrektur der perspektivischen Verzeichnungen können somit verschiedene Ansichten der gleichen Oberfläche
miteinander identifiziert und die jeweiligen Interferenzmuster verglichen werden, siehe die Bilder 11. und 12.

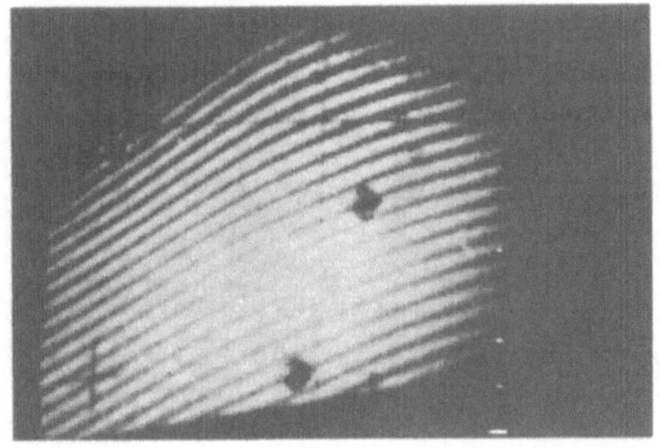

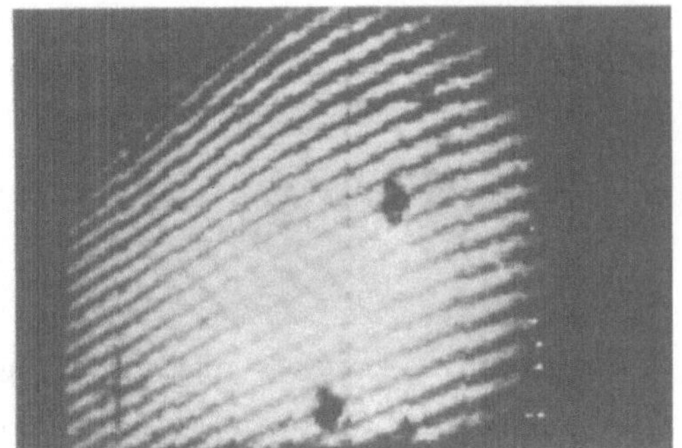

Bild 11. Interferenzmuster

Bild 12. Korrigiertes Interferenzmuster aus Bild 11.

5. Zusammenfassung

Durch die Anwendung einfacher Bildverarbeitungsverfahren auf gestörte holografische Interferenzmuster konnte eine wesentliche Verbesserung dieser Muster erzielt werden, die somit eine zuverlässige quantitative automatisierte Auswertung gewährleisten. Sämtliche angeführten Verfahren verwenden kein oder nur geringes Vorwissen über die Störungen oder die gewünschte Information. Es besteht die Hoffnung, noch effektivere Verfahren bei Verwendung dieses Vorwissens zu erhalten. Die angeführten Beispiele und Verfahren wurden implementiert auf dem modularen Bildanalysesystem MBS-III, welches auf einem 8-bit-Mikroprozessor basiert und von den beiden erstgenannten Autoren entwickelt wurde.

Literatur

/1/ Schumann, W., Dubas, M.; Holographic Interferometry, Springer Series in Optical Sciences 1979
/2/ Ek, L., Biedermann, K.; Implementation of hologram interferometry with a continuously scanning reconstruction beam, Applied Optics, vol. 17 (1978)

/ 3/ Fossati-Bellani, V., Sona, A.; Measurement of three-dimensional
displacements by scanning a double exposure hologram, Applied
Optics, vol.13(1974)

/ 4/ Kreitlow, H., Kreis, Th., Jüptner, W., Fischer, B.; Jahresbericht
zum BMFT-Vorhaben DV 5.803, 1977

/ 5/ Kreitlow, H., Kreis, Th.; Entwicklung eines Gerätesystems zur
automatisierten statischen und dynamischen Auswertung holografischer Interferenzmuster, Proceedings of the "Laser 79",
pp. 426-436, IPC Science and Technology Press Ltd. 1979

/ 6/ Kreis, Th., Kreitlow, H.; Quantitative evaluation of holographic
interference patterns under image processing aspects, S.P.I.E.-
Proceedings, vol. 210, 1979

/ 7/ Kreitlow, H., Kreis, Th.; Automatic evaluation of Young's
fringes related to the study of in-plane-deformations by speckle
techniques, S.P.I.E.-Proceedings, vol. 210, 1979

/ 8/ Rosenfeld, A., Kak, A.; Digital Picture Processing, Academic
Press 1976

/ 9/ Pratt, W.; Digital Image Processing, J. Wiley & Sons 1978

/10/ Kreis, Th., Kreitlow, H., Geldmacher, J.; Optimierung der Glei-
chungssysteme zur quantitativen Auswertung holografischer Inter-
ferogramme, 79. Tagung der DGaO, 1978

ERZEUGUNG VON STRUKTUREN IN DER HALBLEITER-TECHNOLOGIE
(MIKRO-LITHOGRAFIE) - ELEKTRONENOPTISCH

Th. Ricker

AEG-TELEFUNKEN, Forschungsinstitut Ulm
Postfach 1730, 7900 Ulm/Donau

1. Einleitung

Eine komplexe Summe technischer und wirtschaftlicher Gründe - z.B.
geringere Verzögerungszeit oder Verlustleistung einerseits und höhere
Ausbeute pro Scheibe andererseits - veranlaßt die Hersteller integrierter Schaltungen, die Einzeldimensionen der planaren Strukturen
immer weiter zu verringern, wobei die Scheibenfläche oftmals noch vergrößert wird. Dieser Trend stellt Anforderungen an die Mikrolithografie, die über die Leistungsfähigkeit der heute eingesetzten lichtoptischen Verfahren hinausgehen werden.

In Bild 1 sind schematisch die heute praktizierten und für die Zukunft
diskutierten Möglichkeiten der Mikrolithografie zusammengestellt und
in etwa nach zunehmendem Auflösungsvermögen geordnet /1/. Unter den
verschiedenen Wegen, vom geometrischen Entwurf (Layout) zur belichte-

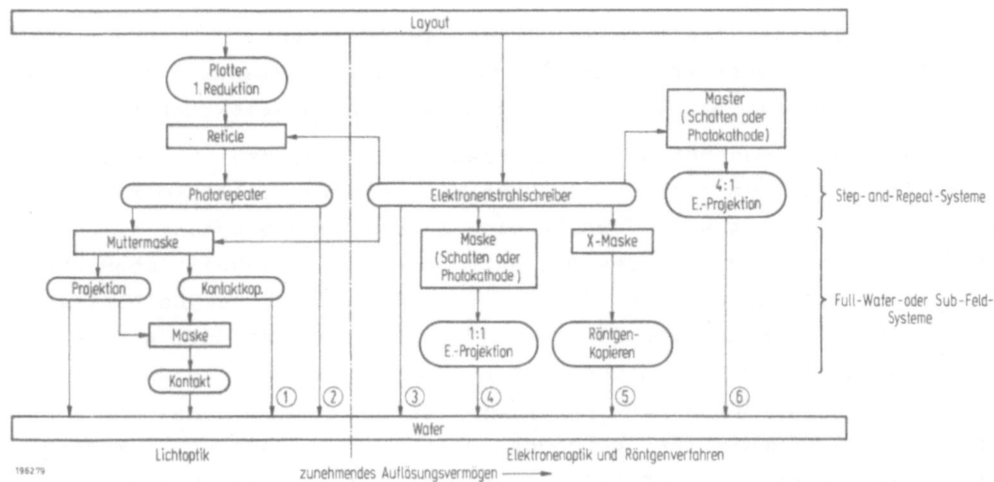

Bild 1: Verschiedene Wege und Verfahren der Mikrolithografie

ten Scheibe (Wafer) zu gelangen, nehmen die Elektronenstrahlschreiber
eine zentrale Stelle ein. Sie verdanken dies zum einen ihrem hohen
Auflösungsvermögen bei hoher Schärfentiefe, zum anderen - und vermutlich überwiegenden Teil - ihrer hohen Flexibilität durch die direkte
Rechnersteuerung des Elektronenstrahls. Im folgenden sollen nun die
verschiedenen elektronenoptischen Belichtungsverfahren kurz beschrieben und die Maschinenkonzepte nach dem erreichbaren Durchsatz bewertet werden. Für die Beurteilung der künftigen Entwicklung der Mikrolithografie sei jedoch bereits hier darauf hingewiesen, daß die hohen
Investitionen und die für die technologischen Folgeprozesse eingefah-
rene Fotolacktechnik den lichtoptischen Verfahren ein großes Beharr-
ungsvermögen verleihen werden.

2. Belichtungsverfahren

Alle Elektronenstrahl-Belichtungsverfahren können zwischen zwei extremen
Kategorien eingeordnet werden /1-3/, nämlich:

(1) Ein fein fokussierter Strahl (Gaußsche Sonde) wird durch ein Aus-
    tast- und Ablenksystem so über die zu belichtende Fläche geführt,
    daß die gewünschten Figuren aus einer Folge sequentiell belich-
    teter Bildpunkte entstehen (vergl. Bildentstehung im Raster-
    Elektronenmikroskop).

(2) Eine teiltransparente Maske mit den gewünschten Strukturen wird
    integral 1:1 oder verkleinert auf die zu belichtende Fläche pro-
    jiziert (vergl. Bildenstehung im Transmissions-Elektronenmikroskop).

Bei beiden Verfahren reicht der Ablenkbereich bzw. das Bildfeld in
keinem Falle aus, um die gesamte Halbleiterscheibe in einem Schritt
zu belichten. Es ist also jeweils eine mechanische Bewegung des Kreuztisches notwendig, um die Gesamtfläche Schritt für Schritt abzuarbei-
ten. Ferner ist zu beachten, daß die Prozeßfolge bei der Halbleiter-
herstellung eine Folge von Maskierungsebenen verlangt, die untereinander eine genaue geometrische Zuordnung ("Justierung") einhalten
müssen. Diese Zuordnung wird durch eine genaue und konstante Kalibrierung der Belichtungsanlage erreicht, was das Schreiben und Erkennen
von Justiermarken und/oder eine laserinterferometrische Kontrolle
der Kreuztischbewegung voraussetzt. An dieser Stelle erst wird über
die Genauigkeit und Kontrolle der gesamten Bildpunktzahl des Schreib-
feldes entschieden.

Das <u>Verfahren (1)</u> hat den Vorteil hoher Flexibilität, da jede beliebige Kontur durch direkte Rechnersteuerung des Strahls geschrieben
werden kann. Durch Variation des Strahldurchmessers kann zudem die Adres-
senstruktur dem verlangten Auflösungsvermögen angepaßt werden. Justiermarken lassen sich durch Abrastern des in Frage kommenden Gebietes
über einen Detektor für reflektierte Elektronen oder Probenstrom gut
erkennen und ausmessen (der Schreiber arbeitet dann als Rastermikro-
skop). Die meisten Laboranlagen arbeiten daher in dieser Weise. Der
große Nachteil dieses Verfahrens liegt in der geringen Schreibgeschwindigkeit, die zu einem geringen Durchsatz solcher Anlagen führt.

Zum Ausfüllen der zu belichtenden Figuren werden zwei Strategien unterschieden (siehe Bild 2):

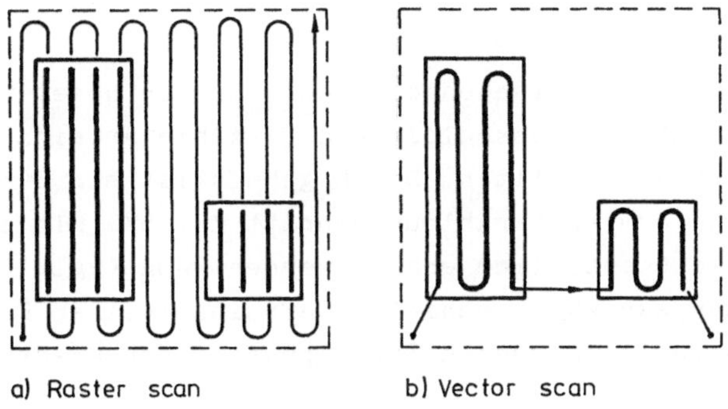

<u>Bild 2:</u>   Verschiedene Schreibverfahren für Elektronenstrahlschreiber

a) Beim Raster scan überstreicht die Ablenkung das gesamte Bildfeld
   mäanderförmig, der Strahl wird nur über den Figuren hellgetastet
   (Bild 2a). Vorteile: konstante Ablenkfrequenz, elektronische
   Invertierbarkeit des Bildes.

b) Beim Vector scan springt der Strahl nur jeweils zu den Figuren und
   füllt diese nach einem Mäander- oder Spiralverfahren aus (Bild 2b).
   Vorteile: Zeitersparnis (nur etwa 25 % der Fläche bestehen aus zu
   belichtenden Figuren), Schreibdichte und damit Dosis können individuell variiert werden.

Das <u>Verfahren (2)</u> hat den Vorteil eines hohen Durchsatzes. Der Einsatz einer starren Maske schränkt jedoch die Flexibilität erheblich ein. Damit eignet sich dieses Verfahren prinzipiell recht gut für die Massenfertigung feiner Strukturen.

Die 1:1-Projektion von Fotokathoden-Masken auf die Halbleiterscheibe in einem homogenen Magnetfeld /4/ erwies sich in ihrer Leistungsfähigkeit als begrenzt wegen der Farbfehler (Austrittsarbeit), der Kontrastübertragung, der geometrischen Verzüge des Feldes und der damit verbundenen Justierschwierigkeiten.

Die verkleinernde Projektion teiltransparenter Masken hat vom elektronenoptischen Standpunkt aus eine vielversprechende Leistungsfähigkeit erreicht (37000 auflösbare Linien pro Bildfeld in einem 1:4-Projektor /5/). Das technologische Problem, eine für Elektronen teiltransparente und dennoch verzugsfreie Maske herzustellen, konnte leider bisher nur unbefriedigend gelöst werden.

Man bemühte sich daher um Zwischenlösungen, die den hohen Durchsatz des Verfahrens (2) auf die maskenlose und flexible Arbeitsweise des Verfahrens (1) übertragen sollten. Das Ergebnis ist ein durch Blenden elektronenoptisch geformter Strahlquerschnitt /3, 6/, mit dem die Schreibgeschwindigkeit erheblich erhöht werden kann (vgl. Bild 3). Üblicherweise werden zur kantenscharfen Definition einer Figur mindestens vier Durchläufe eines runden Strahlprofils vorgesehen (Bild 3a).

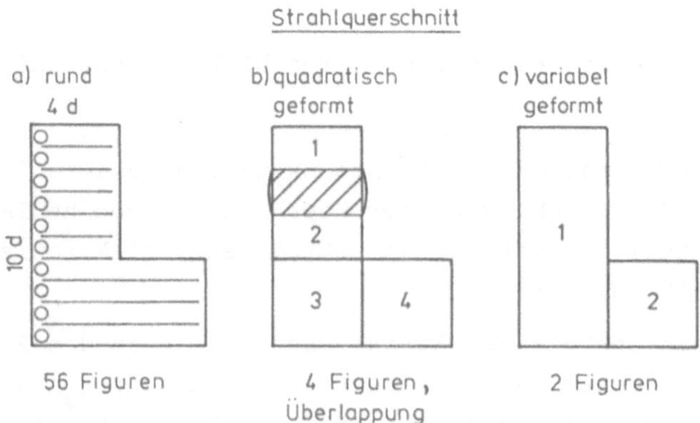

<u>Bild 3</u>: Vorteile eines geformten Strahlquerschnitts für die Schreibgeschwindigkeit.

Beim gleichen Richtstrahlwert der Elektronenquelle und bei gleicher
Kantenschärfe (Steigung des Strahlprofils) kann ein quadratisch geformter Strahl den 16-fachen Strahlstrom erreichen. Ferner ist die Zahl der
zu adressierenden Bildpunkte erheblich verringert (Bild 3b). Verwendet
man schließlich einen variabel rechteckig geformten Strahlquerschnitt,
was durch abgelenkte Projektion zweier quadratischer Blenden aufein-
ander möglich ist /5/, so verringert sich die Adressenzahl weiter
(Bild 3c). Mit dem geformten Strahlquerschnitt wird allerdings die
Flexibilität eingeschränkt: Es können bevorzugt nur noch rechtwink-
lige Strukturen hergestellt werden, was jedoch beim Entwurf komplexer
Schaltungen aus anderen Gründen sowieso angestrebt wird.

3. Grenzen von Auflösung und Bildfeld

Die künftig benötigten Strukturdimensionen liegen in der Größenordnung
von 0,5 bis 1,0 µm. Dies bedeutet eine Kantenschärfe und damit eine
elektronenoptische Auflösung und Positioniergenauigkeit von 50 bis
200 nm. Von der Wellenlänge (verwendet werden Energien von 5 - 30 keV),
der Apertur und den Linsenfehlern her gesehen sind Strahldurchmesser
von einigen 10 nm elektronenoptisch kein Problem, soweit man nicht zu
weit von der optischen Achse abweichen muß.

Die eigentliche Auflösungsgrenze wird bei massiven Proben, ähnlich
wie in der Rastermikroskopie, durch die laterale Elektronenstreuung
vorgegeben. Die vom Substrat rückgestreuten Elektronen und die Sekun-
därelektronen erzeugen in dem elektronenempfindlichen Lack nämlich
auch dort eine Hintergrund-Belichtungsdosis, wo der Primärstrahl gar
nicht auftrifft. Dies führt bei eng benachbarten Figuren zu Maßabwei-
chungen ("Proximity effect"), die eine Auflösungsgrenze schon weit vor
der prinzipiell elektronenoptisch erreichbaren setzt. Die Maßabwei-
chungen können durch individuell variable Dosis zum Teil kompensiert
werden. Grundsätzlich läßt sich die Streugrenze nur umgehen, wenn
man Substratfolien belichtet, die derart dünn sind, daß der Elektronenstrahl von ca. 10 keV sie durchdringt. Auf diese Weise können ultra-
feine Strukturen mit dem Elektronenstrahl hergestellt werden, die man
eventuell für Röntgenmasken, Zonenlinsen oder Josephson-Elemente benötigt.

Etwas anders werden die Überlegungen, wenn man in Betracht zieht, daß
für die Mikrolithografie große Bildfelder und große Ablenkwinkel benötigt werden. Hier müssen die Linsen- und Ablenksysteme so entworfen
werden, daß große Bildfelder verzeichnungsfrei mit einer möglichst
hohen Bildpunktzahl beschrieben werden können /7/. Hinzu kommt, daß
der Aperturwinkel in der Bildebene ausreichnd groß (einige mrad) gewählt werden muß, um bei endlichem Richtstrahlwert der Kathoden (W,
La B_6, Feldemitter?) hohe Strahlströme (einige μA) in kleinen Strahl-
querschnitten (einige 0,1 μm) zu erzielen. Die geometrischen Verzeichnungen müssen bis zur Größe des Auflösungsvermögens kompensiert werden,
weil die elektronenoptischen Bildfelder von der Ausdehnung komplexer
Schaltungen (Chips) überschritten werden und daher ein genaues Zusammensetzen der Bildfelder nach einer Tischbewegung möglich sein soll.
Will man die oben genannten Forderungen erfüllen, so erscheinen derzeit für 0,2 μm Auflösung allenfalls Bildfelder von etwa 2 mm Kanten-
länge realisierbar.

4. Maschinenkonzepte und Durchsatz

Eine fertigungsgerechte Anlage soll sich auszeichnen durch

- hohen Durchsatz auch bei kleinen Dimensionen der zu belichtenden
  Strukturen,

- Rechnersteuerung

- geringe Zeiten für Kalibrierung und Wartung

Tabelle 1 soll eine Übersicht geben über die in Abschnitt 2 beschriebenen Verfahren, die in Abschnitt 3 beschriebenen Grenzen und die Aus-
wirkungen der elektronenoptischen Seite auf das Gesamtkonzept. Der
obere Teil der Tabelle enthält prinzipielle Angaben; im unteren Teil
sind als Anhaltspunkte einige zahlenmäßige Richtwerte angegeben, die
in derzeit eingesetzten Systemen realisiert wurden. Man sieht, daß
Schreiber mit rundem Strahlquerschnitt trotz ihrer hohen Figurenfre-
quenz den geringsten Durchsatz erzielen und die höchste Lackempfindlich-
keit benötigen. Auf der anderen Seite erwiesen sich bisher ausschließlich solche Schreiber mit festem Strahlquerschnitt als praxisgerechte
Systeme mit der nötigen Zuverlässigkeit und Reproduzierbarkeit.

Strahlform	rund (Gauß)	geformt		Maskenprojektion	
		quadratisch	variabel	4:1	1:1
Flexibilität	sehr hoch	hoch		unflexibel	
Schreibgeschwindigkeit	gering	mittel, strukturabhängig		"hoch"	
Justierung	gut	gut		schwieriger	
Proximity effect	kompensierbar	kompensierbar		nicht kompensierbar	
Verzeichnung	←———— bei großen Bildfeldern hoch *) ————→			0**)	
Figurenfrequenz	40 MHz	5 MHz	200 kHz	1 Hz	
Adresse	0,5 μm	2,5 μm (offset 0,5 μm)		>30 000 Linien/ Bild	
Lackempfindlichkeit	1 μC cm^{-2}	10 μC cm^{2}		>10 μC cm^{2}	
Durchsatz $\left[\text{3"Scheiben}/_h\right]$	2	10	5 – 20	20	100

*) bei kleiner Auslenkung ist telezentrischer Strahlengang möglich

**) bei homogenen Feldern

Tabelle 1: Richtwerte für die Leistungsfähigkeit verschiedener elektronenoptischer
Belichtungsverfahren.

Zum Entwurf oder zur Beurteilung eines Maschinenkonzeptes ist jedoch
weit mehr als die elektronenoptische Seite zu berücksichtigen. Neben
Auflösungsvermögen und Genauigkeit der Anlage ist vor allem der Durchsatz zu beachten. Zur gesamten Durchlaufzeit tragen folgende Anteile
bei:

$$\text{Durchlaufzeit} = \frac{\text{(zu belichtende) Fläche}}{\text{Figurenfrequenz x Figurenfläche}}$$

+ Tischbewegungszeit (bei dunkelgetastetem Strahl)

+ Justierzeit (Justiermarkenerkennung)

+ Ladezeit (Scheiben, Speicher des Rechners)

Dabei ist

$$\text{Figurenfläche} = (\text{Strahldurchmesser})^2$$

oder Fläche des geformten Strahlquerschnitts
(hierdurch wird die Auflösung bestimmt!)

$$\text{Figurenfrequenz} \sim \text{Strahlstromdichte} \times \text{Lackempfindlichkeit}$$

(solange < Datenrate

und   < max. Ablenkfrequenz)

$$\text{Tischbewegungszeit} \sim \frac{\text{Scheibenfläche}}{(\text{Bildfeldkante})^2} \quad \text{(Zahl der Schritte}$$

für Step and Repeat-

Systeme)

$$\text{Justierzeit} \sim \frac{\text{notwendige Zahl der Marken}}{\text{Strahlstromdichte} \times \text{Markengröße}}$$

In diesen Abhängigkeiten zeichnen sich zwei Wege einer Optimierung
ab (Bild 4):

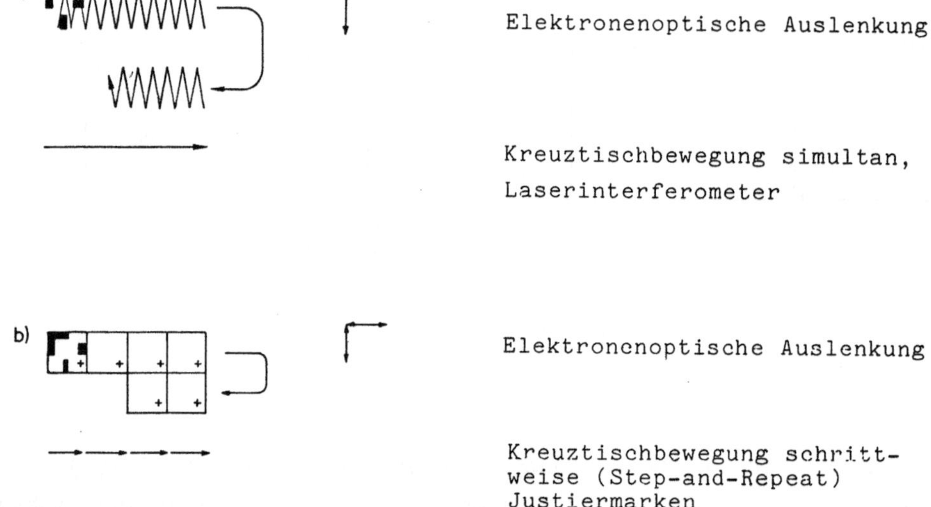

<u>Bild 4</u>: Maschinenkonzepte für simultane oder schrittweise Bewegung
des Kreuztisches.

(a) Man verringert den Anteil der Kreuztischbewegung zur gesamten
Durchlaufzeit ganz erheblich dadurch, daß mit "fliegendem Tisch"
belichtet wird. Praktisch bedeutet dies, daß die elektronenoptische Auslenkung im wesentlichen in einer Koordinatenrichtung erfolgt, während der Tisch simultan sich in der dazu senkrechten
Koordinatenrichtung bewegt. Ungleichmäßigkeiten der Tischbewegung
werden über Laserinterferometer und Korrektur in der elektronenoptischen Ablenkung trägheitslos kompensiert (Bild 4a).

(b) Man verwendet ein möglichst schnelles Belichtungsverfahren (Vector
    scan mit variabel geformtem Strahlquerschnitt) in beiden Koordi-
    natenrichtungen der zu belichtenden Fläche und verringert die Zeit
    für die Tischbewegung (d.h. die Zahl der Schritte) durch Ausnützung
    eines möglichst großen elekronenoptischen Bildfeldes (Bild 4b).

Nach Ansicht des Autors hat das Maschinenkonzept (b) besonders gute
Chancen, wenn die Anforderungen

- kein extremes Auflösungsvermögen

- Maskierungsebenen mit geringerer Figurendichte

- Lacke mit geringerer Empfindlichkeit

verlangen. Auf der anderen Seite glauben wir, daß das Maschinenkonzept
(a) durch die Forderung nach

- hohem Auflösungsvermögen

- hoher Figurendichte in jeder Ebene

- der Entwicklung von empfindlichen Lacken und Kathoden mit
  hohem Richtstrahlwert

günstig beeinflußt wird.

5. Stand der Dinge und Forderungen für die Zukunft

Mit der Fortentwicklung integrierter Schaltungen ist auch die zugehörige Fertigungstechnik und damit die Mikrolithografie in einer dynamischen Entwicklungsphase. Elektronenstrahlschreiber haben schon vor
Jahren in fast alle Entwicklungslabors Einzug gehalten und dienen dort
zur experimentellen Erzeugung feinster Strukturen, teils durch Direktbelichtung der Substrate, teils über die Herstellung von Masken für
das UV- oder Röntgen-Kopieren im Maßstab 1:1 (Bild 5). Gerade für Ent-
wicklungsabteilungen ist die in Bild 5 demonstrierte Flexibilität des
elektronenoptischen Weges gegenüber dem lichtoptischen sehr nützlich.

In der Fertigung zahlreicher Halbleiterhersteller sind heute Elektronen-
strahl-Maskengeneratoren routinemäßig im Einsatz. Die Vorteile dieser
Schreiber bei der Maskenherstellung konnten problemlos in die üblichen
Fertigungsprozesse integriert werden, und man ist zur Zeit noch dabei,
die speziellen Eigenschaften des elektronenoptischen Weges (hohe Maß-
haltigkeit und Überdeckungsgenauigkeit, geringe Fehlerdichte, Möglichkeit verschiedener Strukturen auf derselben Maske, Herstellung von

Mehrfach-Reticles) voll auszunutzen.

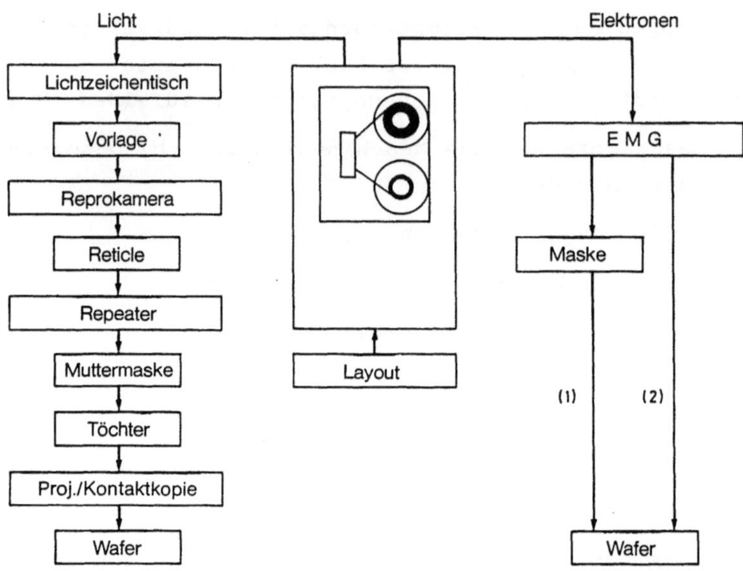

Bild 5: Vorteile des elektronenoptischen Weges gegenüber der Licht-
optik infolge verringerter Zahl der Zwischenschritte (EMG =
Elektronenstrahl-Maskengenerator).

Die direkte Elektronenstrahlbelichtung der Scheiben wird bisher nur
von einem großen Halbleiterhersteller im Fertigungsmaßstab praktiziert
/3/. Unter welchen Umständen dieser Weg zu wirtschaftlichen Vorteilen
führt, ist derzeit umstritten. Die generelle Abhängigkeit der Litho-
grafie-Kosten pro belichtete Scheibe als Funktion der gefertigten
Scheibenzahl ist in Bild 6 dargestellt. Wie man sieht, fallen die
Kosten zur Maskenherstellung bei größeren Stückzahlen kaum mehr ins
Gewicht. Der Schnittpunkt S, ab dem die Herstellung über Masken
(Weg (1) in Bild 5) kostengünstiger wird als die Direktbelichtung,
liegt für den Durchsatz der heute verfügbaren Maschinen zwischen zwei
und drei belichteten Scheiben. Dabei ist allerdings die bei Direktbelichtung zu erwartende Ausbeutesteigerung noch nicht berücksichtigt.

Das im Prinzip und vom Durchsatz her sehr attraktive Verfahren der
Elektronenprojektion konnte bisher an keiner Stelle zur praktischen
Einsatzreife entwickelt werden. Ursache dafür ist, wie bereits erwähnt,
das ungelöste Problem stabiler, aber für Elektronen teiltransparenter

Masken.

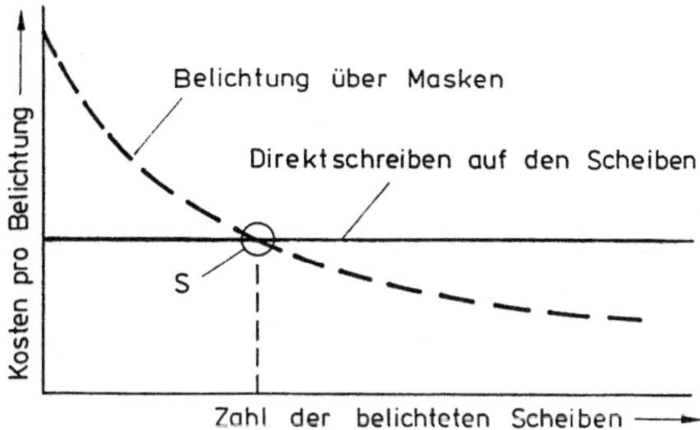

Bild 6: Kostenvergleich zwischen Direktschreiben und Belichten über Masken als Funktion der Stückzahl.

Für die künftige Entwicklung ergeben sich aus heutiger Sicht folgende Forderungen:

- Um die Vorteile der elektronenoptischen Maskenherstellung voll ausnützen zu können, müssen die prozeßbedingten Fehlerdichten (Maskenmaterial, Beschichtung, Lacktechnik, Entwickeln und Ätzen) weiter verringert werden.

- Für die Direktbelichtung von Scheiben müssen aus technologischer Sicht noch Verbesserungen bei prozeßkompatiblen Lacken, beim Richtstrahlwert der Strahlquellen und ihrer Konstanz sowie bei einer effektiven Belichtungsstrategie erzielt werden.

- Für die Direktbelichtung von Scheiben muß aus wirtschaftlicher Sicht der Durchsatz gegenüber den heute verfügbaren Systemen noch etwa um den Faktor 10 gesteigert werden.

Da es noch unsicher ist, wann und wie die beiden Forderungen für die Direktbelichtung erfüllbar sind, wird man weiterhin nach Wegen suchen, feine Strukturen auch auf nicht-elektronenoptische Weise großflächig von Masken auf die Scheiben zu übertragen, wie z.B. durch kurzwelliges UV-Licht oder Röntgenstrahlung.

Die diesem Bericht zugrunde liegenden Arbeiten wurden teilweise vom Bundesministerium für Forschung und Technologie gefördert. Die Verantwortung für den Inhalt liegt jedoch allein beim Autor.

6. Literaturverzeichnis

/1/ J. Hersener und Th. Ricker: Zur Mikrolithographie für planare Bauelemente,
Wiss. Ber. AEG-TELEFUNKEN 52 (1979) 139 und 231

/2/ A.N. Broers: A review of high-resolution microfabrication techniques,
Inst. of Phys. Conf. Ser. 40, Ed. E.Ash, London (1978) 155

/3/ E.V. Weber, R.D. Moore: E-beam exposure for semiconductor device lithography,
Solid State Technology (May 1979) 61

/4/ J.P. Scott: An electron image projector with automatic alignment,
IEEE Trans. ED 22 (1975) 409

/5/ B. Lischke, J. Frosien, K. Anger: Hochauflösende Elektronenlithographie mit Hilfe der Mikroprojektion,
Optik 54 (1979) 325

/6/ H.C. Pfeiffer: Variable spot shaping for electron-beam lithography,
J.Vac.Sci.Technol. 15 (1978) 887

/7/ R. Speidel, G. Kolger, E. Kasper: Optical properties of combined magnetic lenses and deflection systems,
Optik 54 (1979/80) 433

<u>SCHNELLE RECHNERGESTÜTZTE ENTZERRUNG OPTISCH VERZEICHNETER</u>

<u>BINÄRBILDER MIT HILFE EINES INTERAKTIVEN BILDSPEICHERSYSTEMS</u>

<u>FAST COMPUTER AIDED DISTORTION CORRECTION OF BINARY IMAGES</u>

<u>BY THE USE OF AN INTERACTIVE IMAGE STORE SYSTEM</u>

Reiner Schröder

Cambridge Instrument Company GmbH

D - 4600   Dortmund 1

Zusammenfassung:

Das dargestellte Verfahren eliminiert den Einfluß von nicht ausreichend
linearen Abbildungen in Licht- und Elektronenoptik. Dabei wird das Blick-
feld in eine Anzahl kleiner Rasterquadrate aufgeteilt. Mit Hilfe eines
Objektmikrometers werden Koordinatenkorrekturwerte für jedes Rasterquadrat
berechnet und abgespeichert. Die Korrektur des aktuellen Binärbildes geschieht
in einem sehr flexiblen und schnellen interaktiven Bildspeichersystem. Dieser
Halbleiterbildspeicher ist in der Lage, mehrere Binärbilder in verschiedenen
Ebenen gleichzeitig zu halten und über eine ALU in Echtzeit zu verarbeiten.
Das Binärbild wird in den erwähnten Quadraten entsprechend den Meßdaten re-
positioniert.

Summary:

The process presented eliminates the influence of insufficient linearity caused
by light and electron optics. This is done by dividing the field of view into a
number of scanning squares. Correction values for the coordinates of each square
are computed and stored by means of an object micrometer. The actual binary image
is corrected using a very flexible and fast interactive image store system. This
semiconductor image memory is able to store several binary images in different
planes simultaneously and to process them via an ALU in real time.
The binary image is corrected by repositioning the individual squares with
respect to the measured data.

In der Bildverarbeitung stellen uns nicht ausreichend lineare Abbildungen des
licht- und elektronenoptischen Inputsystems häufig vor Probleme, die nach kon-
ventioneller Methode nur mit relativ großem Aufwand gelöst werden können.
Allgemein bekannte Erscheinungsformen dieser Fehler sind Kissen- oder Tonnenver-
zeichnungen.
Eine Verzeichnungskorrektur ist somit für alle Bildverarbeitungsaufgaben interessant,
die möglichst unverzerrte Bilder als Input benötigen. In dieser Arbeit wird
Cambridge Instrument Company GmbH implementiertes Verfahren vorgestellt und erläutert,
das mit Hilfe eines Mikrorechners (PDP 11/03) und eines interaktiven Bildspeicher-
systems die Verzerrungen einer Mikroskop-Kamera-Anordnung eliminiert (s. Abb. 1).

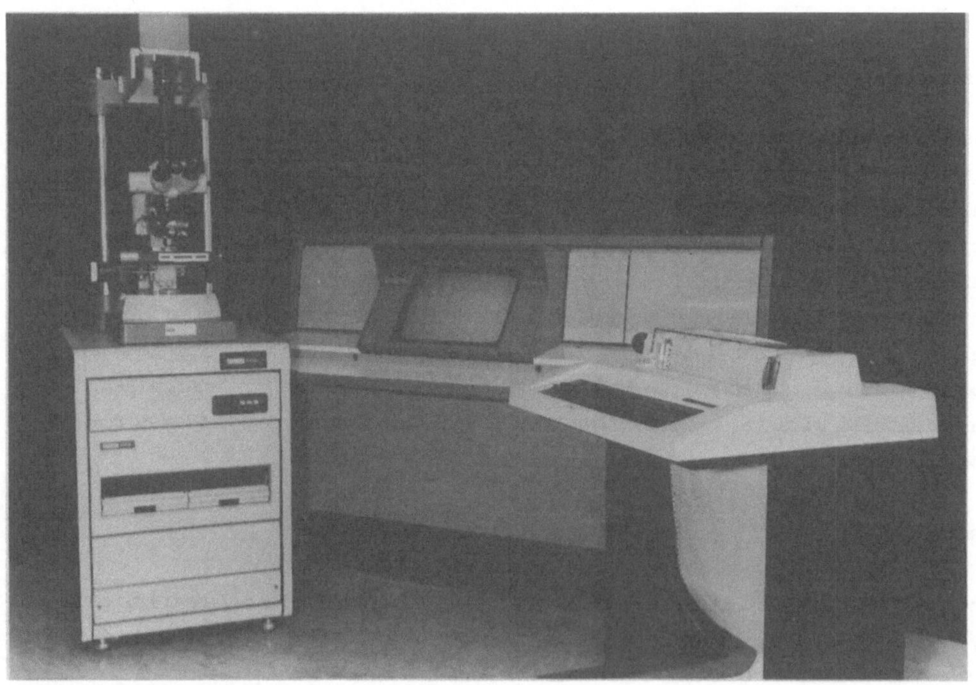

Abb. 1. Mikroskop-Kamera Anordnung mit QUANTIMET 720.

Das Verfahren besteht hauptsächlich aus zwei Phasen:

1. Verzerrungsmessung und Abspeichern von Daten.

2. Entzerrung eines aktuellen Binärbildes im interaktiven Bildspeichersystem gemäß den unter 1. ermittelten Daten.

Das gesamte zu korrigierende Bild wird in eine Anzahl gleich großer Quadrate unterteilt. Die Randbedingung bei der Auswahl der Quadratgröße lautet: die Verzeichnung in einem Quadrat des elektronischen Rasterbildes darf betragsmäßig einen Bildpunkt nich überschreiten. Mit Hilfe eines Objektmikrometers und des automatischen Mikroskoptisches wird für jedes Quadrat ein Zahlenpaar ermittelt, das die Positionskorrektur zwischen verzeichnetem und unverzeichnetem Bild in X- und Y-Richtung darstellt. Die so gewonnene X-Y-Korrektur-Matrix (s. Abb. 2) wird in einem Kalibrierungsfile auf einem Massenspeicher abgelegt.

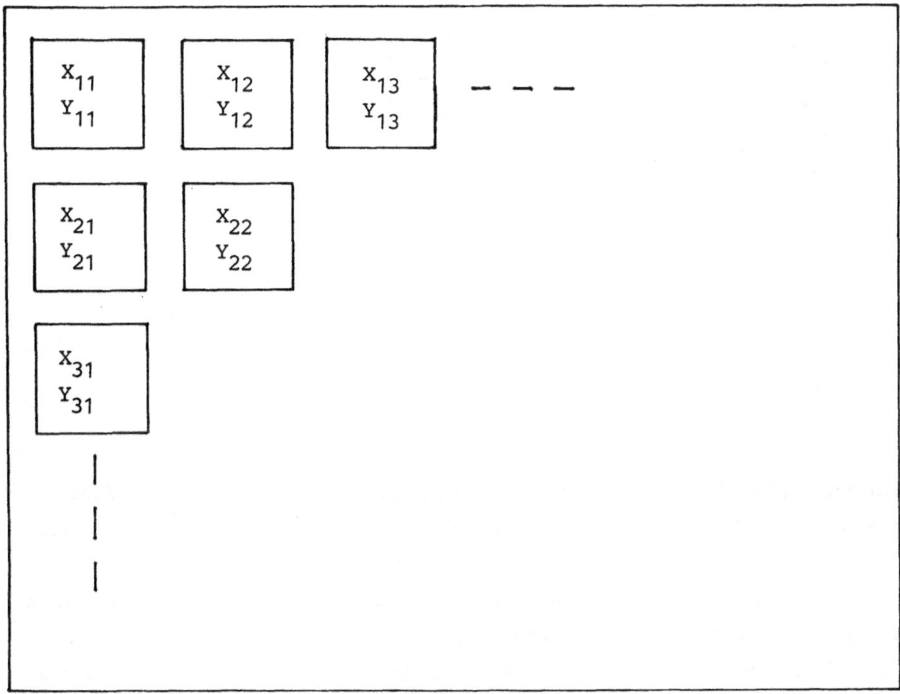

Abb. 2: Zuordnung der Korrekturmatix zum Bild.

Im nächsten Schritt wird ein Binärbild, das z.B. mit einem unserer automatischen Detektoren gewonnen wird, in den interaktiven Bildspeicher geladen und mit Hilfe der Daten-Matrix korrigiert. Aus diesem Grunde sei kurz auf das interaktive Bildspeichersystem (Interactive Image Store System = IISS) eingegengen.
Im Blockschaltbild (Abb. 3) ist als Kern der 768 K-Bytes Halbleiterspeicher zu erkennen. Diese Kapazität reicht aus, um z.B. acht binäre Bilder im QUANTIMET-Format gleichzeitig zu halten und zu verarbeiten (s. Abb. 4).(Man kann natürlich auch beispielsweise ein 8-bit-Grauwertbild speichern.) Am Eingang können aktuelles Bild vom QUANTIMET und Speicherinhalt in der ALU in Echtzeit verknüpft werden. Ausgangsseitige

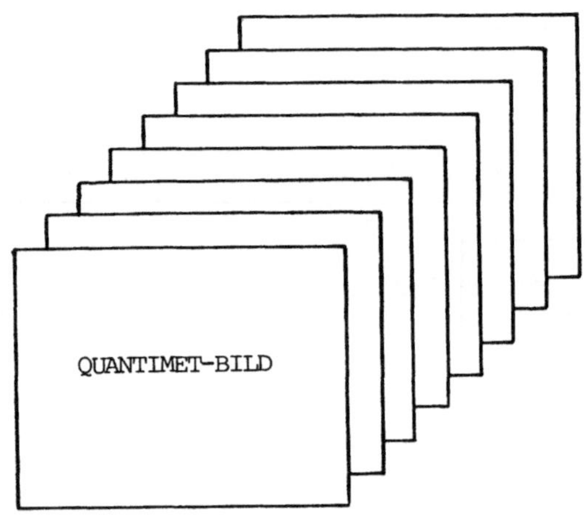

Abb. 4. Bitebenenorganisation des IISS

Manipulationen (Zuordnung von Grauwerten) sind mit Hilfe der LOOK UP TABLES realisierbar. Es sei noch erwähnt, daß sämtliche Speicher-, Verknüpfungs- und Leseoperationen des QUANTIMET-Bildes in Echtzeit erfolgen.
In der Korrekturphase des Verfahrens wird das binäre, von Mikroskop und Kamera verzerrte Bild in Echtzeit in eine Ebene des Bildspeichers geladen.
Anschließend wird es blockweise (1Block = 1 Quadrat) unter Berücksichtigung der abgespeicherten Korrekturwerte - Matrix neu adressiert und an die korrigierte Position in die gleiche Bitebene zurückgeschrieben. Bei Überlappung zweier Quadrate wird maximal 1 Zeile oder Spalte des zuvor geschriebenen Quadrates

überschrieben. 1 Bildpunkt große Lücken werden durch Duplizieren geschlossen.

Abb. 5: Normal verzerrtes Binärbild.

Abb. 6: Entzerrtes Binärbild.

Abb. 5. und 6. zeigen das Binärbild eines Netzmikrometers: einmal normal verzerrt und einmal entzerrt. Die Wirksamkeit des Verfahrens ist besonders an den Bildecken zu erkennen, wo die Verzeichnung relativ stark ist.

ZUR DYNAMIK-KOMPRESSION BEI DIGITALEN BILDERN

Hans-Georg Zimmer
Max-Planck-Institut für experimentelle Medizin
Forschungsstelle Neurochemie, Göttingen

Zusammenfassung

Eine richtungsabhängige zweite Ableitung erlaubt eine rauschunempfind-
liche Dynamik-Reduktion durch eine nichtlineare Hochpaßfilterung. Aus
einer niederfrequenten Hüllkurve des gefilterten Bildes werden Faktoren
für eine multiplikative Reduktion zu hoher Amplituden bzw. helligkeits-
abhängige Verschiebungen des Nullpunktes abgeleitet. Das Verfahren ver-
meidet störend breite und harte Konturen, erhält Helligkeitsinformationen in "ruhigen" Bildteilen und liefert auch im Grenzfall der Binärdarstellung noch lesbare Bilder.

Einleitung

Moderne Scanning-Photometer können mikroskopische Objekte als digitale
Bilder mit mehr als tausend Graustufen aufnehmen /1,2/. Für die Darstellung solcher Daten auf einem Plotter oder Bildschirm stehen in der
Regel nur zwei bis 30 unterschiedliche Graustufen zur Verfügung, wenn
man keine Falschfarbendarstellung benutzt. Das folgende Verfahren zur
Dynamik-Reduktion wurde entwickelt mit dem Ziel, für den menschlichen
Betrachter lesbare Bilder zu erzeugen, die den Detailreichtum des digitalen Bildes erhalten und unter Verzicht auf photometrische Richtigkeit
mit wenigen Graustufen darstellbar sind. Lesbarkeit ist hier subjektiv
gemeint im Sinne der Erkennbarkeit von Strukturen oder Texturen. Das hier
beschriebene Verfahren hat Ähnlichkeiten mit der Konturfindung von Geuen
und Liedtke /3/, dem in Pratt /4/ wiedergegebenen verallgemeinerten statistical differencing von Wallis und erlaubt bei Binärbildern höhere Ortsfrequenzen als das Verfahren von Fujimura /5/.

Anwendungsgebiet des hier beschriebenen Verfahrens sind photometrische
Aufnahmen mikroskopischer Präparate, die durch mechanisches Scannen der
Objekte entstehen, wobei die wirksame Meßblende die doppelte Schrittwei-
te des Scanningschrittes als Durchmesser hat, die Poisson-Verteilung der
Photonen durch das Ziehen der Quadratwurzel aus dem analogen Photometer-
signal berücksichtigt ist /1,2/ und wo durch lineare Filterung für helle
Bildteile ein Signal-Rausch-Verhältnis von 1000 erreicht wird. Die als
Beispiele gegebenen Bilder haben eine Größe von 256 x 256 Bildpunkten.

Eine rauscharme Konturfilterung

Photometrisch auszuwertende Objekte bestehen in der Regel aus ausgedehn-
ten hellen und dunklen Bildteilen, die durch entsprechende Färbung erzeugt werden. Da Menschen Intensitätsverhältnisse nur grob abschätzen
können, verwenden sie für die Zuordnung der photometrischen Daten zu den
Objekten Strukturdetails der Objekte. Deshalb bringt eine Hochpaßfilterung der photometrischen Daten eine Bildverbesserung im Sinne der Ver-
deutlichung hoher Ortsfrequenzen und in der Regel auch eine Reduktion
der Dynamik des Bildes, wenn nämlich der Übergang Hell-Dunkel nicht bei
den höchsten Ortsfrequenzen erfolgt. Das ist bei biologischen Objekten
oft der Fall, aber nicht z.B. bei einem Balkengitter.

Bekannte Verfahren der Hochpaßfilterung benutzen diskrete Realisierungen
z.B. des Laplace-Operators $\frac{\partial^2}{\partial x^2} + \frac{\partial^2}{\partial y^2}$ /6,7/, die empfindlich sind gegen
Bildstörungen durch Rauschen. Deshalb werden hier erstens nicht die In-
tensitäten, sondern deren Quadratwurzeln registriert und als digitale
Bilder gespeichert. Dadurch wird das signal-abhängige in ein signal-unab-
hängiges, additives Rauschen transformiert. Anderenfalls erscheinen helle
Bildteile stärker verrauscht als dunkle /1/.

Als zweite Maßnahme gegen das Rauschen wird die Bildung der zweiten Ableitung verknüpft mit einer Integration in der zur Differentiation senkrechten Richtung. Fig. 1a gibt das Koeffizientenschema der üblichen Realisierung des Laplace-Operators in Form eines linearen Filters, Fig. 1b
das Koeffizientenschema für die hier benutzte zweite Ableitung in x-
Richtung. Das Vorzeichen ist umgekehrt worden, damit Bildpunkte heller

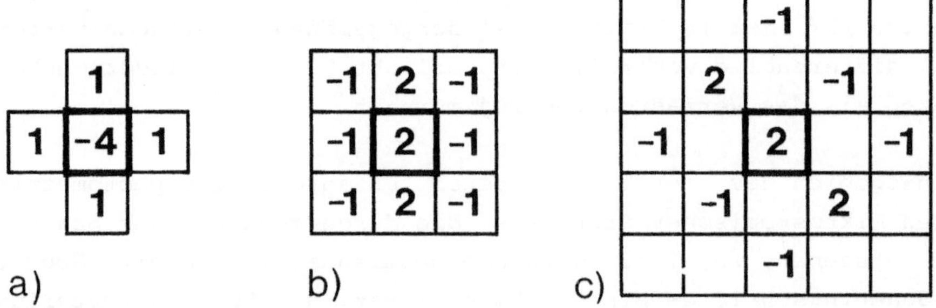

Fig. 1: Koeffizientenschemata für die Konturfilterung. a) Übliche dis-
krete Realisierung des Laplace-Operators $\frac{\partial^2}{\partial x^2} + \frac{\partial^2}{\partial y^2}$. b) Zweite Ableitung
in x-Richtung, c) zweite Ableitung in Diagonalrichtung +45°. Die zweiten
Ableitungen in den Richtungen y und -45° bekommt aus Fig. 1b bzw. 1c
durch Drehung des Schemas um 90°.

wiedergegeben werden, wenn ihre Grauwerte über denen ihrer Umgebung liegen. Fig. 1c gibt das Koeffizientenschema für die Bildung der zweiten Ableitung in der +45°-Richtung, die Koeffizientenschemata für die Richtungen y und -45° bekommt man aus Fig. 1b und 1c durch Drehung um 90°.

Zur Konturfilterung wird jedem Bildpunkt diejenige der vier Ableitungen zugeordnet, die den größten Absolutwert hat. Dadurch wird das Filter nichtlinear und ist nicht mehr mit Hilfe einer Übertragungsfunktion beschreibbar. Subjektiv bekommt man wegen der Betonung von Linienelementen einen besseren Bildeindruck als nach Anwendung des Laplace-Operators. Punktförmige Strukturen werden aber durch die Integration abgeschwächt. Die Differentiation in den Diagonalrichtungen ist notwendig, weil anderenfalls diagonal verlaufende Linien oder Kanten schlechter erkannt werden als solche in Zeilen- oder Spaltenrichtung. Das konturgefilterte Bild enthält positive und negative "Grauwerte". Summe oder Mittelwert der vier Ableitungen ergeben ein lineares Filter, das aber die hohen Ortsfrequenzen schlechter darstellt als das Konturfilter.

Die niederfrequente Hüllfläche

Für die weitere Verarbeitung des konturgefilterten Bildes werden dessen niederfrequente Hüllflächen verwendet. Sie werden in zwei Schritten erzeugt. Zuerst wird jedem Bildpunkt das Maximum der Beträge der konturgefilterten Grauwerte aus einer 7x7-Umgebung des Bildpunktes zugeordnet. Diese Hüllfläche schließt alle Grauwerte ein, ist aber kantig. Deshalb wird in einem zweiten Durchlauf jedem Bildpunkt der Mittelwert aller Punkte der ersten Hüllfläche aus einer 7x7-Umgebung zugeordnet.

Die Mittelwertbildung garantiert nicht, daß alle Grauwerte des konturgefilterten Bildes betragsmäßig kleiner sind als die Werte der Hüllfläche. Das könnte bei der folgenden Dynamik-Reduktion zu einem Klippen des Signals führen. In der Praxis wurde dieser Effekt nicht bemerkt. Auf eine genaue Bestimmung der Hüllfläche wurde wegen des Rechenaufwandes verzichtet.

Multiplikative Dynamik-Reduktion und additive Grauwertkorrektur

Bei der Dynamik-Reduktion wird die Grauwert-Dynamik der Hüllfläche in Beziehung gesetzt zur Grauskala des Ausgabegeräts. Ist für einen Bildpunkt der Grauwert H der Hüllfläche größer als der halbe Graustufenbereich $\frac{D}{2}$ des Ausgabegeräts, dann wird der konturgefilterte Grauwert dieses Bildpunktes mit dem Faktor $\frac{D}{2 \cdot H}$ reduziert. Ist $H \leqslant \frac{D}{2}$, dann wird $v(\frac{D}{2} - H)$ zum konturgefilterten Grauwert des Bildpunktes addiert. Es ist $v = 1$, wenn

für diesen Bildpunkt der Grauwert des Originalbildes größer ist als der
Mittelwert aller Grauwerte des Bildes, sonst ist v = -1. Wenn die lokale
Variation der Grauwerte im konturgefilterten Bild kleiner ist als der
darstellbare Bereich, werden durch diese Maßnahme niederfrequente Informationen über die Grauwerte des Originalbildes in die Darstellung aufgenommen. Das erhöht die Anschaulichkeit der Darstellung und verhindert
eine Überbetonung des Rauschens in "ruhigen" Bildteilen. In dieser addi-
tiven Korrektur statt einer multiplikativen liegt ein wesentlicher Unterschied zu dem von Wallis angegebenen Verfahren (vgl. /4/).

Zur Ausgabe von Halbtonbildern setzt man für D die Anzahl darstellbarer
Graustufen ein und gibt jedem Bildpunkt des verarbeiteten Bildes einen
Offset von $\frac{D}{2}$, damit alle auszugebenden Grauwerte positiv sind. Schwache
lokale Kontraste lassen sich dadurch unterdrücken, daß man D größer wählt
und das verarbeitete Bild vor der Ausgabe auf die zulässige Anzahl von
Graustufen skaliert. Auf diese Weise bekommt die niederfrequente Hellig-
keitsinformation der Originaldaten mehr Gewicht. Für den Bildeindruck ist
es zweckmäßig, daß das Ausgabegerät eine quadratische Charakteristik hat.

Für eine Binärdarstellung setzt man z.B. D = 16, denn für D = 2 ist die
Bedingung $H < \frac{D}{2}$ praktisch nie erfüllt, was zur Folge hat, daß auch ruhige
Bildteile keine niederfrequenten Helligkeitsinformationen bekommen. Je
größer D, desto größer ist der lokale Kontrast, der bei der Binärausgabe
unterdrückt wird. Alle negativen Werte des verarbeiteten Bildes werden
schwarz, die übrigen weiß dargestellt. Eine Veränderung dieser natürlichen Schwelle führt zu einer Überbetonung heller oder dunkler Bereiche
und falschen Orten für die Konturen.

<u>Bildlegende zu Fig. 2</u>
Photometrie eines Diapositivs für den direkten Vergleich der verarbeiteten Bilder mit dem Original. Die Schrittweite des Scanners ist 0,1 mm
und entspricht 0,23 mm bei der hier wiedergegebenen Vergrößerung 2,3x.
a) Reproduktion vom Originalnegativ, b) bis f) Darstellungen des digitalen Bildes, Photographien vom Bildschirm des Computers PDP-12 (DEC).
b) Zehn Graustufen ohne Verarbeitung, c) zehn Graustufen nach dem beschriebenen Verfahren der Dynamik-Reduktion, d) wie c), aber nach Laplace-
Filterung statt der Konturfilterung; e) und f) sind die c) und d) entsprechenden Binärbilder mit D = 10 (siehe Text).
Die in Fig. 2c) z.B. am Ärmel sichtbare Textur ist in unabhängigen Messungen des Diapositivs reproduzierbar und beschreibt zum Teil lokale
Dichteschwankungen der wenigen Silberkörner in diesem Gebiet.

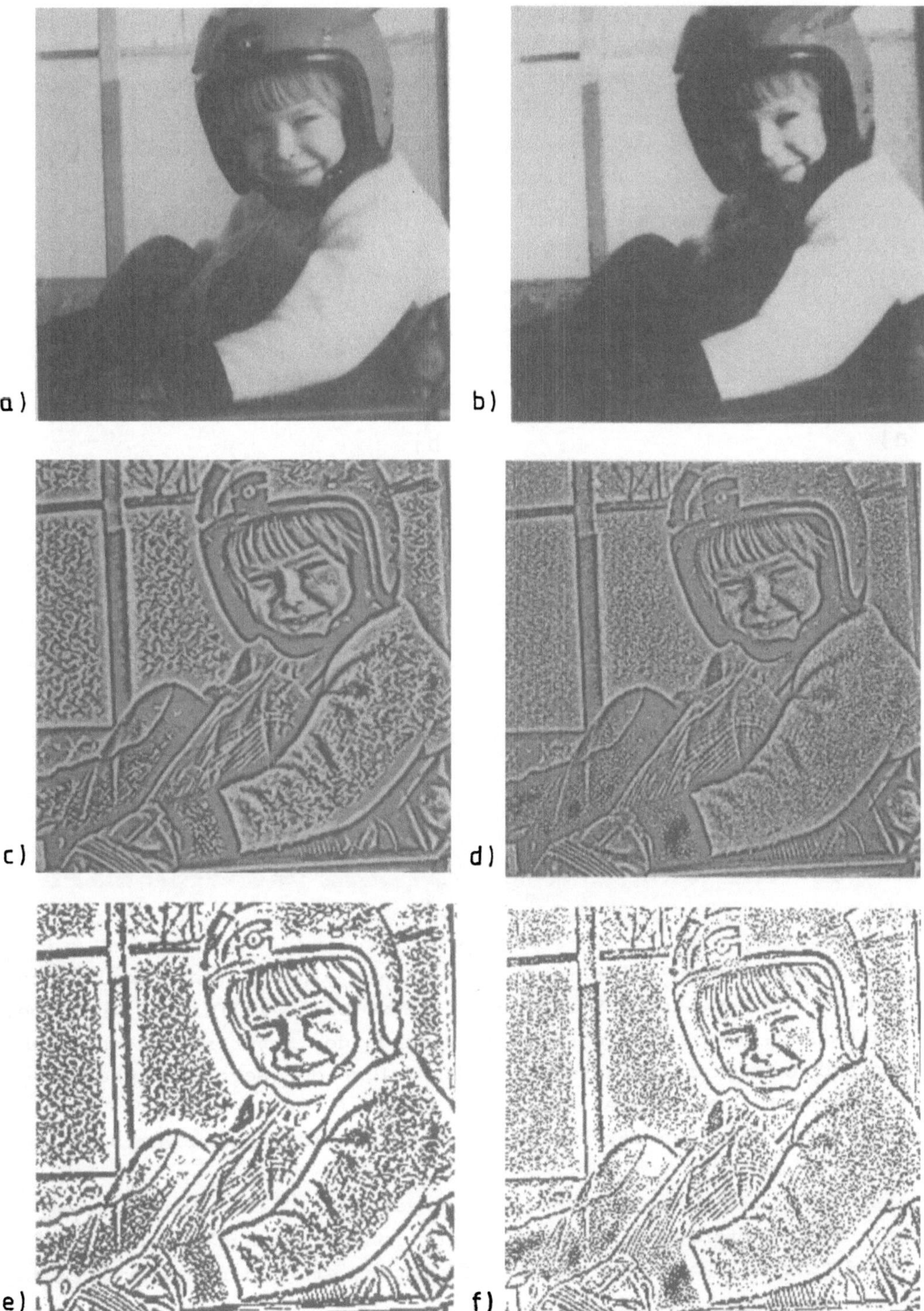

Fig. 2

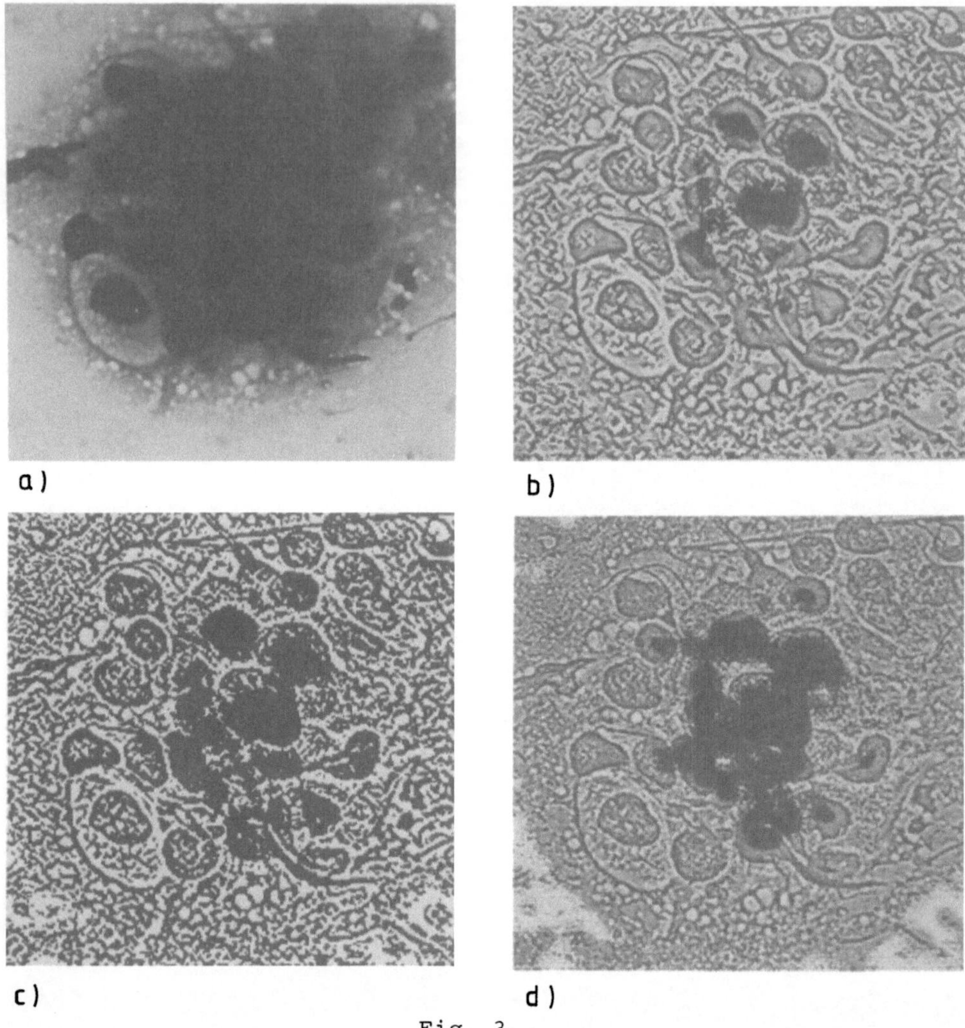

Fig. 3

a) May-Grünwald-Giemsa gefärbter Ausstrich aus einem Lymphknoten. Photographiert in weißem Licht, Vergrößerung 470x. Diese Zellgruppe wurde bei der Wellenlänge 570 nm photometriert, wodurch der Kontrast zwischen dem Hintergrund und den stark absorbierenden Zellen den Wert 1000 überstieg. Die Schrittweite des Scanners ist 0,0005 mm.

b) bis d) Darstellungen der Photometerwerte, Photographien vom Bildschirm des Computers.

b) Darstellung mit D = 20 und Skalierung auf zehn Graustufen nach dem beschriebenen Verfahren der Dynamik-Reduktion, c) Binärdarstellung mit D = 16, d) wie b), aber nach Laplace-Filterung statt der Konturfilterung.

<u>Literatur</u>

/1/ Zimmer, H.-G., Kronberg, H., Bernstein, R., Neuhoff, V.: Improvements in microphotometry by digital signal processing. Pattern Recognition (1980) in press

/2/ Zimmer, H.-G., Kronberg, H., Neuhoff, V.: Signalverarbeitung in der Mikrophotometrie. Microscopica Acta (1980) in press

/3/ Geuen, W., Liedtke, C.-E.: Konturfindung auf der Basis des visuellen Konturempfindens des Menschen. Informatik-Fachberichte 20, 72 - 80, Springer-Verlag, Berlin, 1979

/3/ Pratt, W.K.: Digital image processing, p. 326. Wiley, New York 1978

/5/ Fujimura, K.: A representation of real world images with lines and and solid regions. Proceedings of the 4th International Joint Conference on Pattern Recognition, 613 - 615. Kyoto 1978

/6/ Rosenfeld, A., Kak, A.C.: Digital picture processing, p. 181. Academic Press, New York, 1976

/7/ Kugler, J., Wahl, F.: Kantendetektion mit lokalen Operatoren. Informatik-Fachberichte 20, 25 - 35, Springer-Verlag, Berlin, 1979

Zur Repräsentation von Kontrollstrukturen und
von Wissen in der Musteranalyse

H.Niemann
Universität Erlangen-Nürnberg
Lehrstuhl für Informatik 5 (Mustererkennung)
Martensstr.3, D-8520 Erlangen

Kurzfassung

Zu den wesentlichen Komponenten eines Systems zur Analyse von Mustern gehören unter
anderem ein Kontrollmodul und ein Modul, der Wissen über die strukturellen Eigenschaften der Muster und den Problemkreis enthält. In diesem Beitrag wird die Repräsentation der Kontrollstruktur und des Wissens mit Hilfe von hierarchischen Graphen (h-Graphen) diskutiert. Die Aufgabe des Kontrollmoduls besteht in der Auswahl
weniger geeigneter Suchpfade im Problemlösungsgraphen. An einem Beispiel wird die
Repräsentation des Kontrollmoduls mit einem h-Graphen erläutert. Mit Hilfe von Wissen
ist es möglich, den Suchraum bei der Problemlösung einzugrenzen. Die Repräsentation
von Wissen mit h-Graphen wird ebenfalls durch ein Beispiel erläutert.

1. Einführung

Musteranalyse wurde in [1] als die Beschreibung eines Musters durch einfachere Be-
standteile und deren Beziehungen untereinander definiert. Zwei wichtige Beispiele
sind die Erkennung zusammenhängend gesprochener Sprache [2] und die Auswertung von
Bildern [3]. Die Analyse kann aufgefaßt werden als die Übersetzung der anfänglich
gegebenen Abtastwerte in eine symbolische Beschreibung, die aus dem Grunde erfolgt,
weil eine solche Beschreibung - möglicherweise reduziert auf einige wichtige Aspekte -
für die weitere automatische Verarbeitung geeigneter ist als eine Menge von Abtast-
werten.

Die Analyse von Mustern erfordert flexiblere Systemstrukturen als sie beispielsweise
bei der Klassifikation üblich sind. Die wesentlichen Komponenten eines Analysesystems
zeigt Bild 1. Es enthält eine Datenbank, in der Ergebnisse der Analyse gespeichert
werden und über die die anderen Komponenten gekoppelt sind. Dazu kommen ein Modul,
der von der speziellen Aufgabe weitgehend unabhängige Methoden zur Verarbeitung enthält, ein Modul, der aufgabenspezifisches Wissen enthält, sowie schließlich ein Modul, der die Folge der Verarbeitungsschritte auswählt und dadurch die Kontrolle über
die Analyse ausübt. Beispiele für Methoden sind lineare Filterung zur Reduzierung von
Störungen oder Extraktion von Linienelementen aus einem Grauwertbild. Beispiele für
Wissen sind die Festlegung der strukturellen Eigenschaften von Objekten wie Häusern
und Städten oder die Angabe eines Landschaftsmodells zur Bestimmung der Schatten in
Abhängigkeit von der Uhrzeit. Die Grenze zwischen Methoden und Wissen ist nicht scharf

zu ziehen. Sie entspricht der ebenfalls nicht scharfen Unterscheidung zwischen nie-
deren und höheren Verarbeitungsprozessen, die sowohl beim visuellen System von Lebewesen als auch bei Systemen zur Bildanalyse vorgenommen wird [4].

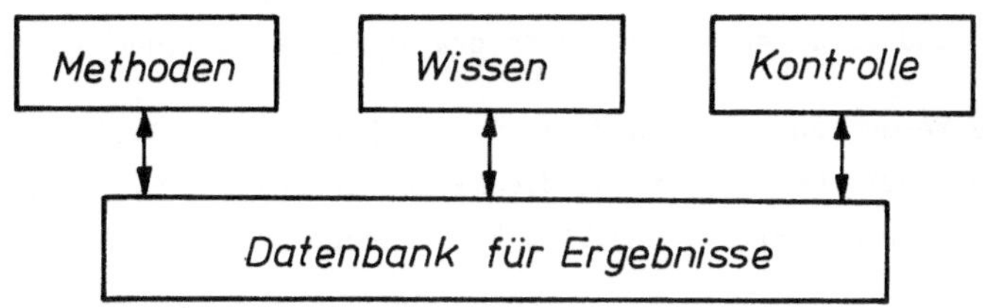

Bild 1   Komponenten eines Systems zur Analyse von Mustern

In diesem Beitrag werden Datenbanken und Verarbeitungsmethoden nicht betrachtet,
sondern nur die Darstellung der Kontrolle und des Wissens mit hierarchischen Graphen.
Die Definition dieser Graphen wird zunächst kurz wiederholt. Dann werden die Darstellung der Kontrolle und des Wissens jeweils an Hand von Beispielen diskutiert.

2. Hierarchische Graphen

Hierarchische Graphen (h-Graphen) wurden zunächst zur Darstellung der Semantik von
Programmen eingeführt [5-7]. Anschaulich ist ein h-Graph ein Graph, dessen Knoten
entweder ein primitives Element enthalten oder einen Graphen, der selbst wiederum
Knoten mit einem Graphen als Inhalt haben kann, so daß eine Schachtelung in beliebiger
Tiefe möglich ist.

Eine formale Definition des h-Graphen basiert auf dem erweiterten gerichteten Graphen,
der im folgenden kurz als Graph bezeichnet wird. Ein solcher Graph ist ein Quadrupel

$$G = \{K, M, q, E\} \qquad , \qquad\qquad (1)$$

wobei die Elemente des Quadrupels definiert sind als

$$
\begin{aligned}
&K: \quad \text{endliche Menge der Knoten} &, \\
&M: \quad \text{endliche Menge von Markierungen der Ecken} &, \\
&q = \{q_1, q_2\}: \quad \text{zwei spezielle Knoten, nämlich Anfangs- und Endknoten} &, \\
&E: \quad K \times M \rightarrow K \text{ , eine partielle Abbildung zur Definition der Ecken oder Kanten.}
\end{aligned} \qquad (2)
$$

Die Menge M dient also über die Abbildung E zur Bezeichnung oder Markierung der Ecken, wobei die Schreibweise

$$E(k_i, m) = k_j \qquad k_i, k_j \in K, \qquad m \in M \tag{3}$$

besagt, daß es eine vom Knoten k_i zum Knoten k_j gerichtete Ecke mit der Markierung
m gibt. Keine Ecke ist zum Anfangsknoten q_1 hin gerichtet, und keine Ecke ist vom
Endknoten q_2 weg gerichtet. Die obigen Definitionen entsprechen im wesentlichen den
für Graphen üblichen und erlauben die bekannte grafische Darstellung eines Graphen G.

Mit $\tilde{K}$ werde nun eine Menge von Knoten und mit Q eine Menge primitiver (nicht zerleg-
barer) Elemente bezeichnet. Es sei $\tilde{G}(K, S)$ die Menge der Graphen G, die sich für
irgendein $K \subseteq \tilde{K}$ und $S \subseteq Q$ aus Gl.(1) ergeben. Ein h-Graph H über $\tilde{K}$ und Q ist das
Tupel

$$H = \{K, \eta\} \quad , \tag{4}$$

wobei η die partielle Abbildung

$$\eta: \tilde{K} \rightarrow Q \cup \tilde{G}(K, S) \tag{5}$$

ist. Für einen Knoten $k_i \in \tilde{K}$ gibt $\eta(k_i)$ den Inhalt des Knotens an. Dieser Inhalt
kann entweder ein primitives, d.h. nicht weiter zerlegbares, Element sein oder ein
Graph, der in Knoten und Ecken zerlegbar ist. Wie aus dem einfachen Beispiel in
Bild 3 hervorgeht kann ein Knoten rekursiv sein, d.h. sich selbst enthalten. Wenn
ein Knoten k_i einen Graphen G_i enthält, so werden alle nach k_i gerichteten Ecken mit
dem Anfangsknoten von G_i verbunden und alle von k_i weg gerichteten Ecken mit dem
Endknoten.

Der h-Graph erlaubt es also, entweder zusätzliche Einzelheiten einzufügen, indem ein
Knoten durch seinen nichtprimitiven Inhalt ersetzt wird, oder von Einzelheiten zu
abstrahieren, indem ein Teilgraph durch einen Knoten ersetzt wird.

3. Kontrolle

Das System in Bild 1 beginne seine Aktivität, wenn zu irgendeiner Zeit ein neues
Muster in die Ergebnis Datenbank eingelesen wird. Der Systemzustand werde jeweils
durch den Inhalt {Daten} der Datenbank gekennzeichnet. Ein Verarbeitungsschritt, der
diesen Inhalt ändert, bewirkt also auch eine Veränderung des Systemzustandes. Die
Menge der auf die Datenbank anwendbaren Transformationen {T} ist bestimmt durch die
vorhandenen Verarbeitungsmodule. Ist beispielsweise eine Transformation nur auf Ketten von Symbolen anwendbar und enthält die Datenbank keine solchen Ketten, so ist
die Transformation nicht anwendbar. Der Inhalt {Daten} der Datenbank schränkt also
die Menge {T} der verfügbaren Transformationen ein auf die Menge {T/{Daten}} der
anwendbaren Transformationen. Wenn in einem durch {Daten} definierten Zustand alle

Transformationen {T/{Daten}} angewendet werden, ergeben sich alle möglichen Folgezu-
stände. Auf diese können wieder alle möglichen Transformationen angewendet werden,
und so weiter bis man entweder in einem Zustand eine symbolische Beschreibung erhält
oder keine neuen Zustände mehr erzeugen kann. Auf diese Weise erhält man einen Suchgraphen, dessen Knoten Systemzustände sind und dessen Ecken Transformationen sind.
Eine "blinde" Suche nach der richtigen Lösung in diesen Graphen scheidet wegen der
kombinatorischen Explosion der Menge der Knoten aus. Statt dessen muß man die Suche
auf einige wenige Pfade in dem Suchgraphen beschränken, wobei natürlich solche Pfade
auszuwählen sind, von denen einer mit großer Wahrscheinlichkeit zum Ziel, nämlich
der symbolischen Beschreibung, führt. Genau dieses ist die Aufgabe des Kontrollmoduls. Eine Möglichkeit zur Darstellung des Kontrollmoduls sind die h-Graphen, die
eine Verallgemeinerung der Bildanalysegraphen ergeben [8].

Die Darstellung der Kontrollstruktur mit h-Graphen wird an einem einfachen Beispiel
diskutiert. Das System in Bild 1 verfüge über n Verarbeitungsmodule und über p Prozessoren zur Ausführung von Algorithmen. Es sei erwünscht, daß irgendeine Auswahl von
bis zu p Prozessen auf irgendwelchen der p Prozessoren ausgeführt werden kann. Es soll
zulässig sein, daß ein Modul gleichzeitig (aber mit verschiedenen Daten) auf mehr als
einem Prozessor aktiv ist, was zum Beispiel auftreten kann, wenn an verschiedenen
Stellen einer gesprochenen Äußerung aus Silben Worte gebildet werden sollen. Bild 2
zeigt einen möglichen h-Graphen, der diese parallele Aktivität initialisiert. Seine
Knoten k0 bis k10 enthalten selbst wieder umfangreiche Einzelschritte, die hier der
Einfachheit halber nicht durch weitere Graphen sondern eine kurze Beschreibung charakterisiert werden:

k0 : initialisiere parallele Verarbeitungsschritte
k1 : Eingabe eines Musters in die Datenbank
k2 : stelle Veränderungen des Inhalts {Daten} fest
k3 : bestimme die auf {Daten} anwendbaren Module
k4 : beurteile die Nützlichkeit dieser Module
k5 : bestimme die Zahl p_f der freien Prozessoren
k6 : prüfe, ob $p_f > 0$
k7 : aktiviere die p_f am höchsten bewerteten Module
k8 : prüfe, ob noch nicht ausgeführte Module warten
k9 : prüfe, ob Endergebnis oder Haltebedingung vorliegt
k10: gib Ergebnis oder Haltebedingung aus

Die Darstellung in Bild 2 ist völlig unabhängig von der Art und Anzahl der vorhandenen
Verarbeitungsmodule. Natürlich wäre beispielsweise der Inhalt von Knoten k4 jedoch von
der Art der Module abhängig. Ebenso ist offen, ob die Verarbeitung "bottom-up" oder
"top-down" verläuft oder gemischt. Dieses hängt von den vorhandenen Moduln und ihrer
Bewertung ab. Ein Kontrollmodul ist natürlich nur dann erforderlich, wenn die Folge

der Verarbeitungsschritte wegen der Komplexität der Muster in Abhängigkeit vom jeweils
zu analysierenden Muster zu wählen ist. Wenn andrerseits eine feste Folge von Schritten für alle oder fast alle Muster eines Problemkreises ausreicht, so werden diese in
einer entsprechenden Systemstruktur fixiert, wodurch ein Kontrollmodul überflüssig
wird.

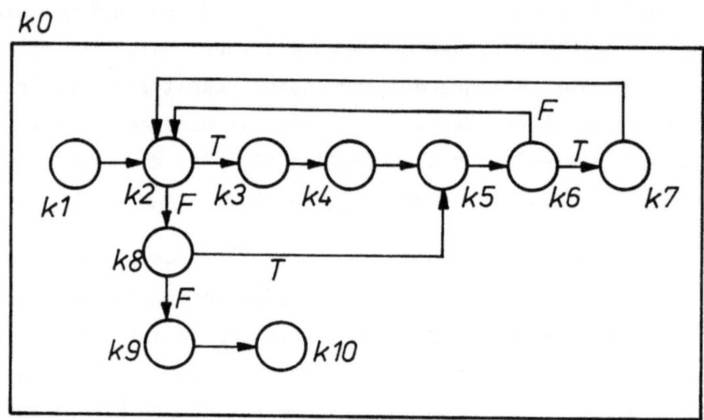

Bild 2   Darstellung eines Kontrollmoduls durch einen h-Graphen

In [9] wird darauf hingewiesen, daß man einen Graphen explizit, d.h. durch Angabe der
Knoten und Ecken, oder implizit, d.h. durch Angabe eines Algorithmus zur Erzeugung
der Knoten und Ecken, definieren kann. In diesem Sinne stellt Bild 2 eine implizite
Definition des Suchgraphen dar, von dem aber bei jeder Analyse nur ein kleiner Ausschnitt explizit erzeugt wird. Die Darstellung der Kontrollstruktur mit h-Graphen
ist besonders zweckmäßig, wenn die Kontrollstruktur selbst als Hierarchie von Strategien aufgefaßt wird, wie es beispielsweise in [10] der Fall ist.

4. Wissen

Wegen der im vorigen Abschnitt erwähnten kombinatorischen Explosion des Suchgraphen
ist es wichtig, möglichst viele Pfade von vornherein auszuschließen. Das kann auf
Grund von Wissen über strukturelle Eigenschaften der Muster und über den Problemkreis
geschehen. Man kann Wissen als die Darstellung von Beschränkungen, die in der Umwelt
vorliegen, auffassen und damit Pfade im Suchgraphen, die zu sinnlosen Mustern führen,
vermeiden.

In den meisten Fällen läßt sich Wissen hierarchisch organisieren, wobei die Hierarchie-
ebenen vom Problemkreis abhängen. Dieses gilt für die Analyse von Bildern, wo man

beispielsweise Szenen, Objekte, Teile von Objekten, Linien oder Flächen oder Texturen,
Linien- und Texturelemente sowie Bildpunkte unterscheiden kann, ebenso wie für die
Analyse von Sprache, wo man zum Beispiel Sätze, Worte, Silben, Laute und Sprachseg-
mente unterscheiden kann. Die Zahl der Ebenen in einer Hierarchie, die Art der Ebenen
und die zu einer Ebene gehörigen Elemente liegen dabei nicht von vornherein fest,
sondern sind vom Entwickler eines Systems zu bestimmen. Wegen dieser hierarchischen
Strukturierung sind h-Graphen zur Darstellung von Wissen besonders geeignet.

Als ein Beispiel für die Verwendung von h-Graphen wird die Spracherkennung genommen,
da auch im HARPY-System hierarchische Darstellungen intensiv genutzt wurden [11].
Bild 3 zeigt eine mögliche Satzstruktur mit den Knoten "Subteil", "Verb", "Präpteil"
und einem leeren Knoten λ. Der Inhalt der Knoten "Subteil" und "Präpteil" ist ebenfalls als Graph dargestellt.

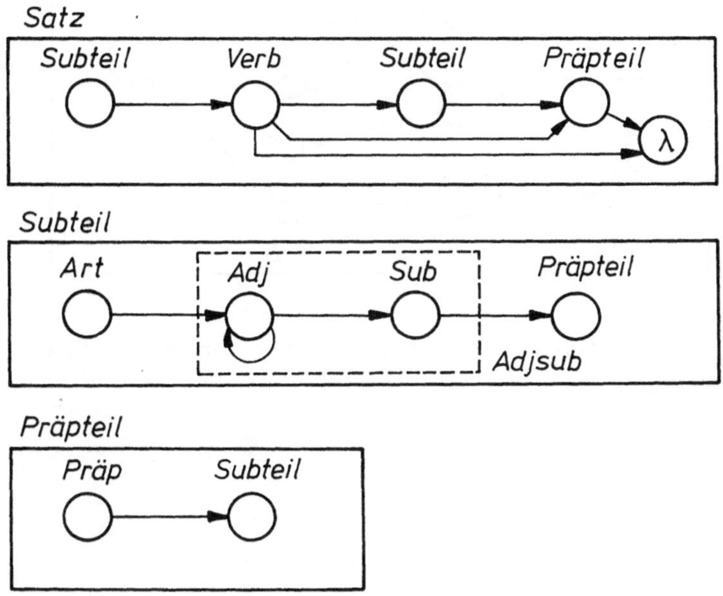

Bild 3   h-Graph einer Satzstruktur mit zwei rekursiven Knoten

Weitere Einzelheiten, die aber hier ausgelassen wurden, ergeben sich durch Festlegung
des Inhalts der Knoten "Adj" oder "Art". Man erhält Sätze, indem man den Graphen vom
Anfangs- zum Endknoten auf irgendeinem Pfad durchläuft und dabei nichtprimitive
Knoten jeweils durch ihren Inhalt ersetzt. Es ist ohne weiteres möglich, das recht
allgemeine Schema in Bild 3 weiter einzuschränken. Beispielsweise kann man Paare

(Adj, Sub) auf einige zulässige beschränken, aber mehrere Adjektive gefolgt von einem Substantiv nicht weiter einschränken, da dieser Fall vergleichsweise selten ist. Das wird erreicht, wenn man den Knoten "Adjsub", der in Bild 3 gestrichelt angedeutet ist, wie in Bild 4 definiert, wobei die Endungen der Adjektive durch einen Strich - dargestellt sind. Eine noch weitere Einschränkung könnte dahin gehen, eine endliche Menge zulässiger Sätze vollständig zu spezifizieren [11]. Auch hier ermöglichen also die h-Graphen die Darstellung von Wissen mit dem jeweils erforderlichen Grad von Spezialisierung.

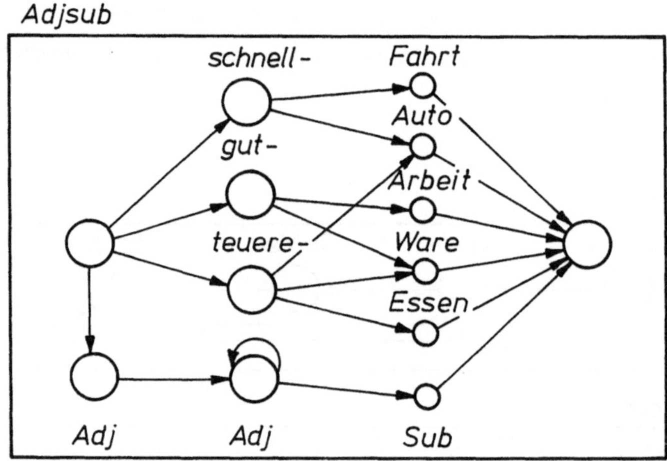

Bild 4   Durch geeignete Definition des Knotens "Adjsub" werden zulässige Paare (Adj, Sub) festgelegt

5. Schlußbemerkung

Für Produktionensysteme wurden Datenstrukturen und Operationen auf diesen definiert. und implementiert, die sehr allgemeinen Manipulationen an h-Graphen entsprechen [12]. Die Darstellung mit h-Graphen liegt näher an der Anschauung, die mit Produktionenregeln näher an der Implementierung. Die beste Form der Darstellung von Kontrolle und Wissen ist noch offen und hängt vermutlich auch vom Problemkreis ab. Graphen werden intensiv für die laufenden Arbeiten zur Analyse von Schaltplänen des Lehrstuhls benutzt [13,14].

Literatur

[1] H.Niemann: Ein Ansatz zur Analyse komplexer Muster. In J.P.Foith (ed.): Ange-
      wandte Szenenanalyse, Informatik Fachberichte 20. Springer-Verlag, Berlin
      Heidelberg New York 1979, 103-109

[2] D.R.Reddy: Speech recognition by machine, a review. Proc.IEEE $\underline{64}$, 501-531 (1976)

[3] H.Niemann: Digital image analysis. In P.Stucki (ed.): Advances in Digital Image
      Processing. Plenum Press, New York 1979, 77-122

[4] H.G.Barrow, J.M.Tenenbaum: Recovering intrinsic scene characteristics from
      images. In A.R.Hanson, E.M.Riseman (ed.): Computer Vision Systems. Academic
      Press, New York 1978, 3-26

[5] T.W.Pratt: A hierarchical graph model of the semantics of programs. Proc.AFIPS
      Summer Joint.Conf. 1969, 813-825

[6] H.Göttler: Zweistufige Graphmanipulationssysteme für die Semantik von Programmier-
      sprachen. Arbeitsberichte des IMMD, Bd.10 Nr.2, Universität Erlangen 1977

[7] H.J.Schneider: Algorithmische Sprachen. Unveröffentlichtes Vorlesungsmanuskript,
      Universität Erlangen

[8] C.A.Harlow: Image analysis and graphs. Comp. Graphics and Image Proc.2, 60-82
      (1973)

[9] N.J. Nilsson: Problem solving methods in artificial intelligence. McGraw-Hill,
      New York 1971

[10] H.P.Nii, E.A.Feigenbaum: Rule-based understanding of signal. In D.A.Waterman,
      F.Hayes-Roth (ed.): Pattern-Directed Inference Systems. Academic Press, New
      York 1978, 483-501

[11] A.Newell: HARPY, production systems, and human cognition. In R.A.Cole (ed.):
      Perception and Production of Fluent Speech. Lawrence Erlbaum Ass., Hillsdale
      1980, 289-380

[12] McCracken: A production system version of the HEARSAY II speech understanding
      system. Dep. of Comp. Science, Carnegie-Mellon University 1978

[13] H.Bunke: Analyse elektrischer Schaltpläne mit einfachen Schaltsymbolen. In
      E.Triendl (ed.): Bildverarbeitung und Mustererkennung, Informatik Fachberichte
      17, Springer-Verlag, Berlin 1978, 126-132

[14] H.Bley: Digitization and segmentation of circuit diagrams. First Scandinavian
      Conference on Image Analysis 14.-16.1.1980, Linköping, Schweden

BILDGRAPHEN FÜR DIE SEGMENTIERUNG VON STROMLAUFPLÄNEN

Heinrich Bley
Universität Erlangen-Nürnberg
Lehrstuhl für Informatik 5 (Mustererkennung)
Martensstr. 3, D-8520 Erlangen

Kurzfassung

Aus Binärbildern von Stromlaufplänen werden durch ein Zeilenvergleichsverfahren Bildgraphen berechnet. Dabei werden zusammenhängende Bildpunkte nach einfachen Kriterien
zu Primärkomponenten zusammengefaßt. Die Primärkomponenten werden als Knoten eines
Graphen dargestellt. Durch Löschen irrelevanter Knoten wird zunächst eine Vereinfa-
chung des Bildgraphen erreicht. Alphanumerische Zeichen werden durch Berechnung der
Zusammenhangskomponenten im Bildgraphen lokalisiert. Liniensegmente, die Grundsymbole
für eine syntaktische Analyse der Linienzeichnung, werden durch Verschmelzen der
Knoten des Graphen nach heuristischen Regeln berechnet.

1. Einleitung

Die Segmentierung von Binärbildern technischer Zeichnungen ist Teil eines Systems für
das Lesen von Stromlaufplänen. Im Rahmen der Arbeiten an diesem System werden am
Lehrstuhl für Mustererkennung der Universität Erlangen die Teilaufgaben bei der Verarbeitung der Zeichnungen von der Bildaufnahme bis zur Berechnung der Symbol- und
Verbindungsliste untersucht /1/.

Die Zeichnungen werden mit einer Image Dissector Kamera aufgenommen. Im ersten Verarbeitungsschritt wird das Binärbild berechnet. Das größte verfügbare Standardformat
ist DIN A4 mit einer Auflösung von 2000 x 1400 Bildpunkten.

Die hier beschriebene Segmentierung des Binärbildes geht von einer Beschreibung des
Bildes durch einen Bildgraphen aus. Methoden der Linienverdünnung oder der Bildverbesserung werden nicht auf das ganze Binärbild angewandt; diese Verfahren sind sehr
rechenintensiv und nicht umkehrbar. Von höheren Verarbeitungsstufen aus können diese
Vorverarbeitungsmethoden aber gezielt auf Bildausschnitte angewendet werden.

2. Berechnung des Bildgraphen aus dem Binärbild

Einfache Gruppen zusammenhängender schwarzer Bildpunkte werden zu Primärkomponenten
zusammengefaßt. Die Primärkomponenten werden als Knoten eines Bildgraphen dargestellt.
Die weiteren Berechnungen zur Segmentierung des Bildes, z. B. Suchen der Schrift-

```
AAA    CCC      DDD      GG      IIIIIIIIII
AAA    CCC      DDD      GGG     IIIIIIIIIIIII
 AA    CCC      DD       GGG            IIIIII
AAA    CCC      DD       GG               HHH
 AA      CCC DDD         GG                HH
AAA       BBBBB          GGG              HHH
 AA       BBBB        EEE FF              HHH
 AA       BBB         EE    FF             HH
 AA       BB         EEEE      FFF          HH
AAA       BBB        EEE         FFF        HH


    a)         b)         c)          d)
```

Bild 1: Zerlegung des Binärbildes. a) überlappende Zeilenabschnitte, verschmolzen zu
1 Primärkomponente, b) und c) Verzweigung, 3 Primärkomponenten, d) geometrische Bedingung, Vergleich des umschreibenden Rechtecks mit der Anzahl schwarzer Bildpunkte,
2 Primärkomponenten.

zeichen, werden auf dem Bildgraphen durchgeführt. Das Binärbild selbst wird nicht
verändert; deshalb ist auf höheren Verarbeitungsstufen ein Rückgriff auf Ausschnitte
des Originalbildes möglich.

Das Binärbild wird zeilenweise verarbeitet. Die Verschmelzung einzelner Bildpunkte
zu Primärkomponenten ist in Bild 1 dargestellt. Dabei sind die Punkte der verschiedenen Komponenten durch unterschiedliche Großbuchstaben markiert. Gruppen zusammenhängender Bildpunkte in einer Zeile werden Zeilenabschnitt genannt. Zeilenabschnitte
aus aufeinanderfolgenden Zeilen können verschmolzen werden, wenn sie überlappen
(Bild 1a). Bei Verzweigungen in Verarbeitungsrichtung (Bild 1b) oder gegen Verarbeitungsrichtung (Bild 1c) werden überlappende Zeilenabschnitte jedoch nicht verschmolzen; Verzweigungen führen zu einer Aufspaltung in mehrere Primärkomponenten. Um eine
Zerlegung des Binärbildes in einfache und kompakte Primärkomponenten zu erzeugen,
werden zusätzliche geometrische Bedingungen eingeführt. Überlappende Zeilenabschnitte
werden nicht verschmolzen, sondern in zwei Primärkomponenten aufgespalten, wenn eine
dieser Bedingungen verletzt wird. Eine einfache geometrische Bedingung vergleicht die
Fläche F des umschreibenden Rechtecks der Primärkomponente mit der Anzahl A schwarzer
Bildpunkte der Komponente. Nur wenn der Quotient F/A kleiner als ein Schwellwert θ
ist, werden die Zeilenabschnitte verschmolzen (Bild 1d). Da F/A $\geqslant$ 1 berechnet das
Programm bei Eingabe eines Schwellwertes $\theta < 1$ als Spezialfall den 'line-adjacency-
graph'/2/.

Eine Markierung der Elemente in der Binärbildmatrix ist nicht erforderlich, da im
Programm bei der Verarbeitung der Zeile i diese Zeile mit der Liste der bis zur Zeile
i-1 berechneten Primärkomponenten verglichen wird.

Bild 2a zeigt die Zerlegung in Primärkomponenten für ein einfaches Beispiel, das Bild
eines Schriftzeichens. Der Bildgraph (Bild 2b) wird als eine Knoten- und eine Kanten-
liste gespeichert. Jede Eintragung in die Knotenliste enthält neun geometrische Parameter, die Bedingungen für Beginn und Ende der Primärkomponente und den positiven
und negativen Grad des Knotens. Der positive Grad eines Knotens ist die Anzahl der
gerichteten Kanten, die von dem Knoten ausgehen. Der Bildgraph ist nicht zusammenhängend. Zusammenhängende Teilgraphen entsprechen Zusammenhangskomponenten im Binärbild. Die Richtung der Kanten gibt die Reihenfolge an, in der benachbarte Knoten aus
dem Binärbild errechnet werden. Der Bildgraph, der so für die Zeichnung in Bild 3
berechnet wurde, enthält 708 Knoten. Durch die Wahl der Parameter für die geometrischen Bedingungen der Zerlegung muß zwischen der Größe des Graphen und der Güte der
Beschreibung des Binärbildes ein Kompromiß gefunden werden.

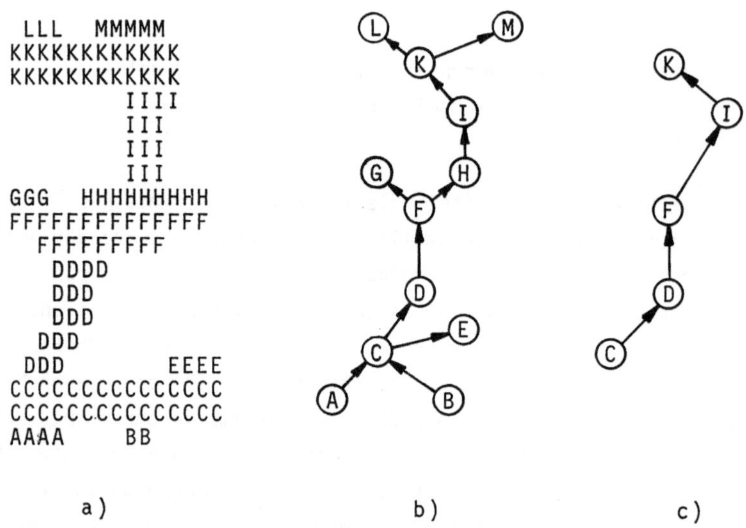

Bild 2: a) Zerlegung des Binärbildes, b) Bildgraph für das Binärbild, c) geglätteter
Bildgraph.

3. Glättung des Bildgraphen

Die aus dem Binärbild errechneten Graphen (Bild 2b, 5b) enthalten viele kleine Primärkomponenten, die keine Information über die zugrunde liegende Linienzeichnung enthalten. In den Bildern 4 und 5 werden die Graphen so dargestellt, daß für jeden Knoten
(Primärkomponente) das umschreibende Rechteck gezeichnet wird. Rechtecke, die an-
einandergrenzen, sind im Graphen durch eine Kante verbunden. Die kleinen, störenden
Primärkomponenten werden durch Randrauhigkeiten in der Zeichnung und durch Quanti-
sierungseffekte erzeugt. Die Glättung des Bildgraphen eliminiert diese Komponenten.

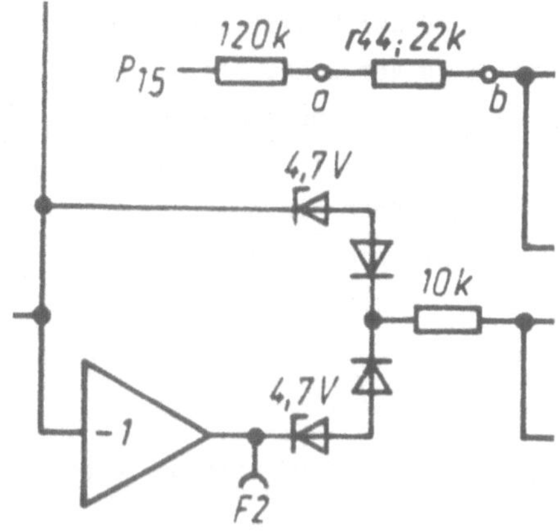

Bild 3: Teil eines Stromlaufplans,
512 x 512 Bildpunkte

Bild 4: Zerlegung und Glättung für einen
Ausschnitt aus Bild 3, diagonale Linien

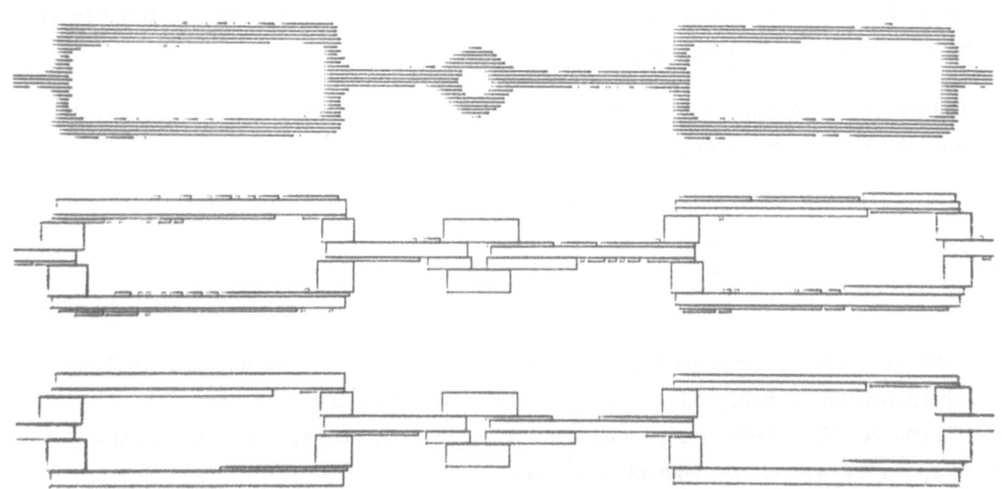

Bild 5: a) Binärbild, Ausschnitt aus Bild 3, b) Zerlegung, umschreibende Rechtecke
der Primärkomponenten, c) Zerlegung nach der Glättung des Bildgraphen

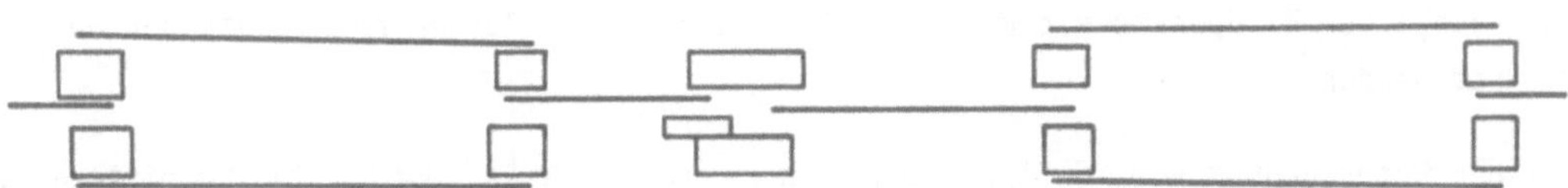

Bild 6: Bildausschnitt nach Berechnung der dominierenden horizontalen Linien. Die
Rechtecke entsprechen Primärkomponenten

Kleine isolierte Komponenten und kleine Komponenten am Rand der Linien werden gelöscht. Wenn Verzweigungen im Graphen entfernt werden, wird versucht, die übrig bleibenden Knoten zu verschmelzen. Der Algorithmus wird im folgenden beschrieben; dabei ist

$d^+(i)$ positiver Grad des Knoten i; Anzahl der von i ausgehenden Kanten
$d^-(i)$ negativer Grad des Knoten i; Anzahl der in i eintreffenden Kanten
$d(i) = d^+(i) + d^-(i)$.

Glättung des Graphen

1: Lösche alle Knoten i vom Grad $d(i) = 0$, die nicht mehr als n Binärbildpunkte enthalten.
2: Lösche alle Knoten i vom Grad $d^+(i) = 1 \wedge d^-(i) = 0$ ($d^+(i) = 0 \wedge d^-(i) = 1$), wenn i mit einem Knoten j vom Grad $d^-(j) > 1$ ($d^+(j) > 1$) verbunden ist, und wenn das umschreibende Rechteck der Komponente i nicht größer als k x l Bildpunkte ist.
3: Verschmelze alle Knoten i mit einem benachbarten Knoten, wenn der positive (der negative) Grad des Knoten i im Schritt 2 auf $d^+(i) = 1$ ($d^-(i) = 1$) vermindert wurde. Prüfe dabei die Bedingungen, die auch für die Berechnung des Graphen aus dem Binärbild (s. o.) verwendet wurden.

Die Bilder 2c, 5c zeigen Beispiele für die Glättung. Der Graph für Bild 3 wird von 708 auf 360 Knoten reduziert (Parameter n = 1, k = 5, l = 2).

4. Suchen der Schriftzeichen

4.1 Teilen des Bildgraphen

Die Schriftzeichen bilden im Vergleich zu den Linien der Zeichnung kleine Zusammenhangskomponenten im Binärbild. Die Suche nach Schriftzeichen basiert deshalb auf der Berechnung von Zusammenhangskomponenten, d. h. auf der Berechnung zusammenhängender Teilgraphen im Graphen des gesamten Bildes.

Die Größe des umschreibenden Rechtecks, die Fläche und die Lage der Zusammenhangskomponenten im Binärbild werden aus den geometrischen Parametern errechnet, die in der Knotenliste für die Graphen gespeichert sind. Für Stromlaufpläne mit einer einheitlichen Schriftgröße kann die mittlere Größe der Schriftzeichen sowie die mittlere Anzahl schwarzer Bildpunkte als Median der Werte für alle Zusammenhangskomponenten berechnet werden.

Bei einer Untersuchung von 25 Stromlaufplänen, Format DIN A2, wurden 496 Schriftzeichen

pro Blatt als Mittelwert gezählt. Da die Linien der Zeichnung nur wenige Zusammenhangskomponenten bilden, sind die obengenannten Mediane mittlere Werte für die
Schriftzeichen.

Mit den so gewonnenen Daten als Schwellwerte wird der Bildgraph in zwei Teile zerlegt: Schriftzeichen und Linienzeichnung, im folgenden als S-Graph und L-Graph bezeichnet. Der L-Graph enthält alle die zusammenhängenden Teilgraphen, die wesentlich
größer sind als Schriftzeichen. Diese Zerlegung ist - bedingt durch Störungen in
der Bildvorlage selbst und bei der Digitalisierung - nicht immer ganz richtig. Für
die ersten Schritte der weiteren Verarbeitung kann diese Zerlegung aber als korrekt
angesehen werden.

4.2 Berechnung der Wortgruppen

Da nicht jede Zusammenhangskomponente im S-Graphen genau einem Schriftzeichen entspricht, müssen für die Segmentierung zunächst die Wörter, d. h. regelmäßige Anord-
nungen von Schriftzeichen, berechnet werden. Dazu wird ein Clustering-Algorithmus
verwendet /3/.

Jede Zusammenhangskomponente wird als Knoten eines neuen Graphen aufgefaßt. Die Knoten
sind paarweise durch eine Kante miteinander verbunden. Die Kanten sind mit dem Abstand der Zusammenhangskomponenten im Binärbild gewichtet. Durch eine Schwellwert-
operation werden alle Kanten entfernt, deren Gewicht größer als ein Schwellwert θ
ist. θ kann aus der vorher berechneten mittleren Schriftzeichengröße bestimmt werden.
Durch diese Schwellwertoperationen ergeben sich zusammenhängende Teilgraphen, die
Wörtern entsprechen.

Der Algorithmus ist so implementiert, daß nur die Kanten mit einem Gewicht < θ erzeugt werden. Dabei wird die Tatsache ausgenutzt, daß die Datei der aus dem Binärbild errechneten Zusammenhangskomponenten nach den Koordinaten der Komponenten geordnet ist.

Für die abschließende Segmentierung der Wörter in Einzelzeichen steht damit eine
hierarchische Beschreibung zur Verfügung: Binärbild-Primärkomponenten – Zusammenhangs-
komponenten-Wörter.

5. Berechnung der Linienelemente

Der L-Graph beschreibt die Linienzeichnung so genau, daß ein Rückgriff auf das Binärbild nur in Ausnahmefällen notwendig ist. Zunächst werden die dominierenden, d. h.
die größeren Linienelemente berechnet: horizontale, vertikale, diagonale Geraden und

Kreissegmente. Diese Linienelemente werden durch Verschmelzen der Knoten des Bildgraphen berechnet.

Der Algorithmus für die Berechnung diagonaler Linienelemente (Bild 4) enthält folgende Teilaufgaben:

1: Suche alle Knoten i vom Grad $d^+(i) = 1 \wedge d^-(i) = 1$, die Primärkomponenten mit umschreibendem Rechteck kleiner k x l Bildpunkte entsprechen.
2: Suche alle Kanten zwischen den Knoten aus Schritt 1.
3: Suche in dem so entstandenen Teil-Bildgraphen alle Ketten, geordnet nach der Länge.
4: Berechne für alle Ketten aus den Parametern der Knoten eine Ausgleichsgerade.
5: Entscheide für Diagonale (ja/nein) und ersetze die entsprechenden Ketten im Bildgraphen durch einen neuen Knoten.

Die Berechnung horizontaler und vertikaler Linienelemente beruht ebenfalls auf der Auswahl einer Teilmenge der Knoten nach heuristischen Regeln. Die Teilaufgaben entsprechen denen für diagonale Linienelemente.

Die Berechnung kleinerer Linienelemente kann sich auf bereits klassifizierte, dominierende Linienelemente stützen (Bild 6).

6. Ergebnisse

Durch ein Zeilenvergleichsverfahren kann aus dem Binärbild ein Bildgraph berechnet werden, der die Grundlage für die Segmentierung der Stromlaufpläne bildet. Für das Beispiel in Bild 3, 512 x 512 Bildpunkte, wurde ein Graph mit 708 Knoten berechnet. Die Programmlaufzeit auf einer PDP 11/34 betrug 40 s. Die Größe des Graphen und die Rechenzeit sind vom Bildinhalt abhängig. Aus diesen Gründen, und wegen der Verwendung unterschiedlicher Anlagen und Programmiersprachen ist der Aufwand für die Berechnung des Bildgraphen nur schwer mit den Ergebnissen anderer Arbeiten vergleichbar /4/.

Die Glättung des Bildgraphen vermindert die Anzahl der Knoten in dem Beispiel von 708 auf 360 Knoten. Die Reduzierung um etwa 50 % konnte auch an anderen Beispielen bestätigt werden.
Durch die Teilung des Bildgraphen können die Verarbeitung der Schriftzeichen und die Verarbeitung der Linien der Zeichnung weitgehend voneinander getrennt werden. Die Suchoperationen auf den Graphen werden durch die Teilung einfacher und schneller.

Mit der Berechnung der Wörter wird die Suche der Einzelzeichen auf ein Segmentierungsproblem zurückgeführt, wie es in ähnlicher Form bei optischen Beleglesern auftritt. Die vorhandenen Datenstrukturen bieten Ansatzpunkte für komplexere Segmentierungsverfahren, die auch bei geringerer Bildqualität Erfolg versprechen.

Die dominierenden geraden Linienelemente der Stromlaufpläne können im Bildgraphen zuverlässig erkannt werden. Erweiterungen für kleinere Strukturen werden untersucht.

Literatur

/1/ H.Bunke, "Analyse elektrischer Schaltpläne mit einfachen Schaltungssymbolen", in E.Triendl (Hrsg.), "Bildverarbeitung und Mustererkennung", 1. DAGM-Symposium, Informatik Fachberichte 17, Springer Verlag, 1978, S. 126-132

/2/ T.Pavlidis, "Structural pattern recognition", Springer Verlag, New York, 1977

/3/ C.T.Zahn, "Graph-theoretical methods for detecting and describing Gestalt clusters", IEEE Trans. on Comp., Vol. C-20, No. 1, Jan. 1971, pp. 68-89

/4/ F.Veillon, "One pass computation of morphological and geometrical properties of objects in digital pictures", Signal Processing, Vol. 1, 1979, pp. 175-189.

<u>Segmentierung von Blutzellbildern unter Berücksichtigung</u>
<u>von a priori Wissen über den Bildinhalt</u>

C.-E. Liedtke, Universität Hannover

1. Einleitung

Segmentierung ist die Zerlegung eines Bildes in solche Teilbilder, die
für den Beobachter des Bildes eine besondere <u>Bedeutung</u> haben. Die
Bedeutung der Teilbilder kann entweder subjektiv begründet sein oder
auch durch Wissen über die Prozesse, die zur Bildentstehung geführt
haben. Die Segmentierung kann deshalb nicht getrennt werden von der
Bedeutungszuweisung zu den Teilbildern, d.h. von ihrer Klassifizierung.

Wenn es nicht möglich ist, die Teilbilder alleine aufgrund der Merkmale zu klassifizieren, die man direkt aus dem Bild gewinnen kann,
wie Grauwert, Farbe, Textur usw., dann ist eine korrekte Segmentierung
des Bildes überhaupt nur dann denkbar, wenn zusätzliche Information
über den Bildinhalt verfügbar ist. Diese zusätzliche Information, die
man also bereits hat, bevor man das Bild überhaupt gesehen hat, nennt
man "a priori Wissen".

Mit Unterstützung der Deutschen Forschungsgemeinschaft arbeiten wir
an einem Projekt, das sich mit der automatischen Klassifizierung von
Leukozyten des peripheren Blutes aufgrund ihrer Mikroskopbilder be-
schäftigt. Es hatte sich hierbei recht schnell herausgestellt, daß
das wesentliche Problem in der Segmentierung des mikroskopischen Zellbildes in Kern und Plasma des Leukozyten, Erythrozyten, Thrombozyten
und Hintergrund liegt. Geringe Unterschiede in der routinemäßigen
Präparatsaufbereitung der Blutausstriche können zu beträchtlichen
Unterschieden in der Färbung und Gesamtabsorption des mikroskopischen
Zellbildes führen. Da die standardisierten Färbeverfahren, wie z.B.
die Pappenheim-Färbung, im Hinblick auf die visuelle Auswertung des
Mikroskopbildes optimiert worden sind, haben die erwähnten Veränderungen zwar nur einen geringen Einfluß auf die visuelle Analyse,
stellen jedoch für eine automatische Auswertung einen beträchtlichen
Unsicherheitsfaktor dar. Um eine korrekte Segmentierung durchführen
zu können, muß deshalb a priori Wissen in den Segmentierungsprozeß
eingebracht werden.

2. Parzellierungsalgorithmus

Als Parzellierungsalgorithmus wird ein schneller Split & Merge-Algorithmus verwendet, ähnlich dem, der bei Pavlidis beschrieben wird. Die Merkmale, die aus dem Bild gemessen werden müssen, und an denen die Einheitlichkeit festgestellt werden soll, müssen die Eigenschaft haben, daß sie innerhalb eines Segments weitgehend konstant bleiben, sich aber von einem Segment zu einem anderen Segment signifikant ändern. Aus einer großen Lernstichprobe von Testregionen ergab sich nach einer Zerlegung des Farbbildes in die Komponenten RGB, daß aufgrund des Merkmals "Grün" Kern, Hintergrund und die gemeinsame Fläche von Plasma und Erythrozyten sehr gut voneinander getrennt werden konnten. Plasma und Erythrozyt ließen sich dagegen voneinander sehr gut durch das Merkmal "X" trennen, das eine Linearkombination der drei Farbauszüge darstellt. Dieses Resultat ist in Abb.1 verdeutlicht. Abb.1b stellt das Merkmal "Grün" und Abb.1c das Merkmal "X" dar. Die Konturen der Parzellen, die aus den beiden Merkmalen mit einem Split & Merge-Algorithmus gewonnen wurden, sind in Abb.1d zu sehen.

3. Assemblierungsalgorithmus

Der Algorithmus, der nach einer heuristischen Strategie die Parzellen zu Segmenten zusammensetzt, benutzt hierzu a priori Wissen über die photometrischen und geometrischen Eigenschaften der Objekte. Ein Blockdiagramm des Algorithmus ist in Abb.2 wiedergegeben. Die Strategie des Segmentierungsverfahrens basiert darauf, daß den einzelnen Parzellen zunächst aufgrund von Verträglichkeitsmaßen Bedeutungen entsprechend den Objektklassen zugewiesen werden und schließlich benachbarte Parzellen mit derselben Bedeutung zu den Segmenten zusammengefaßt werden. Die anfängliche Zuweisung von Verträglichkeitsmaßen sowie die Korrektur dieser Maße innerhalb des Assemblierungsalgorithmus berücksichtigt die verschiedenen Kategorien von a priori Wissen über den Inhalt des mikroskopischen Zellbildes. Die Reihenfolge, in der diese Kategorien abgearbeitet werden, hat einen erheblichen Einfluß auf das Resultat.

Zunächst wird das a priori Wissen über die photometrischen Merkmale berücksichtigt. Jeder Parzelle nach Abb. 1d werden fünf Maße zugeteilt, die die Verträglichkeit der photometrischen Merkmale der Parzellen mit den fünf Bedeutungen Kern eines Leukozyten (1), Plasma eines Leukozyten (2), Erythrozyten (3), Hintergrund (4) und Thrombozyten (5) beinhalten. Abb.3a zeigt das Grauwertbild eines eosinophilen Granulo-

zyten und Abb.3b die Parzellen, die mit dem oben beschriebenen Split &
Merge-Algorithmus gebildet worden sind. Jede Parzelle wurde in Abb.3b
durch einen anderen Grauwert dargestellt. Wenn man allen Parzellen die
Bedeutung zuweist, die dem höchsten Verträglichkeitsmaß aufgrund des
a priori Wissens über die photometrischen Merkmale entspricht, die
Parzellen gleicher Bedeutung zusammenfaßt und mit einem Grauwert
codiert, dann gelangt man zu Segmenten entsprechend Abb.3c. Da es hier
nur auf die korrekte Segmentierung des Leukozyten ankommt, erscheint
das Resultat schon weitgehend korrekt. Der gröbste Fehler liegt darin,
daß das Segment, das den im Bild rechts angelagerten Thrombozyten um-
schließt, fälschlicherweise als Plasma des Leukozyten erkannt worden
ist.

Wie aus dem Blockdiagramm nach Abb.2 ersichtlich ist, erfolgt im An-
schluß an die Auswertung der photometrischen Merkmale die Korrektur
der Verträglichkeitsmaße aufgrund von a priori Wissen über die Nachbarschaftsbeziehungen. Da hierbei immer nur zwei benachbarte Parzellen
betrachtet werden können, muß für die vollständige Untersuchung der
Nachbarschaftsbeziehungen dieser Komplex mehrfach durchlaufen werden,
und zwar so lange, bis keine Korrektur der Verträglichkeitsmaße mehr
registriert wird. Die Nachbarschaftsanalyse untersucht Einschlüsse
und bewertet Parzellen danach, daß bei einer vorgegebenen Bedeutung
für eine Parzelle andere Parzellen mit bestimmten Bedeutungen benachbart sein müssen. Beispielsweise muß die Thrombozytenparzelle in Abb.3
entweder einer anderen Thrombozytenparzelle oder einer Hintergrunds-
parzelle benachbart sein. Dadurch wird für die Parzelle, die den
Thrombozyten in Abb.3 umgibt, die aufgrund der photometrischen Merkmale dominierende Verträglichkeit mit der Bedeutung "Plasma des Leukozyten" abgeschwächt und die Bedeutung "Hintergrund" angehoben. Das
aufgrund der Nachbarschaftsbeziehungen korrigierte Bild ist in Abb.3d
dargestellt.

Zur Zeit wird an der nächsten Stufe gearbeitet, in der durch eine
schrittweise Maskenbildung gesteuert durch Form- und Flächenkriterien
a priori Wissen über diese beiden Merkmale in die Segmentierung eingebracht wird, die gerade bei einer visuellen Auswertung des mikroskopischen Zellbildes eine außerordentlich große Bedeutung haben.

Das a priori Wissen über das Mikroskopbild eines Blutausstrichs beinhaltet Wissen über

a) die Klassen der Objekte, die in dem Bild vorhanden sein können, wie Kern und Plasma der Leukozyten, Erythrozyten, Thrombozyten und Hintergrund,

b) die Eigenschaften der Objekte, wie Farbe, Absorption, Größe, Form usw.,

c) die Beziehungen zwischen den Objekten, wie Einschlüsse (z.B.: Kern ist immer vom Plasma eingeschlossen) und Nachbarschaftsbeziehungen (z.B.: ein Kernteil muß immer einem anderen Kernteil oder einem Plasmateil benachbart sein).

Um ein Objekt als solches gegenüber einem Hintergrund empfinden zu können, muß dieses zumindest teilweise von einer Kontur umgeben sein. Auf dieser Basis gibt es eine Reihe von Segmentierungsverfahren, die primär nach den Konturen suchen, die die Objekte umgeben. Die meisten Konturfindungsverfahren sind lokale Algorithmen, bei denen aus einer vorgegebenen, endlichen Umgebung um einen Punkt darauf geschlossen wird, ob der betrachtete Punkt ein Konturpunkt ist oder nicht. Diese Verfahren haben u.a. zwei wesentliche Nachteile. Zum einen kann nicht sichergestellt werden, daß die gefundene Kontur geschlossen ist. Es muß meist eine Nachbearbeitung in Form von Konturschließungsverfahren angesetzt werden. Zum anderen wird von solchen lokalen Algorithmen Textur fälschlicherweise als eine Vielzahl von Konturpunkten aufgelöst.

Eine andere Gruppe von Segmentierungsverfahren, die diese Nachteile nicht aufweist, basiert auf der Erkenntnis, daß die Objekte in einem Bild oder zumindest Teile der Objekte in gewissen lokalen Merkmalen einheitlich erscheinen. Hier soll im folgenden ein Teilbild, das ein sinnvolles Objekt, wie Kern oder Plasma eines Leukozyten, Erythrozyt, Thrombozyt usw. oder den Hintergrund, darstellt, ein "Segment" genannt werden und eine einheitlich erscheinende Region eine "Parzelle". Das bedeutet, daß Segmente entweder mit Parzellen identisch sind oder sich zumindest aus Parzellen zusammensetzen. Hieraus wurde die folgende Segmentierungsstrategie abgeleitet: In einem ersten Schritt werden aufgrund eines Einheitlichkeitsmaßes auf der Basis eines lokalen Merkmals einheitliche Gebiete, die Parzellen, gefunden. In einem zweiten Schritt werden die Parzellen unter Verwendung von a priori Wissen zu den gesuchten Segmenten zusammengesetzt.

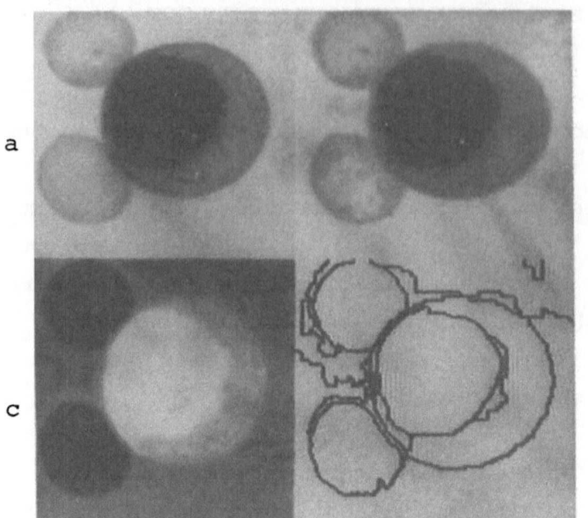

Abb.1, Parzellierung

a) Grauwert des Zell-
   bildes
b) Merkmal "Grün"
c) Merkmal "X"
d) Konturen der Par-
   zellen

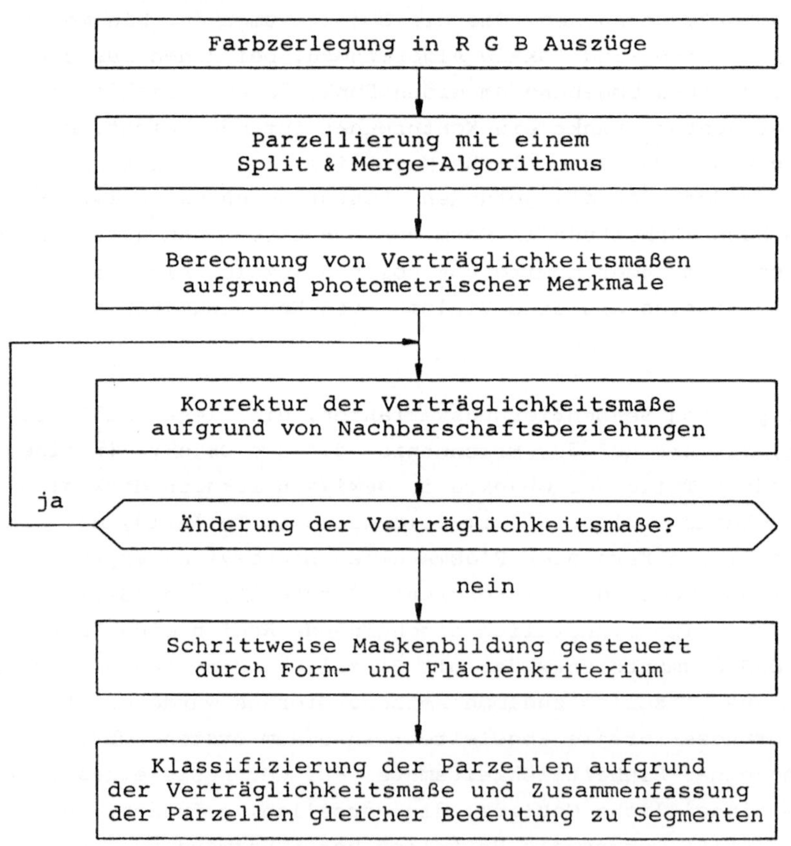

Abb.2, Blockdiagramm des Segmentierungsalgorithmus

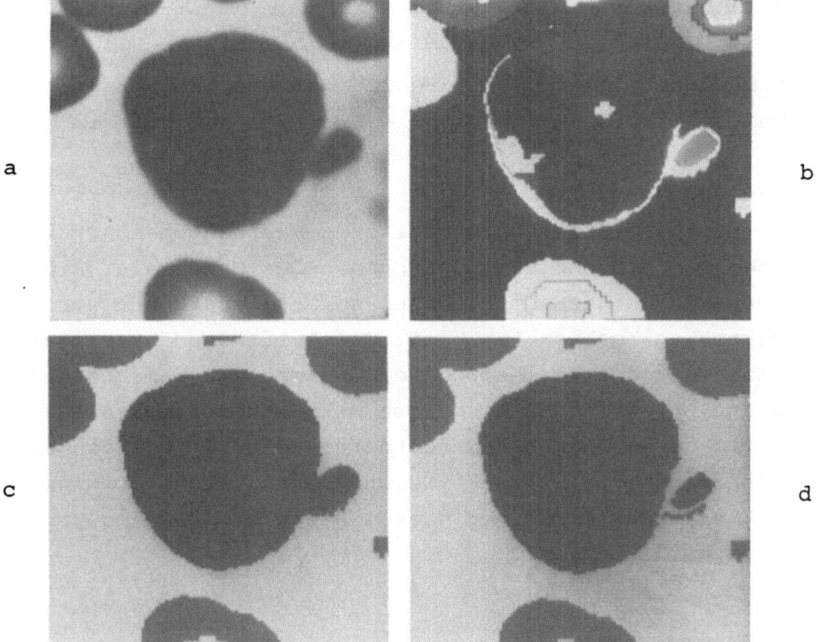

Abb.3, Assemblierung der Parzellen
a) Grauwert des Zellbildes
b) Parzellen codiert durch Grauwert
c) Bedeutungszuweisung aufgrund
   photometrischer Merkmale
d) Korrektur der Bedeutungszuweisung
   aufgrund von Nachbarschaftsbeziehungen

AUTOMATISCHE BILDANALYSE ZUR VERMESSUNG VON KERNSPUREN IN PLASTIK-DETEKTOREN

H.Drechsel, J.Pipper, R.Schucht, J.Beer, W.Heinrich
Universität Gesamthochschule Siegen, Fachbereich Physik

Zusammenfassung

In Plastik-Kernspur-Detektoren entstehen Spuren von stark ionisieren-
den Teilchen durch einen Strahlenschaden des Materials. Diese latenten
Spuren können durch Ätzen mit Laugen soweit vergrößert werden, daß sie
mit dem Mikroskop beobachtbar sind. Das Auffinden derartiger Spuren in
Plastikfolien und die Vermessung von Größen, die dem Energieverlust
des Teilchens proportional sind, ist mit Methoden der Bildanalyse möglich. Es wird der Aufbau eines rechnergesteuerten Mikroskops mit Auto-
fokus beschrieben. Die Bildanalyse und Fokussierung erfolgen mit Software. Die Einsatzmöglichkeiten dieses Systems werden an ersten experimentellen Daten diskutiert.

Einleitung

Geladene Teilchen, die sich durch Materie bewegen, hinterlassen dort
durch Ionisation der Atome eine latente Spur. In dielektrischen Festkörpern bleibt dieser Strahlenschaden entlang der Teilchenbahn zeitlich und örtlich konstant, so daß eine stabile Spur des Teilchens entsteht. Elektronenmikroskopische Untersuchungen zeigen für derartige
Spuren einen Durchmesser des geschädigten Bereichs in der Größe von
~50 Å (1). Unter günstigen Umständen bildet dieser Bereich einen be-
vorzugten Angriffspunkt für Säuren oder Laugen. Durch Ätzen des Materials wird die Oberfläche mit der Geschwindigkeit v_o abgetragen,
während im Bereich des engen Kanals der Spur die Ätzgeschwindigkeit
v_s beträgt. Ist auf Grund des Strahlenschadens $v_s > v_o$ so entsteht
als Ätzfigur ein Kegel mit dem Öffnungswinkel $\sin \alpha/2 = v_o/v_s$.

Der Strahlenschaden im dielektrischen Spurdetektor wächst mit dem
Energieverlust des Teilchens. Der Schwellwert im Energieverlust, von
dem ab ätzbare Spuren entstehen, bestimmt die Empfindlichkeit des Detektors. Oberhalb dieser Schwelle wächst die Spurätzrate und damit die
Länge der Ätzkegel mit dem Energieverlust. Als dielektrische Detektoren mit hoher Empfindlichkeit haben sich dünne Plastikfolien (einige
100μm) verschiedener Materialien wie Zellulosenitrat, Zelluloseazetat
und Polycarbonate wie Lexan, Makrofol und neuerdings auch CR39 bewährt.

Die Schwellen dieser empfindlichen Plastikdetektoren zur Registrierung
von Teilchen liegen allerdings immer noch so hoch (typische Größenordnung: 500 bis einige tausend mal dem Energieverlust eines minimalio-
nisierenden Protons) daß sie bevorzugt zur Registrierung mehrfach ge-
ladener Kerne in der kosmischen Strahlung oder an Schwerionenbeschleu-
nigern eingesetzt werden. Üblicherweise werden viele Plastikfolien auf-
einandergestapelt und so exponiert, daß die Teilchen mehrere Folien
durchqueren bis sie zur Ruhe kommen. Den Abstand des Ätzkegels von dem
Punkt, an dem das Teilchen zur Ruhe kommt, bezeichnet man als Restreichweite. Die Abhängigkeit der Länge des Ätzkegels von der Restreichweite gibt eine Auskunft über die Ladung der Projektilkerne. Zur
Bestimmung der Kegellänge muß die Ätzfigur an der Folienoberfläche,
im Normalfall eine Ellipse, sowie die Position der Kegelspitze mit
einem Mikroskop in dreidimensionalen Koordinaten vermessen werden.
Bild 1 zeigt solche Ätzkegel für ^{40}Ar-Ionen in Zellulosenitrat. Mit

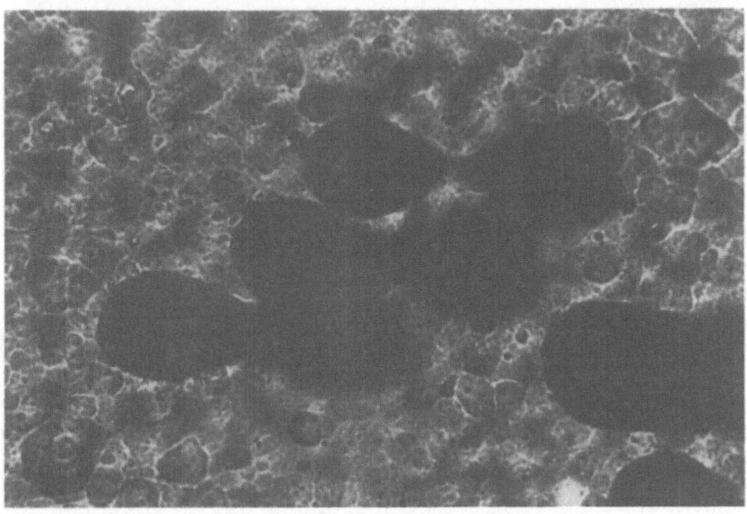

Bild 1: Ätzkegel von ^{40}Ar-Ionen in Zellulosenitrat,
betrachtet im Durchlicht

der Methode, die Länge der Ätzkegel als Funktion der Restreichweite
zu messen, können die Ladungen von Schwerionen mit einer Genauigkeit
von bis zu $\sigma = \pm 0.1$ Ladungseinheiten bestimmt werden (2). Voraussetzung für diese Ladungsauflösung ist ein sorgfältiges Vermessen der
Ätzkegel, wie es zur Zeit nur im manuellen Betrieb mit einem Mikroskop möglich ist. Diese Arbeitsweise schränkt die Anzahl der meßbaren
Daten in den Experimenten stark ein.

Möglichkeiten der automatischen Bildanalyse für die Teilchenspuren

Bei dem Versuch, Teilchenspuren in Plastikdetektoren mit Verfahren der
Bildanalyse zu finden und zu vermessen, erweist es sich als, zumindest
gegenwärtig, unmöglich, den Meßvorgang analog zur Handmessung ablaufen
zu lassen. Diese Schwierigkeit ist hauptsächlich dadurch bedingt, daß
räumliche Koordinaten an bestimmten Punkten der Ätzfigur gemessen werden müssen. Ein Ausweg ergibt sich, wenn man sich darauf beschränkt,
die Ätzfigur z.B. nur an der Oberfläche der Plastikfolie zu betrachten. Dies ist durch eine Beleuchtung im Auflicht leicht zu erreichen.

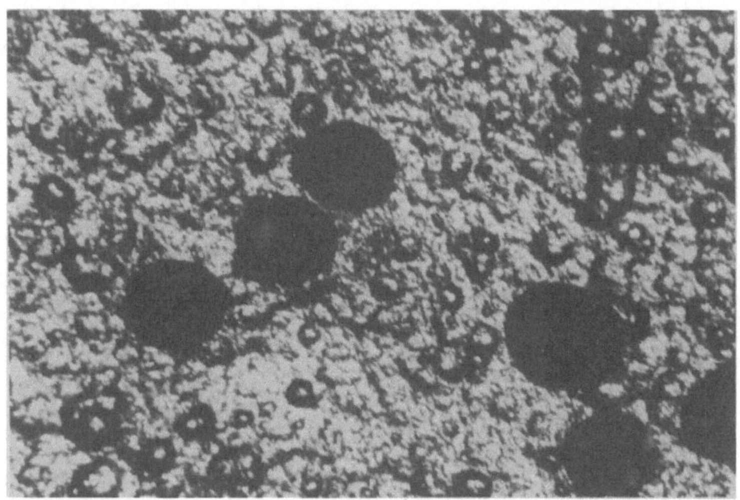

Bild 2: Die gleichen Spuren wie in Bild 1, betrachtet im Auflicht

Bild 2 zeigt die gleichen Spuren wie Bild 1 in dieser Beleuchtung. Als
dunkle Teilchenspuren erscheinen hier nur, wegen des steilen Teilchen-
einfalls, die nahezu kreisförmigen Schnitte der Ätzkegel mit der Folienoberfläche. Diese Objekte vom Untergrund der Strukturen der Folienoberfläche zu unterscheiden und damit zu finden sowie ihre geometrischen Größen wie Position, Fläche und Durchmesser zu bestimmen, sind
mit Verfahren der Bildanalyse relativ leicht möglich. Eine weitere
Möglichkeit besteht darin, bei Teilchenspuren, die nahezu senkrecht
zur Folienoberfläche verlaufen, die Folie längere Zeit zu ätzen. In
diesem Falle treffen sich die von beiden Seiten in die Folie eindrin-
genden Ätzkegel in der Folienmitte und es entsteht ein Loch. Bei Beleuchtung im Durchlicht heben sich diese Löcher deutlich vom Untergrund ab, wie Bild 3 zeigt. Auch derartige Spuren sind leicht mit Verfahren der Bildanalyse zu finden und zu vermessen.

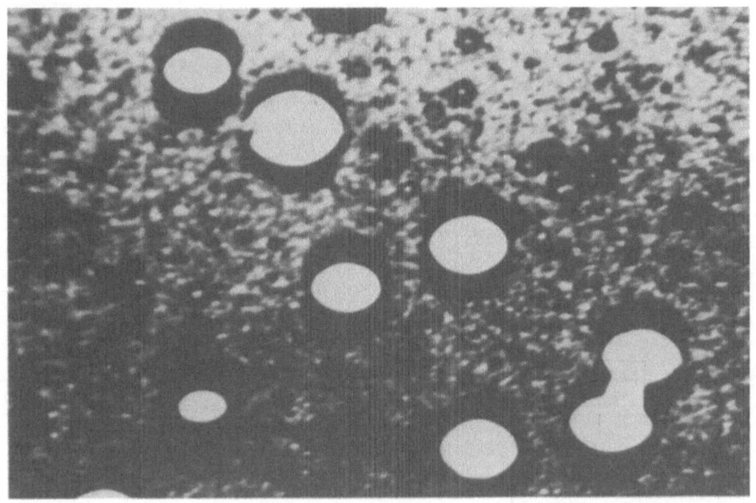

Bild 3: Durchgeätzte Spuren von ^{40}Ar-Ionen in Zellulosenitrat, betrachtet im Durchlicht

Zur Bestimmung der Ladung von Schwerionen, welche Spuren in mehreren aufeinanderfolgenden Plastikfolien hinterlassen haben, wird an Stelle der Kegellänge bei der automatischen Messung die Fläche der Öffnungs- ellipse des Ätzkegels bzw. des durchgeätzten Loches in Abhängigkeit von der Restreichweite vermessen.

Aufbau der rechnergesteuerten Meßapparatur

Die Plastikfolien werden durch ein Mikroskop im Durchlicht oder Auf- licht mit einer Videokamera betrachtet. Bild 4 zeigt schematisch den Aufbau der Meßapparatur. Das Videobild wird von einem Bilddigitali- sierer (4) in 256 x 256 Bildpunkten mit Grauwerten in 16 Stufen digi- talisiert. Ein Mikroprozessor vom Typ Motorola 6800 hat Zugriff auf den Bildspeicher und übergibt die Bildpunkte zeilenweise an eine PDP 11/03. In diesem Rechner laufen zur Zeit die Programme zur Erken- nung der Teilchenspuren und zur Bestimmung ihrer physikalischen Grö- ßen. Nach der Bearbeitung des gesamten Videobildes wird ein weiterer Ausschnitt der Plastikfolie betrachtet. Hierzu wird der schrittmotor- gesteuerte Mikroskoptisch mit einer Arbeitsfläche von 10 cm x 10 cm um den entsprechenden Betrag weiterbewegt. Dazu übergibt die PDP 11/03 die Koordinaten des nächsten Bildausschnittes an einen Mikropro- zessor. Dieser, ebenfalls ein Motorola 6800, bestimmt aus der Diffe- renz der Koordinaten der Zielposition und der augenblicklichen Positi- on die Anzahl der Schritte, um die sich die Motoren bewegen müssen

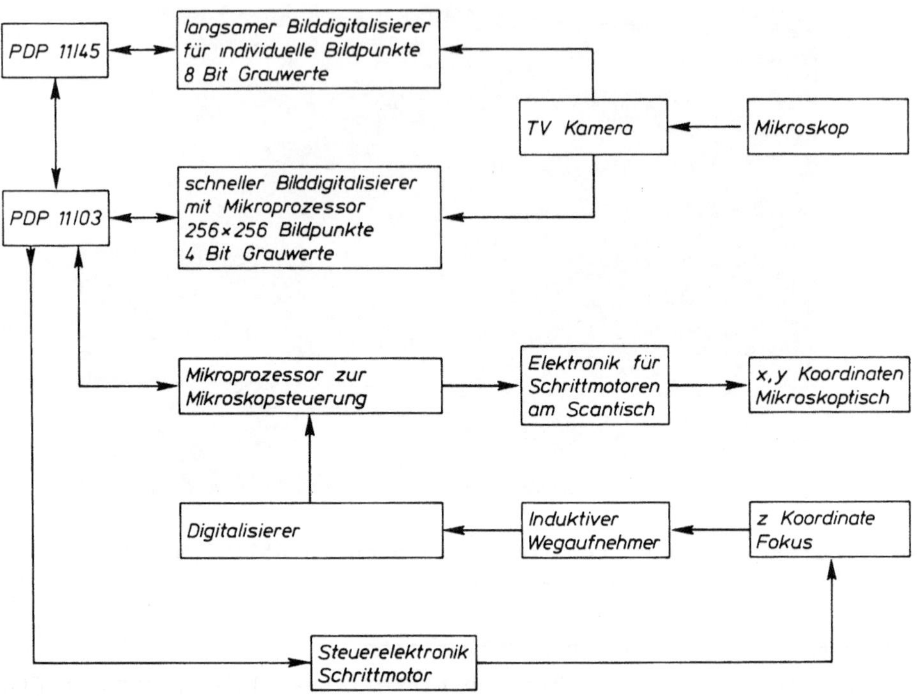

Bild 4: Schematischer Aufbau der Apparatur zur rechnergesteuerten Vermessung der Spuren in Plastikdetektoren

und erzeugt eine entsprechende Impulsfolge, die über eine spezielle Elektronik die Schrittmotoren betreiben. Das Kommando zur Positionierung des nächsten Bildfeldes erfolgt unmittelbar nach dem Digitalisieren eines Bildes und wird dann selbständig vom Mikroprozessor abgearbeitet. In der Zeit, die die PDP 11/03 zur Bearbeitung des vorherigen Bildausschnittes, das im Bildspeicher steht, benötigt,wird das Videobild stabil, so daß es sofort nach Bearbeitung des vorhergehenden Bildes auf Kommando der PDP 11/03 vom Bilddigitalisierer übernommen werden kann.

Zur automatischen Fokussierung des Bildes kann, falls dies erforderlich ist, über eine spezielle Steuerelektronik ein Schrittmotor am z-Antrieb des Mikroskops betätigt werden. Zur Entscheidung, ob das Bild scharf ist, werden gegenwärtig noch über eine PDP 11/45 im

Multiuserbetrieb Daten von einem weiteren Bilddigitalisierer übernommen. Dieser ist in der Lage, individuelle Bildpunkte in 256 Stufen
der Grauwerte zu digitalisieren.

Software zur Identifizierung und Vermessung der Spuren

Die Teilchenspuren können wie die Bilder 2 und 3 zeigen, je nach Spur-
typ und Beleuchtung als Bildbereiche mit extrem großer oder kleiner
Helligkeit erkannt werden. Dazu wird für jede Zeile nach Liniensegmen-
ten gesucht, die diese Bedingung für eine vorgegebene Schwelle im
Grauwert erfüllen. Dann wird überprüft, ob die gefundenen Liniensegmente zu Teilchenspuren gehören, die in der vorhergehenden Zeile bereits vorhanden waren. Falls dies der Fall ist, werden die Bildpunkte
dieser Spur zugeordnet. Wenn ein Liniensegment zu keiner Spur der
letzten Zeile gehört,wird es als eine neue Spur definiert. Spuren,die
in der letzten Zeile noch auftraten aber in der gegenwärtigen Zeile
kein zugehöriges Liniensegment enthalten, werden als abgeschlossenes
Gebiet betrachtet, dem keine weiteren Bildpunkte zugeordnet werden.

Als physikalische Größen der Spuren werden die Fläche als Summe aller
Bildpunkte, die Position in den beiden Tischkoordinaten als der
Schwerpunkt und die Länge der Projektionen der Spuren auf die Koordi-
natenachsen sowie der Umfang der Spur bestimmt. Spuren mit konkaven
Rändern sind erlaubt und werden richtig vermessen. Spuren, die in
ihrem Inneren ein Gebiet haben, welches nicht die Schwellbedingung
erfüllt, werden ausgefüllt.

Beim Vermessen der Spuren wird die Abschattung des Mikroskopbildes zu
den Rändern hin berücksichtigt. Dazu wird die Größe dieser Abschattung als Mittelwert für jeweils ein Feld von mehreren Bildpunkten an
einem Bild mit konstanter Helligkeit vermessen. Die Schwellen im Grauwert für die Identifizierung einer Teilchenspur werden punktweise auf
diese Abschattierung korrigiert.

Ergebnisse

Mit der hier beschriebenen Apparatur werden gegenwärtig die ersten experimentellen Daten aufgenommen. Um die Möglichkeiten, welche die
automatische Bildanalyse zur Vermessung von Kernspuren in Plastikdetektoren bietet, aufzuzeigen, werden daher hier teilweise auch Daten
aus vorhergehenden Experimenten benutzt, bei denen an Stelle der digitalen Bildanalyse mit einer gezielten Software zur Spurerkennung ein
elektronisches, nicht programmierbares Bildanalysegerät, das Quanti-

met, benutzt wurde. Unterschiede in beiden Systemen bezüglich der Auf-
lösung durch unterschiedliche Anzahl von Bildpunkten spielen keine
Rolle, da die experimentellen Bedingungen so gewählt wurden, daß die
Anzahl der Bildpunkte pro Spur vergleichbar ist.

Identifizierung von Teilchenspuren

Eine Teilchenspur ist, wie beschrieben, für die automatische Bildanalyse definiert als eine Fläche mit Helligkeitswerten oberhalb oder unterhalb einer Schwelle. Bild 5 zeigt Ergebnisse, welche für Spuren von
Ar-Ionen im Auflicht gewonnen wurden, die die Folie unter einem Winkel
von 30° gegen die Senkrechte treffen. Die vermessenen Spuren sind also
Ellipsen mit einer geringen Exzentrizität. In der Abbildung ist die
Fläche der Spur gegen den Umfang aufgetragen. Für kreisförmige Spuren
ist der Zusammenhang zwischen diesen Größen durch die eingezeichnete
Kurve gegeben. Bei dieser Messung wurde zusätzlich zu den automatisch
gemessenen Daten für jede Spur von Hand eine Information über die Qualität der Spur eingegeben. Es wurde insbesondere zwischen richtigen
Spuren (Dreiecke in Bild 5) und Objekten, die keine Spuren waren aber als
solche erkannt wurden (Kreise), sowie den seltenen Fällen, wo zwei oder
mehrere Teilchenspuren so dicht zusammenliegen, daß ihre Ätzfiguren
ineinander übergehen (Kreuze), unterschieden. Bild 5 zeigt, daß die

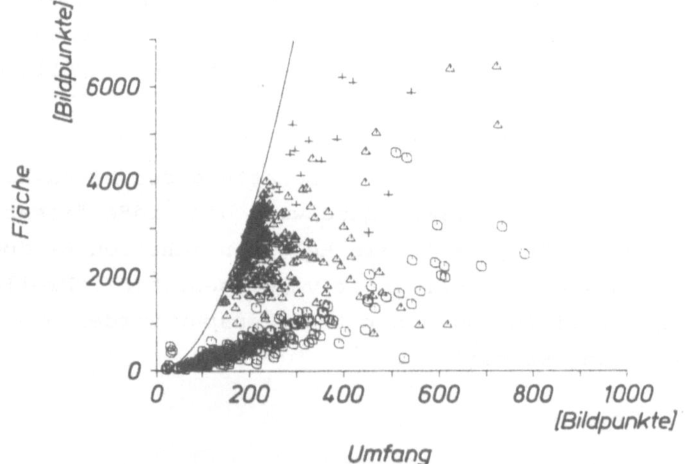

Bild 5: Zusammenhang zwischen Fläche und Umfang für:
     o Objekte, die keine Spuren sind
     Δ Spuren von einem Teilchendurchgang
     + zusammenfallende Spuren von mehreren Teilchendurchgängen
     — Kurve für kreisförmige Spuren

Teilchenspuren und die Objekte, die keine Teilchenspuren sind, sich sauber voneinander trennen lassen. Die Objekte, welche keine Spuren sind, werden durch Unregelmäßigkeiten an der Folienoberfläche erzeugt. Diese Unregelmäßigkeiten sind längliche Gebilde kleiner Fläche. Die eigentlichen Teilchenspuren häufen sich im Bereich der eingezeichneten Kurve. Dabei gibt die Kurve, die für kreisförmige Spuren gilt, eine obere Grenze der Fläche. Wenige Spuren zeigen einen stark überhöhten Umfang im Vergleich zur Fläche. Dieser Fall tritt auf,wenn eine Spur und eine Unregelmäßigkeit der Oberfläche zusammenfallen. Für den Einsatz der automatischen Bildanalyse in Experimenten, bei denen ein Teilchen Spuren in mehreren Folien hinterlassen hat, ist eine weitere Möglichkeit zur sicheren Identifizierung von Teilchenspuren dadurch gegeben, daß Spuren in aufeinanderfolgenden Plastikfolien am gleichen Ort gefunden werden. Die Wahrscheinlichkeit, daß solche Spuren zufällig durch Unregelmäßigkeiten in aufeinanderfolgenden Folien vorgetäuscht werden ist sehr klein.

Automatische Fokussierung des Mikroskops

Als ein scharfes Bild wird ein Bild mit maximalem Kontrast definiert. Hierzu werden Differenzen der Helligkeitswerte zwischen benachbarten Bildpunkten entlang einer Zeile gebildet. Bild 6 zeigt jeweils den maximalen Wert dieser Differenzen in Abhängigkeit von der Position des Schrittmotors für den Fokus. In diesem Fall wurde eine Bildzeile betrachtet, welche eine durchgeätzte Spur schneidet, die im Durchlicht beleuchtet wird. Die scharfe Spitze für den maximalen Kontrast in diesem Bild liegt bei der Position des Schrittmotors,an der das Bild auf dem Fernsehmonitor als scharf erscheint.

Trotz dieses guten Ergebnisses ist eine automatische Fokussierung nicht unproblematisch, da sie sehr zeitraubend ist. Um eine Entscheidung treffen zu können, ob die gegenwärtige Bildposition scharf ist oder nicht, ist es erforderlich, das Bild zunächst einmal in beide Bewegungsrichtungen zu defokussieren und dann zumindest in Ausschnitten erneut zu digitalisieren. Da der Fokus nicht in allen Fällen, insbesondere für nicht durchgeätzte Spuren, durch ein so enges Maximum wie in Bild 6 definiert ist, muß diese Vermessung des Kontrastes an einer größeren Anzahl von Positionen des Schrittmotors erfolgen. Glücklicherweise ist eine automatische Fokussierung nicht in allen Fällen erforderlich.

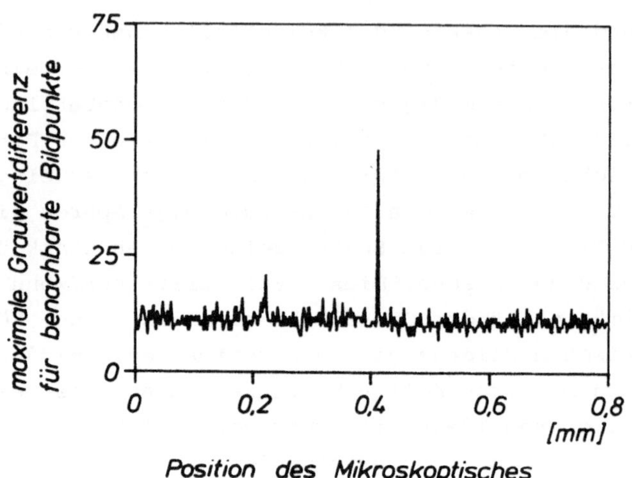

Bild 6: Wert der maximalen Grauwertdifferenz für benachbarte
Bildpunkte entlang einer Zeile in Abhängigkeit von der
Position des Mikroskoptisches (Fokuseinstellung)

Genauigkeit der Ladungsbestimmung für Spuren schwerer Kerne

Die Identifizierung von schweren Kernen erfolgt mit Hilfe der Abhängigkeit der Fläche der Ätzfigur von der Restreichweite des Teilchens. Bild 7 zeigt diesen Zusammenhang für Lexanfolien in Kurven, welche aus einer Eichung mit Teilchen bekannter Ladung folgen. Die Datenpunkte zeigen Spuren der Fragmente von ^{40}Ar-Ionen, welche einen Wassertank verlassen, in dem das Argon abgebremst wurde (5). Solche Fragmente entstehen, wenn ein Ar-Projektil im Wasser auf ein Proton oder einen Sauerstoffkern stößt. Dieses Beispiel zeigt, daß eine eindeutige Zuordnung von Teilchenladungen ohne weiteres möglich ist. Zusätzlich zu den in Bild 7 eingezeichneten Kurven sind weitere Kurven für andere Isotope der angegebenen Kerne möglich. Diese liegen zwischen den hier gezeigten Kurven. Dieser Effekt kann bei der Ladungsbestimmung berücksichtigt werden, indem man so tut als ob es auch nichtganzzahlige Ladungszahlen der Kerne gäbe. Die Häufigkeiten der so bestimmten Ladungszahlen für eine große Anzahl von Fragmenten sind in Bild 8 aufgetragen. Die Breiten der Ladungsverteilungen sind durch zwei Effekte verursacht. Es treten als Fragmente mit größter Wahrscheinlichkeit die Kerne auf, die in Bild 7 angegeben sind. Zusätzlich treten aber auch mit geringer Häufigkeit andere Isotope auf, die als Teilchen ungerader Ladung identifiziert werden und somit die Häufigkeitsverteilungen verbreitern. Zum zweiten ist die Breite der Ladungsverteilung

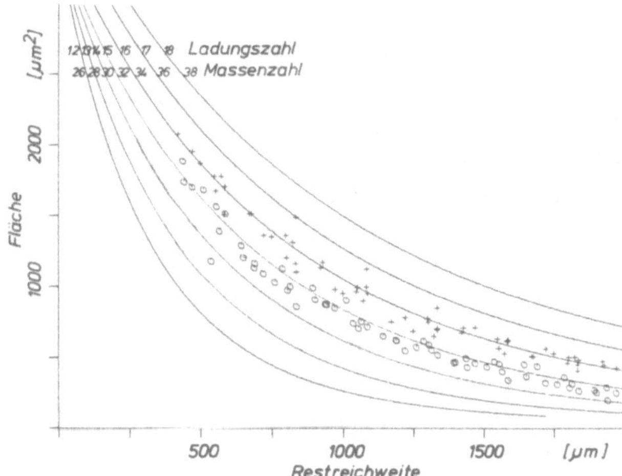

Bild 7: Fläche des Kegelschnittes an der Folienoberfläche als Funktion der Restreichweite für verschiedene Kerne in Lexan,-Theoretischer Zusammenhang aus einer Eichung mit bekannten Schwerionen O,+Meßpunkte für unbekannte Kerne, die als $^{32}_{15}P$ (o) bzw. $^{34}_{16}S$ (+) identifiziert wurden (jeweils 10 Teilchen)

natürlich durch den experimentellen Fehler der Ladungsbestimmung verursacht. Nähert man die Ladungsverteilungen durch eine Gaußverteilung an, so haben diese eine Varianz von etwa $\sigma = \pm O,3$ Ladungseinheiten. Daraus folgt, wenn man die Breite der Ladungsverteilungen einmal ganz den Meßfehlern zuschreibt, für dieses Experiment ein Auflösungsvermögen für die Ladungsbestimmung mit einer oberen Grenze von $\Delta Z = \pm O,3$.

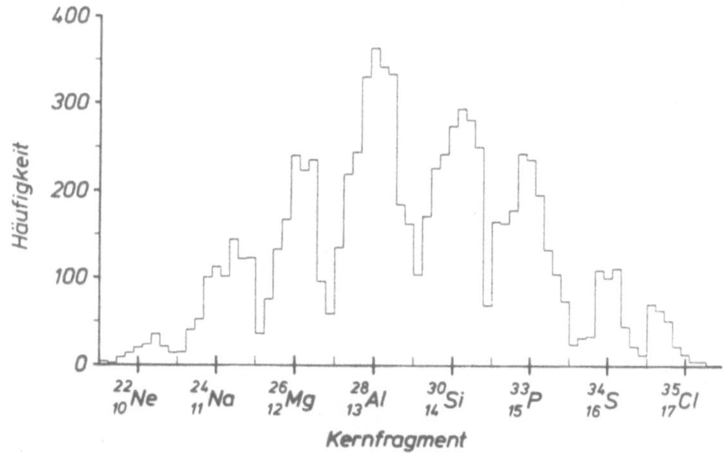

Bild 8: Häufigkeitsverteilung der Ladungen von Fragmenten eines ^{40}Ar Strahls hinter einem Wasser-Target

Literatur

1) P.B.Price, R.M.Walker, Chemical Etching of Charged Particle Tracks
   J.App.Phys.33,3407-3412(1962)

2) K.P.Bartholomä, G.Siegmon, W.Enge,Isotopic Composition of Cosmic
   Ray Iron Nuclei,14th International Cosmic Ray Conference,München
   1975, Conference Papers Vol.1,Seite 384

3) R.L.Fleischer, P.B.Price, R.M.Walker,Nuclear Tracks in Solids,
   University of California Press, Berkeley (1975)

4) B.Schöfer, J.Pipper, W.Heinrich, Ein digitales Video-System mit
   einem Mikroprozessor zur Bildanalyse, dieser Tagungsbericht

5) D.Hildebrand, E.V.Benton, R.P.Henke, W.Heinrich
   Fragmentation of High Energy Argon Ion in Water,In Press in
   Nuclear Tracks.

<u>SEQUENTIELLE BESTIMMUNG MORPHOLOGISCHER MERKMALE</u>
<u>HOLOGRAPHISCH AUFGEZEICHNETER PARTIKEL</u>

G. Haussmann[+], H. Zarschizky
Drittes Physikalisches Institut, Universität Göttingen
[+] jetzt: Lehrstuhl f. Theor. Nachrichtentechnik, TU Hannover

1. Einleitung

Holographische reelle Bilder als analoge optische Bildspeicher ermöglichen einen ersten Einstieg in die 3-D Bildverarbeitung und gestat-
ten es, das Problem der großen Datenmengen, die bei einer vollstän-
digen digitalen Abtastung und Abspeicherung räumlicher Bilder anfal-
len, zu umgehen. Die Bildpunkte $I(x,y,z)$ werden dabei über eine
mechanisch verschiebbare digital adressierbare Kamera direkt aus dem
holographischen Bild in den Rechner eingelesen, wobei ein wahlfreier
Zugriff in allen drei Dimensionen möglich ist. Das entwickelte Verfahren, bei dem das räumliche Bild Ausschnitt für Ausschnit nacheinander in der Tiefe abgearbeitet wird, findet Anwendung bei der Analyse holographisch gespeicherter, dreidimensionaler Partikelfelder
/1/. Nachdem es gelingt, Objekte durch die Detektion der Objektrandschärfe in der Tiefendimension des
holographischen Bildes zu fokus-
sieren /2/, sollen im Rahmen dieses
Beitrages die Probleme diskutiert
werden, die sich bei der Auswertung
eines zweidimensionalen Bildausschnittes in einer bestimmten
Tiefenebene ergeben.

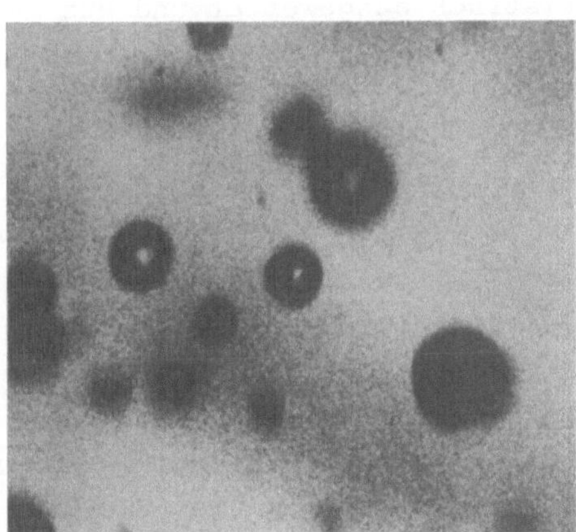

Abb. 1
Bildausschnitt eines Hologramms mit
transparenten Luftblasen in Wasser
in einer bestimmten Tiefenebene des
reellen Bildes

2. Segmentierung des Bildausschnittes

Bei der Verarbeitung von Bildern mit einfachen, weitgehend homogenen
Partikeln reduziert sich das Problem der Segmentierung auf die Tren-
nung der Bildpunkte in Objekt- und Hintergrundpunkte. Im kontrast-

reichen Teil des Bildes mit nur einem fokussierten Objekt im Bildausschnitt weist das Intensitätshistogramm eine ausgeprägte Bimodalität

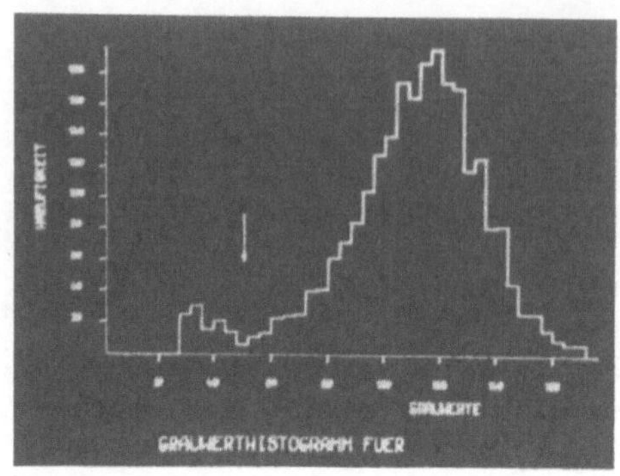

Abb. 2

Intensitätshistogramm eines
Bildausschnitts mit einer scharf-
gestellten Blase. Eine Segmentierungsschwelle wird in das Minimum
zwischen die Histogrammoden gelegt.

auf, die es ermöglicht, eine
Schwelle in das Minimum zwischen
die Moden zu legen und die Segmentierung ausschließlich auf der Basis dieser Intensitätsschwelle
durchzuführen (siehe Abb. 2).
Sind jedoch weitere unscharfe Partikel im Bildausschnitt vorhanden
oder sind die Teilchen klein gegen
die Bildfläche, so kann aufgrund
mangelhafter Bimodalität des Histogramms entweder überhaupt keine
Schwelle festgelegt werden oder sie
bekommt einen eher zufälligen Wert
zugeordnet.
Nachdem ein zusätzliches Segmentie-
rungskriterium auf der Basis einer
lokalen Statistik, wobei die Homogenität der Partikel ausgenutzt werden sollte, insbesondere an den Objekträndern zu keinen befriedigenden
Ergebnissen geführt hat, wird auf dem jetzigen Stand des Verfahrens
das Histogramm des Bildausschnitts statistisch ausgewertet und aus dem
Erwartungswert über das Einbringen von a-priori-Wissen eine stabile
Segmentierungsschwelle berechnet.

3. Auswerteprogramme

Durch die Anwendung von Auswerteprogrammen auf den Bildausschnitt in
einer bestimmten Tiefenebene erhält jedes dort vorhandene Objekt Meßwerte für Fläche und Umfang, die x- und y-Koordinaten des Schwerpunk-
tes, die z-Koordinate aus der Verschiebetischstellung, eine objektgebundene Maßzahl für die Randschärfe sowie die Objektpunktzahl in einer
Randzeile oder -spalte zugeordnet. Aufgrund der beschränkten Speicher-
kapazität des benutzten Prozeßrechners konnten ausschließlich sequen-
tielle Algorithmen implementiert werden, wobei jeweils drei Bildzeilen
direkt aus dem holographischen Bild in den Kernspeicher eingelesen,
Ketten zusammenhängender Objektpunkte gebildet und mit einheitlichen
Marken versehen sowie Zeiger gesetzt werden, wenn bisher getrennt
markierte Objekte sich vereinigen (siehe Abb. 3).
Größere transparente Objekte weisen häufig einen hellen Fleck in der

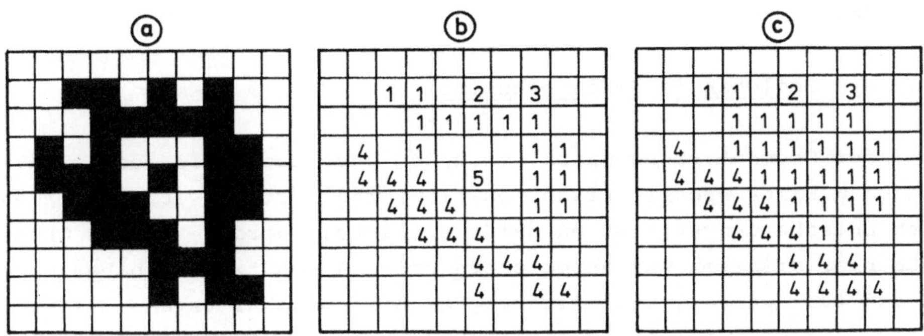

Abb. 3

Prinzip des Algorithmus zur Bestimmung morphologischer Partikelparameter
a) Binäres Objekt
b) Markierung zusammenhängender Objektpunkte
   Zeiger 2 → 1 und 3 → 1 in Zeile 3, Zeiger 1 → 4 in Zeile 5
c) Ausfüllen der Löcher im binären Objekt

Mitte auf, der von dem ungestreut durch das Partikel hindurchtretenden
Licht herrührt, als Hintergrund interpretiert wird und auf diese Weise
Flächen- und Umfangswerte verfälscht. Ein Programm kann daher auf die
bereits markierten Bildzeilen angewandt werden, das Ketten gleicher Marken oder durch Zeiger verknüpfter Marken miteinander verbindet und so die Löcher ausfüllt (Prinzip siehe Abb. 3c). Aufgrund des sequentiellen Vorgehens können dabei allerdings nur die bis zur aktuellen Zeile gewonnenen Informationen verwertet werden, was u.U. zu fehlerhaften Resultaten führen kann. Für die vorliegende Aufgabe erfüllt das Verfahren jedoch im wesentlichen die gestellten Anforderungen (siehe auch Abb. 6).

Die objektgebundene Schärfemaßzahl des Teilchenrandes wird

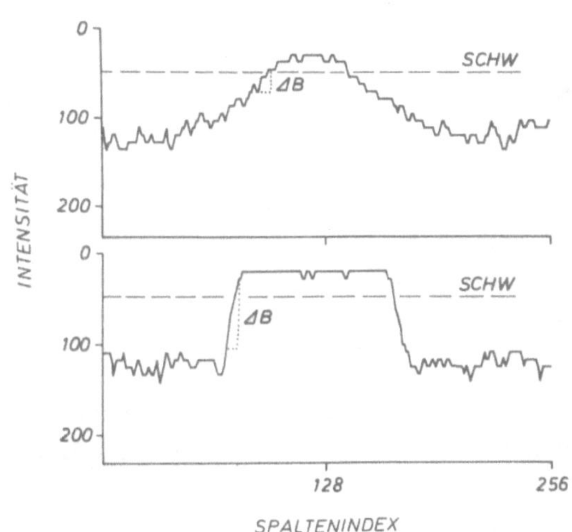

Abb. 4

Bestimmung der objektgebundenen Maßzahl der Objektrandschärfe auf der
Basis der Segmentierungsschwelle

auf der Basis der Segmentierungsschwelle in Form der durchschnittlichen Kantensteigung berechnet (siehe Abb. 4).

4. Mehrere Teilchen im Bildausschnitt

Da bei der Segmentierung unter Umständen auch unscharfe oder unvollständig am Bildausschnittsrand positionierte Partikel erfaßt werden,
müssen Entscheidungskriterien dafür entwickelt werden, welche Objekte
der Rechner erfassen und abspeichern soll. Abschätzungen haben ergeben, daß für den Fall unvollständig am Bildausschnittsrand positio-
nierter Teilchen der Fehler der Fächenmessung dann unter 5% bleibt,
wenn weniger als 1/4 der Umfangspunkte in einer Randzeile oder -spalte
liegen /3/.
Zur Klärung der Frage, bis zu welchem Defokussierungsgrad unscharfe
Partikel noch erfaßt werden können, soll die Abhängigkeit der ermit- -

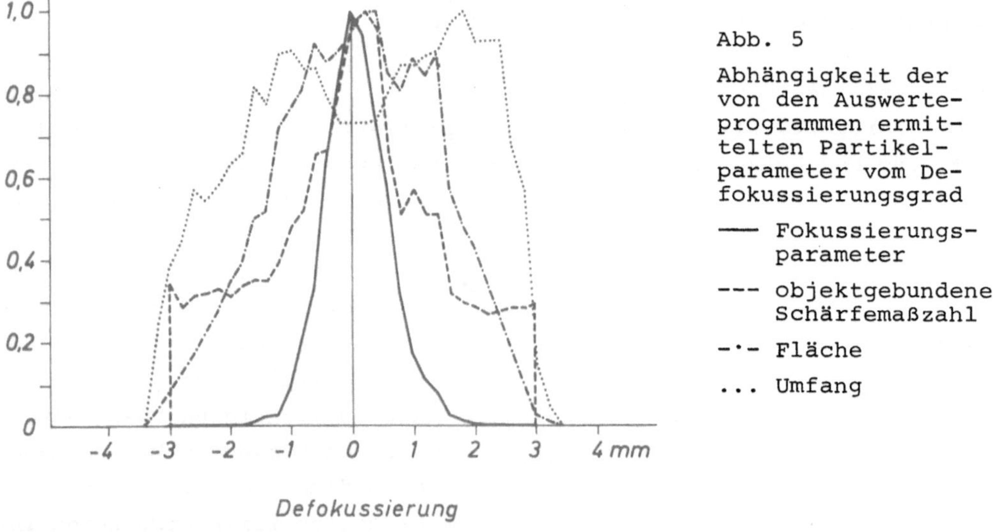

Abb. 5
Abhängigkeit der
von den Auswerte-
programmen ermit-
telten Partikel-
parameter vom De-
fokussierungsgrad

—— Fokussierungs-
parameter

--- objektgebundene
Schärfemaßzahl

-·- Fläche

... Umfang

telten Partikelparameter von der Defokussierung untersucht werden.
Ein typisches Beispiel für ein größeres Teilchen ist in Abb. 5 dargestellt. Dabei zeigt sich, daß
- die Fläche im Bereich der größten Partikelschärfe ein lokales Maximum, der Umfang dagegen ein lokales Minimum aufweist,
- die objektgebundene Schärfemaßzahl einen monotonen Verlauf besitzt
  und damit zur Beschreibung der Teilchenschärfe gut geeignet ist.
Eine Auswertung mehrerer Versuche hat ergeben, daß im Bildausschnitt
alle Teilchen erfaßt und ihre Daten abgespeichert werden können, deren
Schärfemaßzahl in einem Verhältnis zu der des eigentlich fokussierten

Teilchens von mindestens 0.65 steht. Der Meßfehler kann dann in nahezu allen Fällen mit höchstens 10% abgeschätzt werden. Durch die Erfassung auch derjenigen Teilchen, die im Bildausschnitt keine maximale Schärfemaßzahl aufweisen, wird sichergestellt, daß sie bei der Analyse selbst dann nicht verloren gehen, wenn der Rechner sie nicht getrennt anfokussiert.

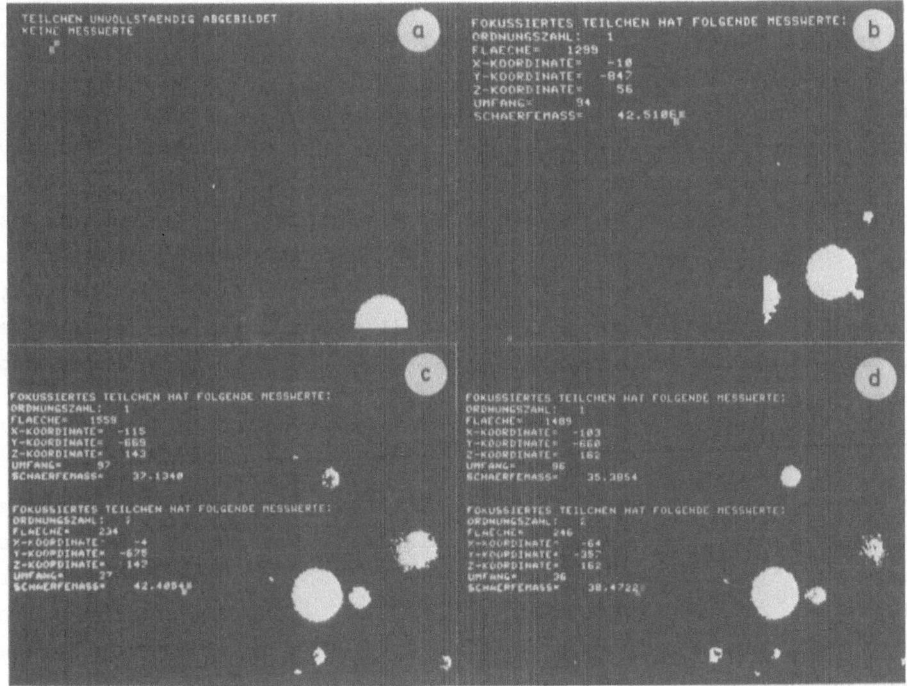

Abb. 6

Typische Situation des automatischen Versuchsablaufes mit mehreren Teilchen im Bildausschnitt
a) Teilchen am Bildausschnittsrand wird unterdrückt
b) Teilchen am Bildrand und unscharfes Teilchen werden unterdrückt
c) Bildausschnitt mit mehreren scharfen und unscharfen Teilchen
d) Bildausschnitt wie in c), jedoch in einer anderen Tiefenebene
   (Abstand der Tiefenebenen: 1.9 mm)

In Abb. 6a bis 6d sind typische Situationen des automatischen Versuchsablaufs dargestellt, wobei die erkannten Teilchen als Binärbild zusammen mit den morphologischen Daten der erfaßten Partikel auf einem Sichtschirmgerät ausgegeben werden.

5. Die Statistik der Meßwerte

Die nicht perfekte mechanische Stabilität des optischen Aufbaus sowie
das Rauschen in den Photomultipliern der Kamera haben eine mangelhafte
Reproduzierbarkeit der aus dem optischen Bildspeicher eingelesenen Daten zur Folge. Daher müssen die aus dem Histogramm bestimmten Segmen-
tierungsschwellen und damit auch die Meßdaten der Partikel als Zu-
fallsvariable interpretiert werden. Ihre Statistik ist für ausgewählte
Teilchen in Testhologrammen untersucht worden /3/. Dabei zeigt sich,
daß der Fehler bei der Flächenmessung bei Partikeldurchmesserwerten
von 100 µm bis 800 µm, von Ausnahmen abgesehen, unter 6 % liegt. Während sich die x- und y-Koordinaten aus dem Bildausschnitt relativ genau berechnen lassen (absoluter Fehler unter 50 µm), muß bei der Festlegung der Tiefenkoordinate aus der mechanischen Verschiebetischstellung mit einer Unsicherheit bis zum halben Teilchendurchmesser gerech-
net werden. Zur Kontrolle des automatischen Analyseverfahrens wurden
außerdem noch die vom Rechner ermittelten Durchmesserwerte mit manuell
bestimmten verglichen, wobei sich eine gute Übereinstimmung ergab.

6. Anwendungsbeispiel

Mit Hilfe des implementierten automatischen Versuchsablaufs wurden Ho-
logramme von schnell bewegten Luftblasen in Wasser, die mit Hilfe eines Rubin-Impuls-Lasers aufgezeichnet wurden, teilweise analysiert.
Dabei wurde die x-y-Projektion des auszuwertenden Bildvolumens in
gleichgroße, sich großzügig überlappende Bereiche eingeteilt, die
nacheinander in der Tiefe analysiert wurden.
Im Verlauf der Auswertung kommt es dabei relativ häufig vor, daß Partikel in den Überlappungsbereichen der Bildausschnitte, durch Pseudo-
fokussierungen oder durch eine niedrig gewählte Schwelle zur Unterdrückung unscharf abgebildeter Teilchen mehrfach erfaßt und mit ihren
Meßwerten abgespeichert werden. In einem abschließenden Arbeitsgang
werden derartige Mehrfacherfassungen an den nahezu identischen Koor-
dinatenwerten erkannt und auf den Meßwertsatz mit der maximalen Ob-
jektschärfemaßzahl reduziert.
Das Gesamtergebnis der Auswertung eines Teils des Hologramms kann in
Abb. 7 mit der fotografischen Rekonstruktion des virtuellen Bildes
verglichen werden. Die Tiefenkoordinate ist in diesem zweidimensionalen Plot nicht dargestellt, sie steht jedoch ebenfalls zur Verfügung.
Der Rechner hat nahezu alle im untersuchten Volumen vorhandenen Partikel erfaßt und nach Lage und Größe vermessen. Der durchschnittliche
Rechenaufwand lag bei 30 sec, er ist im allgemeinen jedoch von der

Partikeldichte und der Hologrammqualität abhängig.

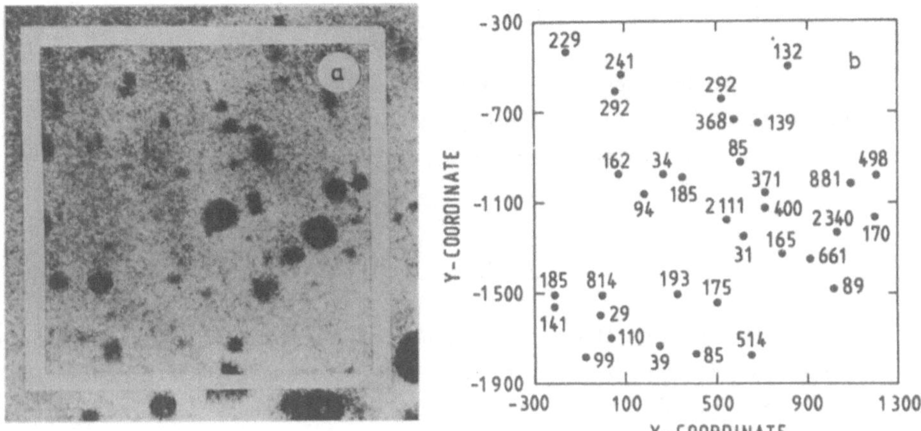

Abb. 7

Vergleich der vom Rechner ermittelten Flächen- und Koordinatenwerte
mit der fotografischen Rekonstruktion des Testhologramms
a) Fotografie des virtuellen Bildes
b) Ergebnis der automatischen Ausertung
   (die Zahlen geben die Flächenwerte an)

Das Verfahren kann auf dem augenblicklichen Entwicklungsstand auf Partikelfelder mit nicht zu großer Teilchendichte angewandt werden.
Schwierigkeiten bereiten noch nichtsphärische und zusammenhängende
Teilchen. Mit dem Einsatz von Prozeßrechnern mit größerer Kernspei-
cherkapazität dürfte es jedoch in Zukunft möglich sein, komplexere
nichtsequentielle Algorithmen zu implementieren und auf diese Weise
diese Schwierigkeiten zu überwinden.
Die vorliegende Untersuchung wurde mit Mitteln der Deutschen Forschungsgemeinschaft durchgeführt.

7. Literaturverzeichnis

/1/ G. Haussmann, W. Lauterborn, Informatik-Fachberichte, Vol. 17,
    Springer, Berlin 1978, S. 275 - 280.

/2/ G. Haussmann, Informatik-Fachberichte, Vol. 20, Springer,
    Berlin 1979, S. 94 - 100.

/3/ G. Haussmann, Dissertation, Göttingen 1979.

A MULTIPROCESSOR-SYSTEM FOR THE ACQUISITION AND ANALYSIS OF VIDEO IMAGE SEQUENCES

R. Brennecke, H.J. Hahne, P.H. Heintzen

Department of Pediatric Cardiology and Biomedical Engineering,
Universitäts-Kinderklinik Kiel, W.Germany

Abstract

We give a preliminary report on the organization, architecture and programming of an image processing system optimized for the high speed storage, handling and analysis of digitized time-varying video image sequences. Typical known video processor architectures are characterized by dedicated data paths. Spatial multiplexing is used for system reconfiguration. The multiprocessor architecture described here uses a time-multiplexed synchronous bus for easy system expansion. Control and computational tasks are distributed among several levels of software and corresponding hardware to simplify efficient programming. The basic data structure supported is the data stream. Data streams are assembled and distributed under programm control. Performing I/O- and computational tasks can be visualized as passing these structured data streams through a chain of programmed processors. We expect that this concept , which is supported by hardware, will simplify the efficient programming of concurrent I/O- and computational processes required for fast execution of image sequence processing tasks.   Applications from medical X-ray image processing are given.

Design Goals

From an operational point of view, video-image sequence analysis is characterized by the large amount of data to be stored, examined and analyzed. In our applications, the enhancement and analysis of dynamic X-ray images from the heart and the circulation, the primary data base is 10 to 60 Mbyte of video information accumulated in approximately 10 seconds. The interactive development of new algorithms using a sequential computer is extremely time-consuming even if one succeeds in finding a hierarchical or cone-like structure of data processing algorithms. This is also true for the critical evaluation of new algorithms on the basis of a sufficiently large set of different video scenes. Moreover, many clinical applications require the enhancement and preliminary analysis of a video scene in real-time or in a few minutes.

From our applications we derived the following goals for an image sequence processing system:

1.) Digital real-time storage of video image sequences with a minimum resolution of
    256*256*8 bit per field, 50 TV-fields per second, for 10 seconds. Presently,
    intermediate analog (video-tape) storage of data introduces tape-noise and
    time-base jitter.
2.) Real-time data reduction by entropy-coding and spatial and temporal windowing.
    Applying redundancy reduction (1), X-ray image data may be stored with a higher
    resolution than specified above (2,3).
3.) Image restoration for the compensation of errors introduced by the X-ray imaging
    system (4).
4.) Change detection by regional cross correlation (3,5).
5.) Image enhancement by logarithmic image subtraction, temporal integration, tempo-
    ral filtering (3,6,7,8,9) and grey-level histogram modification (8).
6.) Quantitative extraction of motion parameters such as time of arrival of a flow
    perturbation or relative regional blood flow (10,11,12).
7.) Display of results (stills and digital loop movies).

The system described below is optimized to handle these tasks. Since it is programmable and the bus structure allows easy expansion, we expect that it can be
adapted to many other problems.

<u>System Architecture</u>

Typical video processors (8,13,14,15) combine an A/D-converter, a D/A- converter,
multiple semiconductor memories, arithmetic units and look-up tables. The system is
usually synchronized to one of the external data sources (e.g. video camera).
System reconfiguration is performed by spatial multiplexing (data switches).

In image sequence analysis applications, the storage capacity provided by economi-
cally feasible semiconductor memories is often too limited to store digitized primary data and intermediate and final results. Therefore, in the multiprocessor system
described, a digital secondary memory (fast digital disk system) will be closely
coupled to the video processor. The system is internally synchronized and uses buf-
fered I/O-processors to interface to externally synchronized video sources and
sinks. Finally, a time multiplexed synchronous bus and a large semiconductor memory
are shared by all processors to facilitate dynamic system reconfiguration and the
addition of processors. The system is at the same time I/O- and computation- ori-
ented and thus is called Image Sequence Acquisition and Analysis Computer (ISAAC).
Fig.1 is a block diagram of the configuration of the ISAAC processor showing the
characteristics described above.

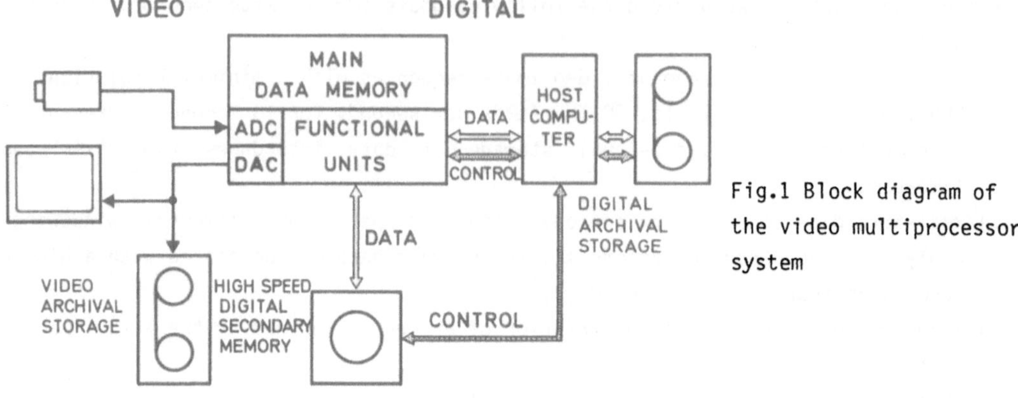

Fig.1 Block diagram of the video multiprocessor system

The system can be regarded as a digital video interchange. Data processing by programmable functional units may occur while transferring data between I/O-ports and the main memory. This (MIMD-) multiprocessor system is programmed by a minicomputer system (host computer). The host additionally performs complex computations on data preprocessed by the video processor. In response to results, it controls the disk system and selected registers of the video processor.

The following discussion will center on the problem of the coordination or synchronization of the activities of the functional units. The organization of functional units and the main memory is discussed shortly.

<u>Functional</u> <u>Units</u>. Computational and I/O-processes may operate concurrently. They are allocated to a number of specialized programmable functional units (FU). During a setup-phase, each FU is programmed by the host computer. Fig. 2A shows the structure of two typical FUs. Independently from their internal structure (serial pipeline or parallel processor), each FU is activated by loading a data word (typically 8 byte) into its input buffer. Synchronized by the system clock, the FU performs the programmed operations and loads the result into the output buffer. Thus the problem of coordinating the activities of the FUs is equivalent to maintaining several concurrent data streams between input and output buffers of I/O-processors, computational units and partitions of the main memory.

In some FUs, the function performed is modified in response to a function key supplied to the control input (Fig. 2A) together with each input data word. This key is decoded from the buffer address code (SDL-code) defined in the description of system control given below. This feature allows the instantaneous modification of functions performed by these FUs (17). If, for instance, several data streams time-share a single FU, the operation performed by the FU may depend on the source of each data word. Function key pipelining is done in parallel to data pipelining (Fig. 2A).

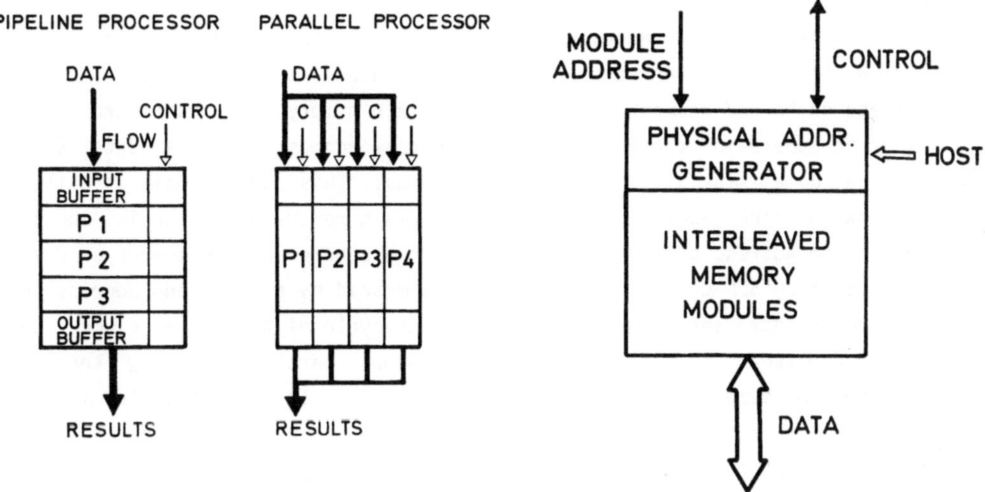

Fig.2A Structure of functional units   Fig.2B Main memory management unit

Main Memory Organization. The main functions of the central semiconductor memory management are to buffer large data blocks, to perform data block transformations (e.g. line sequential write, row sequential read), and the exchange of data blocks between FUs (including repetitive or recursive processing of data by the same FU). These tasks do not require random access of the FUs to main memory addresses. Instead, large blocks of data are stored or accessed according to repetitive patterns. The central memory management unit of the ISAAC system takes these considerations into account. The FUs do not access the physical address space, but call the address of one of 16 address generators. When its 4 bit address is called, each address generator calculates a new 20 bit address from the previously calculated address according to a scheme programmed by the host computer. Data are exchanged between the corresponding memory location and the data-port of the memory (Fig. 2B). Under control of an address generator, the data of a three-dimensional array (matrix) in physical address space may be scanned. The generator changes the starting point after each matrix scan automatically and in this way shifts the matrix through a larger matrix. Standard dynamic MOS-memory is used to allow the economical storage of about 50 TV-fields (256*256*8 bit per field). By demultiplexing and interleaving, a maximum bandwidth of 320 Mbit/s is attainable.

System Control. Fig. 3 is a block diagram of the internal organization of the ISAAC-system. The FUs and the main memory are connected to a data and to a control

bus. The system is coordinated by signals from a central control unit (operation
sequencer) and from the system clock generator. Since the FUs are synchronized by
the data flow, the task of the sequencer is to maintain concurrent data streams
between these units and between the FUs and the main memory. Each data transfer is
initiated by the operation sequencer by applying the addresses of a data source
buffer and a data sink buffer to the control bus. This address pair is called a
source/destination link (SDL-Code). Similarly, a main memory partition is accessed
by specifying the address of the corresponding address generator as source or desti-
nation address in an SDL-Code. The SDL-code is compared by all FUs and address generators to their addresses. During the subsequent cycle of the system clock , data
are transferred between the addressed buffers or memory partitions using the data
bus.   At the same time, a new SDL-code is transmitted. The data transfer initial-
izes the operations of the addressed FUs. While these operations proceed, data may
be transfered between other FUs. Thus, data transfers and data processing occur
simultaneously using a time-multiplex scheme.

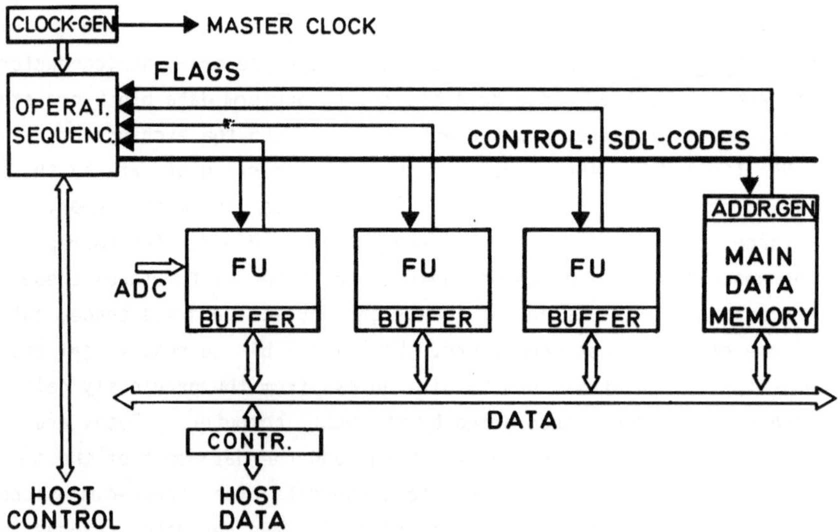

Fig.3 Control and data flow in the multiprocessor system

The sequencer obtains the relevant status information of the FUs and the address
generators -the filling of data buffers- by monitoring flags set by these units.
Thus there is a similar communication between processors and bus control unit as in
a conventional bus system managed by a hardware arbiter implementing a priority
scheme. However, the bus controller of the ISAAC system uses a different scheme of
bus allocation.
Fig.4 describes the organization of the operation sequencer. Synchronized by the

system clock, the sequencer reads a control list, which is assembled by the host. Reading is strictly sequential. The list containing approximately 80 lines is read in a cyclical mode for more than 1000 times during a typical process. In each line, one source/destination address pair (SDL-code) is specified. Each line of the list may directly address a pair of FUs as described above. However, some of the codes in the stream read from the list may alternatively be changed by the code modifier schematically shown below the list. Depending on the pattern of flag signals of the FUs and the address generators and on external interrupts, four modifications may occur:

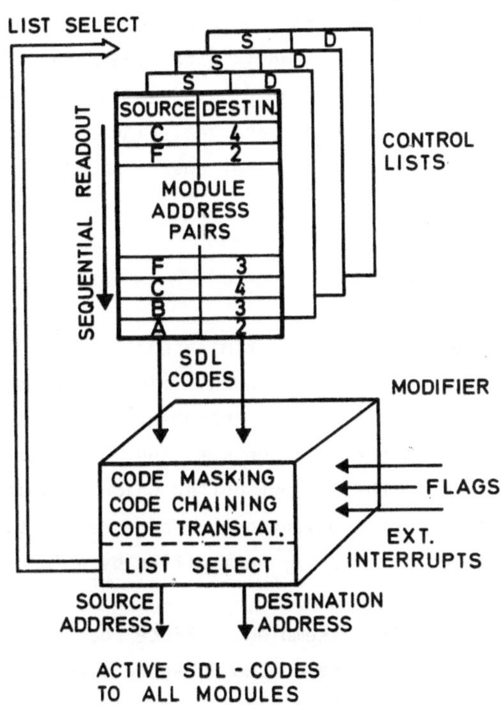

Fig.4 Structure of the central control unit (operation sequencer)

1.) <u>Code Masking</u>: Transmission of an SDL-code is inhibited, if the corresponding source buffer is empty or the simultaneously addressed sink buffer is full.

2.) <u>Code Chaining</u>: An SDL-code may be masked as long as another code is inhibited (masked). This simplifies e.g. the synchronization of an internal data stream with external data.

3.) <u>Code-Translation</u>: Instead of masking a code, the code may be translated into a different code, which is not inhibited. In this way, the waste of the corresponding bus cycles is avoided. More generally, selected entries of the sequencer list are conditionally transformed.

4.) <u>List-Selection</u>: After each complete passage of the control list, the modifier unit may select a different list in response to flags or external interrupts. In this way, the system may be reconfigured by changing all links (SDL-codes) between FUs and main memory modules. The response time for the list change is less than 16 μs.

Conditions leading to a list change occur in time-intervals of 2ms to 2s typically and are handled in the ISAAC system by a MOS- microprocessor.

The described system coordination is similar to the polling scheme sometimes regarded as applicable only to low performance microprocessor systems. In general purpose applications, system response time may be slow and system throughput low if only a small fraction of the flags interrogated during polling are active. In image sequence processing applications, however, large interrelated data blocks are handled and thus system requirements for a considerable time period are easily specified. Thus, the operation sequencer will meet unexpected conditions requiring code masking only for a small fraction of system cycles. Moreover, by using a look-ahead scheme, the modifier unit is never idle while waiting for a flag signal. The control scheme is adapted to changing conditions by the operations of code translation and list selection.

Comparing the described system to a video-processor using a conventional priority arbiter and an asynchronous bus (18) shows no disadvantages of the modified polling scheme. In addition to the features provided by a priority arbiter, the operation sequencer and the modifier unit give the programmer deterministic control over data stream structures and thus, among other things, allow him to emulate some of the features of data assembly and data distribution networks used in data flow machines (16,17). The list sequencer supports the programmed implementation of an interleaving scheme for main memory storage (19). Tests of hardware and real-time software are simplified by the synchronous bus protocol and by the cyclical operation mode of the control list.

Programming and Applications

In programming the ISAAC- system, three main levels may be discriminated:

Level 1: Definition of the functions of the FUs (by control codes, microprograms, look-up tables) and of the address generators (word-count and increment registers) which manage main memory partitions. After loading these parameters, the FUs independently perform operations on data transferred to their input buffer which in some cases may have the character of subroutines of conventional software (e.g. histogram construction). The operation performed by a FU may be modified by a function key supplied with each data word .

Level 2: The control list of the list sequencer is assembled. Since data are transferred to the FUs under control of this list, one or two SDL-code lines may have the function of a subroutine call. The control list is easily assembled since it does not contain jump or branch instructions and since interrupt processing is performed by selection of different lists (level 3). A single control list mirrors the transient configuration of the processor for a substantial period of time (10^4 to 10^7 buscycles typically). We call this time interval a process-field period (comparable to the term TV-field period). Level 2 programming also includes the definition of condition codes and look-up tables for the sections of the code-modifier performing selective code-chaining and code-translation operations (Fig. 4).

Level 3: Definition of the condition code patterns for list selection. Comparing these patterns to the actual condition flags (internal flags and external interrupts) the list selector changes between lists and thus links or interleaves several (typically three to eight) process-field periods.

This enumeration shows the modularity of both hardware and corresponding software provided by the ISAAC-system. The operations and subroutines (level 1) performed during a process-field period are linked by the control list (level 2). Several control lists or the equivalent process-fields are dynamically linked by the list selector (level 3).

The primary data structure supported is the data stream. A set of concurrent data streams is assembled and directed using level 2 programming. Data buffering and data block transformations, computational and I/O- processing are performed by passing these data streams through memory structures and FUs specialized using level 1 programming. The multiprocessor is periodically reconfigured using level 3 programming. This allows the adaptation of the system e.g to a changing balance between I/O- and computational requirements.

We expect that this modularity supported by the hardware will simplify the programming of the ISAAC multiprocessor without detailed knowledge of the hardware system. The synchronous bus structure is open for the addition of processors ("subroutine modules") where necessary and when new LSI-circuits become available which are optimized for a set of signal-processing tasks.

The system is expected to be fully operational early in 1981. One of its applications will be cardiac image enhancement by picture subtraction, an algorithm presently performed in this clinic using an off-line image processing system (8). In an image generated after injection of contrast material into a heart chamber (dye image), the opacified cardiovascular structures are superimposed by irrelevant background shadows (chest). The interfering background can be eliminated, if one finds from the image series preceeding the injection a "background image" generated at the same respiratory phase. A technique described earlier (3) subtracts from each dye image the stored background image showing maximum cross correlation with this opacified image in a region of interest. Each of about 120 dye images (TV-fields) has to be cross-correlated with at least 32 background fields in a region containing more than 2000 pixels.
Fig. 5 shows this process schematically. The tabel lists process-field periods and for each process-field period the concurrent data streams involved. During the first period, every fourth background image of the background series (or the average of groups of four TV-fields) is stored in main memory. When contrast material injection starts, the modifier unit switches to the control list defining the second process-field. Now, at any time the three most recent dye images are stored in memory and cross- correlation and subtraction proceed as shown in Fig. 5. Subtraction data are histogram-equalized according to a look-up table derived by the histogram unit from the previous subtraction image. After D/A-conversion, the resulting

enhanced image series is displayed and stored on video tape. The optimum background images are selected by the host on account of the correlation data provided by the correlator (approximately 100 byte per TV-field). Optionally, the digital data are stored on the fast disk system for further processing.

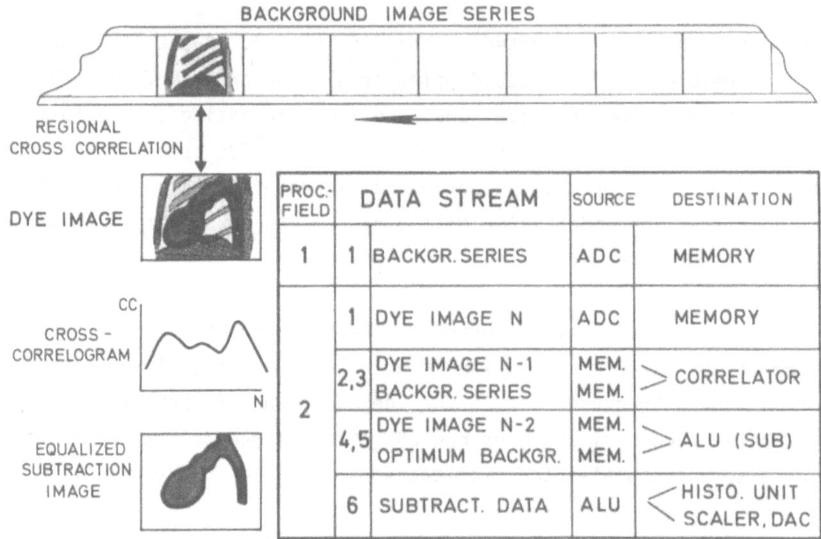

PROC.-FIELD		DATA STREAM	SOURCE	DESTINATION
1	1	BACKGR. SERIES	ADC	MEMORY
2	1	DYE IMAGE N	ADC	MEMORY
	2,3	DYE IMAGE N-1	MEM.	CORRELATOR
		BACKGR. SERIES	MEM.	
	4,5	DYE IMAGE N-2	MEM.	ALU (SUB)
		OPTIMUM BACKGR.	MEM.	
	6	SUBTRACT. DATA	ALU	HISTO. UNIT / SCALER, DAC

Fig.5 Data stream description for an image subtraction/correlation process.
ALU: Arithmetic logic unit

The data stream description of the process shown in the table (Fig.5) is translated into an SDL-code list (Fig.4) in a straightforward way (level 2 programming). The list selector changes from field-period 1 to 2 when contrast material injection starts (level 3). In a more efficient program, an additional third process field (control list) could correspond exclusively to the correlation process. This process field would be activated during the vertical blanking period of each TV-field after the start of dye injection. In this way, the correlator could use the total bandwidth of the bus when only computational and no I/O- transfers are required. Code chaining can be utilized to interleave data of the streams 2 and 3 (4 and 5). Thus, operand pairs arrive at the functional units in structured streams simplifying the architecture and the programming of these processors.
Examples demonstrating the performance of the algorithm have been published in an earlier report (3).

Acknowledgement

This project is supported by the Deutsche Forschungsgemeinschaft.

References

(1) Pratt WK: Digital Image Processing. John Wiley, New York 1978
(2) Brennecke R, Hahne HJ, Heintzen PH: Verbesserung der Speicherung videoangio-
kardiographischer Bildserien durch digitale Signalverarbeitungsverfahren.
Biomedizinische Technik, Ergänzungsband 23: 73, 1978
(3) Brennecke R, Hahne HJ, Moldenhauer K, Bürsch JH, Heintzen PH: Improved digital
real-time processing and storage techniques with applications to intravenous
contrast angiography. Proc Comp Cardiol, IEEE Computer Society, Long Beach
1978, pp. 191-194
(4) Hahne HJ, Bürsch JH, Grönemeyer D, Heintzen PH: Die Berechnung von Funktions-
angiogrammen unter Berücksichtigung röntgenologischer Abbildungsfehler.
Biomedizinische Technik, Ergänzungsband 24, 191-192, 1979
(5) Rosenfeld A: Automatic detection of changes in reconnaissance data. Proc 5.th
Convention on Military Electronics, 1961, pp. 492-499
(6) Heintzen PH, Brennecke R, Bürsch JH, Lange P, Malerczyk V, Moldenhauer K,
Onnasch D: Automated video-angiocardiographic image analysis.
Computer (IEEE) 8 : 55-64, 1975
(7) Brennecke R, Brown TK, Bürsch JH, Heintzen PH: Digital processing of videoan-
giographic image series using a minicomputer. Proc Comp Cardiol, IEEE Computer
Society, Long Beach 1976, pp. 255-260
(8) Brennecke R, Brown TK, Bürsch JH, Heintzen PH: A system for computerized
video-image preprocessing with applications to angiocardiographic
roentgen-image series. In: Digitale Bildverarbeitung (Ed. HH Nagel)
Springer, Berlin- Heidelberg-New York 1977, pp. 244-262
(9) Kruger RA, Mistretta CA, Houk TL, et al: Computerized fluoroscopy in
real-time. Radiology 130: 49, 1979
(10) Höhne KH, Böhm M, Erbe W: Computerangiographie. Fortschr. Röntgenstr. 129,
667-672, 1978
(11) Bürsch JH, Hahne HJ, Brennecke R, Hetzer R, Heintzen PH: Funktions-Angiogramme
als Ergebnis der densitometrischen Analyse digitalisierter Röntgenbildserien.
Biomedizinische Technik, Ergänzungsband 24, 189-190, 1979
(12) Brennecke R, Hahne HJ, Moldenhauer K, Bürsch JH, Heintzen PH: A special purpose processor for digital angiocardiography. Design and applications. Proc
Comp Cardiol 1979 , IEEE Computer Society, Long Beach, in press
(13) Ledley RS, Kulkarni YG, Park CM et al: Texac, a powerful new picture pattern
recognition computer. Proc. Conf. Pattern Recognition and Image Processing,
IEEE Society, Long Beach 1978
(14) Kruger RA, Mistretta CA, Lancaster J et al: A digital video processor for
real-time x-ray subtraction imaging. Optic Eng 17, 652, 1978
(15) Andrews HC: Semiconductor advances boost digital image processing system performance. Computer Design, Sept. 1979, pp. 23-102
(16) Missunas DP (Ed.): Workshop on Data Flow Computer and Program Organization.
Computer Architecture News ACM SIGARCH, Vol. 6, no.4, October 1977
(17) Schaffner MR: Processing by data and program blocks.
IEEE Trans. Comput., C-27, 1978, 1015
(18) Nicolae GC, Höhne KH: Multiprocessor system for real-time digital processing
of video-image series. Elektron. Rechenanl. 21 : 171-183, 1979
(19) Gilbert BK, Storma MT, James CE et al.: A real-time hardware system for digital processing of wide-band video images. IEEE Trans.Comput. 25: 1089, 1976

OBJEKTERKENNUNG DURCH EINEN KYBERNETISCHEN LERNVORGANG
AM BEISPIEL EINES RÖNTGENBILD-ANALYSATORS

M. Prammer, H. Pichler
Institut für Allgemeine Elektrotechnik
Technische Universität Wien/Österreich

1. Zusammenfassung

Das Röntgenbild-Verarbeitungssystem, das derzeit an der TU Wien entwickelt wird, enthält einen Analysator zur Erkennung relevanter Kontur-
information im Schädel-, Kiefer-, und Gesichtsbereich. Dieser Algorithmus orientiert sich am menschlichen Erkennungsvorgang. Segmentierung
mit Hilfe einer Standardvorlage (Prototyp) und die Möglichkeit, durch
gezielte Rückfragen eine Selbstoptimierung durchzuführen, simulieren
den biologischen Lerneffekt.

2. Systemkonfiguration

In Abb. 1 ist das System vereinfacht dargestellt. Die Bildvorlage wird
von einer handelsüblichen TV-Studiokamera mit selektiertem Vidikon abgetastet, an einen eigenentwickelten Echtzeit-Speicher/Prozessor (RTP)
weitergegeben und am Monitor dargestellt. Über eine Parallelschnitt-
stelle (31.000 Worte/sec) hat der Hauptrechner PDP 11/34 freien Schreib-/
Lesezugriff zu allen Bildpunkten. Das Bildformat hat 512 x 512 pixels
mit 8 bit Digitalisierungstiefe plus 2 bit Overlay für Cursor und Marken.
Das Fernsehraster entspricht der CCIR-Norm (50 Halbbilder/sec) mit auf
7 MHz erweiterter Bandbreite und quadratischem Bildfeld. Diese Einschränkung ist aufgrund der Primärbildinformation - Fern/Seiten-(tsd-)
Aufnahmen des Kopfes - zulässig.

Auf dem Hauptrechner läuft RSX-11M, VDOS (View Data Operating System)
und AXIS (Automatic X-ray Interpreting System). VDOS enthält die Peri-
pherie-Treiber, einen grafischen Editor, File Services und Graphic
Utilities. AXIS führt die röntgenbildspezifischen Operationen durch.
Die PDP 11/34 ist mit 124 K Worten Kernspeicher voll ausgebaut und ver-
fügt über 3 Plattenspeicher (RK05) und einen RK07-Trommelspeicher. Im
Time-Sharing-Betrieb wird der Hauptrechner von einer DEC System 20-
Rechenanlage unterstützt.

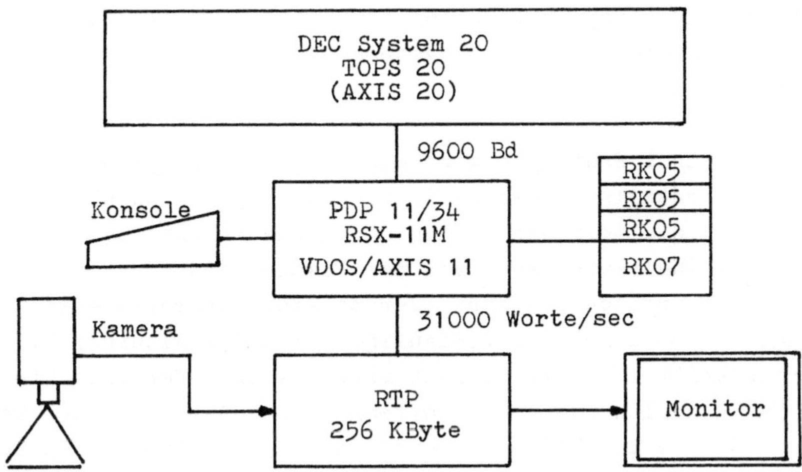

Abb. 1: Systemkonfiguration

3. Grundlagen

Voll ausgebaut ist die Hardware seit Anfang 1980 verfügbar. Alle folgenden Ausführungen sind die Darstellung der grundlegenden Arbeitsweise, die theoretisch und in Simulationsexperimenten schon früher erarbeitet wurde.

Die relevanteste Information einer tsd-Schädel-Röntgenaufnahme besteht vor allem aus den Konturlinien bestimmter Skeletteile, dem Weichteilprofil und der Zahnstellung. Diese Information ist überlagert von störenden Effekten wie Doppelkonturen aufgrund Asymmetrie, Muskeln, Sehnengeflechten.

Das beschriebene System verwendet folgende zahlenmäßige Darstellung:

- Eine begrenzte Anzahl (typ. 32) spezieller Punkte, die Referenzpunkte (RP), werden mit hoher Genauigkeit in absoluten Koordinaten aufgezeichnet. Sie sind
  a) markant, somit relativ schnell aufzufinden und
  b) medizinisch i. a. von Bedeutung und z. B. zur Konstruktion eines Wachstumsvektorgramms geeignet.

- Der anschauliche Zusammenhang wird durch Standardlinien (SL) hergestellt, die mit den Referenzpunkten verknüpft sind, aber nicht deren extrem hohe Genauigkeit aufweisen. Jede Standardlinie beginnt bei einem Referenzpunkt, von wo aus in relativen Koordinaten adressiert wird.

Dieses Datenformat entspricht sowohl dem Übernahmeprotokoll zwischen
Analysator und nachfolgenden Sub-Systemen, als auch der Prototyp-
Darstellung.

Die Verwendung eines Prototyps wird als <u>primäres Erkennen</u> bezeichnet
(ausführliche Darstellung vgl. /1/). Sie ist möglich durch die relativ
geringe Varianz, die zwischen Fällen der gleichen Altersgruppe zu er-
warten ist. Der Analysator kann von der Fiktion ausgehen, Bild und
Prototyp seien identisch und dann schrittweise konkretisieren.
Abb. 2 zeigt als Beispiel den vorläufigen Prototyp Altersgruppe 16 - 18
Jahre, Durchschnitt m/w. Die derzeit verwendeten Referenzpunkte sind
markiert. Das Modell wurde von D.Hoffmann und G.Watzek an der Univer-
sitätsklinik Wien entwickelt. Verwendet wurde dazu ein BOLTON-Standard
aus /11/, der mit Hilfe einer Normalaufnahme erweitert und geeignet
segmentiert wurde.

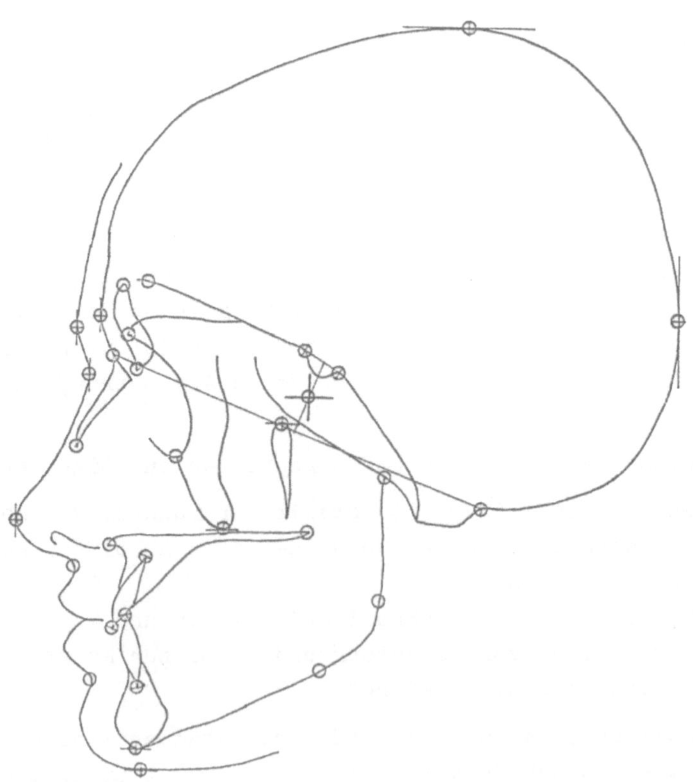

<u>Abb. 2</u>: Prototyp-Beispiel

4. Prototyp-Erstellung

In Abb. 3 ist die Prototyp-Erstellung als Flußdiagramm dargestellt.
Eine vom Röntgenologen ausgewählte Standardvorlage wird aufgenommen
und aufbereitet. Mit Hilfe eines Übersetzer-Programms werden daraus
die benötigten maschinenadäquaten Datenstrukturen entwickelt.

Die Aufbereitung besteht aus folgenden Schritten:
- Tiefpaß mit relativ hoher spatialer Grenzfrequenz (3 x 3 pixels),
- Erstellen des Histogramms der Helligkeitsverteilung,
- daraus Optimierung des Kontrasts durch Dehnen der Grauwertskala,
- und die Anwendung eines nichtlinearen Filters aus /3/, (S.197 - 200),
  das rauschunterdrückend wirkt bei gleichzeitiger Verbesserung der
  Kanteninformation.

Ein Röntgenologe und ein Operator arbeiten mit dem Cursor des VDOS-
CRT-Editors zur Markierung der Referenzpunkte. Die Standardlinien wer-
den im "Trace"-Modus des CRT-Editors Punkt für Punkt digitalisiert.
Die Linien werden also nicht - wie oft üblich - durch Polygonzüge er-
setzt, sondern mit der durch den TV-Raster vorgegebenen größtmöglichen
Auflösung dargestellt.

Die endgültige Prototyp-Darstellung besteht aus 3 Dateien:

- Referenzpunktdatei: feste Record-Länge (4 Worte), freier Zugriff.
  Ein Record enthält: RP-Identifikation, RP-Status, Koordinaten.
- Standardliniendatei: variable Record-Länge, sequentiell.
  Ein Record entspricht einer Linie. Im 8-Worte-Line-Header ist u. a.
  die SL-Identifikation enthalten. Alle Punkte sind relativ zu ihren
  Vorgängern adressiert. Ein 4 bit-Feld gibt die 8 Elementarrichtungen
  oder Steuerbefehle wie Anfang, Ende, Verzweigung, Löschen, an. Die
  Maximallänge einer Linie ist 992 Punkte.
- Assoziationseinheitendatei: feste Record-Länge (4 Worte), freier
  Zugriff. Diese Datei wird vom Operator geschrieben und compiliert.
  Ein Record enthält: RP-Identifikation, SL-Identifikation, Verknüp-
  fungsvorschrift. Als Verknüpfung wird verwendet: "Anfang von", "Ende
  von", "Verzweigung", "Extremum", u. a. m.

Alle Koordinaten sind verschiebbar (relocatable). Als Ursprung des
sekundären Koordinatensystems dient der aus 4 Referenzpunkten errech-
nete Wachstums-Nullpunkt (Konstruktion in Abb.2). Damit wird die Darstellung translationsinvariant.

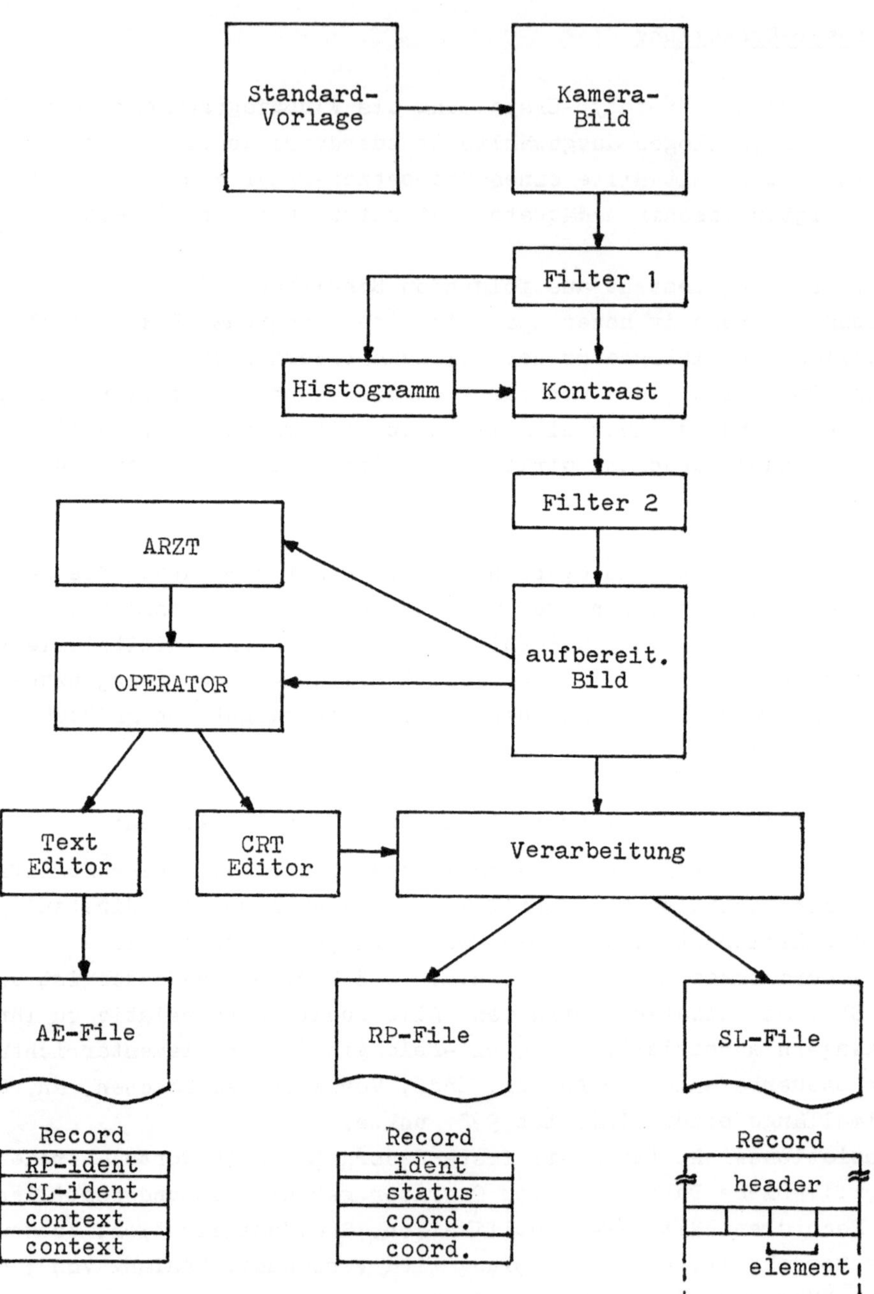

Abb. 3: Prototyp-Generierung

5. Verarbeitung

Jedes digitalisierte Bild soll eindeutig und fehlerfrei als Kombination
von Referenzpunkten und Standardlinien dargestellt werden. Der notwendige Informationsfluß ist in Abb. 4 dargestellt.
Die Vorverarbeitung (Filter, Kontrast) ist ähnlich der der Prototyp-
vorlage. Zusätzlich wird ein software-realisierter Shadow-Corrector
durchlaufen. Der Verarbeitungsblock besteht aus Operatoren, die teils
globale, teils lokale Information erkennen können. Die Abfolge ist nicht
starr, da alle Module untereinander kompatibel sind. Zwischenergebnisse
werden im "Mailbox"-Verfahren mit Sender- und Empfängeradresse auf dem
Argument-Stack abgelegt.

Die typische Vorgangsweise ist folgende:

HUNT und TRACE sind Suchalgorithmen (Makrooperatoren), die Bildteile
auf signifikante Aussagen der Mikrooperatoren durchsuchen. Als Mikro-
operatoren werden verwendet: Gradient, Laplacian, Prewitt-Edge-Detector,
Template-Matcher, Texture-Analyzer. HUNT sucht in schmalen Sektoren,
TRACE folgt aktuellen Konturen.
Haben diese beiden Makros die ersten Referenzpunkte gefunden, werden
durch MAP die Prototyp-Standardlinien koordinatentransformiert und als
Verbindungslinien der RP's gezeichnet. FLEX paßt diese Linien schließlich den wirklichen Bildkonturen an. FLEX ist ein abgeänderter Plan-
Follower (vgl. /7/) und unempfindlich gegenüber zerhackten oder doppel-
ten Konturen. Gefundene RP's und SL's werden in Output-Dateien trans-
feriert. Sie liefern Ansatzpunkte für HUNT und TRACE zur Suche neuer
Punkte.

Die Aufrufe der Makrooperatoren erfolgen durch ein Source-File, das in
Echtzeit interpretiert wird. Der dafür entwickelte M-Code enthält Aufrufe für die Makrooperatoren als Anweisungen. Weiters sind bedingte
Sprünge möglich, die bei Versagen eines Operators (keine oder mehr-
deutige Aussage) zu anderen Algorithmen oder einer Anforderung eines
externen Eingriffs verzweigen.
Die Verwendung von Standard-Makro- und Mikro-Operatoren erlaubt es,
komplizierte Suchsequenzen baukastenartig zusammenzusetzen und zu ver-
bessern.
Die entstandenen RP- und SL-Dateien werden mit einer Text-Datei (Name,
Alter, Krankengeschichte des Patienten) kombiniert und als Patienten-
datei abgelegt.

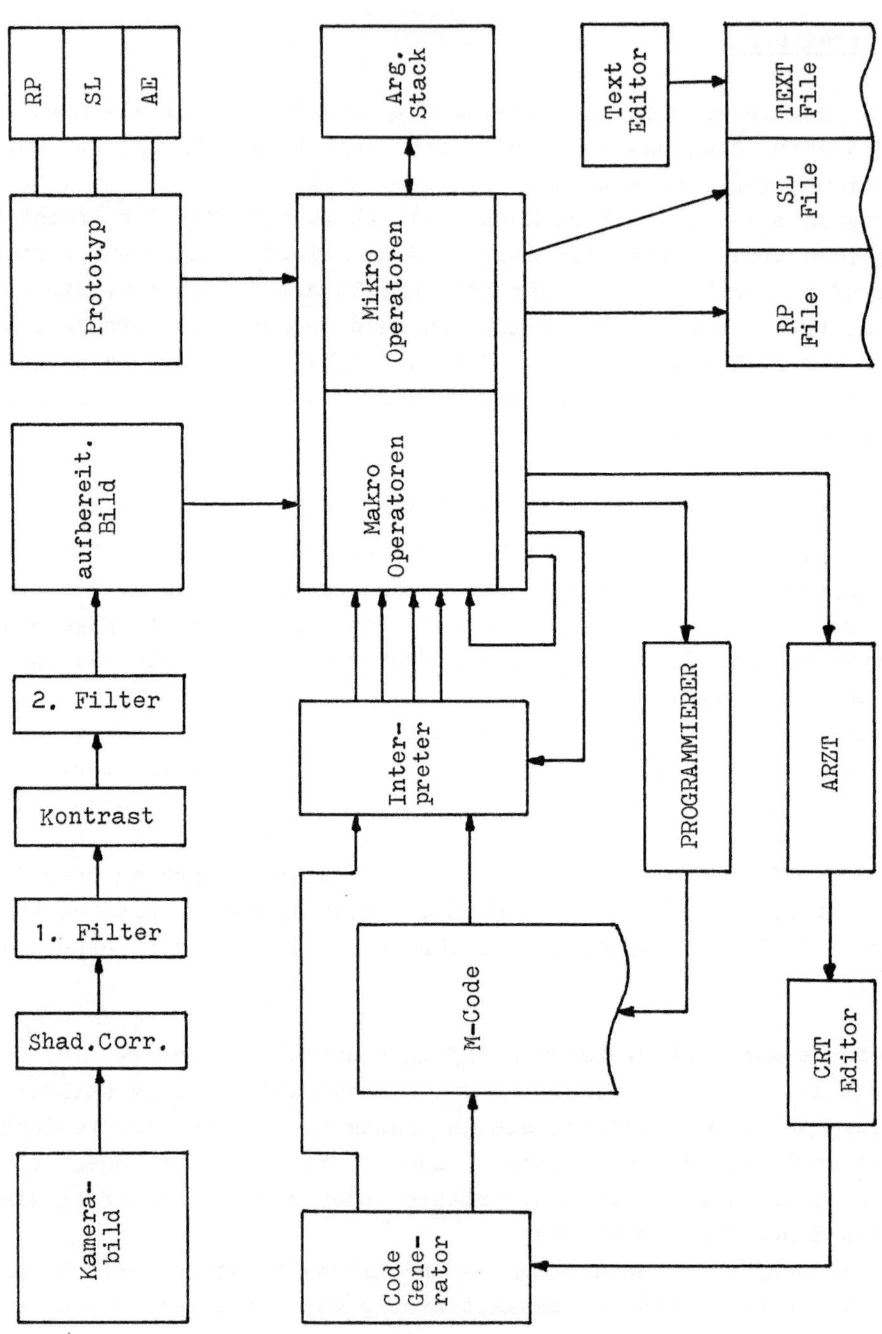

Abb. 4: Informationsfluß

6. <u>Optimierung und Lernfähigkeit</u>

Wird, wie in Abb. 4, Mensch und Maschine zu einem kybernetischen System
zusammengefaßt, entsteht eine Rückkopplung, die es dem Arzt ermöglicht,
die ihm an sich unbekannte Maschinenstruktur zu optimieren.
Jeder Makrooperator kann, wenn er die zugewiesene Aufgabe nicht lösen
kann, folgendermaßen reagieren:

- interne Justierung (Bsp.: Kontrastadaption)
- Auslösung eines bedingten Sprunges durch den Interpreter, was zur
  Folge haben kann:
  - Aufruf vorbereiteter Recovery-Routinen,
  - vorzeitiger Programmabbruch oder
  - Anforderung der Hilfe des Arztes und/oder
  - Änderung des M-Codes.

Der M-Code (modifizierender Code) bzw. Interpreter und Code-Generator
unterstützen das <u>Lernen mit Ermutigung</u> /1/ folgendermaßen:

- Parallele Algorithmen können programmiert werden. Jeder Durchlauf
  ergibt eine Erfolgsbilanz, die bessere Kalküle vorreiht und erfolg-
  lose schließlich eliminiert.
- Parameterwerte, die a priori nur schätzbar sind (z. B. Schaltschwel-
  len), werden durch Probieren justiert und permanent im M-File gespeichert.
- Rekursiver, auf sich selbst bezogener Austausch von Anweisungen und
  Blöcken geht über den vom Programmierer überschaubaren Ablauf hinaus
  und führt u. U. zu neuen Problemlösungen.

Die folgende Seite gibt einen Auszug aus einer M-Code-Liste wieder.
Beginnend bei oberer Bildrandmitte sucht der HUNT-Operator (Zeile 1002)
nach unten fortschreitend nach einer querenden schwarz/weiß-Flanke und
damit nach der oberen Kalottenhälfte (vgl. Abb. 2). Diese Kontur wird
nach ihrem höchsten Punkt (RP03) und den Punkten mit vertikalen Tangen-
ten (RP02, RP04) abgetastet. Zwischen diesen Punkten werden die Linien
SL02 und SL03 gezogen und angepaßt.
Findet HUNT keinen geeigneten Punkt, wird zur Zeile 1501 verzweigt.
Mit 10 Werten wird die Ansprechschwelle des Edge Detectors (MOD =)
ausprobiert (1000 ... Prewitt; 4 ... low/high, horizontal bleibt konstant). Ist auch dann kein Punkt gefunden, wird die manuelle Zuweisung
über ASK angefordert. Hierauf muß ein Arzt den Cursor auf RP03 posi-
tionieren. Soll dieser Lernvorgang von Dauer sein, so muß der Rechner
- was hier nicht gezeigt ist - anschließend versuchen, die Positionierung nachzuvollziehen.

```
C          BEARBEITUNG DER OBEREN KALOTTENHAELFTE     M-CODE   V1.2   BL1
C          -----------------------------------------------
C
C          ELEMENTE:        RP #02,#03,#04              SL #02,#03
C*******************************************************************************
C INITIALISIERUNG, LOESCHEN DER SCRATCH PAD'S
C
1000      START
          RESET
          PRINT     ' RESTART AT LABEL "1000"'
C-----------------------------------------------------------------------------
C AUFFINDEN EINES PUNKTES AUF DER KALOTTENKONTUR
C
1001      SET       HHH=0255,VVV=0000
1002      HUNT      DIR=1000,MOD=1054,DST=0003,ERR=1501
C-----------------------------------------------------------------------------
C SUCHEN DES HOECHSTEN PUNKTES (=RP #03)
C
          TRACE     DIR=0000,MOD=1054,LIN=0002,DST=0003,ERR=1005
          GOTO      LAB=1006
1005      TRACE     DIR=3000,MOD=1058,LIN=0003,DST=0003,ERR=1510
1006      DEFINE    RFP=0003
C-----------------------------------------------------------------------------
C VON RP #03 ENTLANG DER KONTUR ZU RP #02 UND RP #04
C
1010      SET       RFP=0003
          TRACE     DIR=0000,MOD=1054,LIN=0003,DST=0004,FLG=0001
1015      SET       RFP=0003
          TRACE     DIR=3000,MOD=1058,LIN=0002,DST=0002,FLG=0002
          IFNOT     FLG=0001,LAB=1520
          DEFINE    RFP=0004
          IFNOT     FLG=0002,LAB=1520
          DEFINE    RFP=0002
C-----------------------------------------------------------------------------
C EINTRAGEN UND MODIFIZIEREN DER IDEALKONTUREN, ENDE
C
1020      MAP       LIN=0002,ERR=1541
1021      MAP       LIN=0003,ERR=1545
1022      FLEX      LIN=0002,ERR=1551
1023      FLEX      LIN=0003,ERR=1555
          PRINT     ' SEQUENCE "1000" COMPLETE'
          STOP
C*******************************************************************************
C ROUTINE ZUR MODIFIZIERUNG DER HUNT-ANWEISUNG
C
1501      PRINT     ' MODIFICATION AT LABEL "1002"'
          ALTER     LAB=1002,POS=0004,INC=0010,MAX=1094,ERR=1502
          GOTO      LAB=1001
1502      ALTER     LAB=1002,POS=0004,NEW=1054
          ALTER     LAB=1002,POS=0006,NEW=1502
          ALTER     LAB=1002,POS=0004,DEC=0010,MIN=1004,ERR=1503
          GOTO      LAB=1001
1503      ALTER     LAB=1002,POS=0004,NEW=1054
          ALTER     LAB=1002,POS=0006,NEW=1501
C-----------------------------------------------------------------------------
C MANUELLE ZUWEISUNG IST ERFORDERLICH
C
1510      PRINT     ' PLEASE ENTER RP #03'
          ASK       DST=0003
          DEFINE    RFP=0003
          PRINT     ' THANKS - CONTINUING'
          GOTO      LAB=1010
```

Diese Arbeit entstand im Rahmen eines Projekts des österreichischen
Fonds zur Förderung der wissenschaftlichen Forschung.

__Lit.:__

/1/   Steinhagen,H.E./Fuchs,S.: Objekterkennung;
                                 VEB Verlag Technik, Berlin, 1976

/2/   Bartels,P.H./Subach,J.A.: Significance Probability Mappings and
                                 Automated Interpretation of Complex
                                 Pictorial Scenes;
                                 Digital Processing of Biomedical Images
                                 Plenum Press, New York, 1976

/3/   Kuwahara,M. et al.:   Processing of RI-Angiocardiographic
                                 Images;
                                 Digital Processing of Biomedical Images
                                 Plenum Press, New York, 1976

/4/   Sklansky,J.:   Boundary Detection in Medical Radio-
                                 graphs;
                                 Digital Processing of Biomedical Images
                                 Plenum Press, New York, 1976

/5/   Fischler,M./Elschlager,R.:The Representation and Matching of
                                 Pictorial Structures;
                                 IEEE Transactions on Computers,
                                 vol. C-22, 1973

/6/   Martelli,A.:   An Application of Heuristic Search
                                 Methods to Edge and Contour Detection;
                                 Communications of the ACM, vol. 19, 1976

/7/   Kelly,M.D.:   Edge Detection in Pictures by Computer
                                 Using Planning;
                                 Machine Intelligence, vol. 6, 1971

/8/   Abdou,I.E./Pratt,W.:   Quantitative Design and Evoluation of
                                 Enhancement/Tresholding Edge Detectors;
                                 Proceedings of the IEEE, vol. 67, 1979

/9/   Pavlidis,Th.:   Hierarchies in Structural Pattern
                                 Recognition;
                                 Proceedings of the IEEE, vol. 67, 1979

/10/ Walker,G.F./Kowalski,G.J.:A Two-dimensional Coordinate Model for
                                 the Quantification, Description, Analysis,
                                 Prediction and Simulation of Craniofacial
                                 Growth;
                                 Growth 35, vol. 35, 1971

/11/ Broadbent,H., sen./
      Broadbent,H., jun./
      Golden,W.H.:   Bolton-Standard of Dentofacial Develop-
                                 mental Growth;
                                 T. V. Mosby Comp., St. Louis, 1975

GENORMTE FARBMESSUNG UND AUTOMATISIERTE ZYTOPHOTOMETRIE

IN AZUR B - EOSIN GEFÄRBTEN PRÄPARATEN [1]

Rüter A. [2], Wittekind D. [3], Harms H., Aus H.M.

Computergestüzte Zytophotometrie Einheit des SFB 105 [4]

ZUSAMMENFASSUNG:

Farbe ist ein oft entscheidendes Merkmal in der visuellen Diagnose gefärbter Zell-Präparate. Die gegenwärtigen Methoden der computergestützten Zytophotometrie sind unzureichend die in der Routine ver-
wandten, feinen Farbunterschiede zu erfassen. Dieses Projekt beschäf-
tigt sich mit der standardisierten, von Meßsystem-Charakteristika unabhängigen, Farbauswertung an Azur B - Eosin gefärbten Präparaten, um
vom menschlichen, subjektiven Urteil abzukommen. Erste Ergebnisse an
Kernen und Nukleolen zeigen, daß die Absorptionsminima und -maxima der
Komponenten der Farblösung keine geeignete Information für die computergestützte Analyse am gefärbten Präparat sind und daß nicht von maximalen Kontrasten zwischen unterschiedlichen Zellbereichen bei festen
Wellenlängen für alle Zellen eines Präparates ausgegangen werden kann.
Eine exakte, reproduzierbare, zytophotometrische Analyse der Farbeigenschaften erfordert das Erfassen des gesamten sichtbaren Spektrums
in Übereinstimmung mit dem genormten CIE-DIN-Farbsystem.

[1] Diese Arbeit ist unterstützt durch die Deutsche Forschungsgemeinschaft, Sonderforschungsbereich 105 Würzburg und Az: 01 VH 056- ZA/
NT/MT 225a, Bundesministerium für Forschung und Technologie
[2] Die Arbeit ist Teil der Promotions-Arbeit von A.Rüter
[3] Anatomisches Institut der Universität Freiburg
[4] Institut für Virologie und Immunbiologie der Universität Würzburg,
Versbacher Str. 7, 8700 Würzburg

EINLEITUNG:

Eine computergestützte Analyse von gefärbten Zellpräparaten basiert
heute hauptsächlich auf der Ausnutzung von Absorptionsminima und -ma-
xima der verwendeten Farbstoffkomponenten /3,4,7-10/. Die meist
schmalbandigen Filter werden so gewählt, daß ihre Transmissionsmaxima
mit den Absorptionsminima oder -maxima der jeweils zu untersuchenden
Farbkomponente übereinstimmen. Die bei Färbeprozeduren angewendeten,
meist aus mehreren Komponenten bestehenden Farblösungen führen zu Fär-
beeffekten, die zur Differenzierung in Zellklassen, zur Beurteilung
von Zellbereichen, und damit zur Diagnose herangezogen werden.

In der Hämatologie sind Färbungen vom Typ Romanowsky-Giemsa immer
noch von überragender Bedeutung und nichts spricht dafür, daß innerhalb absehbarer Zeiträume eine andere Färbemethode die beherrschende
Position der Giemsa-Färbungen in Frage stellen könnte.
Neuerdings konnte nun gezeigt werden /1/, daß die in den Romanowsky-
Giemsa-Farblösungen der im Handel vorhandenen Farbstoffe nicht alle
den gleichen Einfluß auf das Färbeergebnis ausüben. Nur zwei Farbstoffe "tragen" die Färbung: Azur B und Eosin Y. Das kationische, blaue
Azur B gemeinsam mit dem anionischen, roten Eosin ergeben an "geeigneten" Substraten den Romanowsky-Giemsa-Effekt (RGE). Kennzeichnend für
den RGE ist die Farbe <u>purpurrot</u>= "Magenta Red"= purple, mit dem Absorptionsmaximum bei 545-550 nm (Sumner und Evans 1973 /23/, Comings
1975 /24/, Wittekind 1979 /2/. Diese Farbe "Magenta" wird weder von
Azur B noch von Eosin Y alleine an Blutausstrichen erzielt. Das wesentliche "geeignete Substrat" ist der Zellkern.
Die Purpurfarbe des Zellkernes kontrastiert mit der Farbe Blau in Zytoplasmen von Zellen, die reichlich RNA enthalten (Lymphozyten, Stamm-
zellen, auch Tumorzellen). Auch am zustandekommen der Farbe Blau sind
Azur B und Eosin beteiligt, nur beruht die Entwicklung dieser Farbe
offensichtlich auf anderen Bindungsmechanismen, auf die hier nicht näher einzugehen ist.
Die Reproduzierbarkeit der Romanowsky-Giemsa-"Staining pattern" wird
nun sehr erheblich durch die Anwesenheit jener anderen Thizianfarbstof-
fe beeinträchtigt, die man stets in mehr oder weniger großer Zahl, in
den Handelsfarbstoffen findet. Zu ihnen gehören: Methylenblau, Azur A,
Azur C, manchmal auch Thionin. Ferner wirkt sich auf das Färberesultat
auch eine zu niedrige Azur B/Eosin Y Relation aus. Quotienten von 10:1
bis 5:1 ergeben sehr gute Resultate, 2:1 oder gar 1:1 hingegen nicht.
Die in der Literatur so wohlbekannte Launenhaftigkeit der Giemsa-Färbungen hat in der unkontrollierten Beeinträchtigung der Azur B-Eosin-

Effekte durch die Anwesenheit jener überflüssigen Farbstoffe bzw. in
einer zu hohen Eosin-Konzentration ihre Ursache.
Die Entscheidung, welche Farblösung und Färbeprozedur in der Praxis
verwendet werden, basiert bisher letztlich auf Gewohnheit und anderen
subjektiven Gesichtspunkten, gelegentlich sogar auf ästhetisch bestimmten Eindrücken /13/. Dies führte zu unüberschaubaren Differenzen bei
Angaben für die computergestützte Analyse, bei welcher Wellenlänge
welche Zellkomponente zu erfassen und zu bewerten sei (Green: 412,525,
560 /3/; Brenner: 420,490,550,600 /8/; Lemkin-Lipkin: 420,546 /4/;
Young: 420,530,570 /9/; Ringhardtz: 530,590 /5/; /20/), obwohl es sich
in allen Fällen um Romanowsky-Farblösungen handelt. Außer der variab-
len Zusammensetzung der Farblösungen (Metall-Salz-Kontamination) be-
einflussen auch die Präparation (Antigerinnungsmittel, Alter der Zellen) und die Färbeprozedur (Fixation, Puffer pH-Wert, Temperatur, Zeit)
das Färbeergebnis /6/.
Solche Gegebenheiten werfen nicht nur Probleme für die computergestützte Analyse auf, sondern stellen auch die Vregleichbarkeit der in
verschiedenen klinischen Laboratorien auf visuellem Weg erreichten
Diagnosen in Frage /6/. Um diesem in seiner Bedeutung erkannten Problem abzuhelfen, werden seit Jahren erfolgreiche Versuche gemacht,
Farblösungen herzustellen, die den vollen RGE erbringen und zugleich,
wegen der hohen Qualität der verwendeten Farbstoffe Azur B und Eosin Y
die Standardisierung der Giemsa-Färbungen ermöglichen sollen /1,11,12/.

UNTERSUCHUNG:

Ein Ausstrich eines sanguinolenten Aszites wurde mit gereinigtem Azur
B - Eosin Y gefärbt /1,11,12/.
Aus dem in eine Axiomat-Zytophotometrie-Einheit /18,19/ eingebrachten
Präparat wurden acht Zellkerne (Abb. 1) gescannt, die mindestens eine
Nukleole enthielten. Die Zellen sind bewußt nicht nach biologischen
Kriterien gewählt worden, sondern nur in der Absicht ein möglichst
breites Spektrum der im Präparat sichtbaren Farbeigenschaften von Ker-
nen und Nukleolen zu erfassen (Abb. 1). Die Messung wurde für jeden
Kern 24 mal im sichtbaren Wellenlängenbereich von 380-740nm mit
schmalbandigen Interferenzfiltern durchgeführt. Wichtig ist hierbei
u.a. die sorgfältige Bestimmung der Transmissionseigenschaften der
Filter und eine strenge Linearität des Empfängers durch die Korrektur
der Verschiebung des absoluten Schwarzpunktes der Kamera in Anhängig-
keit von der Temperatur. Die Filter wurden mit einem Perkin-Elmer
Zweistrahl-Spektrophotometer 555 untersucht. Die HW-Breiten lagen zwi-

schen 8,2 und 13,6nm. Die Abstände zwischen den spektralen Durchlaß-
stellen (Projektionen der Schwerpunkte der Filtertransmissions-Kurven
auf die Wellenlängen-Achse), den Stützstellen für die Farbbestimmung,
betrugen 9 bis 21nm. Um die aus den Daten gesuchten Transmissionsver-
halten aller Meßpunkte von spektralen Einflüssen des Meßsystems wei-
testgehend unabhängig zu machen, wurde zusätzlich im Präparathinter-
grund (zellfreier Bereich als Weiß-Referenz) eine 60·60 Meßpunkte große Stelle mit den 24 Filtern gemessen. Aus diesen Daten berechneten
Programme die spektrale Transmission (24 Stützstellen) für die Norm-
lichtart E ("energiegleiches Spektrum") /16,17/. Für weitere Details
siehe auch /14,15/.

Aus jeweils einem der Datensätze im Bereich 540-600nm wurden für jeden
Kern interaktiv Masken für das Kernchromatin als auch für die jeweils
vorhandenen Nukleolen erstellt. Mit Hilfe dieser Masken wurden für jeden der 8 Kerne und jede Nukleole die mittleren Spektren und deren mi-
nimale und maximale Abweichung berechnet (Abb. 2). Weiterhin wurden
aus den Transmissionswerten jedes Meßpunktes, festgelegt durch die 24
Stützstellen, mit Hilfe der NORMspektralwertkurven $\overline{x}(\lambda)$, $\overline{y}(\lambda)$, $\overline{z}(\lambda)$
/16,17/ die Farbart (x,y) und der Hellbezugswert Y berechnet. Die aus
diesen Datensätzen, ebenfalls mit Hilfe der erstellten Masken, bestimmten mittleren Farbarten, wieder mit minimaler und maximaler Abweichung
(Abb. 3C), sind in Abb. 3B dargestellt.

Für jede Nukleole eines jeden Kernes wurden die Differenzspektren zwischen mittlerem Kernspektrum und mittlerem Nukleolenspektrum errechnet
(Abb. 4).

Aus Platzgründen werden nicht alle Daten der untersuchten Kerne dargestellt und besprochen.

Abb. 1:

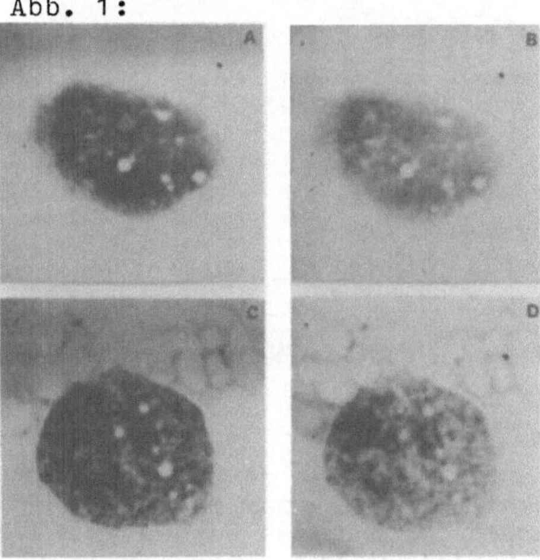
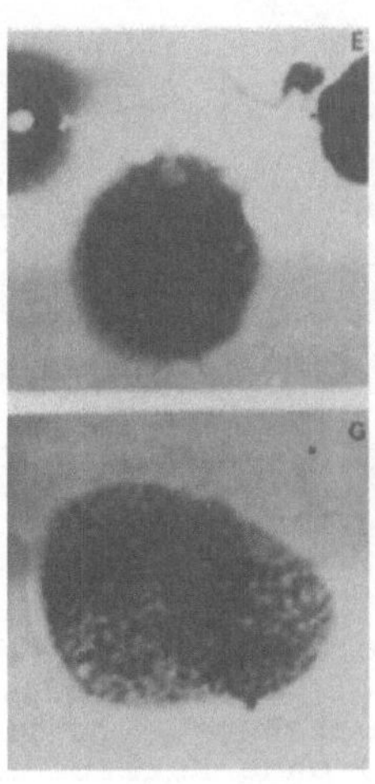
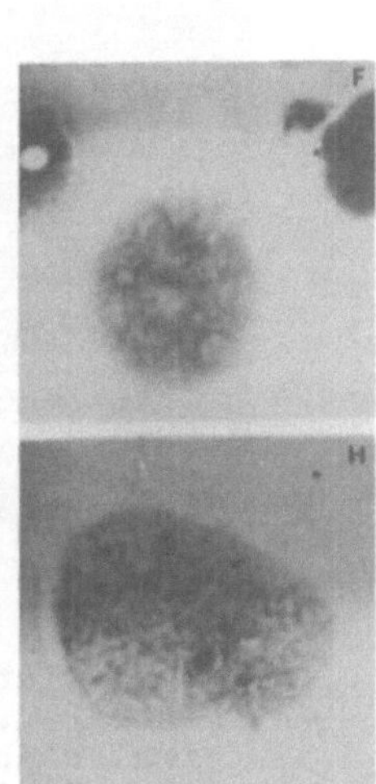

<u>Abb. 1</u>: 4 der 8 untersuchten Zellkerne (Kern Nr. 1 (A.B), 4 (C,D), 5 (E,F), 8 (G,H)) jeweils bei 541nm (A,C,E,G) und 601nm (B,D, F,H) vom Monitor der TV-Kamera fotografiert. Meßauflösung 8 Pixel/ μm in x- und y-Richtung.

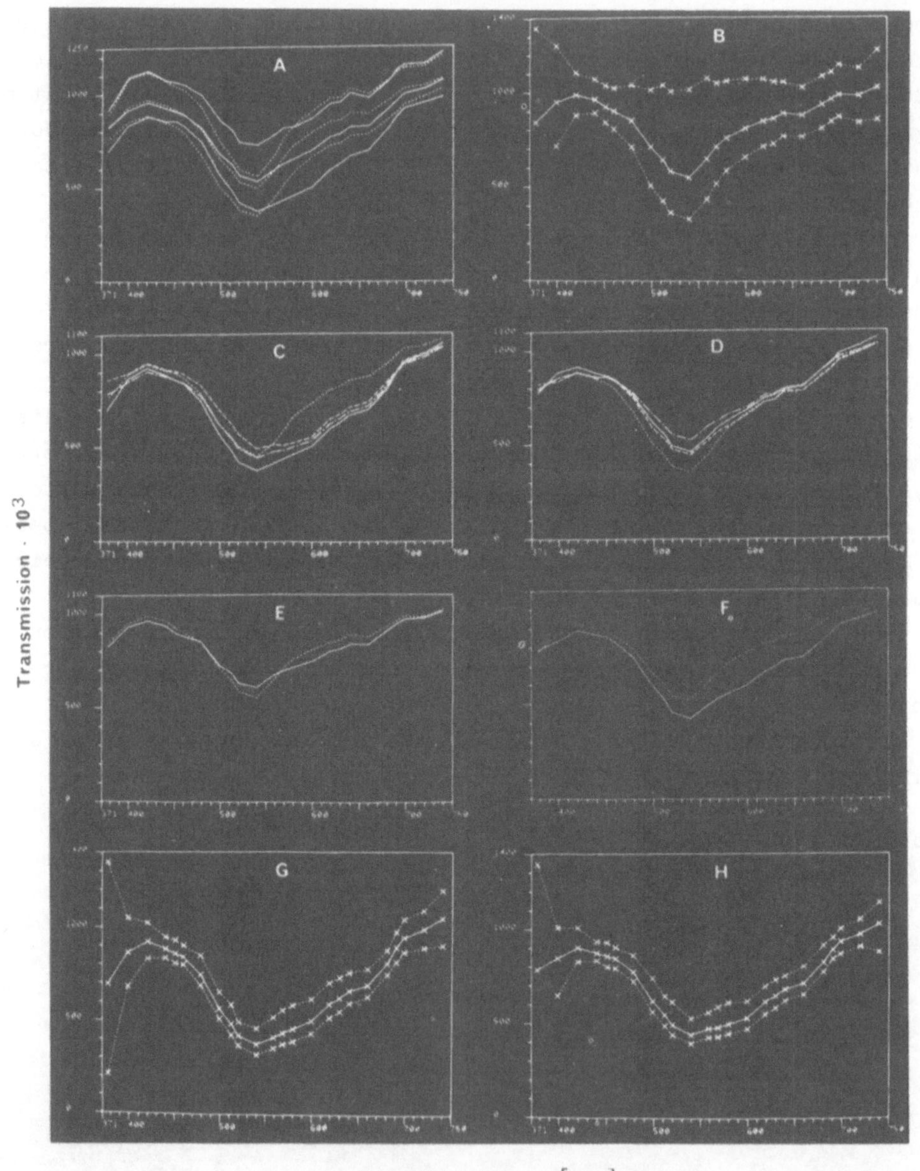

<u>Abb. 2</u>: A: mittlere Spektren der Mittelwert-Spektren der 8 gemessenen Kerne (....) und ihrer Nukleolen (———) mit maximaler und mi- nimaler Abweichung. B: mittleres Spektrum des Kernes Nr.1 (Abb. 3A,B) ohne Nukleolen mit maximaler und minimaler Abwei-

chung. Die Kreuze markieren die Stützpunkte, festgelegt durch
die 24 Interferenzfilter. C-F: mittlere Spektren der Kerne
(....) und der dazugehörigen Nukleolen 1 (———) und, falls
vorhanden, Nukleolen 2 (-.-.) und Nukleolen 3 (----) für Kerne
Nr. 8 (C), 5 (D), 1 (E) und 4 (F). G,H: mittlere Spektren der
Nukleolen 1 (G) und 2 (H) des Kernes Nr.8 mit minimaler und
maximaler Abweichung. Die Kreuze markieren die 24 Stützpunkte.

ERGEBNIS:

Die Nukleolen fallen in Farbsättigung und Farbton unterschiedlich aus
(Abb. 3B). Die mittleren Farbtöne aller Nukleolen sind, vor allem bei
größerer Farbsättigung, blauer als die der zugehörigen Kerne. Es gibt
zwar Berührungspunkte der Farbarten von Nukleolen und Kernen (10-31,
61), die Nukleolen sind aber in bezug auf ihren Kern deutlich blauer
(10-11,12), (30-31,32), (60-61). Es ist eine, besonders bei den Nukleolen auffallende, Tendenz zu beobachten, daß mit zunehmender Farbsättigung sich die Farbtöne von Magenta in Richtung Blau verschieben. Die
eingezeichneten, gestrichelten Linien sollen nur diese Tendenz ver-
deutlichen.

Die Differenzspektren in Abb. 4 geben den Abstand zwischen mittlerem
Kernspektrum und mittlerem Spektrum einer seiner Nukleolen wieder. Damit sind die jeweiligen Auslenkungen der Punkte von 0 auf diesen Kurven nichts anderes als der im Mikroskop sichtbare Kontrast zwischen
Kern und Nukleole in Abhängigkeit von der Wellenlänge.
Aus den CIE-DIN-Norm-gerecht gemessenen Daten folgt, daß die Kerne Nr.
3 und 5 den größten Kontrast zwischen Kernchromatin und Nukleolen eindeutig bei 541nm aufweisen (Abbn. 2D,4B). Dagegen ist bei den Kernen
4,6 und 8 maximaler Kontrast eindeutig bei 601 nm zu erzielen (Abbn.
2C,2F,4C). Es gibt aber auch Kerne (1,2,7), bei denen sich die Frage
nach maximalem Kontrast zwischen diesen beiden Wellenlängen schwer
entscheiden läßt. Bei Kern 1 ist zur Nukleole 2 (am Rand) der Kontrast
bei 541nm maximal, zur Nukleole 1 bei 541nm und 601nm etwa gleich gering (Abb. 4D).
Maximale Kontraste liegen in keinem Fall im Bereich der Absorptionsminima 380-460nm und 660-740nm (Abbn. 2C-F,4A).

Die Hellbezugswerte der Kerne mit geringerer Farbsättigung (Abb. 3B)
liegen zwischen 67 und 75 und fallen mit zunehmender Sättigung bis zu
Y=52 bei Kern Nr.5 ab. Die entsprechenden Werte Y der ungesättigten
Nukleolen liegen zwischen 70 und 83 und fallen ab bis zu 48-56 für die
relativ sehr farbgesättigten Nukleolen von Kern 8. Dies stimmt mit dem
visuellen Eindruck überein.

Abb. 3:

Das CIE-DIN-Farbart-Dreieck für die Normbeleuchtung E ("energiegleiches Spektrum"), x=0,3333 y=0,3333
A: Bereiche der in B und C dargestellten Farbarten in bezug auf alle natürlichen Farbarten. B: mittlere Farbarten der gemessenen Kerne und Nukleolen. Die Zehnerpotenz entspricht der Nr. des Kernes, die letzte Stelle gibt die Nr. der Nukleolen an (Kern selbst =0).
C: Bereich der Farbarten für die Kerne 8 (——), 5 (...) und 3 (---) und der dazugehörigen Nukleolen (die jeweils kleineren Bereiche). Eingezeichnet sind die mittleren Farbarten der Kerne und Nukleolen:
     Kern 8,   Kern 5,   Kern 3.

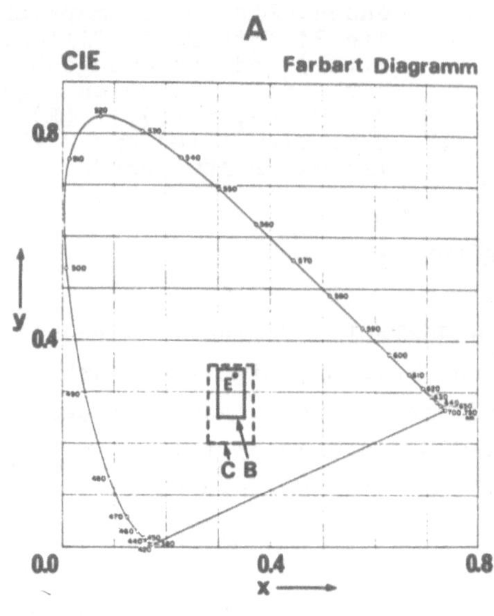

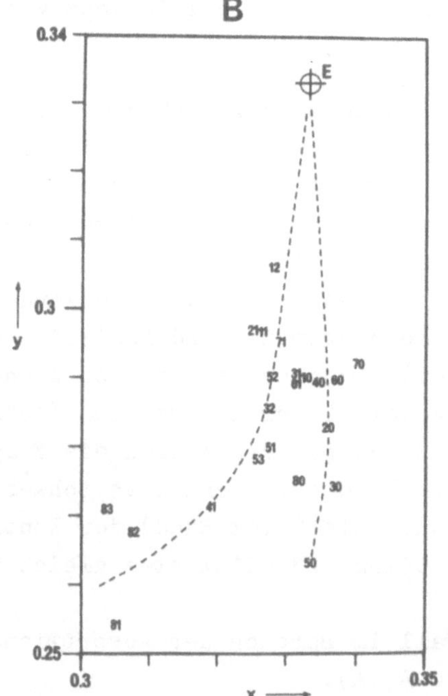

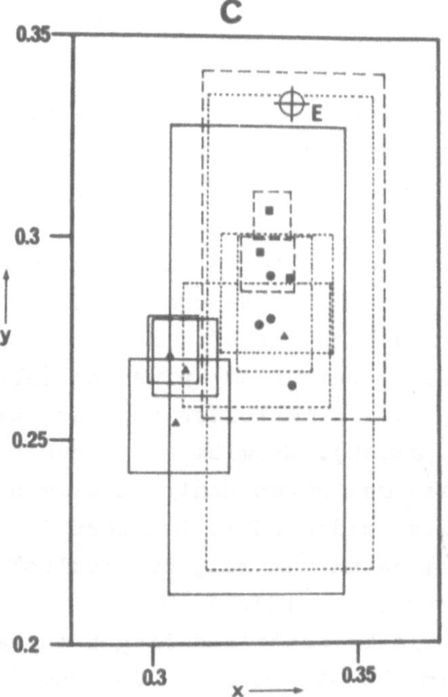

Bei Kern 1 fällt auf, daß bei der Kurve der maximalen Transmission alle Transmissionswerte größer 1 sind (Abb. 2B), obwohl sich die Spektren von Kern und Nukleolen "normal" zueinander verhalten (Abb. 2E). Es muß Meßpunkte geben, deren Hellbezugswert Y größer als 100 ist. Dem

Referenz-Weiß im Präparat wurde durch die genormte Auswertung der Hellbezugswert Y=100 zugeordnet /14,15/. Das bedeutet, es gibt Punkte im Kern, die heller als das "Weiß" sind. Betrachtet man Abb. 1, so sieht man Löcher (Vakuolen) im Zellkern, die diese Vermutung bestätigen. Gleiches ist auch bei Kern 4 festzustellen (Abb. 1C,D). Dies stimmt mit der Tatsache überein, daß der Bereich der Farbarten dieser beiden Zellen den Weißpunkt "E" einschließt (Abb. 3C).

Betrachtet man die mittleren Transmissions-Spektren für alle Kerne und alle Nukleolen (Abb. 2A), so fällt auf, daß sämtliche Kurven ihr Minimum bei 541nm haben, obwohl sie im Mikroskop anders aussehen. Dies stimmt mit allen mittleren Spektren der einzelnen Kerne und Nukleolen überein (Abb. 2C-F). Ebenfalls haben alle Kurven von Kernen und Nukleolen ein Transmissionsmaximum bei 420nm und die Transmissions-Kurven steigen vom Minimum 541nm bis zu einem maximalen Wert bei 741nm stetig an. Die Bandbreite der Spektren der 8 Kerne im Präparat (Abb. 2A) ist entschieden größer als der Unterschied zwischen mittleren Spektren eines jeden Kernes und der dazugehörigen Nukleolen (Abb. 2C-F). Die Transmissions-Kurve des Chromatins von Kern Nr.8 verläuft im Bereich 560-740nm deutlich über denen der Nukleolen; das Kernplasma hat mehr rote/magenta Farbtöne im Gegensatz zu den magenta bis blauen Nukleolen (Abb. 1G,H). Die Spektren der 3 Nukleolen von Kern 8 (Abb. 2C) laufen vergleichbar. Es besteht ein Unterschied in der Steilheit der Kurvenverläufe, was mit kleinen Unterschieden in der berechneten Farbsättigung und im Farbton im CIE-Farbart-Dreieck identisch ist (Abb. 3B,C) (Spektrum der Nukleole Nr.1 tiefer liegend (460-680nm) als das von Nukleole 2, d.h. größere Farbsättigung von 81 gegenüber 82 (Abb. 3C)).

Vergleicht man die Aussagen mit den Spektren von Kern 5 (Abb. 2D), so haben hier die Nukleolen in bezug auf ihren Kern den gleichen Rot-Anteil (590-740nm). Dies bedeutet, die Farbart der Nukleolen ist ähnlich der des Kernes; der Farbton liegt nur etwas mehr bei Blau (Abb. 3B,C). Der Farbart-Bereich der Nukleolen liegt hier, im Gegensatz zu Kern Nr. 8, innerhalb des Farbart-Bereiches des Kernchromatins (Abb. 3C). Die Transmissions-Kurve im Bereich 440-580nm liegt, bei sonstiger Gleichheit, deutlich unter denen der Nukleolen. Im Gegensatz zu Kern 8 ist hier die Farbe des Kernchromatins gesättigter als die seiner Nukleolen (Abbn. 3C,D;4). Diese Unterscheidung läßt sich auch bei anderen Kernen machen (Abb. 2). Das Spektrum der Nukleole 2 von Kern 5 hebt sich gegenüber den anderen beiden durch flacheren Verlauf hervor, die Farbsättigung ist geringer, die Nukleole liegt am Rand des Kernes (Abb.

1E,F).

Das mittlere Spektrum des Kernes 4 (Abb. 1C,D) hat im Verhältnis zu
dem der Nukleole kaum mehr Rot-Anteile (570-690nm) (Abb. 2F). Umgekehrt, die Nukleole hat kaum weniger Rot, was nicht überraschen kann,
denn die Nukleole ist vom Kernchromatin überlagert (Abb. 1C,D).

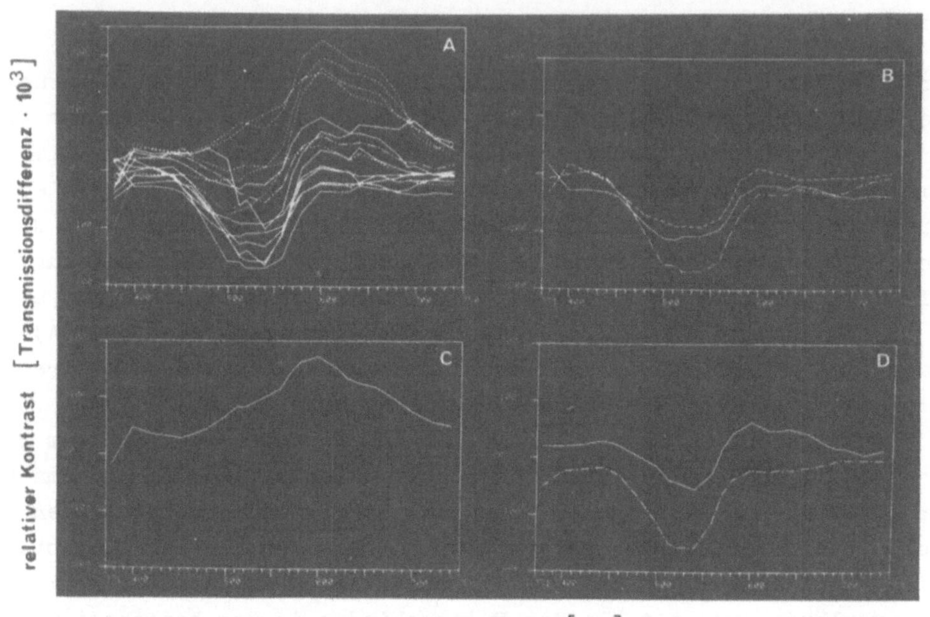

Abb. 4: A: Differenzspektren = mittlere Kernspektren - mittleres
Spektrum einer jeweils zugehörigen Nukleole. (....) von Ker-
nen 4,6,8, (-.-.) Differenzspektrum von Kern 1 und Nukleole 1.
B-D: Differenzspektren von Kernen 5 (B), 4 (C) und 1 (D).
Kerne (....), Nukleolen 1 (———), falls vorhanden, Nukleolen
2 (-.-.), Nukleolen 3 (----).

DISKUSSION:

1) Computergestützte Farbanalyse, die allein auf den Absorptionsminima
und -maxima der Komponenten der Farblösung beruht, ist ungeeignet.
2) Farbanalyse unter alleiniger Ausnutzung des Kontrastes bei einzelnen Wellenlängen (ca. 540 und 600nm bei Azur B - Eosin) genügt
nicht in allen Zellen.
3) Nur die genormte, dem Menschen entsprechende, Erfassung des gesamten sichtbaren Spektrums erlaubt in der computergestützten Zytophotometrie alle wichtigen Farbinformationen zu erfassen. Zur weiteren
Auswertung sind Differenzspektren, wie von anderer Seite bereits

vorgeschlagen /6/, sinnvoll.

Sämtliche mittlere Spektren, sowohl von den Kernen als auch von allen
Nukleolen haben ein Absorptionsminimum bei 421nm, die größte Absorption bei 541nm; von diesem Absorptionsmaximum steigen die Transmissionswerte stetig bis 741nm an. Die letzten Ziffern hängen von den Stütz-
punkten ab, festgelegt durch die verwendeten Interferenzfilter. Die
benachbarten Stützpunkte liegen bei 400,441,522,560 und 721nm. Das
Differenzspektrum von mit gereinigtem Azur B- Eosin gefärbten und von
mit gereinigtem Azur B gefärbten Kernen hat sein Absorptionsmaximum
bei etwa 540-545nm /6 App.2/. Betrachtet man sich mittlere Spektren
von Nukleolen samt ihrer minimalen und maximalen Abweichungen (Abb.
2G,H), so ist bei allen Nukleolen charakteristisch die relativ geringe
Variation der Farbart (Abbn. 1,3C) bezogen auf die Varianz der Kerne
(Abb. 2B). Die Meßpunkte innerhalb der Nukleolenflächen unterscheiden
sich vornehmlich durch ihre Helligkeit (entspricht einer Multiplikati-
on aller Stützpunkte der Spektren mit einem Faktor). In den Nukleolen
ist trotz der blauen (besser blaueren) Farbtöne das Absorptionsmaximum
bei 541nm dominierend. Betrachtet man die Differenzspektren aus Kernen
und Nukleolen, so fällt auf, daß die Kerne mit besonders gesättigten
Nukleolen bzgl. des Kernes (Nr.4,8) den deutlich größten Kontrast zwischen Kernen und Nukleolen bei 601nm haben. Wieder ist die letzte Stelle durch die Interferenzfilter bestimmt; benachbarte Stützstellen 581
und 621nm. Dem entspricht das Absorptionsmaximum im Azur B gefärbten
Zellkern bei ca. 592nm, im Zellplasma bei 596nm /6 App.2/.
Diese Feststellungen unterstreichen eine Aussage /6/, daß eine Bewertung der auf dem RGE beruhenden Färbemuster durch die Differenzspektren zum Azur B- bzw. Eosin-Spektrum ausgedrückt werden können.

Das Vorkommen von Löchern ,u.a. Vakuolen, in den Zellkernen, deren
Hellbezugswert größer 100 ist, weist darauf hin, daß auch im Präparat-
hintergrund im Bereich der gefärbten Zellen Farbstoff auf dem Glasträger "liegt". Die Adsorption von Farbstoffen an Substraten ist ein phy-
sikalisch-chemischer, recht komplexer Prozeß. Der Weißbezug soll die
Daten von den Veränderungen durch Charakteristika des jeweiligen Meßsystems befreien; nicht aber von den Einflüssen der Färbung, die sollen ja gerade erfaßt werden. Ein mikroskopisch freier Bereich zwischen
den Zellen ist von der Färbung beeinflußt. Darum muß der Weißbezug eine makroskopisch von Farblösung freie Stelle auf dem gleichen Glasträger sein. Nur so ist die vollständige Vergleichbarkeit zwischen mehreren Präparaten möglich.

Die Veränderung des Farbtones mit zunehmender Sättigung (Abb. 3B)
zeigt, daß alle 3 Farbparameter (Ton, Sättigung, Helligkeit) mit der
Menge des Farbstoffes variieren, die von den Zellen beim Färbeprozeß
aufgenommen wird /21,22/. Ein deutlich unterschiedlicher Farbton von
gleichen Zellbereichen in unterschiedlichen Arealen eines Präparates
müssen kein Hinweis auf biologische Unterschiede sein. Es muß in der
computergestützten Analyse von einer gemeinsamen Betrachtung aller
drei Farbparameter (Ton, Sättigung, Helligkeit) ausgegangen werden, da
sonst mit falschen Ergebnissen zu rechnen ist.

Die gemessenen 8 Kerne liegen im gleichen Präparat in einem 3,4·2,1
mm^2 großen Areal. Die Frage, ob die unterschiedlichen Farbcharakteri-
stika der Kerne und Nukleolen durch unterschiedliche biologische Eigenschaften, verschiedene Zellrassen oder kleinere biologische Varian-
zen, oder unterschiedliche Konzentrationen der Farblösung an den betreffenden Präparatstellen beim Färbeprozeß hervorgerufen wurden, soll
und muß hier offen bleiben. Es wurden zur Untersuchung nur isoliert
liegende Kerne aus dem Präparat gemessen. Die Anwendung von Ribonukle-
ase und Desoxiribonuklease zur streng getrennten Untersuchung von
Kernchromatin und Zytoplasmen steht aber noch bevor.

Unabhängig davon läßt sich feststellen, daß ein Computer-Algorithmus
zur zytophotometrischen Auswertung der Farbeigenschaften von Zellbereichen, hier Kernen und Nukleolen, der:
1) auf den Absorptionsmaxima für Azur B und Eosin basiert, berücksichtigt nicht, daß sowohl Kerne als auch Nukleolen im gefärbten Präparat das gleiche Absorptionsmaximum (ca. 541nm) haben. Die Absorptionsminima stimmen ebenfalls überein (ca. 421, 741nm).
2) auf der Auswertung der im Präparat erfaßbaren maximalen Kontraste
   zwischen Kernen und Nukleolen aufbaut, kann mit den daraus gewonnenen Meßwerten nicht in der Lage sein, die entscheidenden feinen Unterschiede in den spektralen Farbeigenschaften zu erfassen. Die vi-
   suell deutlich unterschiedlichen Kerne 4 und 8 (Abbn. 3C,D und G,H)
   haben beide maximalen Kontrast bei 601nm (Abb. 4A). Auch eine Modi-
   fizierung des Algorithmus durch den Kontrast bei 541nm wäre unzureichend (Vergleiche die beiden oberen Kurven Abb. 4A .... (Kern 8)
   und Abb. 4C (Kern 4)).
3) nur mit Modifikationen optimal für jeweils eine Zell-Gruppe funk-
   tionieren kann, setzt eine Diagnose vor der computergestützten Auswertung voraus und ist damit untauglich. Anzumerken ist hier, daß
   es sich um ein standardisiert herstellbares Präparat handelte /1,
   11,12/.

Nur eine genormte Auswertung des gesamten sichtbaren Spektralbereiches erlaubt die Erfassung und Auswertung der feinen Unterschiede zwischen den Zellbereichen. Die Unterschiede zwischen den beiden Nukleolen eines Kernes (1) (Abb. 1C,D) zeigen die ganze Problematik. Eine computergestützte Analyse von Zellkompartimenten muß immer in bezug auf deren Umgebung, auf den jeweiligen Kern, auf die jeweilige Zelle, unter Erfassung und Berücksichtigung des im Präparat vorliegenden Färbeergebnisses erfolgen.

ANMERKUNG:

Für die technische Assistenz von M.Haucke und hilfreiche Unterstützung durch F.Meinl (C.Zeiss, München) sei hiermit herzlich gedankt.

LITERATUR:

/1/ Wittekind D, Kretschner V, Löhr W: Kann Azur B-Eosin die May-Grünewald-Giemsa-Färbung ersetzen ?. Blut Bd.32: 71-78, 1976

/2/ Wittekind D. in: Clinical and Hematological Laboratory, 1979

/3/ Green JE: Parallel processing in a pattern recognition based image processing system: the Abbott ADC-500 tm differential counter. In: 1978 Proc. of IEEE Computer Society Conf on Pattern Recognition and Image Processing, S.492, IEEE Inc., New York, 1978

/4/ Lemkin P, Lipkin L: Use of the positive difference transform for RBC elimination in bone marrow smear analysis. Analyt Quant Cytol 1, 67, 1979

/5/ Ringhardtz I, Atwood JG, Paul GT: The diff 3 automated blood smear analysis system: an instrument description. Report LM-54, Perkin Elmer Corp., Norwalk

/6/ Protokoll des Bureau Communautaire des Références (BCR)- Working Group on Biomedical Analysis. Meeting 12.2.80, Brüssel. BCR Projekt Nr.183: Reference Methods - Azur B und Eosin Y for Staining of Blood Cells.
Appendix 1: Characteristics of Romanowsky-Giemsa Stains and Romanowsky-Giemsa-Effekt
Appendix 2: Recommendations for a Azur B Reference Preparation

/7/ Tycko DH, Ambalagan S, Liu HC, Ornstein L: Automatic leukocyte classification using cytochemically stained smears. J Histochem Cytochem 24:1, S.178-194, 1976

/8/ Brenner JF, Dew BS, Horton JB, King Th, Neurath PW, Selles WD: An automated microscope for cytologic research, a preliminary evaluation. J Histochem Cytochem Bd.24:1, S.100-111, 1976

/9/ Young IT, Irving I, Paskowitz I: Localization of cellular structures. IEEE Trans Biomed Eng. BME-22, Nr.1, 1975

/10/ Aggarwal RK, Bacus JW: Multi-spectral approach for scene analysis of cervical cytology smears. J Histochem Cytochem, Bd.25:7, S. 668-680, 1977

/11/ Löhr W, Sohmer I, Wittekind D: The azur dyes. Their purification and their physicochemical properties. I. Purification of azur A. Stain Technology 49: 359, 1974

/12/ Löhr W, Grubhofer N, Sohmer I, Wittekind D: The azur dyes. Their purification and physicochemical properties. II. Purification of azur B. Stain Technology 50: 149, 1975

/13/ Romeis B: Mikroskopische Technik. 16. neubearb. Aufl., R.Oldenbourg, München - Wien, S.149, 1968

/14/ Rüter A, Aus HM, Harms H: Die genormte Farbmessung mit dem Lichtmikroskop als Erweiterung der zytophotometrischen Methodik. Informatik-Fachberichte 20, Springer-Verlag Berlin New York, S.294-312, 1979

/15/ Rüter A, Harms H, Aus HM: Standardized color measurement in automated cytophotometry with the light microscope. Proc Int Conf on Pattern Recognition of Cell Images, Chicago 1979. Pattern Recognition (in Druck)

/16/ Colorimetry. Publication CIE Nr. 15 (E 1.3-1), 1971

/17/ DIN Normblatt 5033 Teil 1-9: Farbmessung

/18/ Harms H, Rüter A, Aus HM: A microprocessor controlled Axiomat microscope for aquisition of cell images. Proc Int Conf on Pattern Recorgnition of Cell Images, Chicago 1979 (in Druck)

/19/ Aus HM, Rüter A, Harms H: On-line image analysis of biological cells as viewed in a light microscope. DECUS-Europe, London, 1977

/20/ Ruthmann A: Methoden der Zellforschung. Franck'sche Verlagsbuchhandlung Stuttgart, S.177, 1966

/21/ Habermalz F: Farbmetrische Untersuchung mikroskopischer Farbstoffe und Färbungen. Microscopica Acta 80 Nr.3, S.199-205, 1978

/22/ Klein-Wisenberg Av: Farbmetrik in der Histochemie - Begriffe und Verfahren. Proc Symp der Gesellschaft für Histochemie, Gargellen, 1979 (in Druck)

/23/ Sumner AT, Evans HJ: Mechanism involved in the banding of chromosoms in Quinacrin and Giemsa. Exp Cell Res 81, S.214-222, 1973

/24/ Comings DE: Mechanism of chromosom banding. IV optical properties of Giemsa dye. Chromosoma 50, S.89-110, 1975

ZUR ÜBERTRAGUNGSFUNKTION VON SCANNINGMIKROSKOPPHOTOMETERN[+]

Horst Linge
Max-Planck-Institut für experimentelle Medizin, 34oo Göttingen

1. Einleitung

Für die digitale Analyse mikroskopischer Bilder ist es wichtig zu wissen, wie gut das digitale Bild das aufgenommene Objekt repräsentiert. Ist die Übertragungsfunktion eines Scanningmikroskopphotometers (SMP) bekannt und besitzt sie im betrachteten Ortsfrequenzbereich keine Nullstellen, so läßt sich ein zum Bildaufnahmesystem inverses Filter konstruieren, mit dessen Hilfe sich die Objekte aus ihren Bildern rekonstruieren lassen, sofern das Abtasttheorem nicht verletzt wurde. Im folgenden soll gezeigt werden, unter welchen Bedingungen das Scanningmikroskopphotometer als lineares Bildaufnahmesystem betrachtet werden kann und wie sich dessen Übertragungsfunktion experimentell bestimmen läßt.

Die Datenerfassung mit unserem SMP ist in Fig.1 skizziert. Bei diesem Aufbau kann die vom Abtasttheorem geforderte Bandbegrenzung an drei Stellen beeinflußt werden.

1) Das elektrische Ausgangssignal des Photomultipliers gelangt über einen Radizierer und einen Tiefpaß an den Eingang des Analog-Digital-Wandlers. Durch das Radizieren des Intensitätssignals I gelangt man zu einem Signalmodell $\sqrt{I} = \sqrt{I_o} + n$, in dem sich das Photonenrauschen als additive Größe n beschreiben läßt /1/. In dem nachfolgenden Tiefpaß wird das Photonenrauschen im Frequenzbereich oberhalb der halben Abtastfrequenz unterdrückt. Dieser Tiefpaß wirkt nur auf das Zeitsignal $\sqrt{I}$, bewirkt aber keine Bandbegrenzung in zwei Dimensionen für das Ortssignal.

2) Die Apertur des optischen Systems beeinflußt das Ortssignal in beiden Raumrichtungen /2/. Die Abhängigkeit der Übertragungsfunktion von der Apertur wird hier nicht betrachtet, sondern in einer späteren Arbeit untersucht. Diese Abhandlung beschränkt sich auf den Fall inkohärenter Beleuchtung mit einer numerischen Apertur o,3 bei zehnfacher Objektivvergrößerung.

[+]Mit Unterstützung der Deutschen Forschungsgemeinschaft

3) Bei dieser Bildaufnahmeoptik ist der Einfluß der Apertur auf das Ortssignal vernachlässigbar klein gegenüber dem Einfluß der Meßblende. Sie blendet in der reellen Zwischenbildebene einen kreisförmigen Bildbereich aus, dessen Strahlungsintensität über eine Feldlinse in den Photomultiplier gelangt. Das so gewonnene Bild läßt sich beschreiben als Faltung des Objekts f(x,y) mit der Aperturfunktion der Meßblende h'(x,y) /3/. Die digitale Fouriertransformation des Bildes liefert ein diskretes Spektrum, das bis auf mögliches aliasing einer diskreten Abtastung des kontinuierlichen Spektrums $F(\omega_1,\omega_2)\cdot H'(\omega_1,\omega_2)$ entspricht. Das Spektrum einer kreisrunden Meßblende ist bis auf einen Normierungsfaktor gleich einer Besselfunktion 1.Ordnung geteilt durch ihr Argument. Die Bandbegrenzung des Ortssignals durch eine Meßblende erfüllt das Abtasttheorem nicht streng. Das hat zur Folge, daß das digital berechnete Bildspektrum durch aliasing gestört ist, dessen Größe nicht nur von der Geometrie der Meßblende sondern auch vom Spektrum des Objekts abhängt. Prinzipiell läßt sich das aliasing durch eine Grautonbewertung der Meßblende verringern /4/.

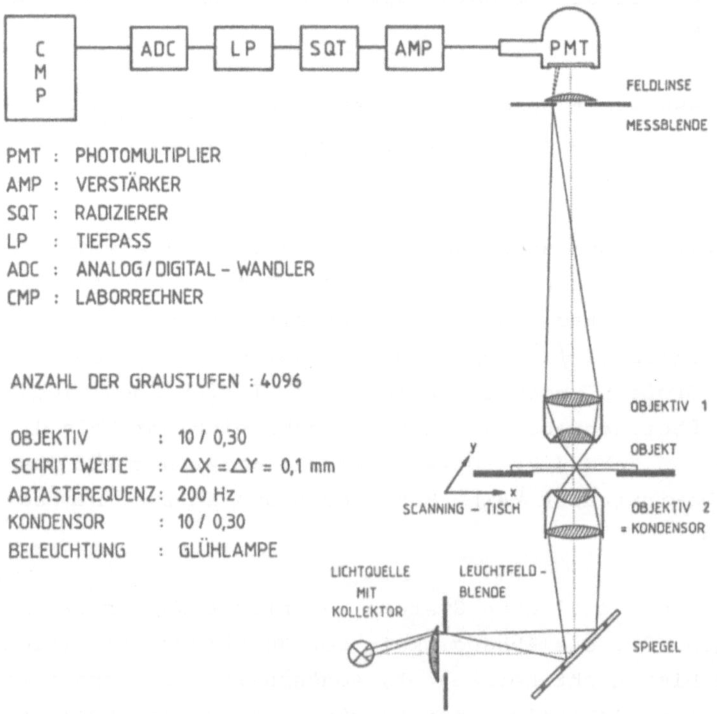

Fig.1:

Schematischer Aufbau des Scanningmikroskopphotometers und Datenerfassungssystems

2. Messung der Übertragungsfunktion

2.1. Der direkte Ansatz

In einem ersten Ansatz zur Bestimmung der Übertragungsfunktion des
Scanningmikroskopphotometers wurde der Quotient

$$H(\omega_1, \omega_2) = \frac{G(\omega_1, \omega_2)}{F(\omega_1, \omega_2)}$$

aus der diskreten Fouriertransformierten (DFT) $G(\omega_1, \omega_2)$ eines gemessenen Testbildes und der DFT $F(\omega_1, \omega_2)$ eines im Rechner konstru-
ierten Vergleichsbildes berechnet. Hierbei ist $\omega_1 = \frac{2\pi m}{M}$, $\omega_2 = \frac{2\pi n}{N}$,
mit m als Zeilen- und n als Spaltenindex, M = N = 256 als Zeilen- und
Spaltenzahl. Als Testobjekte wurden stark fluoreszierende Flecke
von o,32 mm und o,12 mm Durchmesser benutzt, die die Dynamik eines
Selbstleuchters besitzen, um zu einem möglichst guten Signal/Rausch-
Verhältnis zu kommen. Damit im Spektrum des Vergleichsbildes keine
störenden Nullstellen auftreten, muß das Testobjekt hinreichend klein
sein. Wenn aber die Dimensionen der Testobjekte etwa die Größenordnung
der Abtastschrittweite besitzen, approximiert das diskrete Spektrum
des im Rechner erzeugten Vergleichsbildes das kontinuierliche Spektrum
des Testobjekts zu ungenau, so daß dieser direkte Ansatz zur Bestimmung der Übertragungsfunktion aufgegeben wurde.

2.2. Eine indirekte Methode

Die gesuchte Übertragungsfunktion $H(\omega_1, \omega_2)$ ist die Abtastung des
Spektrums $H(\Omega_1, \Omega_2)$ der Punktbildfunktion (PSF) zwischen der Frequenz O und der halben Abtastfrequenz. Nach dem Projektionssatz der
Fouriertransformation ist das Spektrum einer Linienbildfunktion (LSF)
ein eindimensionaler Schnitt durch die gesuchte Übertragungsfuktion
/5/. Mit der Kenntnis der LSF für alle Richtungen ist auch $H(\Omega_1, \Omega_2)$
bekannt. Meßtechnisch läßt sich die ideale Linie nicht besser realisieren als ein punktförmiges Objekt, aber die LSF ist die Ableitung
der Kantenbildfunktion (ESF) in Richtung senkrecht zur Kante. Das
Spektrum eines differenzierten Kantenbildes liefert darum ebenfalls
einen eindimensionalen Schnitt durch die Übertragungsfunktion. Scharfe
Hell-Dunkel-Kanten sind als mikroskopische Testobjekte mit hoher Genauigkeit herstellbar. Die numerische Differentiation bei der digitalen
Verarbeitung eines Kantenbildes führt jedoch zu Approximationsfehlern,
da der Differentialquotient an jedem Bildpunkt durch den Differenzen-
quotient zweier aufeinanderfolgender Grauwerte gebildet wird.

Eine analytische Differentiation der Fourierentwicklung würde diesen
Approximationsfehler vermeiden. Allerdings sind die Bedingungen für
die Vertauschbarkeit von Fouriertransformation und Differentiation auf
begrenzten Bildern in der Regel nicht erfüllt, weil das Zusammenstoßen
heller und dunkler Bildteile an den Bildrändern die gleichmäßige Kon-
vergenz der Fourierentwicklung verhindert. Außerdem stört der Bildrand
das Spektrum des interessierenden Objekts. Bringt man aber einander
gegenüberliegende Bildränder der Kante auf denselben Grauwert, indem
man dem Kantenbild eine Rampe überlagert (Fig.2), so konvergiert die
Fourierentwicklung dieses modifizierten Kantenbildes gleichmäßig, und
der Rand stört das Spektrum des interessierenden Objekts nicht mehr.
Differenziert man das Spektrum der so modifizierten Kantenbildfunktion
analytisch, indem man alle Koeffizienten der Fourierentwicklung mit der
zugehörigen Kreisfrequenz $i\omega$ multipliziert, erhält man einen eindimensionalen Schnitt durch die Übertragungsfunktion, der nur noch mögliche Fehler durch aliasing enthalten sollte.

Die dritte Möglichkeit zur Bestimmung der Übertragungsfunktion, bei
der Testgitter mit sinusförmigem Grauwertverlauf eingesetzt werden,
scheidet im mikroskopischen Bereich wegen der zu fordernden Genauigkeit aus.

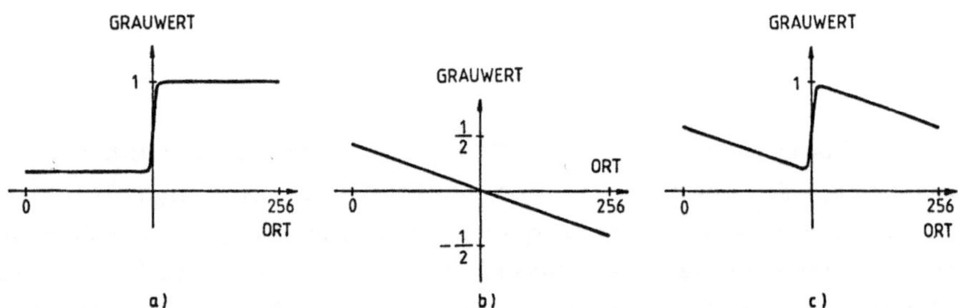

Fig.2:
a) Kantenbild, b) Rampe, c) modifiziertes Kantenbild

3. Meßergebnisse

Als Testobjekte dienten Kanten, die auf einen Glasträger aufgedampft
sind. Sie wurden mit der in Fig.1 gezeigten Apparatur abgetastet, wobei
in jedem Falle das Signal $\sqrt{I}$ digitalisiert wurde, weil hierin das
Photonenrauschen signalunabhängig ist. Zunächst war zu prüfen, ob die
Übertragungseigenschaften des SMP ebenfalls für die Quadratwurzel aus
der Intensität signalunabhängig sind oder ob die Intensität im Bild-

aufnahmesystem linear übertragen wird. Dazu wurde das Signal I und $\sqrt{I}$
mit der im Abschnitt 2.2. beschriebenen Methode ausgewertet. Die Übertragungseigenschaften sind bei $\sqrt{I}$ abhängig davon, ob die Kanten in
Abtastrichtung einen Hell-Dunkel- oder Dunkel-Hell-Übergang darstellt
und wie die Kante relativ zum Abtastraster liegt. Die Ergebnisse für
die Intensität sind im Rahmen der zu erreichenden Genauigkeit bild-
unabhängig und erfüllen somit die Bedingungen an ein lineares System.
Entsprechend der theoretischen Erwartung für optische Übertragungs-
systeme mit inkohärenter Beleuchtung /2/ hat sich damit bestätigt, daß
das Scanningmikroskopphotometer die Intensität linear überträgt. In
Fig.3a ist ein Schnitt durch den Betrag der Übertragungsfunktion für
die Intensität und die entsprechende Kurve für $\sqrt{I}$ zu sehen.

Auf der Frequenzachse ist jeweils die Größe $\bar{\omega}_1 = \omega_1 \cdot \dfrac{M}{2\pi} = m$ oder
$\bar{\omega}_2 = \omega_2 \cdot \dfrac{N}{2\pi} = n$ aufgetragen. Der Richtung $(0, \bar{\omega}_2)$ entsprechen die
Abtastzeilen, der Richtung $(\bar{\omega}_1, 0)$ die Abtastspalten. Sofern nichts
anderes vermerkt ist, beträgt der Durchmesser der Meßblende bezogen
auf die Objektebene 0,244 mm.

In Fig.3b wird der Betrag der Übertragungsfunktion des SMP in Richtung
der Hauptachsen mit dem idealen Spektrum der Meßblende als Sollkurve
verglichen. In der Richtung $(0, \bar{\omega}_2)$ sieht man deutlich die zusätzliche
dämpfende Wirkung des elektrischen Tiefpasses LP (Fig.1). Die geringere
Abweichung der Übertragungsfunktion in $(\bar{\omega}_1, 0)$-Richtung von der Sollkurve kann wahrscheinlich auf aliasing zurückgeführt werden. Es soll
noch untersucht werden, ob ein weiterer systematischer Fehler für diese
Abweichung mitverantwortlich ist. Die Reproduzierbarkeit der Übertragungsfunktion ist im Rahmen der vorliegenden Untersuchungen sehr gut.
In dem Fehlerbalken an der Sollkurve drückt sich die Meßungenauigkeit
beim Bestimmen des Durchmessers der Meßblende aus.

Die Fig.3c und 3d zeigen, daß die Beträge der Übertragungsfunktion in
der Richtung $(\bar{\omega}_1, 0)$ dem idealen Spektrum der Meßblende bei verändertem
Blendendurchmesser gut folgen.

In Fig.3e werden die Beträge der durch numerische und analytische
Differentiation gefundenen Übertragungsfunktionen in $(\bar{\omega}_1, 0)$-Richtung
miteinander verglichen. Bei all diesen Vergleichen lagen die zur numerischen Differentiation gehörenden Kurven unter denen, die durch
analytische Differentiation gewonnen wurden. Ob diese systematische
Abweichung nur auf die Approximationsfehler des numerischen Verfahrens

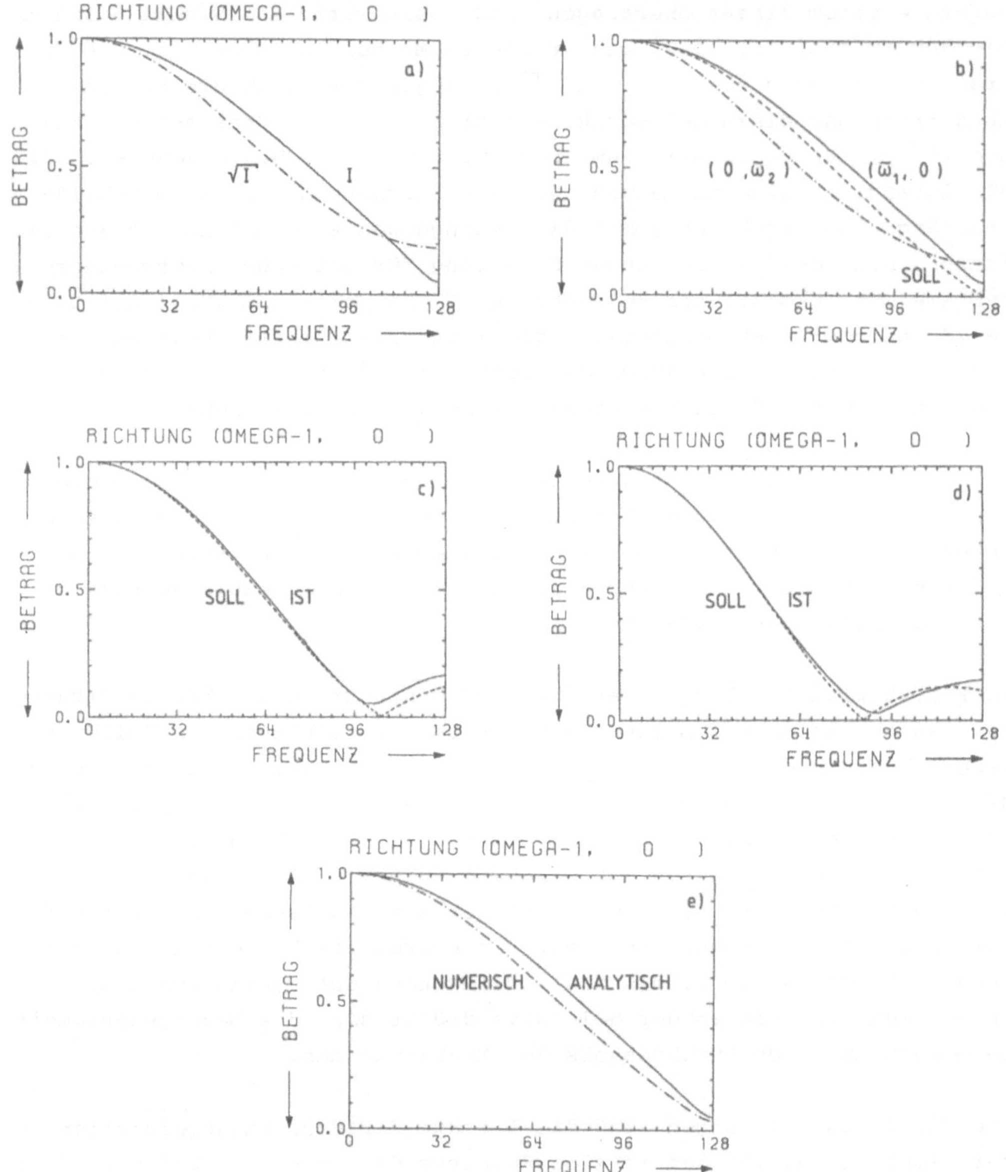

Fig.3:

Schnitte durch den Betrag der Übertragungsfunktion

a)   Vergleich zwischen $\sqrt{I}$ und I

b)   vergleich zwischen Zeilen-, Spaltenrichtung und Sollkurve

c,d) Vergleich zwischen Spaltenrichtung und Sollkurve, für Meßblenden
     mit dem Durchmesser c) 0,300 mm und d) 0,367 mm

e)   Vergleich zwischen numerischer und analytischer Differentiation

zurückzuführen ist, ist noch nicht bekannt.

Zusammenfassung

Aus den Spektren der Meßwerte und eines idealen Vergleichsbildes läßt sich die Übertragungsfunktion nur ungenau bestimmen, da größere Objekte Nullstellen im interessierenden Spektralbereich besitzen und hinreichend kleine Objekte zu einem schlechten Signal/Rausch-Verhältnis führen. Bessere Ergebnisse liefert der indirekte Weg über die Fouriertransformation eines differenzierten Kantenbildes. Nach einer Addition des Kantenbildes und einer Rampe, die die gegenüberliegenden Bildränder auf denselben Grauwert bringt, ist die Differentiation sogar analytisch durchführbar. Dieses elegante Verfahren erlaubt es, die Übertragungsfunktion besonders einfach zu bestimmen und ihre Abhängigkeit von den Geräteparametern zu untersuchen. Es hat sich gezeigt, daß das Scanningmikroskopphotometer im Fall inkohärenter Beleuchtung die Intensität linear überträgt und das Spektrum des Objekts mit dem Spektrum der Aperturfunktion der Meßblende gewichtet. Der Durchmesser der Meßblende ist ein Parameter, der bei inkohärenter Beleuchtung die Übertragungsfunktion bestimmt.

Ich möchte Herrn Dipl.-Ing. R. Bernstein am Lehrstuhl für Nachrichtentechnik der Universität Erlangen-Nürnberg danken, daß er einen Teil der zur Auswertung nötigen Software zur Verfügung stellte.

Literatur

/1/ H.-G. Zimmer, H. Kronberg, R. Bernstein, V. Neuhoff: Improvements in microphotometry by digital signal processing. Im Druck bei "Pattern Recognition".
/2/ J.W. Goodman: Introduction to Fourier Optics. Mc Graw-Hill 1968, Kap.6
/3/ W. Schneider, W. Fink: Integral sampling in optics. Optica Acta, $\underline{23}$, 1976, p. 1011-1028
/4/ T. Kato, Y. Watanabe, K. Tanaka, S. Hashimoto, S. Ohteru: A Note on the Integral Sampling Proposing New Aperture Function. Proceedings of the 4th International Joint Conference on Pattern Recognition, p. 533-535
/5/ K.R. Castleman: Digital Image Processing, Prentice-Hall INC., Englewood Cliffs 1979, p. 268-270

PASSIVE SPATIAL LIGHT MODULATOR

F. Laeri, B. Schneeberger, T. Tschudi

Institute of Applied Physics, University of Berne
Sidlerstrasse 5, 3012 Bern, Switzerland

Abstract

A passive real time spatial light modulator (SLM), using an oil layer as phase modulator of a radiation field, is described. Experiments with a SLM as incoherent to coherent image transformer were performed, revealing the limits in resolution and response speed.

Introduction

Several works published in the past [1-9] investigated the aptitude of deformable oil layers for spatial light modulators (SLM). It is known [11-13] that temperature variations in an oil layer are leading to surface deformations. In the systems described [1-10] the power of the input radiation field of the SLM is converted into localized heat by absorption. This absorption occurs either in the oil layer itself [2-7] or in a special absorbing layer [1,8,9]. The first method constrains the input spectral sensitivity range to the region of the absorption bands of the oil. The second method allows more flexibility in the selection of the input spectral sensitivity range. With epoxy resin absorbing layers [1,8,9] the SLM is sensitive to IR input radiation. The sensitivity can be shifted to the blue or even UV with metal or semiconductor absorbing layers. In this paper we present a SLM with gold and ZnSe absorbing layers. Several other principles are known to work successfully [10,14] but in contrast to those the oil film SLM works without any further energy supply. Oil film SLM's are pure passive devices which reveal no long term storage ability. Rise and fall times lie in the order of 0.1 ... 1 s.

Principle of operation of the SLM

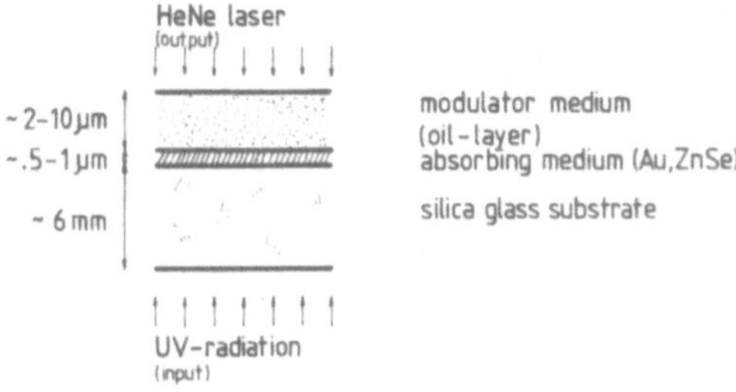

Fig. 1)   Arrangement of the SLM

Fig. 1 shows the basic arrangement of the SLM. The absorbing medium, gold or ZnSe actually, is vacuum deposited on a silica glass substrate (diameter ~80mm). Silica glass is needed to avoid absorption losses of the input UV-radiationpart in the substrate. The incoming radiation penetrates the substrate and is absorbed in the absorbing medium. The absorbed power in this layer is converted into heat. A power distribution in the plane of the absorbing medium is translated in a temperature distribution which is transfered to the modulator medium by heat conduction. The modulator medium consists of silicon oil [15]. The surface tension coefficient of the oil depends on the temperature. The varying temperature in the oil film induces variations of the surface tension in the oil surface which on their part cause a thickness modulation of the oil layer. In this manner, the input power distribution modulates the thickness of the oil layer. This thickness profile of the modulator medium changes the phase of the readout light field. The readout was performed with a HeNe laser.

It is mandatory that the readout process should not affect the readin. In practice this means that the readout radiation field should not be absorbed either by the absorbing layer nor the modulator medium. The optical properties of the absorbing materials gold and ZnSe are shown in fig. 2. The materials absorb radiation above the plasma frequency (gold) or the band gap energy (ZnSe), respectively. In the region of the readout wavelength (633 nm HeNe laser line) the former is a good reflector and the latter is nearly transparent. The ZnSe-curve in fig. 2 exhibits some oscillations above

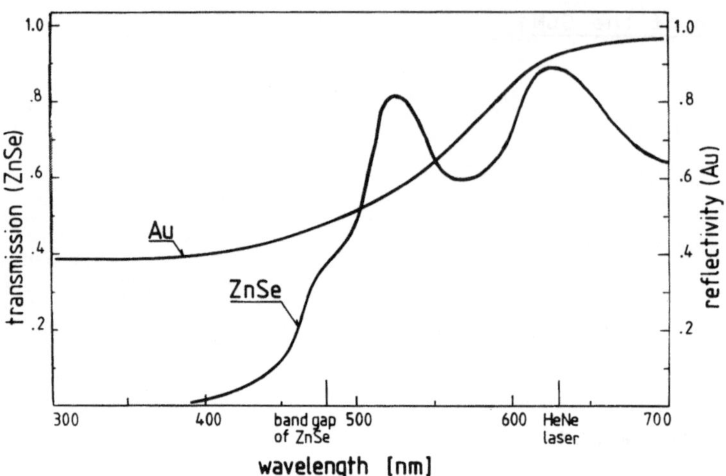

Fig. 2) Transmission spectrum for ZnSe ($\sim$ 1 µm thick) on a silica glass substrate and typical reflection spectrum of gold. The part which is not transmitted or reflected is supposed to be absorbed.

500nm. They are due to interference effects in the thin ZnSe film [16]. Choosing the proper layer thickness, the transmission for the readout wavelength can be localized at a transmission maximum.

Experimental details

As light source with high output intensity in the blue to near-UV spectrum region we used a mercury lamp. To project the test pattern to the SLM, a lens with good correction and transmission for the mentioned spectrum is necessary. The silicon oil we used in the SLM exhibits a rather high vapor pressure and tends to evaporate when exposed to free air. Therefore a sealed housing has been constructed to enclose the oil layer in a saturated silicon oil atmosphere. Fig. 3 shows the inside of the SLM-housing with the oil layer mounting mechanism. The bar, denoted "moving bar" in fig. 3, produces the oil layer in the following way [9]: Through the slim tube on its lower side some oil drops are injected into the gap between bar and SLM substrate. As a result of capillary forces, the oil drops trapped in the gap disperse along the gap. Driven by the hydraulic cylinder (left), the bar moves up and down and leaves a thin oil layer on the

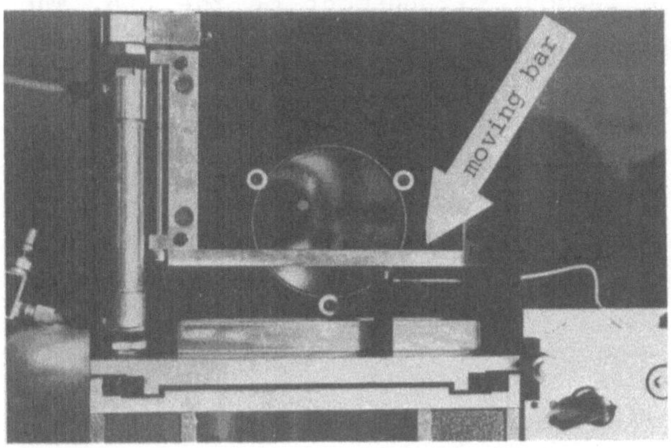

Fig. 3)   Inside of the SLM housing. The horizontal bar (arrow) moves
          up and down and leaves a thin oil layer on the substrate.

SLM substrate. The oil layer thickness is controled by the gap width
and the downward speed of the bar. Oil layers with a thickness between 2 and 10 µm have been obtained with good reproducibility. As
long as the housing is well sealed and the atmosphere inside is
saturated, the oil layer thickness remains unchanged during several
minutes. Only for layers thicker than approx. 10 µm a downward flow
of the oil was observed. Thinner layers adhere to the substrate.

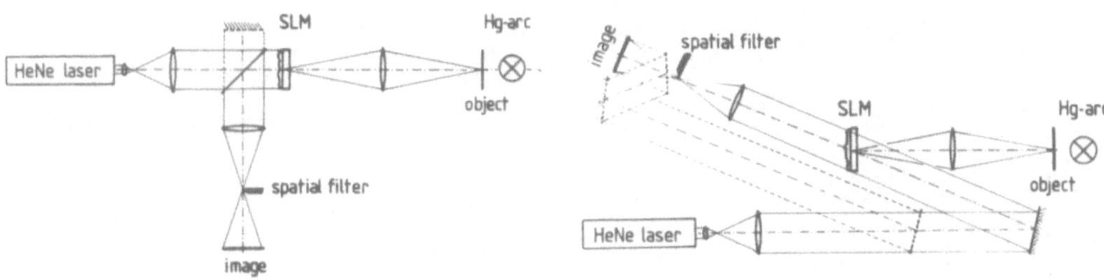

Fig. 4)

Incoherent to coherent image
translator with the SLM with
gold absorber. The readout
laser beam is reflected on the
gold layer. The arrangement was
extended to an interferometer
(dashed lines) for measuring
the oil-layer thickness.

Fig. 5)

Same as fig. 4 but with ZnSe
absorber which transmits the
readout laser beam.

Figs. 4 and 5 illustrate the readout arrangement of the SLM. The arrangement of fig. 4 was used for the SLM with gold absorbing layer. Here, the absorbing layer acts as a mirror for the readout HeNe laser beam. Because ZnSe is transparent at this wavelength, the set up of fig. 5 was used. Needless to say that the sensitivity for the detection of a given oil layer deformation is higher in the arrangement of fig. 4. Compared to the arrangement of fig. 5, the readout laser beam passes twice the oil layer and undergoes twice the phase modulation.

Experimental results

To determine the optical properties of the SLM, a test pattern was projected into the SLM, where the former was illuminated by a high pressure mercury lamp. The illuminance in the input plane of the SLM corresponds to a value of approx. 10'000 Lumen per m^2. The spatial frequency of the outer diameter of the test pattern corresponds to 1 linepair/mm and increases in inverse proportion to the diameter. For some applications, e.g. for visualization, the readout image can be transformed from a phase into an intensity image by means of spatial filtering.

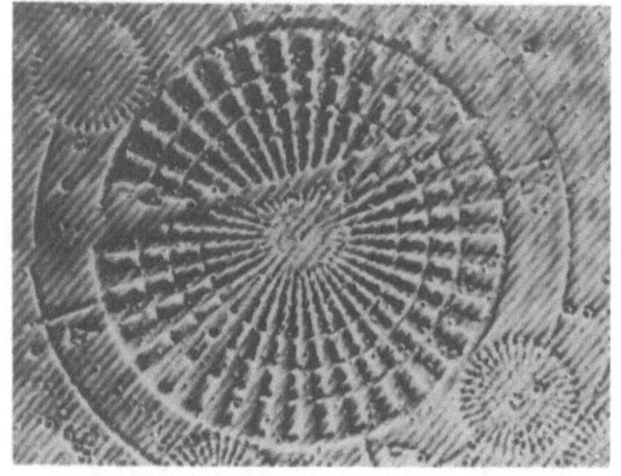

Fig. 6)
Filtered readout image from the gold absorbing layer. Oil layer thickness approx. 4 μm.

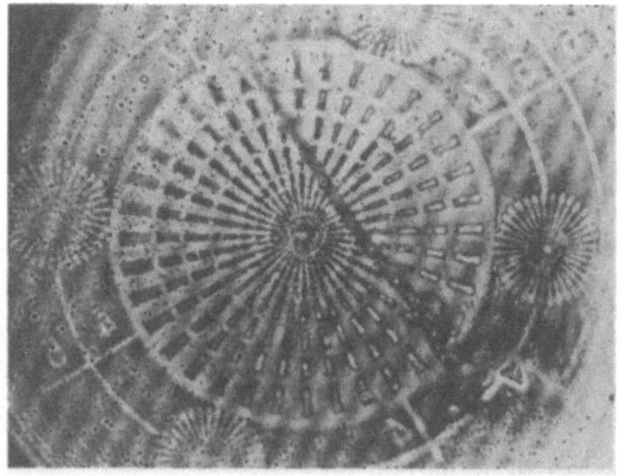

Fig. 7)
Filtered readout image from the ZnSe absorbing layer. Oil layer thickness approx. 2 μm.

Fig. 6 shows the intensity image read out from the SLM with gold absorber. The resolution limit lies at 6,6 LP/mm and is only little affected by the oil layer thickness. In this case the resolution limit is determined by the high thermal diffusion in the gold layer. Screening of the gold layer would interrupt the heat diffusion. But to improve resolution to about 30 LP/mm, the screening must be very fine, about 100 LP/mm. Such a screening is technically difficult to achieve over a field of 5 x 5 cm. It is easier to use absorbing materials which have lower thermal conductivity. ZnSe has a 22 times lower thermal conductivity than gold (ZnSe: 14W/m.K, Au: 318W/m.K at room temperature). With ZnSe absorbing layers we obtained the resolution limit of 20 LP/mm (fig. 7).

With this absorber, a well defined dependence of the resolution limit upon the oil layer thickness was observed. This indicates that with the ZnSe absorber resolution is mainly determined by the hydrodynamics of the oil film and not by thermal diffusion in the absorbing layer. Best resolution of 20 LP/mm was obtained with the thinnest oil layer of 2 µm. The response time of the SLM depends also on the oil layer thickness and is independent of the absorbing material. We observed a modification from about 0,1s for a 10 µm layer to about 5 s for the 2 µm layer. Evidently also the modulation depth of the oil layer for a given input illuminance depends on the layer thickness.

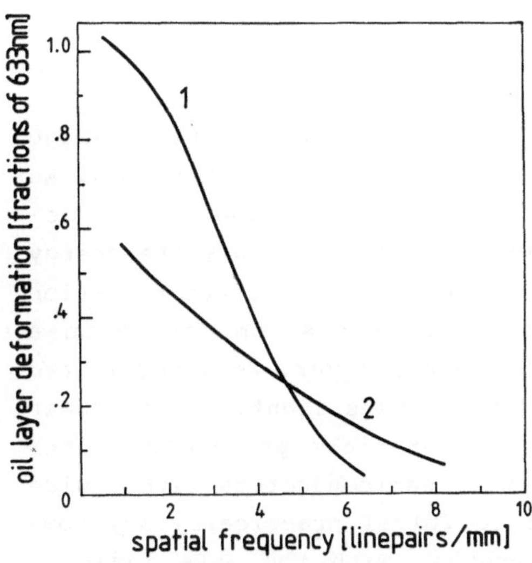

Fig. 8) Oil layer deformation as function of the spatial frequency measured at an illuminance corresponding to about 10'000 Lux. Curve 1 for gold absorber and 6 µm oil layer and curve 2 for ZnSe absorber and 4 µm oil layer.

Fig. 8 shows the surface deformation of the oil film (Au- and ZnSe-absorbing medium) measured with the interferometer set up sketched in figs. 4 and 5.

Several authors tried to describe the hydrodynamical behaviour of their deformable oil layers. But for our experimental situation and results it is not possible to adapt any of these models. Ref. [3] used the approach of Landau, Lifschitz [17]. A similar model is described in Ref. [18]. Both models are based on the Navier-Stokes equation with neglected nonlinear terms $(\vec{v} \cdot \mathrm{grad})\ \vec{v}$. These models ascribe the fluid motion mainly to the presence of density gradients. Pearson [11] and other authors [12,13] showed that surface tension forces alone are sufficient to cause local flows in a fluid layer (Marangoni instability) and that they are the dominant forces. Indeed our oil film surface is deformed in spite its vertical position. The fact that our thin oil layer does not flow downwards along his substrate means that for such a kind of motion the oil layer is build up only from a Prandl boundary layer. The velocity gradients in boundary layers are large. So space derivatives of the fluid velocity induced by surface tension gradients can no longer be neglected. Especially the nonlinear terms $(\vec{v} \cdot \mathrm{grad})\ \vec{v}$ in the Navier-Stokes equation must be included in the analysis. But this renders the solution of the problem with analytical methods virtually impossible.

Conclusions

A spatial light modulator (SLM) suitable for coherent optical image processing or incoherent to coherent image transfer is presented. An oil film acts as phase modulator of a laser beam. The SLM we described is a strict passive device, which means that only the energy of the input radiation field is used to influence an output radiation field. The energy absorption of the input radiation occurs in a separate medium in close contact with the oil layer. We investigated gold and ZnSe layers as absorbing media for blue light. Due to their low thermal conductivity, semiconductor materials produce a better resolution than metal layers. There exist semiconductors with a wide variety of bandgap energies in order to fulfil practically any combinations of input and output wavelengths. With the ZnSe layer, a spatial resolution of 20 LP/mm was achieved. Due to the relatively slow response time of the oil layer in the order of 0,1 ... 1 sec, this SLM is suitable for applications, where no high response speed is crucial but compact construction, together with powerless operation and low cost, are decisive.

Acknowledgements

We thank H.P. Weber and F. Heiniger for their helpful discussions and many suggestions as well as A. Friedrich for his essential engineering contribution in the hardware construction.

References

1)   B. Schneeberger, F. Laeri, T. Tschudi, F. Mast,
     Opt. Commun. $\underline{31}$, p. 13 (1979)

2)   G. Da Costa and J. Calatroni,
     Appl. Opt. $\underline{17}$, p. 2381 (1978)

3)   G. Da Costa and J. Calatroni,
     Appl. Opt. $\underline{18}$, p. 233 (1979)

4)   G. Da Costa and J. Calatroni,
     Proc. of ICO-11 Conference, Madrid, Sept. 10-17 (1978), p. 779

5)   M. Cormier, M. Blanchard, M. Rioux, R. Beaulieu,
     Appl. Opt. $\underline{17}$, p. 3622 (1978)

6)   M. Rioux, M. Blanchard, M. Cormier, R. Beaulieu,
     Appl. Opt. $\underline{17}$, p. 3864 (1978)

7)   J.C. Loulerque, Y. Pomeau, Y. Levy,
     Proc. of ICO-11 Conference, Madrid, Sept. 10-17 (1978), p. 775

8)   F. Mast, V. La Roche,
     Proc. Int. Electro-Optical Design Conference, Brighton (1971)

9)   F. Mast,
     "A New Non-scanning IR-Image-Converter in the 8-14 µm Region
     (Panicon^R)"
     Gretag Ltd., 8105 Regensdorf, Switzerland, 9 April 1969

10) Y.V. Andre, J.P. Chambaret, M.A. Franco, B.S. Prade,
     Appl. Opt. $\underline{18}$, p. 2607 (1979)

11) J.R.A. Pearson,
     J. Fluid Mech. $\underline{4}$, p. 489 (1958)

12) C.V. Sternling and L.E. Scriven,
     A.I.Ch.E.Journal $\underline{5}$, p. 514 (1959)

13)   For further references see
       C. Normand, Y. Pomeau and M.G. Velarde,
       Rev. Mod. Phys. $\underline{49}$, p. 581 (1977)

14)   For a review of non oil film SLMs see
       Opt. Engineering $\underline{17}$, No. 4, July-August (1978)

15)   Dimethylpolysiloxan SI 200, Viscosity 1,5 cSt, Société
       industrielle des silicones; 10 Avenue Franklin D. Roosevelt,
       Paris 8e, France

16)   J.C. Manifacier, J. Gasiot, J.P. Fillard,
       J. of Phys. E $\underline{9}$, p. 1002 (1976)

17)   L. Landau and E. Lifschitz,
       Fluid Mechanics, vol. 6 of the course of Theoretical Physics,
       Pergamon Press 1963, p. 236

18)   A.V. Hershey,
       Phys. Ref. $\underline{56}$, p. 204 (1939)

B. Reuter und P. Vöhringer
Gesellschaft für Strahlen- und Umweltforschung mbH, D-8042 Neuherberg
und Institut für Medizinische Optik, Universität München, D-8000 München

EINLEITUNG

Die Beugung und Streuung von Laserlicht an isolierten Zellen wird in Durchflußsystemen bereits routinemäßig zur schnellen Erfassung der Zellgröße verwendet. Durch Auswertung des Beugungsbildes sind morphologische Zellparameter erfaßbar, die bereits
eine Klassifizierung der Zellen ermöglichen /1/. Die notwendige Forderung, daß immer
nur ein Objekt im Beleuchtungsstrahl sein darf ist bei Durchflußsystemen in optima-
ler Weise erfüllt. Für die seit einigen Jahren in vielen Forschungsanstalten mit
großem Aufwand betriebene Automatisierung der Auswertung zytologischer Präparate,
die bei den Vorsorgeuntersuchungen zur Krebsfrüherkennung gewonnen werden, sind diese Verfahren jedoch nur bedingt geeignet. Eine schnelle Auswertung - angestrebt
sind etwa 10 Minuten für ein Präparat mit der Fläche 2 cm x 4 cm - erfordert die Abtastung mit großen Objetkfeldern, die viele Objekte enthalten können. Naheliegend
ist daher die Verwendung optischer Ortsfrequenzfilter in der Beugungsbildebene zur
Betonung von bestimmten morphologischen Parametern, die eine gute Trennschärfe bezüglich der Zellklassifizierung besitzen und in der Bildebene erfaßt werden. Leider
verhindert das mit der Verwendung von kohärenten Lichtquellen zur Mikroskopbeleuch-
tung verbundene Auftreten von kohärenten Rauscheffekten im allgemeinen quantitative
Messungen.

In einem Mikroskopaufbau zur kohärent optischen Filterung an biologischen Präparaten konnten diese große Schwierigkeiten beseitigt werden durch
1. Verwendung von rauschunempfindlichen Ortsfrequenzfilterverfahren
2. Verwendung einer räumlich instationären Punktlichtquelle und zeitliche Mittelung
   der gefilterten Bildintensität.
Als Filterverfahren scheint die Bandpaßfilterung optimal geeignet zu sein, da sie
größenselektiv wirkt /2/, rauschunempfindlich ist und die Verwendung einer kreisför-
mig bewegten Punktlichtquelle erlaubt /3/. Abbildung 1 zeigt als Beispiel einen mit
einer Fernsehkamera in einem kohärenten Mikroskop registrierten Bildausschnitt (Größe 210µm x 170µm) aus einem Zervikalabstrichpräparat der mehrere Leukozyten, eine
normale Zelle und eine atypische Zelle enthält. Die bei feststehender Quelle (1mW
HeNe Laser) auftretenden hochfrequenten Störungen können durch zeitliche Mittelung
bei rotierender Quelle weitgehend beseitigt werden. Die maximalen Schwankungen der

Objektfeldausleuchtung sind dann kleiner als 5%. Dergleiche Bildausschnitt mit Bandpaßfilterung zeigt deutlich die Markierung der Position einer Krebszelle. Das Intensitätsmaximum liegt im Zentrum der bandpaßgefilterten Zelle. Im folgenden soll untersucht werden, inwieweit mittels Bandpaßfilterung atypische Zellen in Zervikalabstrichpräpraten detektiert werden können. Als Kriterium für die Malignität der Zelle soll dabei die Überschreitung einer vorgegebenen Bildintensität gelten.

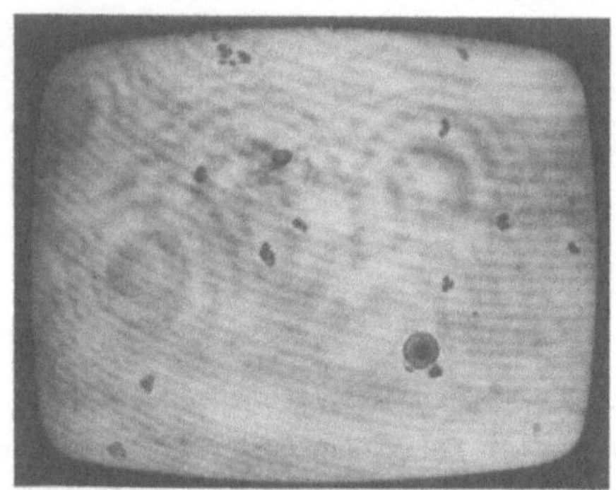

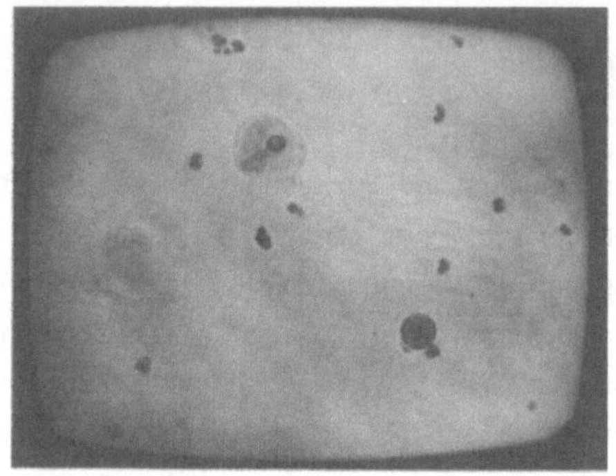

Abb. 1 Bandpaßfilterung an einem Zervikalabstrichpräparat.
Oben links: Bildausschnitt bei kohärenter Beleuchtung, oben rechts: Bildausschnitt bei bewegter Punktlichtquelle, unten links: gleicher Bildausschnitt nach Bandpaßfilterung.

ZELLMODELL

Wir wollen für vorgegebene Zelltypen den Bandpaß ermitteln, der jeweils eine maximale Intensität im Zentrum der gefilterten Zelle liefert. Dazu gehen wir von einem einfachen rotationssymmetrischen Zellmodell bestehend aus Zellkern und Zellplasma aus (Abb. 2). Die Amplitudentransparenz T und die Phasenverschiebung Φ sind über den Zellkern (K) und das Zytoplasma (P) jeweils als konstant angenommen. Die komplexe Amplitudentransparenzfunktion lautet somit

$$T\,(r) = (T_K\, e^{i\Phi_K} - T_P\, e^{i\Phi_P})\, \text{circ}\, (r/R_K) + (T_P\, e^{i\Phi_P} - 1)\, \text{circ}\, (r/R_P) + 1 \tag{1}$$

164

wobei circ $(r/R) = \begin{cases} 1 & \text{wenn } r \leq R \\ 0 & \text{wenn } r > R \end{cases}$

und R_K bzw. R_P der Radius von Zellkern bzw. Zellplasma bedeuten. In diesem Modell ist die komplexe Amplitudentransparenz allein durch die 6 Zellparameter T_K, T_P, Φ_K, Φ_P, R_K, R_P bestimmt. Eine Zellklassifikation die nur diese 6 Parameter verwendet ist natürlich nur dann aussichtsreich, wenn die einzelnen Zelltypen sich deutlich in diesen Parametern unterscheiden. An 129 normalen Zellen und an 140 atypischen Zellen wurden daher diese 6 Parameter bestimmt. Die Zellen wurden von Zytologen aus 5 Zervikalabstrichpräparaten (Pap-Klassen II - IV) ausgewählt und klassifiziert. Die Mittelwerte sind zusammen mit den mittleren quadratischen Abweichungen für jeweils zwei Zellklassen mit normalen (INT: intermediär und PAR: parabasal) und mit atypischen (CIS: carcinoma in situ und DYS: dysplastisch) Zellen in Abbildung 3 mittels Polygondarstellung gezeigt. Anstelle der Amplitudentransparenz T ist das Quadrat, die gemessene Intensitätstransparenz angegeben. Die Darstellung ist normiert auf den jeweiligen Parametermittelwert aller gemessenen Zellen (Polygonzug unten links).
Die Darstellung macht deutlich, daß für eine Klassifikation alle 6 Parameter erforderlich sind. Die Phaseninformation, die nur bei der kohärent optischen Echtzeitverarbeiten zugänglich ist, stellt z. B. eine Separation zwischen Intermediärzellen und dysplastischen Zellen in Aussicht. Die Tatsache, daß

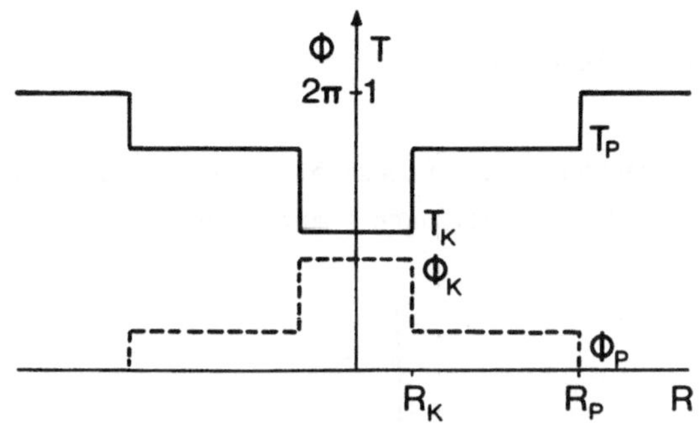

Abb. 2 Vereinfachtes Zellmodell mit radialem Verlauf der Phase Φ und der Amplitudentransparenz T.

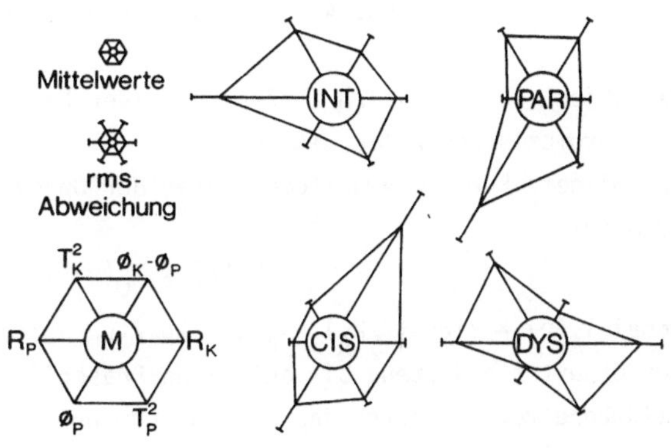

Abb. 3 Polygondarstellung der Mittelwerte und der mittleren quadratischen Abweichungen der 6 Zellparameter für 4 Zellklassen.

dieser Parameter die größte Schwankungsbreite besitzt ist verständlich, weil er für
die routinemäßige Zytodiagnostik keine Rolle spielt und daher bei der Standardisierung der Präparation nicht beachtet wird. Die Abweichungen bezüglich der anderen
Parameter innerhalb eines Präparates und zwischen verschiedenen Präparaten sind für
einen Zelltyp annähernd gleich. Die Parameter, Amplitudentransparenz und Radius
sind normal verteilt.

BANDPASSFILTERUNG

Zur Berechnung der Intensität im bandpaßgefilterten Bild für die Modellzelle wählen wir die in Abbildung 4 angegebene Anordnung.

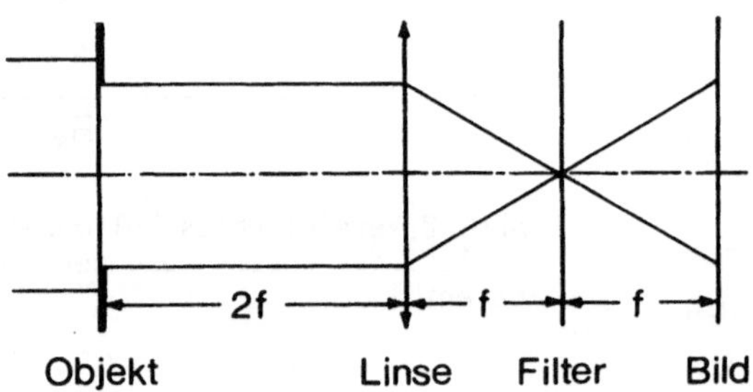

Abb. 4 Anordnung zur Ortsfrequenzfilterung

Das Objekt befindet sich im Zentrum einer Kreisapertur und wird mit einer ebenen
monochromatischen Welle mit konstanter Amplitude 1 beleuchtet und im Maßstab 1:1
abgebildet. Für die Amplitude hinter der Objektebene gilt dann wegen der Rotations-
symmetrie

$$U_0(r) = T_0(r) + T_A(r) \qquad (2)$$

wobei $T_A(r) = \mathrm{circ}\ (r/R_A)$, R_A der Aperturradius und T_0 die Amplitudentransparenz
des Objektes bedeuten. Bis auf einen Phasenfaktor ist dann die Amplitude in der
Bildebene gegeben durch das Faltungsprodukt

$$U_B(r') = U_0(r') * FT\ \{T(s)\}$$

das in einen Objektanteil und einen Aperturanteil zerlegt werden kann.

$$U_B(r') = T_0(r') * FT\ \{T(s)\} + T_A(r') * FT\ \{T(s)\} \qquad (3)$$

$T(s)$ ist dabei die Filterfunktion in der Ortsfrequenzebene und die Ortsfrequenz
$s = (1/f\lambda\ )\rho$ ist eine Funktion des Radius ρ in der Filterebene.
Für einen Bandpaß mit der Transparenz 1 zwischen den Ortsfrequenzen s_T und s_H gilt
die Filterfunktion

$$T(s) = \mathrm{circ}\ (s/s_T) - \mathrm{circ}\ (s/s_H) \qquad (4)$$

Die Amplitudenverteilung für eine bandpaßgefilterte Apertur wurde von Hutzler /2/ berechnet. Diese Rechnungen zeigen, daß bei geeigneter Dimensionierung der Hochpaß-komponente des Bandpasses (s_H)der Aperturbeitrag in der Bildebene mit Ausnahme des Randbereiches vernachlässigt werden kann. Für eine nichttransparente Kreisscheibe vom Radius R im Zentrum der Objektebene erhält man unter dieser Voraussetzung mittels Reihenentwicklung /4/ und Grenzwertbildung /5/ die Amplitude im Zentrum des gefilterten Objekts zu

$$\lim_{r'\to 0} U_B(r') = U_{T,H}(R) = -2 \sum_{k=0}^{\infty} (J_{2(k+1)}(2\pi s_T R) - J_{2(k+1)}(2\pi s_H R)) \tag{5}$$

wobei J_n die Besselsche Funktion bedeutet. Die Intensität im Zentrum des gefilterten Objekts wird dann

$$I_{T,H}(R) = |U_{T,H}(R)|^2 \tag{6}$$

Die Amplitudentransparenz für das Zellmodell (Gleichung 1) enthält als ortsabhängige Anteile die Summe von circ-Funktionen. Analog zur Berechnung der Intensität im Zentrum einer nichttransparenten Kreisscheibe (Gleichung 6) führt daher die Auswertung von Gleichung 3 mit Gleichung 1 und 4 zur Intensität im Zentrum einer gefilterten Modellzelle die sich schreiben läßt als

$$I_B(0) = |A|^2 I_{T,H}(R_K) + |B|^2 I_{T,H}(R_P) + (AB^* + BA^*) U_{T,H}(R_K) U_{T,H}(R_P) \tag{7}$$

mit den Abkürzungen

$$|A|^2 = T_K^2 + T_P^2 - 2T_K T_P \cos(\Phi_K - \Phi_P)$$

$$|B|^2 = T_P^2 + 1 - 2T_P \cos \Phi_P$$

$$AB^* + BA^* = 2T_K T_P \cos(\Phi_K - \Phi_P) - 2T_K \cos \Phi_K + 2T_P \cos \Phi_P - 2T_P^2$$

Die Gesamtintensität ist nach Gleichung 7 nicht nur eine Summe der Einzelbeiträge von Kern und Plasma, sondern sie enthält auch einen dritten Term, der sowohl vom Kernradius wie vom Plasmaradius abhängt.
Die Optimierung eines Bandpasses zur Filterung von Zellen eines Zelltyps erfolgt nun derart, daß für die gemessenen Parametermittelwerte des betreffenden Zelltyps aus den Gleichungen 7 und 5 die Grenzfrequenz des Tiefpasses s_T ermittelt wird, der eine maximale Intensität $I_B(0)$ bewirkt. Die Grenzfrequenz des Hochpasses s_H wird so gewählt, daß der Aperturanteil im gefilterten Bild möglichst gering ist.
Aus Gleichung 7 ist darüberhinaus die Intensität im Zentrum einer Modellzelle als Funktion der Ortsfrequenz des Tiefpasses s_T berechenbar. Durch Vergleich solcher für unterschiedliche Zellklassen bestimmten Kurven ist damit der Bandpaß berechen-

bar, der die beste Separation der Zellen unterschiedlicher Klassen in Aussicht
stellt. Gleichung 7 läßt erkennen, daß durch die Einbeziehung der Phaseninformation wesentlich höhere Maximalintensitäten (bis zu einem Faktor 4) im gefilterten
Bild möglich sind. Vergleiche an Modellzellen mit und ohne Phasenbeitrag zeigen,
daß die Objektphase im Mittel eine um einen Faktor 20 erhöhte Intensität im Ob-
jektzentrum bewirkt.

EXPERIMENTELLES

Der Mikroskopaufbau zur kohärent optischen Filterung ist in /6/ beschrieben. Zur Unterdrückung des kohärenten Rauschens wird zusätzlich der parallele Beleuchtungsstrahl eines HeNe Lasers über ein rotierendes Prisma abgelenkt. Bei einem Keilwin-
kel von 15' ist der Durchmesser des resultierenden Ringquellenbildes in der Beugungsbildebene klein gegen den Durchmesser der Hochpaßkomponente des Bandpaßfilters.
Die bewirkte Bewegung des Beugungsbildes hat keinen meßbaren Einfluß auf das Ergebnis der Filterung /3/.
Die Messungen erfolgen an klassifizierten Zervikalabstrichpräparaten mit monodis-
perser Zellschicht und kontrollierter Färbung /7/. Diese Präparate wurden speziell
für die digitale Zellbildanalyse hergestellt. Die unter Verwendung der an solchen
Präparaten gemessenen Zellparameter durch Computersimulation der Bandpaßfilterung
am Zellmodell optimierten Bandpässe wurde photographisch hergestellt. An 169 normalen und 214 atypischen Zellen wurden für diese Bandpässe die Intensitäten im Zen-

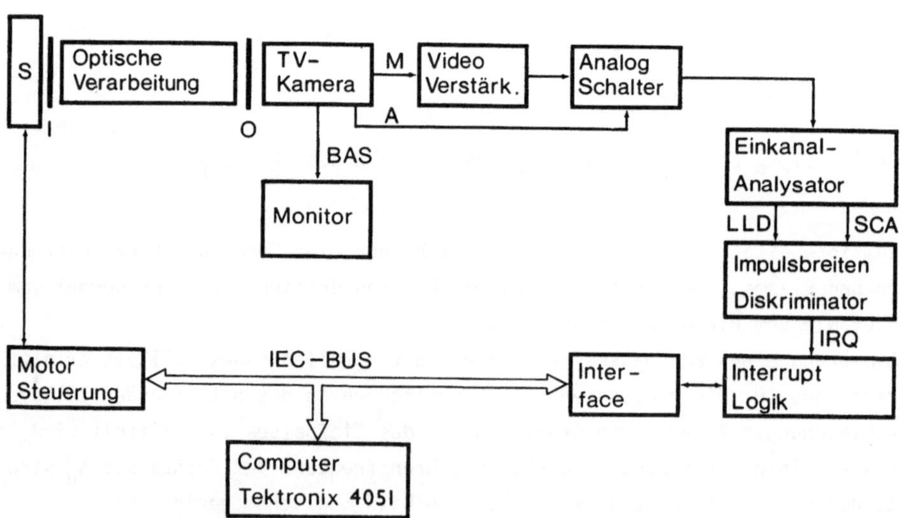

Abb. 5 Anordnung zur automatischen Verarbeitung von zytologischen Präparaten.
S: Scanningtisch, I: Objektebene, O: Bildebene, M: Meßsignal, A: Austastsignal,
LLD, SCA: Schwellwertsignale, IRQ: Haltesignal.

trum der gefilterten Bilder bestimmt.

Die Registrierung in der gefilterten Bildebene erfolgt mittels einer Fernsehkamera mit eingebautem Newicon. Zur vollautomatischen Durchmusterung der Präparate dient das in Abbildung 5 skizzierte System. Ein Mikrocomputer steuert über einen schnellen Zeiss-Scanningtisch (Frequenz 10 kHz, Schrittweite 0,25µm) den Präparatevorschub und registriert die Objektfeldkoordinaten wenn Ereignisse vorliegen, d.h. wenn die Maximalintensität im bandpaßgefilterten Bild innerhalb eines vorgegebenen Intensitätsbereichs liegt. Über einen Impulsbreitendiskriminator können zusätzlich Ereignisse, die von aneinandergelagerten Objekten herrühren, eliminiert werden. Die Verarbeitungszeit für ein Bildfeld beträgt 150 ms, wenn ein Ereignis registriert wird, 30 ms, wenn kein Ereignis vorliegt.

ERGEBNISSE

Abbildung 6 zeigt die Korrelation zwischen den berechneten und den gemessenen Intensitäten für 72 bandpaßgefilterte Krebszellen. Sie enthalten 2 Typen von atypischen Zellen und entstammen Präparaten der Pap-Klasse IV. Die Berechnung erfolgte aus Gleichung 7 bei Verwendung der an einzelnen Zellen gemessenen 6 Parameter. Die aufgetragenen Intensitäten sind jeweils normiert auf die Umfeldintensität in der ungefilterten Bildebene. Die theoretischen und experimentellen Werte gelten für einen Bandpaß,der für eine Modellzelle mit den Parametermittelwerten der atypischen Zellen vom Typ carcinoma in situ ein maximales Signal liefert. Die gute Korrelation der Werte ist ein Indiz für die weitgehende Gültigkeit des Zellmodells.

Für beide Zelltypen sind die Zellen über den gesamten Intensitätsbereich verteilt. Sie sind damit

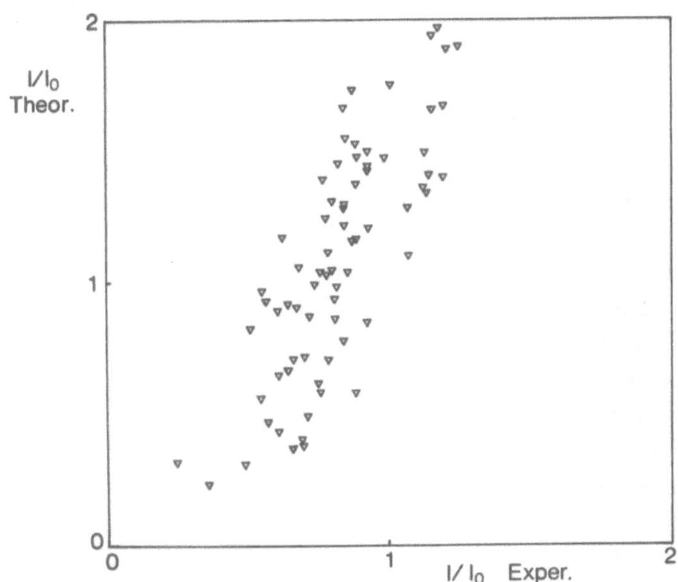

Abb. 6 Korrelation zwischen den theoretischen und experimentellen Werten der Intensität im Zentrum bandpaßgefilterter Krebszellen.

nicht voneinander separierbar.
Diese Tatsache wurde auch bei
der Verwendung anders dimensi-
onierter Bandpaßfilter bestätigt. Es konnte kein Filter gefunden werden, das unter atypischen Zellen die Selektierung
von Zellen einer Klasse ermöglicht. Völlig andere Verhält-
nisse findet man bei normalen
Zellen. Durch Computersimulation wurde jeweils ein Bandpaß
ermittelt, der die selektive
Erkennung von Intermediärzellen
bzw. von Parabasalzellen erlaubt. Bei diesen Bandpässen
lagen die gemessenen Intensitäten von 90% aller atypischen
Zellen unterhalb der zur Detektion der Normalzellen notwendi-
gen Schwelle.

Abbildung 7 zeigt ein Beispiel
für die Detektion von atypischen Zellen ohne Klassenunter-
scheidung. Es wurde ein Filter
verwendet, das für Zellen vom Typ
carcinoma in situ optimiert war. Aufgetragen ist die Häufigkeitsverteilung
der normierten Intensität im Zentrum
gefilterter Zellen bei einer Gesamtzahl von 138 atypischen Zellen aus 4
Zellklassen (schraffierter Bereich)
und 110 normalen Zellen vom Typ intermediär. Abhängig von der Wahl der Diskriminationsschwelle für die Objekterkennung wird ein gewisser Prozentsatz
der normalen Zellen mitdetektiert (die
sogenannte falsch positiv Rate f+) und
ein gewisser Prozentsatz der atypischen Zellen nicht mehr erfaßt (die
sogenannte falsch negativ Rate f-).

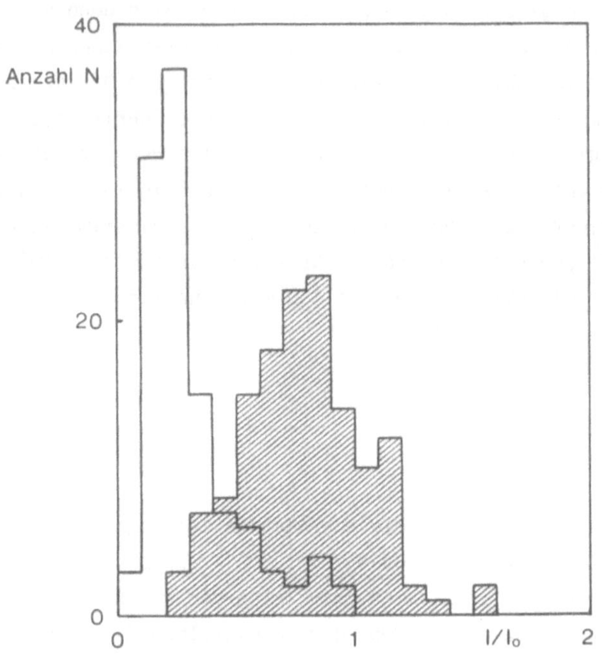

Abb. 7 Häufigkeitsverteilung der experimentell
bestimmten Intensität für bandpaßgefilterte
Krebszellen (schraffierter Bereich) und Intermediärzellen.

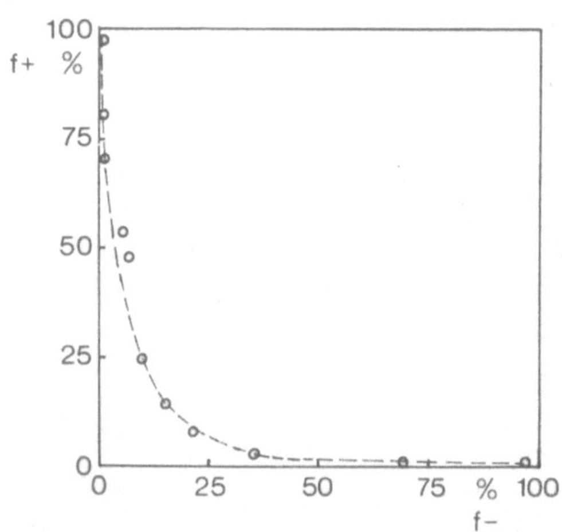

Abb. 8 Experimentell ermittelte Erkennungsraten für die Bandpaßfilterung an 248 Zellen. f+ :falsch positiv Rate, f- :falsch
negativ Rate.

Die gegenseitige Abhängigkeit dieser Raten zeigt Abbildung 8. Diese Darstellungsweise gibt einen guten Einblick in die Leistungsfähigkeit des Verfahrens und ermöglicht die Festlegung einer Diskriminationsschwelle bei vorgegebenen Erkennungsraten.

Die Tabelle zeigt schließlich Ergebnisse für die Durchmusterung größerer Präparatbereiche. Unter Verwendung eines Bandpasses, der wiederum für Zellen vom Typ carcinoma in situ optimiert ist, wurden mit der in Abbildung 5 dargestellten Anordnung die Koordinaten von Bildfeldern registriert, bei denen die maximale Intensität 50% des Intensitätswertes in der ungefilterten Apertur übersteigt. Bei dem untersuchten Präparat der Pap-Klasse IV wäre somit die f- Rate 16%. Die Objektfeldgröße wurde mit 90µmx 110 µm klein genug gewählt um sicherzustellen, daß höchstens ein Objekt pro Bildfeld die Schwelle überschreitet. Die gefundenen Objekte wurden sodann klassifiziert. Danach sind von den normalen Zellen, die detektiert wurden, über 60% Intermediärzellen, der Rest zumeist Histiozyten und Granulozyten, sowie überlagerte Leukozyten. Die Artefakte bestehen zu 90% aus stark absorbierenden Schmutzteilchen, der Rest sind Phasenartefakte. Trotz des hohen Anteils von Artefakten unter den detektierten Objekten ist der Informationsreduktionsfaktor d.h. das Verhätnis Gesamtzahl der Objekte zur Anzahl der detektierten Objekte beachtlich. Bei der in diesem Beispiel verwendeten Objektfeldgröße von 90 µm x 110 µm wird für die automatische Abtastung eines 1 cm^2 großen Präparateausschnitts eine Zeit von 46 Minuten benötigt, davon 40 Minuten allein für die Präparateverschiebung.

Präparat	abgetastete Bildfelder	Zahl der Objekte	detektierte Objekte		
			normale Zellen	atyp. Zellen	Artefakte
Pap-II normal	5096	20180	156	0	176
Pap-IV verd.	2249	4278	13	74	306

Tabelle: Ergebnis der automatischen Durchmusterung eines Präparatbereiches für ein normales und ein verdächtiges Zevikalabstrichpräparat.

SCHLUSSFOLGERUNGEN

Die vorliegenden Ergebnisse zeigen, daß eine Klassifikation der atypischen Zellen nach Untergruppen mittels optischer Bandpaßfilterung nicht möglich ist. Mit einkanaliger optischer Bandpaßfilterung und einfacher elektronischer Nachverarbeitung können aber Positionen atypischer Zellen mit falsch positiv Raten kleiner 10% schnell detektiert werden. Eine Reduktion der dabei detektierten normalen Zellen ist über ein zweites Bandpaßfilter in einem parallelen optischen Zweig möglich. Das beschriebene System zur kohärent optischen Verarbeitung von zytologischen Präparaten bietet sich

an 1. zur Vorselektion von Zellen für die digitale Zellbildauswertung
   2. zur Selektion von Bildfeldern mit atypischen Zellen für die zytologische Diffe-
      rentialdiagnostik.
Vor einer praktischen Anwendung müssen die bisherigen Ergebnisse auch bei Einbeziehung von Präparaten aus den Frühstadien der Karzinom-Entwicklungsreihe statistisch ab-
gesichert werden.

DANKSAGUNG

Wir danken Herrn Prof. H. J. Soost (Institut für Klinische Zytologie, TU München)
für die Überlassung von klassifizierten Zervikalabstrichpräparaten, Frau R. Becker
für die Messungen der Zellparameter und Frl. A. Bock für die Klassifizierung der
detektierten Objekte.

LITERATUR

/1/ Türke, B., Seger, G., Achatz, M., v.Seelen, W., Appl. Optics 17, 2754-2761(1978)
/2/ Hutzler, P.,Appl. Optics 16, 2264-2271 (1977)
/3/ Reuter, B., Wess, O.,Proceedings of ICO-11 Conf., Madrid 1978, 275-278
/4/ Hutzler, P.,'Kohärent optische Filtermethoden und ihre Anwendung in der Mikros-
    kopie', Dissertationsschrift, Darmstadt 1976, S.92
/5/ Sommerfeld, A.,Partielle Differentialgleichungen der Physik, Bd.4, 6.Aufl.,
    Akadem. Verlagsgesellschaft, Leipzig 1966, S.84
/6/ Kinder, J., Reuter, B., Hutzler, P.,Proc. 2nd Int. Conf. on the Automation of
    Cancer Cytology and Cell Image Analysis, Chicago 1979, 69-73
/7/ Otto, K., Höffken, H., Soost, H.-J.,J. Histochem. Cytochem., 27,14-18 (1979)

UNTERSUCHUNGEN VON FILTER- UND KONTURFINDUNGS-ALGORITHMEN AUF PROJIZIERTEN KÖRPERPHANTOMEN MIT ÜBERLAGERTER POISSON-STATISTIK

S.J. Pöppl, G. Herrmann, M. Schedy
H. Schedy
Institut für Medizinische Informatik
und Systemforschung der Gesellschaft
für Strahlen- und Umweltforschung
D 8000 München, Arabellastraße 4/III

Zusammenfassung

Bei der Anwendung bildanalytischer Verfahren in der Herzszintigraphie
stellt die automatische Konturfindung des abgebildeten Objektes einen
besonderen Problemkreis dar. Einerseits verunschärft die begrenzte Auflösung der Gammakamera und der radioaktive Zerfallsprozeß das abzubil-
dende Objekt, andererseits sind die wahren Organkonturen für Vergleiche von Algorithmen nicht ohne weiteres erhältlich. Es werden an Kör-
perphantomen, die mit Poisson-Statistik verrauscht wurden, verschiedene Filter- und Konturfindungsalgorithmen untersucht und gegenüber-
gestellt. Jede Bildverarbeitungsoperation wird durch Intensitätsprofile des verrauschten und unverrauschten Bildes charakterisiert.

Einleitung

Gegenstand der Herzszintigraphie ist es, das Verteilungsmuster radio-
aktiv markierter Substanzen im Herzen zu untersuchen. Ein Szintigramm
ist die Abbildung einer räumlichen Aktivitätsverteilung auf eine zweidimensionale Bildebene.

Zur Darstellung des Herzinnenraumes während der verschiedenen Bewe-
gungsphasen (Myocardmotilitätsszintigraphie) wird Technetium 99 eingesetzt, für die Darstellung der Herzwände (Myocardperfusionsszintigra-
phie) kommt Thallium 201 zum Einsatz.

Die Abbildung mit Hilfe einer Gammakamera erfolgt im allgemeinen zu
fest definierten Herzaktionszeitpunkten, die durch das Elektrokardio-
gramm ermittelt werden können /1/:

Volle Herzkontraktion: Endsystole
Volle Herzerschlaffung: Enddiastole

In der Routinediagnostik wird das Herz modellmäßig als Rotationsellip-
soid beschrieben. Aufbauend auf den dadurch aus Projektionen des Her-
zens ermittelten enddiastolischen und endsystolischen Volumina kann
ein diagnostisch bisher nur invasiv ermittelbarer und sehr wichtiger
Funktionsparameter - die prozentuale Auswurfsmenge bei Kontraktion -
berechnet werden. Dies setzt quantitativ verarbeitbare Organkonturen
voraus.

Erzeugung von Phantomen

Waren bisher viele Verfahren mehr auf die Verbesserung der Lesbarkeit,
bzw. Interpretation von Szintigrammen ausgerichtet, so macht die
Entnahme quantitativer Meßgrößen aus den Szintigrammen eine Validie-
rung der verschiedenen Verfahren unumgänglich. Es wurden daher
verschiedene Körperphantome (räumliche Kante, Zylinder, Schachbrett
und Hohlkugel) auf dem Digitalrechner erzeugt, mit Poisson-Statistik
verrauscht und ihre Projektionen in Form einer Bildmatrix dargestellt. Abbildung 1 zeigt die Projektion einer Hohlkugel mit einer
Wandstärke von 10 Bildpunkten.

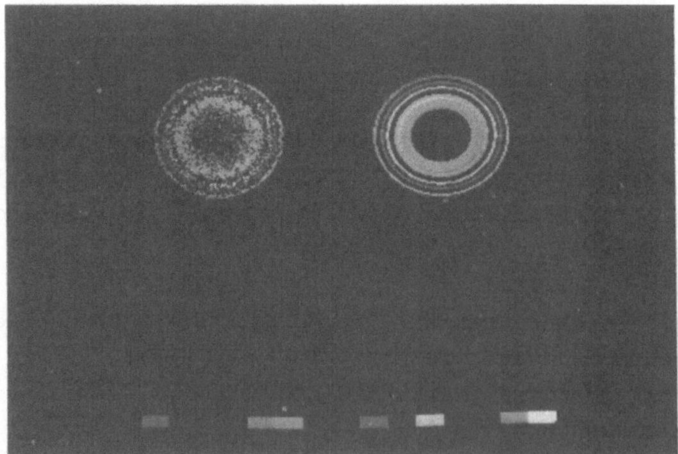

Abb. 1: Projektion einer Hohlkugel mit einer Wandstärke von 10 Bildpunkten.
(Schwarz-Weiß-Wiedergabe einer Farbdarstellung)
Links: Hohlkugel mit überlagertem Poissonprozeß. Rechts: Hohlkugel unver-
rauscht. Die Intensitätsskala nimmt von links nach rechts zu.

Die dargestellte Bildmatrix besteht aus 128 x 128 Bildpunkten mit insgesamt 256 möglichen Intensitätsstufen. Abbildung 2 zeigt einen Schnitt (Intensitätsprofil) bei der 55. Bildzeile. Auf den Abszissen sind in allen Teilbildern die Spaltennummern auf den Ordinaten die Intensitäten (Grauwerte) aufgetragen. Der linke obere Teil zeigt den Schnitt durch das verrauschte Phantom.

Die rechte Bildseite zeigt die Intensitätsprofile bei Anwendung eines 3 x 3 Medianfilters.

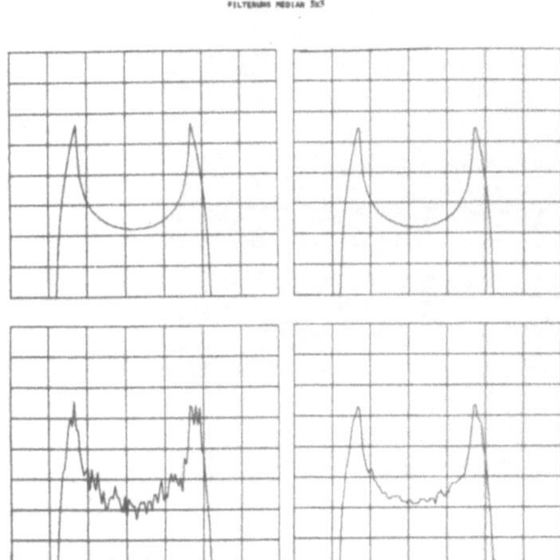

Abb. 2: Schnitt in der 55. Bildzeile durch das Hohlkugelphantom

Abszissen: Spaltennummern
Ordinaten: Intensitätswerte

Links oben: Unverrauschtes Phantom
Rechts oben: Unverrauschtes Phantom gefiltert (MEDIAN-Filter)

Links unten: Verrauschtes Phantom
Rechts unten: Verrauschtes Phantom gefiltert (MEDIAN-Filter)

Filterung

Die in Abbildung 2 angewandte Medianfilterung ist ein nichtlinearer Bildoperator /2,3/.

$\underline{X}$ sei das Objektfeld (zu filterndes Bild), $\underline{Y}$ das Bildfeld (gefiltertes Bild) mit je n x n Bildpunkten. Eine Maske M mit m x m Bildpunkten wobei der Mittelpunkt der Maske m_{rs} ist, wird Zeile für Zeile über das zu filternde Bild bewegt. Die Abbildungsvorschrift ist dazu folgendermaßen:

Alle Maskenpunkte m_{11}, m_{12} ... m_{MM} werden dem Betrag nach geordnet, so daß sich die Zahlenfolge u_1, u_2 ... $u_M{}^2$ ergibt, für die gilt

$$u_1 \leq u_2 \leq u_3 \cdots \leq u_{M^2}$$

Dann errechnet sich ein gefilterter Bildpunkt Y_{rs} zu

$$Y_{rs} = Z_F$$

mit $F = (M^2+1)/2$ und $M = 3, 5, 7 \ldots$

Dieses Verfahren glättet alle Strukturen vollständig, deren Ausdehnung
innerhalb von $\underline{M}$ nicht mehr als $(M-1)/2$ Bildpunkte beträgt. Bildkanten
dagegen werden nicht verunschärft. Abbildung 3 zeigt die Anwendungen
verschiedener Medianfilter auf das verrauschte Hohlkugelphantom.

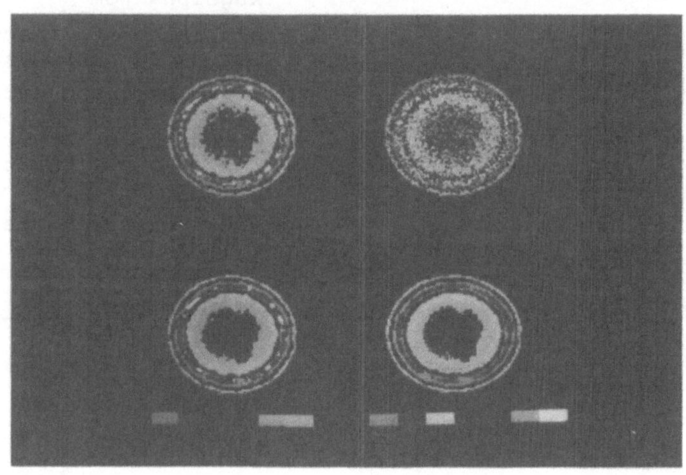

Abb. 3: Verrauschtes Hohlkugelphantom und Medianfilter

Quadrant   I: Verrauschtes Hohlkugelphantom
Quadrant   II: Filterung mit Medianfilter 3x3
Quadrant III: Filterung mit Medianfilter 3x3 (2 mal angewandt)
Quadrant IV: Filterung mit Medianfilter 5x5

Einige sehr ermutigende Experimente /4/ mit rekursiven Wiener Optimal-
filtern 2. Grades sowie Untersuchungen über das Amplitudenspektrum
und ein eventueller Einsatz auf Mikroprozessoren führten zu der Über-
legung einen rekursiven digitalen Bandpaß zur "Kontrastanhebung" ein-
zusetzen. Aus der Standard z-Transformation einer gedämpften cos-
Schwingung läßt sich ein Digitalresonator bzw. Digitalbandpaß ableiten.
Das Transformationspaar lautet:

$$\text{Zeitfunktion} \qquad e^{-at} \cos \omega_0 t$$

$$\text{Standard-z-Transformation} \qquad \frac{1-e^{-aT} \cos \omega_0 T \, z^{-1}}{1-2e^{-aT} \cos \omega_0 T \, z^{-1} + e^{-2aT} z^{-2}} \qquad (1.1)$$

Führt man in (1.1) die Abtastfrequenz f_a, die Resonanzfrequenz f_0 und die Bandbreite b des Resonators (Frequenzwerte wo die Amplitude jeweils auf $1/\sqrt{2}$ des Maximalwertes gesunken ist) so gilt /5/:

$$f_a = \frac{1}{T};\; f_o = \frac{\omega_o}{2\pi};\; b = \frac{a}{\pi};\; aT = \pi b/f_a \tag{1.2}$$

Die Übertragungsfunktion wird dann zu

$$H(z) = A\,\frac{1 + B_z^{-1}}{1 - Dz^{-1} - Ez^{-2}} \tag{1.3}$$

wobei

$$\begin{aligned} B &= -\exp(-\pi b/f_a)\,\cos(2\pi f_o/f_a) \\ D &= 2\,\exp(-\pi b/f_a)\,\cos(2\pi f_o/f_a) \\ E &= -\exp(2\pi b/f_a) \end{aligned} \tag{1.4}$$

FILTER NACH STANDARD Z-TRANSFORMATION

Übertragungsfunktion

$$H(Z) = A\,\frac{1 + Bz^{-1}}{1 - Dz^{-1} - Ez^{-1}}$$

A = Faktor b = Bandbreite

B = -exp(-πb/fa)cos (2πfo/fa)

D = -2exp(-πb/fa)cos (2πfo/fa)

E = -exp(-2πb/fa)

FILTERTYPEN

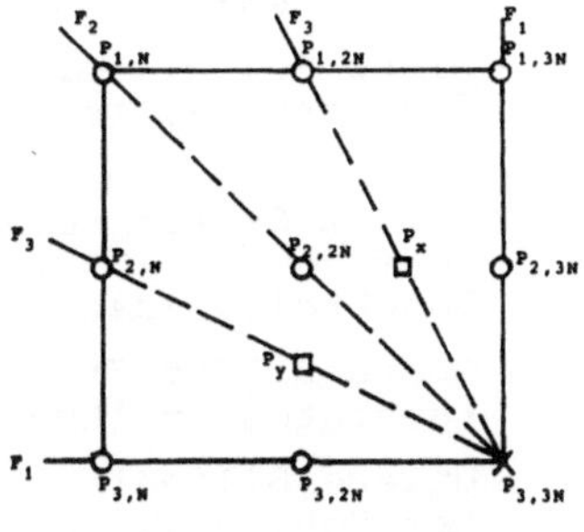

Abb.4: Digitaler Bandpaß

Im oberen Teil ist die Übertragungsfunktion dargestellt. Der untere Teil zeigt den digitalen Bandpaß als einen 3 x 3-Operator mit den verschiedenen Filtertypen F_1, F_2 und F_3.

Das Filter ist als rekursives Filter 2. Grades ausgelegt. Sollen die Filtereigenschaften wie Mittenfrequenz und Bandbreite in allen Richtungen gleich sein, so müssen die Koeffizienten A, B, D und E in (1.3 und 1.4) unterschiedlich sein.

A wird im allgemeinen so gewählt, daß bei der Resonanzfrequenz der Betrag der Übertragungsfunktion einen festen Wert z.B. 1 hat.

Weiterhin gilt:

Filtertyp F1 $\qquad f_{a1} = f_a$

Filtertyp F2 $\qquad f_{a2} = f_a/\sqrt{2}$ $\hfill$ (1.5)

Filtertyp F3 $\qquad f_{a3} = f_a/\sqrt{1.25}$

Die Koeffizienten D und B sind sehr ähnlich, es gilt:

$$D = -2B \hspace{3cm} (1.6)$$

Kürzere Rechenzeiten ergeben sich wenn nur 3 Filter (3 Richtungen) bei zwei Filtertypen (F_1, F_2) verwendet werden. Abbildung 4 zeigt den digitalen Bandpaß als 3 x 3 Operator. Im Rahmen dieser Anwendungen wird der digitale Bandpaß als Doppelbandpaß (Kaskadenschaltung) eingesetzt. Abbildung 5 zeigt die Anwendung des rekursiven Doppelbandpaß auf das verrauschte und unverrauschte Hohlkugelphantom. Die Frequenzangaben stellen das Verhältnis der betrachteten Frequenz zur Abtastfrequenz f_a in Prozent (relative Frequenzen) dar.

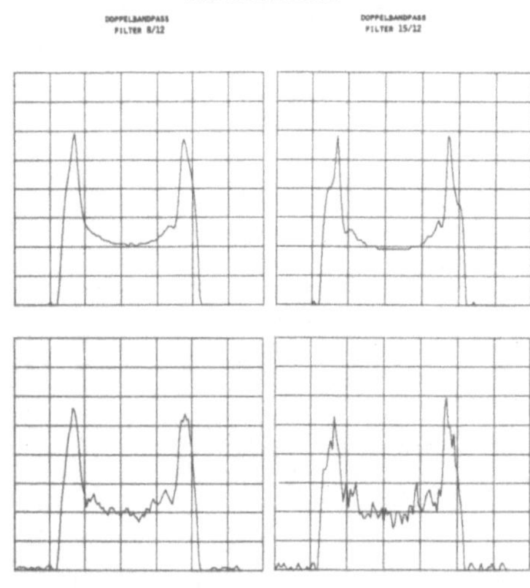

Abb. 5:

Schnitt in der 55. Zeile durch das Hohlkugelphantom

Abszissen: Spaltennummern
Ordinaten: Intensitätswerte

Linke Seite: relative Mittenfrequenz 8%, relative Bandbreite 12%

Rechte Seite: relative Mittenfrequenz 15%, relative Bandbreite 12%

Obere Bildhälfte: Unverrauschtes Hohlkugelphantom

Untere Bildhälfte: Verrauschtes Hohlkugelphantom

Die Abbildung 5 zeigt im Schnittbild, daß für die Kontursuche wichtige Strukturen durch die Bandpaßfilterung angehoben werden, wie sich auch aus einem Vergleich mit Abbildung 2 ergibt.

Gradientenbildung und Kontursuche

Eine sehr beliebte Näherung für die Gradientenberechnung ist der sogenannte Robertsgradient /6/. Bei der Anwendung auf die Phantome, insbesondere auf das Hohlkugelphantom, zeigte sich, daß der Robertsgradient für gleichmäßig abgestufte Intensitätsübergänge nicht geeignet
ist. Deshalb wird ein gewichteter symmetrischer Gradient eingesetzt.
Die x- und y-Komponenten des symmetrischen Gradienten werden berechnet nach:

$$\Delta_y = f(i+1,j+1)+f(i,j+1)+f(i+1,j+1)-(f(i-1,j-1)+f(i,j-1)+f(i+1,j-1))$$

$$\Delta_x = f(i+1,j-1)+f(i+1,j)+f(i+1,j+1)-(f(i-1,j)+f(i-1,j-1)+f(i-1,j+1))$$

i-1, j-1	i-1, j	i-1, j+1
i, j-1	i, j	i, j+1
i+1, j-1	i+1, j	i+1, j+1

Der Betrag des Gradienten berechnet sich aus Δ_x und Δ_y

$$G(i,j) = \sqrt{\Delta_x^2 + \Delta_y^2}$$

Durch die Wahl von mehr Nachbarpunkten gegenüber dem Robertsgradient
ist dieser Gradient rauschunempfindlicher. Um eine verbesserte Roh-
kontur zu erhalten, wird eine Gewichtung eingeführt, die von der Intensität des Punktes (i,j) abhängig ist.

In Abbildung 6 ist ein sequentielles Kontursuchverfahren dargestellt,
das eine Weiterentwicklung von /3/ darstellt. Alle möglichen Kandidatenpunkte des Bildfelds $\underline{y}$ sind in einer Matrix (z.B. nach Gradienten-
operation) gespeichert. Folgende Verarbeitungsschritte werden ausgeführt (s. Abb. 6):

- *Wähle in den Umgebungspunkten 1-5 alle Punkte aus, deren Intensitäten über einer Schwelle T_1 liegen und die sich vom Maximum aus 1-5
um weniger als T_2 unterscheiden. Dies sind mögliche Kandidaten für
den neuen Konturpunkt.*

- *Falls sich unter den Punkten 2-4 Kandidatenpunkte befinden, wähle
hieraus den neuen Konturpunkt (höchster Intensitätswert).*

- *Sonst wähle aus den verbleibenden Punkten 1 oder 5 den neuen Konturpunkt.*

- *Die nicht verwendeten Kandidatenpunkte werden als mögliche Verzweigungen in einem Stück gespeichert.*

- *Wenn unter den Punkten 1-5 kein neuer Konturpunkt auffindbar ist,
wird Punkt 6 geprüft. Liegt sein Intensitätswert über T_1, sind die
Punkte 3 und 6 keine Konturpunkte.*

Ein Verfahren, daß zum Vergleich angewendet wurde, stellt die Relaxationsmethode nach Rosenfeld /7/ dar.

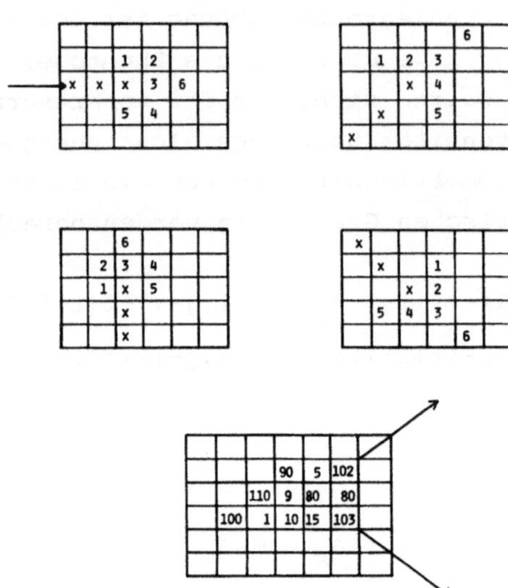

Abb. 6:

Sequentielles Konturfindungsverfahren
Die mit x bezeichneten Punkte
sind die zuletzt aufgefunde-
nen Punkte der Kontur. Im Bereich 1-6 wird nach möglichen
Konturpunkten gesucht.

Ergebnisse

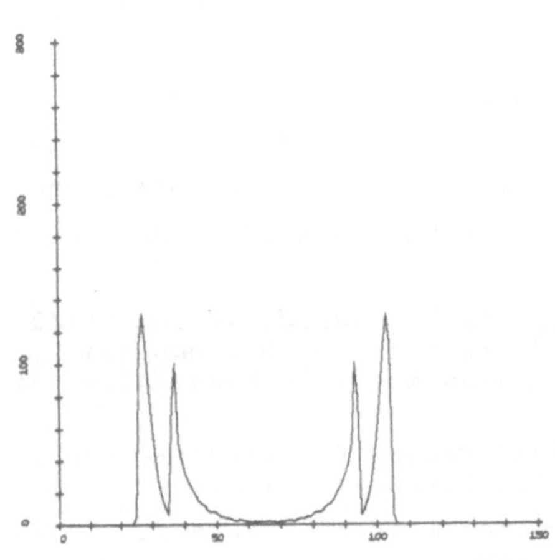

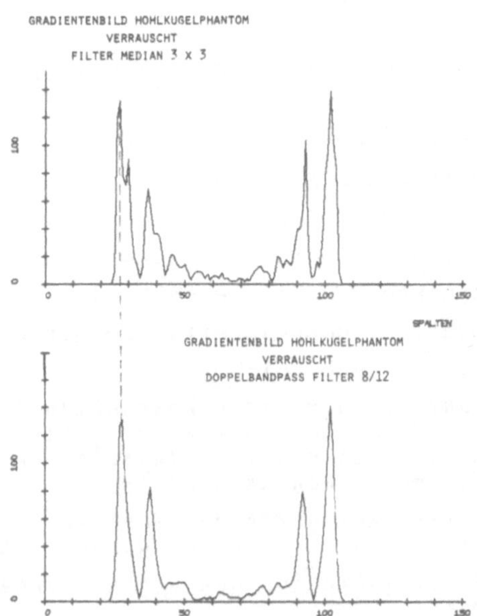

Abb. 7: Gradientenschnittbild der 55. Bildzeile (Abszisse Spaltennum-
mer, Ordinate Gradientenwert) des Hohlkugelphantoms.
Links: Gradientenverlauf bei unverrauschtem Phantom
Rechts: Gradientenverlauf bei verrauschtem Phantom nach Filterung mit Medianfilter 3 x 3 und rekursivem Doppelbandpaß (rel. Mittenfrequenz 8%, rel. Bandbreite 12%).

180

Abbildung 7 zeigt Gradientenschnittbilder der 55. Bildzeile bei unverrauschtem und verrauschtem Hohlkugelphantom. Die Gradienten wurden mit
dem beschriebenen gewichteten Gradientenverfahren berechnet. Die Vorteile des Doppelbandpaßfilters werden beim Vergleich der Gradienten-
profile deutlich.

Abbildung 8 zeigt die Konturen des projizierten Hohlkugelphantoms bei
verrauschtem und unverrauschtem Phantom.

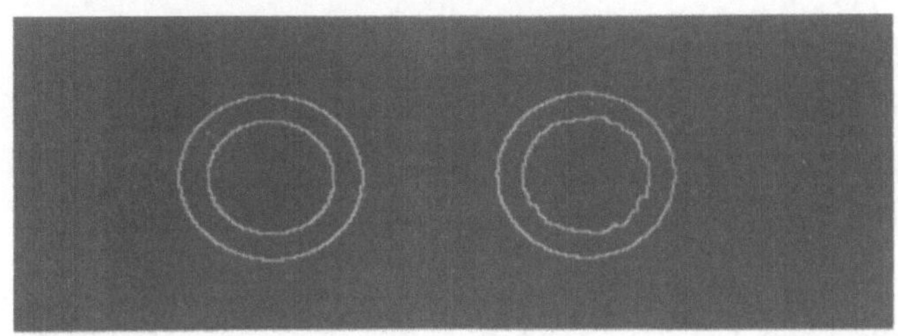

Abb. 8: Konturen des projizierten Hohlkugelphantoms, die mit dem
beschriebenen Konturfindungsverfahren berechnet wurden.
Links: Unverrauschte Hohlkugel
Rechts: Verrauschte Hohlkugel (Doppelbandpaßfilterung,
Gradientenbildung, Konturfindungsverfahren)

Den Erfolg der beschriebenen rekursiven Bandpaßfilterung einschließ-
lich Gradientenbildung und Konturberechnung zeigt Abb. 9.
Dieses Myocardperfusionsszintigramm das in LAO 45° Lage EKG-getriggert
aufgenommen wurde, zeigt die Intensitätskonturen in der Enddiastole
und Endsystole des linken Ventrikels. Abbildung 10 zeigt die mit der
Relaxationsmethode erhaltenen Konturen (Szintigramm in Enddiastole)
bei verschiedenen Iterationen.
Abbildung 11 zeigt einen Schnitt in der 55. Bildzeile durch das Szintigramm, die Wirkung der verschiedenen Filter ist deutlich erkennbar,
was sich auch in den unterschiedlichen Gradientenprofilen zeigt (Abbildung 12).
Beide Abbildungen sprechen für den Einsatz des rekursiven Bandpaßfilters.

Die Verfasser danken Herrn Dr. H. Koffler für viele fruchtbare
Diskussionen.

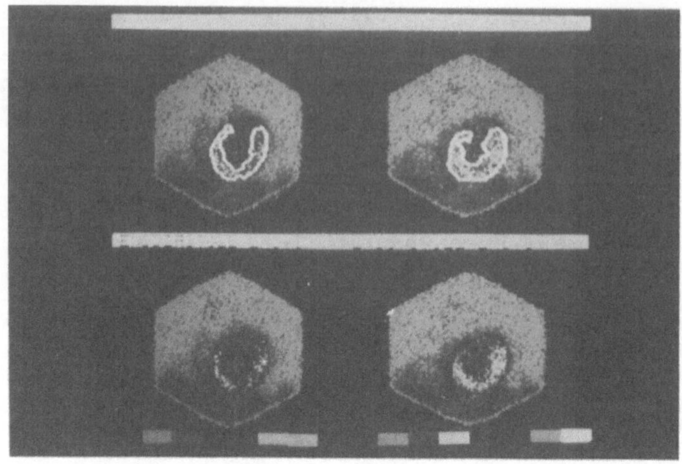

Abb. 9: Myocardperfusionsszintigramm des linken Ventrikels in
LAO 45° Lage mit automatisch ermittelten Konturen.
Links unten: Szintigramm in Enddiastole, darüber mit
                Konturen
Rechts unten: Szintigramm in Endsystole, darüber mit
                Konturen

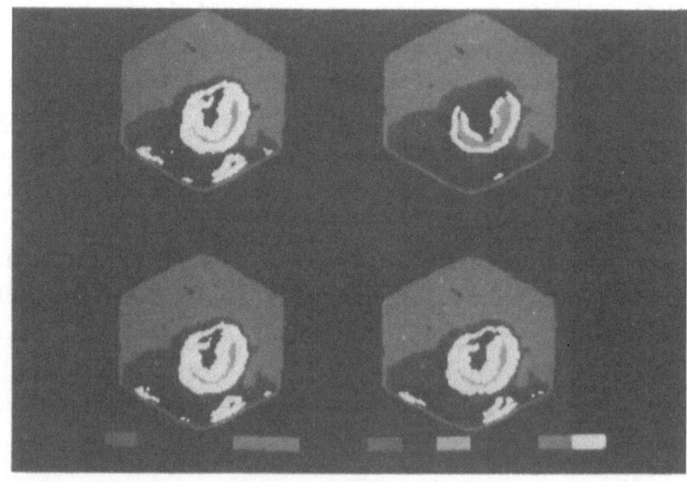

Abb. 10: Ergebnisse der Konturermittlung beim Szintigramm (Enddiastole) aus Abbildung 9 mit der Relaxationsmethode/7/
bei verschiedenen Iterationen.

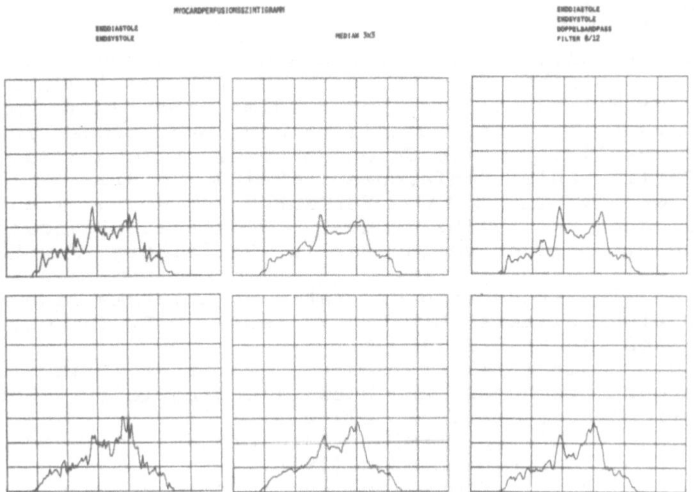

Abb. 11: Schnitt durch Myocardperfusionsszintigramm aus Abbil-
dung 9 in der 55. Bildzeile.
Obere Bildreihe von links nach rechts:
Enddiastole: Original, Medianfilterung, Bandpaßfilterung
Untere Bildreihe von links nach rechts:
Endsystole: Original, Medianfilterung, Bandpaßfilterung

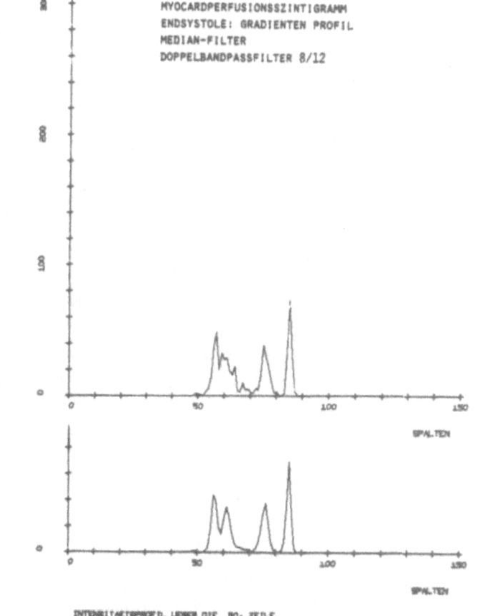

Abb. 12: Gradientenprofil des
Myocardperfusionsszintigramms
in der Endsystole (55. Bildzeile)

Oben: Gradient nach Median-
      filterung
Unten: Gradient nach Bandpaß-
       filterung

Literaturverzeichnis

/1/ Adam, W.E. et. al.: Nuklearmedizinische Verfahren in der Herz-
diagnostik. Deutsches Ärzteblatt Nr. 3, 107-113 (1978).
/2/ Pöppl, S.J.: Methods in one- and twodimensional signal processing.
In: Biomedical pattern recognition and image processing (eds.:
K.S.Fu, T. Pavlidis). Life Sciences Research Report 15, Verlag
Chemie, Berlin Dahlem Konferenzen, 69-109 (1979).
/3/ Abele, L. et al: Ein digitales Verfahren zur Konturfindung und
Störbeseitigung bei Zellbildern. In: Digitale Bildverarbeitung
(Ed.: Nagel), Springer-Verlag Berlin, Heidelberg, New York,
29-36 (1977).
/4/ Wahl, F. et al.: Processing of static scintigrams with adaptive
digital optimum filters. MEDINFO 77 (eds.: D.B. Shives, H. Wolf)
North Holland, 1039-1042 (1977).
/5/ Koffler, H.: Digital filters and how to derive their block diagram, Siemens Forschungs- und Entwicklungsbericht 1, Springer
Berlin, Heidelberg, New York, 227-235 (1972).
/6/ Rosenfeld, A. et al.: Digital picture processing. Academic Press
New York, San Francisco, London (1976).
/7/ Rosenfeld, A. et al.: Scene labeling by relaxation operations.
IEEE Transactions on Systems, man, and cybernetics, Vol. SMC-6,
No.6, 420-433, (June 1976).

Optische Zeichenerkennung mit kohärenter Komponentenfilterung

F. Merkle
Institut für Angewandte Physik I
Universität Heidelberg

Zusammenfassung

Die analogen kohärent-optischen Filtermethoden sind eine Möglichkeit
Objektmuster zu erkennen und zu klassifizieren. Für jedes Objekt wird
hierbei ein ihm angepaßtes holographisches Ortsfrequenzfilter benötigt.
Dieser Nachteil, vorallem bei großen Mustervielfalten wird durch die
Verwendung von Komponentenfiltern, die gleichzeitig mehreren Objekten
angepaßt sind umgangen. Damit läßt sich die Filterzahl auf ld N reduzieren. Die Herstellung dieser Komponentenfilter wie auch die Korrelationen werden dabei analog optisch durchgeführt. Experimente zeigen
Korrelationssignalverhältnisse von 1:0,4. Damit kann eine Schwellenbedingung für den binären Erkennungsprozeß gesetzt werden.

I. Einleitung

Zeichen und Muster können mit der kohärent-optischen Filtermethode
nach Van der Lugt [1,2,3] identifiziert werden. Dabei wird die Intensitätsverteilung eines Objektes $o(x,y)$ fouriertransformiert ($O(x,y)$)
und auf das Filter mit der Transparenz $F(x,y)$ abgebildet. Das trans-
mittierte Licht hat dann die Intensität I

$$I = \iint O(x,y) \cdot F(x,y)\,dxdy.$$

Wird als Filter ein Fourierhologramm des Objektes $o(x,y)$ mit einer
ebenen Referenzwelle verwendet,so kann ein Erkennungsvorgang mit der
in Abb. 1 gezeigten Anordnung eines kohärent-optischen Korrelators
erfolgen. Die Intensität der rekonstruierten Referenzwelle wird maximal, wenn das Referenzzeichen des Filters $F(x,y)$ das Objekt $O(x,y)$
selbst ist. Um damit ein Objekt aus einem festen Datensatz identifizieren zu können, muß die Filteranzahl gleich der Vielfalt der verschiedenen Objekte sein ("matched filtering").

Dieses Verfahren wurde weiterentwickelt, um die Anzahl der Filter-
schritte zu reduzieren. Wird der Erkennungsprozeß binär durchgeführt,
sind K = ldN Filter ausreichend [4] , wenn N Objekte zu identifizieren
sind. Jedem Objekt wird dann ein Intensitätscode I_{nk} zugeordnet.

$$I_{nk} = \iint O_n(x,y) \cdot F_k(x,y)\,dxdy \qquad \begin{aligned} n &= 1\ldots N \\ k &= 1\ldots K \end{aligned}$$

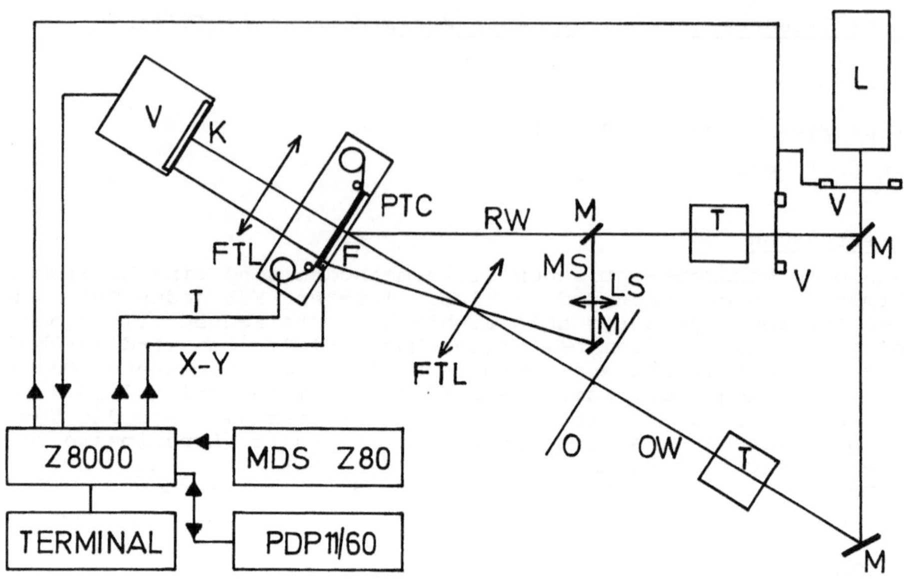

Abb. 1: Hybrider optisch-digitaler Korrelator
(RW: Referenzwelle, OW: Objektwelle, MS: Markierungsstrahl,
L: Laser, M: Spiegel und Strahlteiler, LS: Linse, FTL: Fou-
riertransformationslinse, T: Strahlaufweitung, V: Verschluß
PTC: Mikroprozessorgesteuerte Photothermoplastkamera (T:
Steuerung Filmtransport, x-y: Steuerung automatische Filter-
justierung), V: Vidicon, O: Objektebene, F: Filterebene,
K: Korrelationsebene)

Dabei ist jedes F_k k Objekten O_n angepaßt. I_{nk} wird dann die logische
1 zugeordnet, wenn O_n eine der Komponenten von F_k ist, ansonsten die
logische 0. Dieser Prozeß ist in mathematischer Betrachtungsweise eine
Skalarproduktbildung.

II. Optisch generierte Komponentenfilter

Bei dem hier beschriebenen Verfahren werden die Komponentenfilter ana-
log-optisch hergestellt. Dadurch unterscheidet sich das Verfahren von
der inköhärenten "Principal Component Filtering" Methode [4,5], bei
der die Filter digital berechnet werden.

Als optisches Komponentenfilter $F_k(x,y)$ wird das mittlere Fourierspek-
trum eines Objektsatzes

$$\sum_{i=1}^{I} O_i \qquad i \in n$$

gebildet. O_i sind die einzelnen Objekte. Durch Fouriertransformation
(Abb. 2) und anschließendes Umkopieren erhält man eine Amplituden-
transmission

$$t = \left| \sum_{i=1}^{I} O_i \right|^2 \ , \quad O = F\{o\}.$$

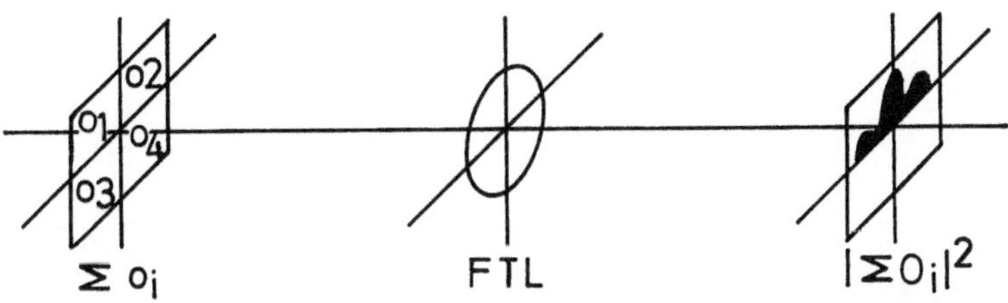

Abb. 2: 1. Fouriertransformation bei der Herstellung der Komponentenfilter.

t enthält die Interferenzterme (Kreuzkorrelationen) der komplexen
Größen O_i. Eine weitere Fouriertransformation (Abb. 3) liefert

$$F\{|O_i|^2\} = \sum_{i=1}^{I} O_i * \sum_{j=1}^{I} O_j$$

$$= \sum_{i=1}^{I} (O_i * O_i) + \sum_{\substack{i=1 \\ i \neq j}}^{I} \sum_{j=1}^{I} (O_j * O_j).$$

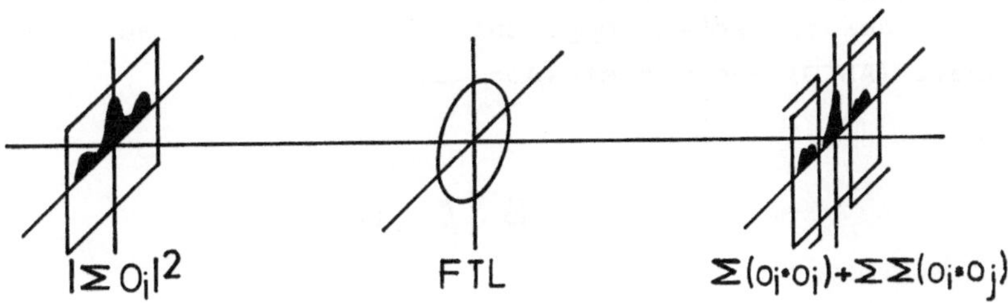

Abb. 3: 2. Fouriertransformation. Ausblendung der Kreuzkorrelations-
terme.

Wird der zweite Summand, der um den Abstand der Einzelobjekte gegen
den ersten verschoben ist, durch eine Maske abgedeckt, so ergibt
eine weitere Fouriertransformation (Abb. 4)

$$F\{\sum_{i=1}^{I} (O_i * O_i)\} = \sum_{i=1}^{I} [F\{O_i * O_i\}]$$

$$= \sum_{i=1}^{I} (|O_i|^2)$$

$$= F_{nk}(x,y).$$

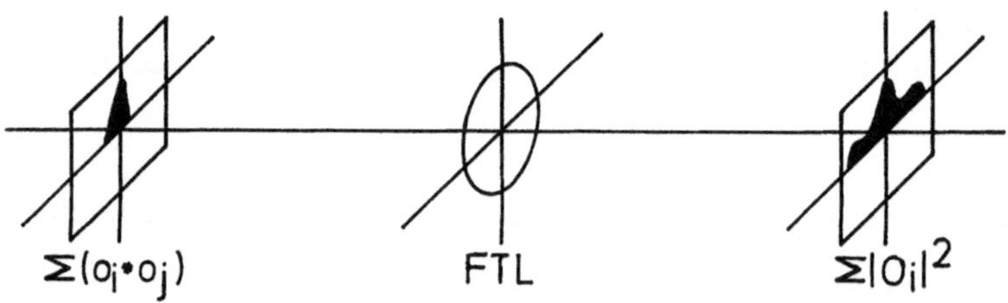

Abb. 4: 3. Fouriertransformation zur Komponentenfilterherstellung

Wird dieses Spektrum holographisch, d.h. hier mit ebener Referenzwelle
aufgenommen, so eignet es sich zur Filterung der Objekte O_i. Bei der
Korrelation mit jedem dieser Objekte ergibt sich ein Autokorrelations-
signal. Andere Objekte liefern Kreuzkorrelationssignale. Damit ist
eine binäre Objekterkennung möglich.

III. Experimentelle Ergebnisse

Die Methode der optischen Komponentenfilterung wird auf den einfachen
Zeichensatz (ABCD) angewendet (Abb. 5).

A B C D

Abb. 5: Zeichensatz

Ein Komponentenfilter ist den Buchstaben A und B angepaßt. Abb. 6a und
b zeigt die mit einem Vidicon aufgenommenen Korrelationssignale der
Buchstaben A und C. Die Intensitäten werden durch Auslesen der in

a)   b)

Abb. 6a und b: Mit dem Vidicon aufgenommene Korrelationssignale des
Buchstabens A (a) und C (b). Das Filter ist den Zeichen
A und B angepaßt.

Abb. 6a und b markierten Zeile gemessen. Ihre Intensitätsprofile sind
in Abb. 7a und b dargestellt. Man erkennt deutlich den Intensitätsun-

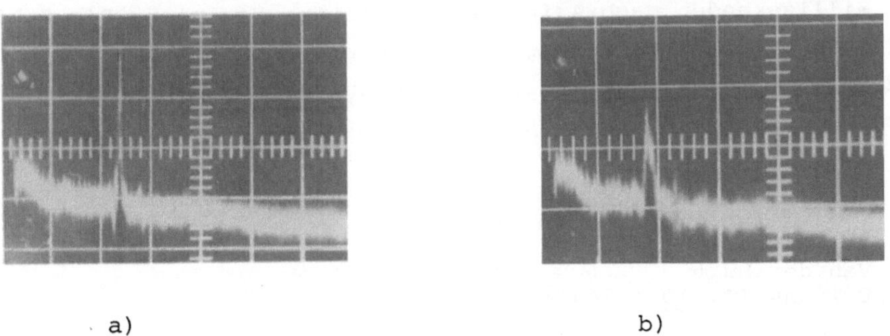

a)   b)

Abb. 7a und b: Intensitätsprofile der in Abb. 6 a und b markierten
Zeilen.

terschied zwischen Autokorrelation (A) und Kreuzkorrelation (C).
Abb. 8 zeigt die Intensitätsmessungen für das A-B-Filter. Es kann eindeutig eine Schwellenbedingung gesetzt werden. Bei größeren Objekt-
vielfalten, bzw. komplizierteren Strukturen, muß eine Intensitätscode-
optimierung erfolgen, d.h. die Objektsätze zur Filterherstellung
müssen so gewählt werden, daß die I_{nk}'s von Auto- und Kreuzkorrelation
möglichst weit differieren. Entsprechende Experimente befinden sich in
Vorbereitung.

IV. Diskussion

Nach den bisherigen experimentellen Ergebnissen läßt sich mit dem Kon-
zept der optischen Komponentenfilterung ein binärer Mustererkennungs-

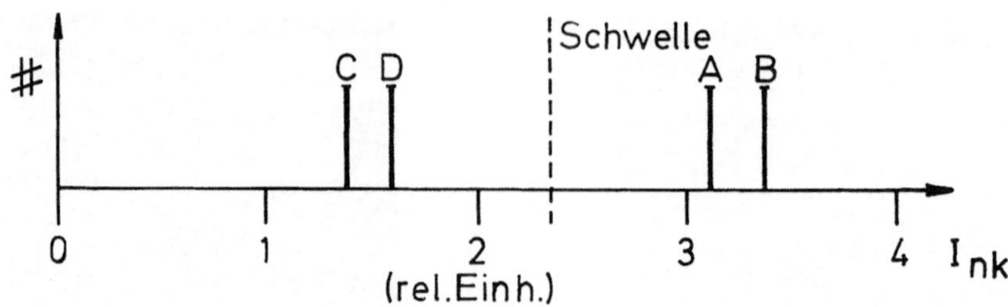

Abb. 8: Korrelationssignalintensitäten der Buchstaben A,B,C,D bei Verwendung des A-B-Filters.

prozeß durchführen. Die Nachteile durch die Kohärenz des Lichtes bei
dem hier beschriebenen Verfahren, speziell Justierprobleme beim Fil-
terwechsel, werden durch eine sich automatisch justierende Thermoplast-
kamera (siehe Abb. 1) beseitigt [6]. Das von dem Vidicon aufgenommene
Korrelationssignal (siehe Abb. 6a) wird durch mikroprozessorgesteuer-
tes Verschieben der Filmbühne optimiert. Der Erkennungsprozeß kann
ca. 20 Millisekunden nach Aufnahme des Filters beginnen. Die Zyklus-
zeit für den Filterherstellungs- und Erkennungsprozeß beträgt ca. 10
Sekunden. Damit eignet sich diese Filterungsmethode zum Einsatz innerhalb eines hybriden optisch-digitalen Prozessorsystems.

Literatur

[1] A. Van der Lugt
    IEEE Trans IT, 10 (1964) 139

[2] F. Merkle, H. Muuss, H. Stöckel
    Optik 49, (1977) 213

[3] F. Merkle, H. Muuss
    Optik 51 (1978) 189

[4] B. Braunecker, A.W. Lohmann
    Opt. Comm. 11 (1974) 141

[5] R. Hauck
    Informatik-Fachberichte 17 (1978) 45
    Springer-Verlag Berlin Heidelberg New York

[6] F. Merkle, T. Karte, J. Bille
    (Mikroprozessorgesteuerte photothermoplastische Filteraufzeichnung)
    wird veröffentlicht

EIN DIGITALES VIDEO-SYSTEM MIT EINEM MIKROPROZESSOR ZUR BILDANALYSE

B.Schöfer, J.Pipper, W.Heinrich

Universität - Gesamthochschule Siegen, Fachbereich Physik

Zusammenfassung

Unter Verwendung hochintegrierter elektronischer Bausteine wurde ein
preiswertes und leistungsfähiges digitales Video-System aufgebaut. Die
Bildanalyse erfolgt mit einem Mikroprozessor (M 6800). Eigenschaften
wie Position, Fläche, Umfang und Durchmesser von Bildobjekten, deren
Grauwert oberhalb einer vorgegebenen Schwelle liegt, werden mit einer
einfachen Software ermittelt.

Einleitung

Die Bildanalyse von Objekten, deren Grauwert sich vom Untergrund ab-
hebt, ist seit Jahren mit Geräten möglich, die mit fest verdrahteten
elektronischen Schaltungen arbeiten. Eigenschaften wie Position, Fläche, Umfang und Durchmesser von Bildobjekten können mit derartigen Apparaturen vermessen werden. Die Anwendung dieser Geräte in weiten Bereichen ist durch ihren Preis eingeschränkt. Durch die Entwicklung von
hochintegrierten elektronischen Bauelementen und von Mikroprozessoren
ist es möglich geworden, preiswerte digitale Videosysteme aufzubauen,
bei denen die Bildanalyse mit einer speziellen Software erfolgt. Derartige Systeme erreichen zwar nicht die hohen Bildverarbeitungsge-
schwindigkeiten, die mit fest verdrahteten Apparaturen möglich sind,
eröffnen aber andererseits, da sie frei programmierbar sind, die Möglichkeit, spezielle auf das Problem angepaßte Verfahren der Bildanalyse zu benutzen. Der Aufbau eines derartigen Gerätes und seine Erwei-
terungsmöglichkeiten werden hier dargestellt.

Aufbau des Systems

Bild 1 zeigt schematisch den Aufbau des hier beschriebenen Systems und
seine Verbindung mit einem größeren Rechnersystem. Kernstück für die
Bilddigitalisierung ist ein schneller Videodigitizer vom Typ TRW 1007
(1), der das am Eingang anstehende Videosignal, angestoßen durch einen
Konvertierungsimpuls, in 33 nsec/Bildpunkt digitalisiert. Der Grauwert, der dem Videosignal zu diesem Zeitpunkt entspricht, wird in
2^8 = 256 Stufen digitalisiert. Von diesen acht Bit werden zur Zeit
nur die vier höchsten Stellen der binären Zahl, also 16 Stufen des
Grauwertes, verarbeitet. Sie werden in einem Speicher (Typ 2114) abgelegt, der in Einheiten von 8 Bit adressierbar ist. Dazu werden je-

weils 2 x 4 Bit in einem Register gesammelt.

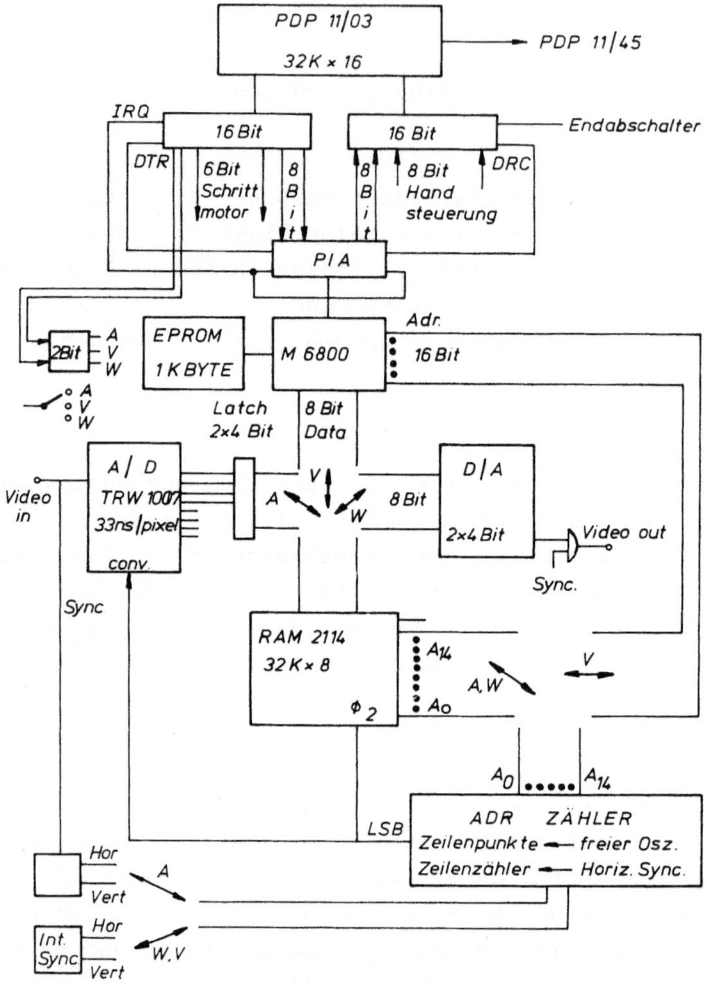

Bild 1: Schematischer Aufbau des Videosystems und Kopplung an
einen Prozeßrechner

Die zeitliche Zuordnung des Videosignals zu einzelnen Bildpunkten erfolgt durch einen Adressenzähler. Er enthält zwei Zähleinheiten, eine
für die Zeile des Videobildes und eine für den Bildpunkt innerhalb
einer Zeile. Durch das Vertikal-Synchron Signal des Videobildes werden beide Zähler initialisiert. Durch das Horizontal-Synchron Signal wird der Zeitenzähler angestoßen und der Bildpunktzähler initialisiert. Zwischen zwei Horizontal-Synchron Signalen werden einzelne

Zeilenpunkte durch einen freien Oszillator definiert. Die Frequenz des
Oszillators bestimmt die Anzahl der Bildpunkte pro Zeile. Wegen des
beschränkten Speichers sind dies zur Zeit 256 Punkte. Von jedem Halbbild der Videokamera werden 256 Zeilen digitalisiert. Das niedrigste
Bit (LSB) des Punktzählers gibt den Taktimpuls für den Speicher und
den Analog-Digital Wandler. Die Inhalte der Zähler zu diesen Zeitpunk-
ten definieren die Adresse von jeweils zwei aufeinanderfolgenden Bildpunkten im Speicher. Während der Aufnahme wird jedes Halbbild digitalisiert und der Inhalt des Speichers laufend überschrieben.

Die oben beschriebene Aufnahme (A) eines Bildes ist eine von drei möglichen Betriebsarten. Weitere Möglichkeiten sind Wiedergabe (W) und
Verarbeitung (V) des im Bildspeicher abgelegten Bildes. Zur Veränderung der Betriebsweise werden Adress- und Datenleitungen, wie es sym-
bolisch in Bild 1 angedeutet ist, mit Hilfe von Tri-State-Bausteinen
umgeschaltet. Die Wahl des gewünschten Betriebszustandes kann sowohl
manuell als auch rechnergesteuert über eine Datenleitung erfolgen.

Die Wiedergabe des im Speicher vorhandenen Bildes erfolgt mit Hilfe
der beschriebenen Adressierlogik. Für diesen Fall werden alle Synchronsignale intern erzeugt. Die Speicherinhalte von 8 Bit werden in
die Information von jeweils 2 Bildpunkten zerlegt und über einen Digi-
tal-Analog Wandler in ein analoges Videosignal umgewandelt. Nach Bei-
mischung der Synchronsignale kann das Bild auf einem Monitor betrachtet werden.

Die Verarbeitung (Betriebszustand V) der Bilder erfolgt über einen Mikroprozessor. Dies ist zur Zeit ein Motorola 6800 (2). Er hat einen
Adressraum von 2^{16} Bytes. Da neben dem Bildspeicher auch ein Programmspeicher vorhanden sein muß (1k EPROM), wurde, bedingt durch diesen
Baustein, der Bildspeicher zunächst auf 32 K Byte beschränkt. In ihm
werden 256 x 256 Bildpunkte mit 4 Bit Grauwerten abgespeichert. Der
Mikroprozessor kann über die Adressleitung auf jeden Bildpunkt im
Speicher zugreifen und den Bildinhalt mit einer speziellen Software
zur Bildanalyse abarbeiten. Über einen peripheren Interface Adapter
(PIA) ist er mit einem anderen Rechner, einer PDP 11/03 verbunden,
die ihrerseits an eine PDP 11/45 gekoppelt ist. Die PDP 11/03 kann
Daten, insbesondere auch ganze Bilder, mit dem Mikroprozessor austau-
schen. Zusätzlich steuert sie Schrittmotoren an, die das zu betrachten-
de Objekt unter der Videokamera verschieben können.

Bildanalyse

Vom Mikroprozessor können über verschiedene Programme Veränderungen
des Videobildes vorgenommen werden. Solche Veränderungen, die für jeden Bildpunkt erfolgen, sind:Verschieben der Helligkeit, Setzen von
Schwellen in der Helligkeit, Invertieren des Bildes sowie Austausch
eines ganzen Bildes mit der PDP 11/03. Programme zur Bildanalyse ge-
statten es, Objekte, die in ihrer Helligkeit über oder unter einer
vorgegebenen Schwelle liegen, zu erkennen und deren Flächen, Umfang
und Durchmesser sowie Schwerpunktskoordinaten zu bestimmen.

Das Gerät wird zur automatischen Vermessung der Spuren von Schwerionen
in Plastikfolien benutzt (3). Bild 2 zeigt das analoge Videobild von
zwei Spuren, die mit einem Mikroskop betrachtet werden.

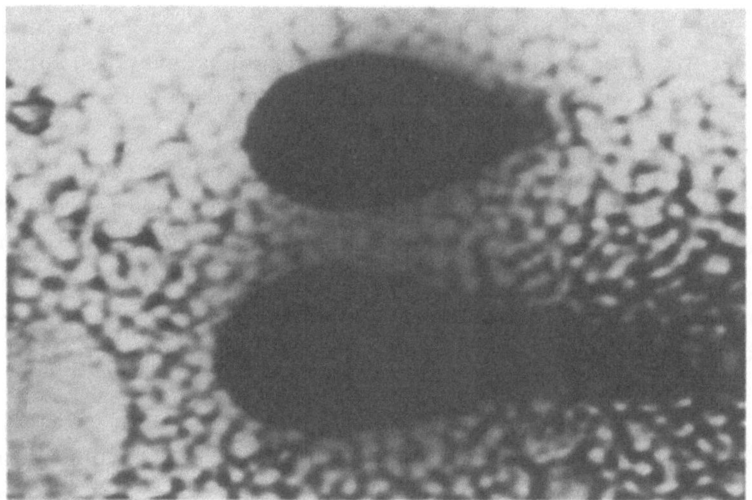

Bild 2: Videobild von Schwerionenspuren in einer Plastikfolie

Bild 3 zeigt das digitalisierte Bild nach der Bildanalyse. Als Spuren
erkannte Bildbereiche sind weiß eingekreist.

Die Genauigkeit mit der geometrische Größen von Objekten vermessen
werden können, wurde am Beispiel von Flächen untersucht. Durch mehr-
faches Digitalisieren des gleichen Videobildes konnten Mittelwerte
und Meßfehler der Flächen verschiedener Objekte bestimmt werden
(Bild 4). Der Fehler der Flächenmessung ist bedingt durch Randpunkte,
die bei aufeinanderfolgenden Messungen einmal dem Objekt zugeordnet
werden, ein anderes mal nicht. Die Anzahl solcher Randpunkte und damit der Fehler der Flächenmessung nimmt prozentual mit der wachsen-

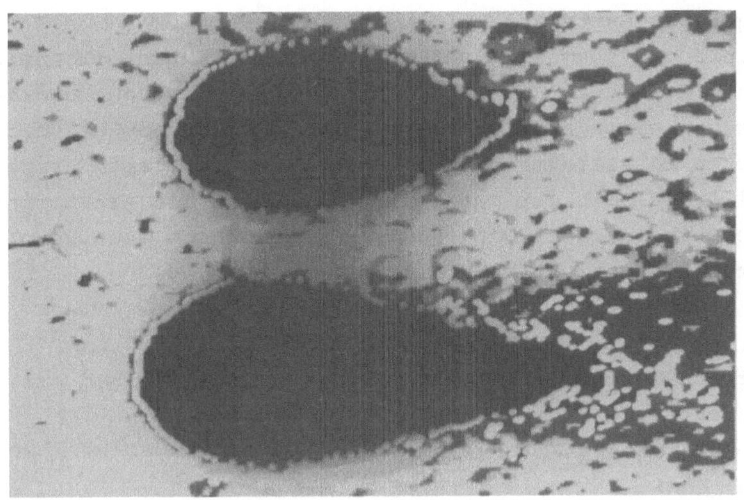

Bild 3: Die Information aus Bild 2 in digitalisierter Form, vom Mikroprozessor vermessene Flächen mit einem Grauwert oberhalb
einer Schwelle sind weiß umrandet

den Fläche ab. Dadurch gibt es eine obere Grenze für die Meßfehler,
die in Bild 4 durch die Kurve angedeutet ist.

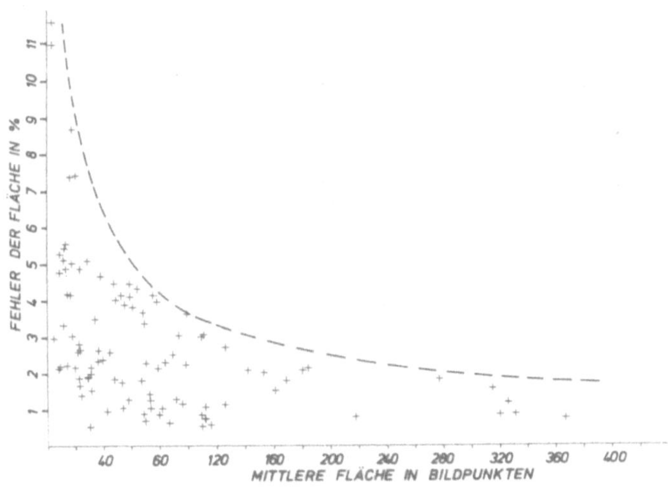

Bild 4: Prozentualer Fehler der Flächenmessung als Funktion der Fläche

Erweiterungen des Systems

Das beschriebene System wird zur Zeit erweitert. Der Bildspeicher wird auf 512 x 512 Bildpunkte mit 8 Bit Grauwerten ausgebaut und der Mikroprozessor gegen einen neueren Baustein (Motorola M 68000), der über einen größeren Adressraum verfügt, ausgetauscht. Diesem Prozessor, der auch schneller ist als der zur Zeit verwendete, wird ein umfangreicher Programmspeicher zur Verfügung gestellt, so daß er auch kompliziertere Programme zur Bildanalyse abarbeiten kann.

Literatur:

(1) Monolithic Video A/D Converter TDC 1007, TRW LSI Products, Redono Beach, California, USA

(2) MC 6800 Microcomputer: System-Design-Data, Motorola, Phoenix, Arizona, USA

(3) H.Drechsel, J.Pipper, R.Schucht, J.Beer, W.Heinrich, Automatische Bildanalyse zur Vermessung von Kernspuren in Plastik-Detektoren, dieser Tagungsbericht.

<u>BESTIMMUNG MORPHOLOGISCHER MERKMALE AN BIOLOGISCHEN</u>

<u>ZELLEN IN EINEM DURCHFLUSS-SYSTEM IN ECHTZEIT</u>

H. Becker

Fachbereich Physik, Universität Essen

Die Problemstellung ist es, biologische Zellen aufgrund ihrer morphologischen Merkmale schnell zu differenzieren, wie es z.B. bei der Krebsfrühdiagnostik (Pre-screening) gefordert wird, wo die schnelle Erfassung möglichst umfangreichen Materials unerlässlich ist.

Die Merkmalserfassung erfolgt am Fraunhoferschen Beugungsbild der Partikel, während sie in einem Durchflusskanal durch den beleuchtenden Laserstrahl strömen.

Formal werden die sog. optischen Momente, d.h. die Differenzialquotienten des Beugungsbilds an der optischen Achse, gemessen. In eindimensionaler Schreibweise:

sei $0(x)$ die (i.A. komplexe) Objekttransparenz,und

$$I(\nu) = \left| \int_{-\infty}^{+\infty} 0(x)e^{-2\pi i\nu x}dx \right|^2 \quad \text{der Intensitätsverlauf im Beugungsbild,}$$

schliesslich $c(s) = \int_{-\infty}^{+\infty} 0(x)0^*(s-x)dx = \int_{-\infty}^{+\infty} I(\nu)e^{2\pi i\nu s}ds$ die Autokorrelationsfunktion

AKF der Objekttransparenz. Dann gilt für das n-te Moment der AKF:

$$M_c(n) = \int_{-\infty}^{+\infty} s^n c(s)ds = \frac{1}{(-2\pi i)^n} \frac{\partial^n}{\partial\nu^n} \left. I(\nu) \right|_{\nu=0} .$$

Unter Verwendung der so definierten optischen Momente sowie anderer einfacher Messgrössen des Beugungsbilds lassen sich die gem. Tabelle 1 angegebenen morphologischen Merkmale der Partikel simultan bestimmen.

<u>Erläuterungen zu den Merkmalsbestimmungen:</u>

Zur Messung des *Trockensubstanzgehalts*, d.h. die im Zellvolumen enthaltenen Proteine, wird der gesamte von der Zelle gestreute Energiefluss gemessen, z.B. über einen Teilerwürfel.

Der *Zelldurchmesser* bzw. Zellvolumen bei sphärischen Teilchen läßt sich nach einem einfachen Verfahren bestimmen, wobei der Quotient von unter 2 Beugungswinkeln im Streufeld gemessenen Intensitäten bestimmt. Für einen weiten Brechungsindexbereich der Teilchen ist dieses Verfahren unabhängig von diesem. Da man bei geeignetem Strömungskanalquerschnitt durch die resultierenden Druckverhältnisse eine Vororientierung nichtsphärischer Zellen erhält, erhält man deren *Exzentrizität* durch Bestimmung des Merkmals "Durchmesser" in senkrecht aufeinanderstehenden Richtungen.

Ein Mass für die *Granularität* der Zelle ist die Abweichung der AKF von der einer homogen struktuierten Zelle gleicher Grösse und Form. Dazu mißt man die Äquivalentbreite des Beugungsbilds, d.h. die Intensität an der optischen Achse dividiert durch den gesamten gestreuten Energiefluss sowie den Teilchendurchmesser.

Bei unsymmetrischer Objekttransparenz $0(x)$ ist die AKF $c(s)$ hermitisch. Das Auftreten

Tabelle 1

MERKMAL von $O(x)$	EIGENSCHAFT DES OBJEKTS $O(x)$	EIGENSCHAFT DER AKF	MESSGRÖSSE IM BEUGUNGSBILD
Trockensubstanzgeh.	$\iint \lvert O(x,y)\rvert^2 dxdy$	$c(0,0)$ d.h. Höhe am Ursprung	$\iint I(\nu,\mu)d\nu d\mu = \iint \lvert O(x,y)\rvert^2 dxdy = c(0,0)$ (gesamter gestreuter Energiefluss)
Granularität	$\iint \lvert O_{gran}\rvert^2 < \iint \lvert O_{homog}\rvert^2$	Durchhängende Flanke $I(0)/c(0) < D$	$\sigma = \dfrac{I(0)}{c(0)\cdot D} = \dfrac{I(0)}{\int I(\nu)d\nu\cdot D}$ 1)Äquivalentbreite von $I(\nu)$ 2)Durchmesser D
Exzentrizität	D_x/D_y	Ungleiche Äquivalentbreite der AKF in x- und y-Richtungen.	$M_c(0,2)/M_c(2,0)$ Messung des 2. Moments der AKF,d.i. die Krümmung von $I(\nu,\mu)\big\rvert_{\nu=\mu=0}$
Durchmesser	D	Ausdehnung	Messung der gestreuten Intensität in 2 Punkten.(nach Hodkinson /5/) $I(\nu_1,0)$ und $I(\nu_2,0)$
Asymmetrie		Imaginärteil der AKF $\neq 0$	Asymmetrie von $O(x) \Longrightarrow$ Asymmetrie von $I(\nu,\mu)$. (Bei symmetrischem $O(x)$ ist die AKF und damit auch ihre FT,$I(\nu,\mu)$,reell und symmetrisch.)
Zellgrobstruktur		2.Moment von $O(x)$ $M_f(2,0)$ bzw. $M_f(0,2)$	Wie bei *Exzentrizität*,zusätzlich $I(0)$.

eines Imaginärteils und damit eine Asymmetrie des Beugungsbilds ist ein Maß für die *Asymmetrie* der Partikel. Messgrösse sind ungerade Momente, d.h. ungerade Differentialquotienten des Beugungsbilds an der optischen Achse.

Eine *Zellgrobstruktur*, z.B. Größe, Lage oder Fragmentierung eines Kerns, läßt sich aus dem normierten 2. Moment der AKF bestimmen $M_C(2)/M_C(o)$,. welches, wie man zeigen kann, gerade das 2. Moment der Objektstruktur $M_f(2)$ ist. Gemessen werden der 2. Differentialquotient und die Intensität am Ursprung.

Experimente:

Exemplarisch sei dies für 2 Merkmale dargestellt; in einem Durchflussaufbau wurden an sphärischen Eichteilchen, deren Brechungsindex vom Durchmesser abhängt, in einem Grössenbereich von 1o bis 16o µm der Durchmesser und der Trockensubstanzgehalt bestimmt. Die Auswertung geschah in Echtzeit durch den an die Detektorelektronik angeschlossenen Rechner. Der Durchmesser dieser Objekte wurde auf ± 3% genau bestimmt (Darstellung s. Fig.1. Aufgetragen ist der im Durchfluss gemessene über dem im Mikroskop bestimmten Durchmesser). Die Standardabweichung bei der Bestimmung des Trockensubstanzgehalts lag bei ± 1o%. In Fig. 2 sind über dem gleichzeitig bestimmten Teilchendurchmesser der im Interferenzmikroskop gemessene Brechungsindex sowie der im Durchfluß gemessene Wert des pro Partikelvolumeneinheit gestreuten Energieflusses, d.h. Trockensubstanzgehalt pro Partikelvolumen, welches ja dem Brechungsindex entspricht, aufgetragen.

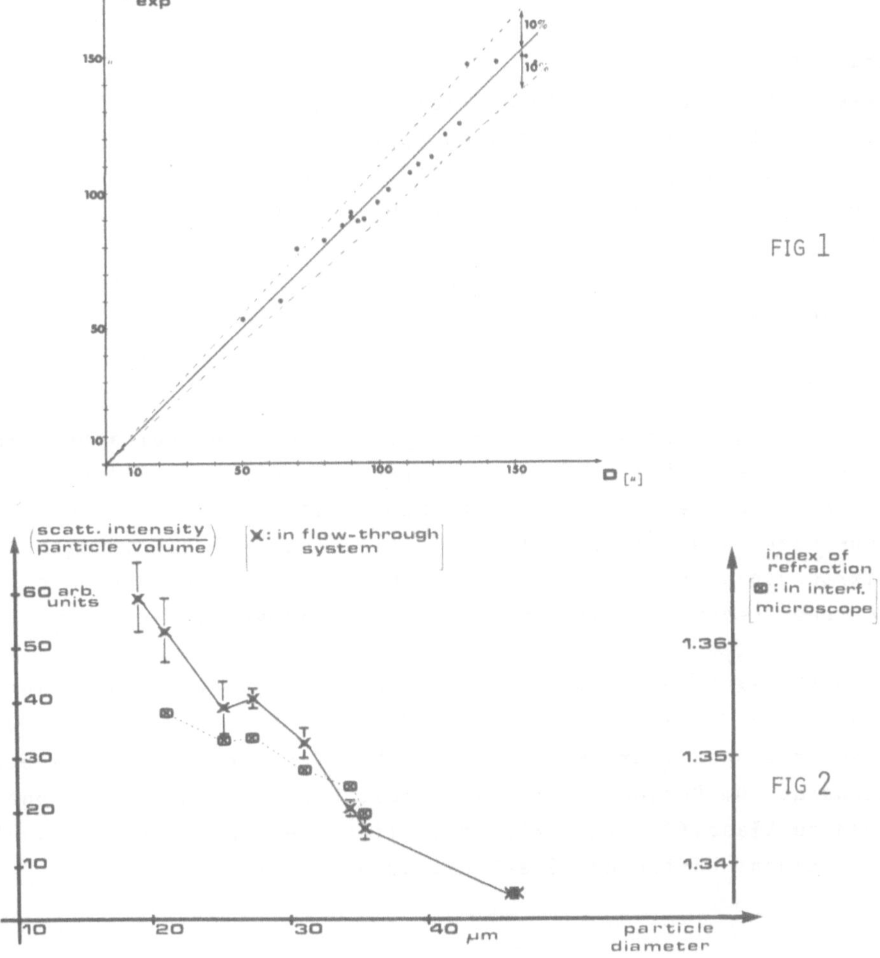

ERMITTLUNG VON RICHTUNGSFELDERN IN TEILCHENVERTEILUNGEN DURCH OPTISCHE RAUMFREQUENZANALYSE

R. Butt
Drittes Phys. Institut
Universität Göttingen
Bürgerstr. 42
D-3400 Göttingen

K. Hinsch
Fachbereich IV
Universität Oldenburg
Postfach 2503
D-2900 Oldenburg

Zusammenfassung

An computergezeichneten Modellvorlagen wird gezeigt, daß sich eine
Orientierungsanalyse einer Anordnung von vielen gleichartigen Objekten mit ortsabhängiger Richtungsverteilung im Raumfrequenzbereich
durchführen läßt. Die erforderliche zweidimensionale Fouriertransformation des Bildes erfolgt kohärent-optisch.

Abstract

Determination of directional fields in particle distributions by analysis of the optically obtained spatial frequency spectrum.
The average direction of orientation as a function of position in an
arrangement of many identical computer-drawn patterns is determined
by analyzing the spatial frequency spectrum. The necessary two-dimensional Fourier transformation of the image is implemented optically.
Applications of interest are named.

1. Einleitung

Eine häufige Aufgabe der Bildanalyse ist es, aus Aufnahmen vieler in
einer Ebene verteilter Objekte deren mittlere Orientierungsrichtung
als Funktion des Ortes zu bestimmen. Beispiele dafür sind: Elektrische oder magnetische Partikel in Feldern, Teilchen in einer Strömung,
Mikroorganismen in einem Lebensraum mit ortsabhängigen Umweltbedingun-
gen oder Lebewesen mit ausgeprägtem Schwarmverhalten.

Die Orientierung der Objekte in einer Bildvorlage soll aus deren
Raumfrequenzspektrum bestimmt werden, das sich auf einfache Weise optisch gewinnen läßt. Bisher wurden Raumfrequenzanalysen hauptsächlich
verwandt, um Periodizitäten in Strukturen zu erkennen |1| oder Teil-
chen zu klassifizieren |2|. Im vorliegenden Fall werden wesentlich
zwei Eigenschaften des Spektrums ausgenutzt:

a) Die Intensität im Raumfrequenzspektrum eines Objektes ist von dessen Ort in der Vorlage unabhängig, dieser hat nur Einfluß auf die Phase der Lichtverteilung im Spektrum, so daß die Überlagerung der Spektren von gleichen Objekten, die an verschiedenen Stellen sind, im Spektrum eine bestimmte Modulation hervorruft. Bei statistisch verteilter Position der Objekte ist dies als Granulation sichtbar.

b) Die Drehung des Objektes in der Vorlagenebene ruft eine entsprechende Drehung seines Spektrums hervor. Unterschiedliche Orientierung in der Vorlage überträgt sich also direkt auf das Spektrum.

Aus diesen Eigenschaften folgt, daß das Spektrum einer zufälligen Anordnung von unterschiedlich orientierten Einzelobjekten eine Richtungsmittelung der Einzelspektren darstellt, woraus sich unter Umständen die mittlere Richtung und die Streuung gewinnen lassen. Um ortsabhängige Richtungsverteilungen zu bestimmen, wird die Vorlage in geeignete Teilbilder zerlegt und dann werden deren Spektren betrachtet. Die mittlere Orientierung im Bildausschnitt wird z. B. durch eine sichtbare Vorzugsrichtung im Spektrum angezeigt. Für die quantitative Auswertung wird die Winkelabhängigkeit des Spektrums in einem geeigneten Raumfrequenzbereich gemessen und durch Korrelation mit einer Referenzkurve der mittlere Orientierungswinkel bestimmt. Die Leistungsfähigkeit der Methode wird an Modellobjekten untersucht.

2. Versuchsaufbau

Die Modellvorlagen sind fotografische Negative mit hellen Objekten auf dunklem Untergrund, deren Originalbilder von einem computergesteuerten Plotter hergestellt wurden. Sie werden mit parallelem kohärenten Licht beleuchtet, so daß in der Brennebene einer Linse das Raumfrequenzspektrum (Beugungsbild) beobachtet werden kann (Abb. 1).

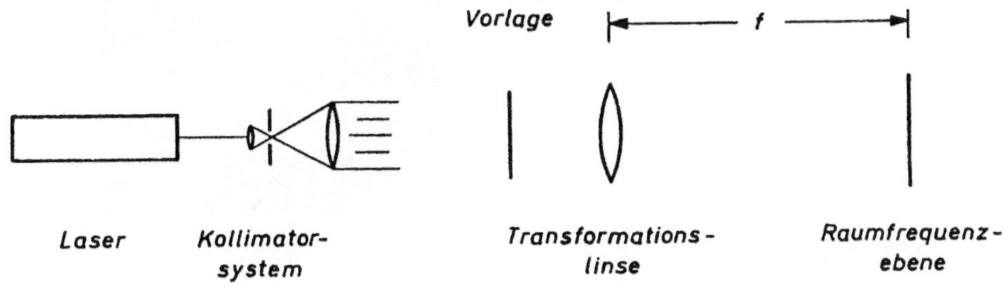

Abb. 1: Aufbau zur optischen Fouriertransformation

Die Vorlagen haben eine Größe von 18 mm x 18 mm und enthalten eine große Anzahl statistisch verteilter Objekte, deren Orientierung sich, der Einfachheit halber, nur mit einer Ortskoordinate ändert. Mit einer verschiebbaren Spaltblende von 2 mm Breite werden nacheinander verschiedene parallele Streifen der Vorlage beleuchtet, so daß jeweils Bereiche mit unterschiedlicher Orientierung erfaßt werden. Qualitativ lassen sich meist schon bei visueller oder fotografischer Beobachtung des Beugungsbildes Aussagen über die mittlere Orientierung machen, wenn die Blende langsam über die Vorlage geschoben wird.

Für die quantitative Auswertung wird die Winkelabhängigkeit des Spektrums auf einem Kreis um den Koordinatenursprung in der Raumfrequenzebene (Schnittpunkt der optischen Achse) mit einer Fotodiode gewonnen. Um Probleme bei der Justierung des Abtastkreises zu vermeiden, steht die Diode während der Messung fest und es wird die Vorlage mit dem von der Blende freigegebenen Bildausschnitt von einem Schrittmotor gedreht, so daß sich das Spektrum langsam an der Fotodiode vorbeidreht. Als Abtastöffnung vor der Diode wurde ein radialer Spalt von 2 mm Länge und ca. 0.3 mm Breite bei einer Linsenbrennweite von 500 mm gewählt, um das kohärente Rauschen etwas zu glätten. Meßprozeß und Datenaufzeichnung wurden weitgehend automatisiert.

3. Modellobjekte und Spektren

Als Testobjekt wird ein Pfeil in Form eines spitzwinkligen Dreiecks gewählt. Abb. 2a zeigt einen Ausschnitt aus dem Originalbild für eine solche Vorlage mit örtlich statistisch verteilten aber ausgerichteten Pfeilen. Die Vorlage als verkleinertes Negativ dieses Bildes enthält

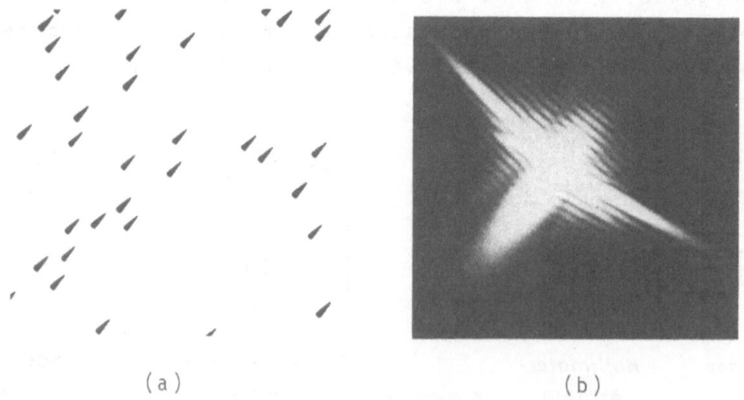

(a) (b)

Abb. 2: (a) Originalbild einer Modellvorlage mit ausgerichteten Pfeilen (Ausschnitt), (b) zugehöriges Raumfrequenzspektrum

bis zu 600 Einzelobjekte. Das zugehörige Raumfrequenzspektrum ist in
Abb. 2b zu sehen. Das Testobjekt (der Pfeil) zeigt eine eindeutige
Vorzugsrichtung, wodurch auch Objekte, die um 180° gedreht sind, unterschieden werden können. Dies wäre z. B. nicht der Fall bei einem
rechteckigen Objekt. Um diese Unterscheidung auch im Spektrum durchführen zu können und um generell eine gute Winkelbestimmung zu ermöglichen, muß der Raumfrequenzbereich (d. h. der Abstand von der optischen Achse im Spektrum), bei dem die Analyse durchgeführt wird, sehr
sorgfältig gewählt werden. Wie in Abb. 2b zu sehen ist, sollte der
Abstand auf diesem Bild mindestens 4 mm sein, da sich erst hier der
Einfluß der im spitzen Winkel zueinander stehenden Beugungskanten des
Pfeils zeigt. Bei zu großem
Abstand besteht die Gefahr,
daß die Lichtintensität zu niedrig und das Signal zu stark
verrauscht wird. Für die Messungen wurde der Bereich von 4
bis 6 mm gewählt. Abb. 3 zeigt
die Lichtintensitätsverteilung
(0° liegt in Richtung nach
rechts unten und der Winkel
läuft im Uhrzeigersinn), die
auch als Referenzkurve für die
Auswertung anderer Vorlagen
eingesetzt wurde.

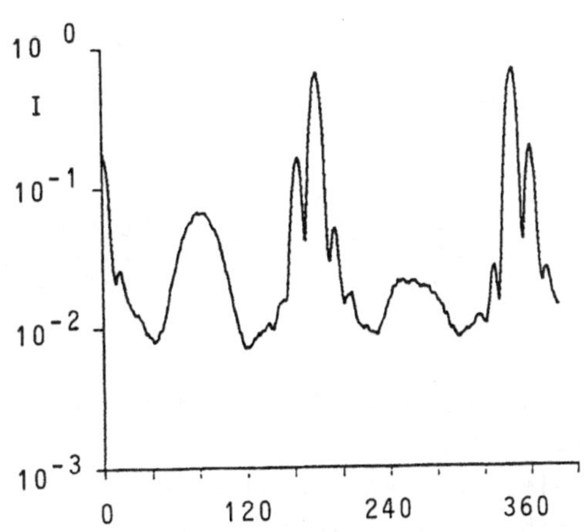

Abb. 3: Intensität I als Funktion
des Winkels im Spektrum von Abb. 2b
(Abstand vom Zentrum 6.5 mm)

3.1 Vorlagen mit Bereichen entgegengesetzter Orientierung

Untersucht wurde eine Vorlage mit Modellobjekten, die Bereiche entgegengesetzter Orientierung enthält (z. B. als Muster für Bereiche unterschiedlicher Magnetisierung). Abb. 4a zeigt einen horizontalen Ausschnitt aus dem Originalbild. Erst nach längerer Betrachtung erkennt
das Auge darin die Gebiete mit wechselnder Orientierung. Die Abbildung
zeigt außerdem die Lage der 18 senkrechten Teilbilder (Spalte), in die
die Vorlage für die Auswertung zerlegt wurde, indem die Abtastblende
zur Auswertung in die jeweilige Position 1 bis 18 gebracht wurde.

Abb. 4b zeigt Spektrum, Helligkeitsverteilung und Korrelationskurve der Musteranordnung für die Teilbilder 7,8 und 9. Während Bild 7

2 4 6 8 10 12 14 16 18

1 3 5 7 9 11 13 15 17

Abb. 4a: Horizontaler Ausschnitt aus dem Originalbild für eine Vorlage mit Bereichen entgegengesetzter Orientierung. Angegeben
sind auch die Positionen der senkrechten Spaltblende (tat-
sächliche Breite 2 mm) bei der Richtungsauswertung.

vollkommen einen Bereich mit nach oben, Bild 9 einen Bereich mit nach
unten weisenden Pfeilen enthält, umfaßt Bild 8 beide Orientierungen
in gleicher Anzahl. Dies ist an den Spektren und Helligkeitskurven gut
zu sehen. Zur quantitativen Auswertung wurden die jeweiligen Hellig-
keitsverteilungen mit der Standardverteilung aus Abb. 3 korreliert
und die Lage des (oder der) Korrelationsmaximums zur Richtungsidenti-
fizierung herangezogen. Die entsprechenden Korrelationskurven zeigt
die Abbildung ebenfalls, woraus die Richtungen gut zu entnehmen sind.

3.2 Vorlagen mit ortsabhängigen stetigen Winkeländerungen

In der Modellvorlage ändert sich der Orientierungswinkel des Pfeils
proportional zur horizontalen Koordinate so, daß über der gesamten
Bildbreite eine Winkeldrehung von 0° bis 360° erfolgt. Das verwendete
Bild zeigt Abb. 5a. Die Winkeländerung ist in diesem Fall schon deutlich zu erkennen und führt zu einem Eindruck von Stromlinien. Schiebt
man die Schlitzblende von 2 mm Breite über die Vorlage von 18 mm Ge-
samtbreite, so ist die Richtung der Pfeile in dem jeweils ausgeleuch-
teten Teilbild über einen Winkelbereich von 40° gleichverteilt. Das
Spektrum ist daher etwas verschmiert, läßt aber eine mittlere Richtung
erkennen. Wenn die Blende langsam über die Vorlage geschoben wird, so

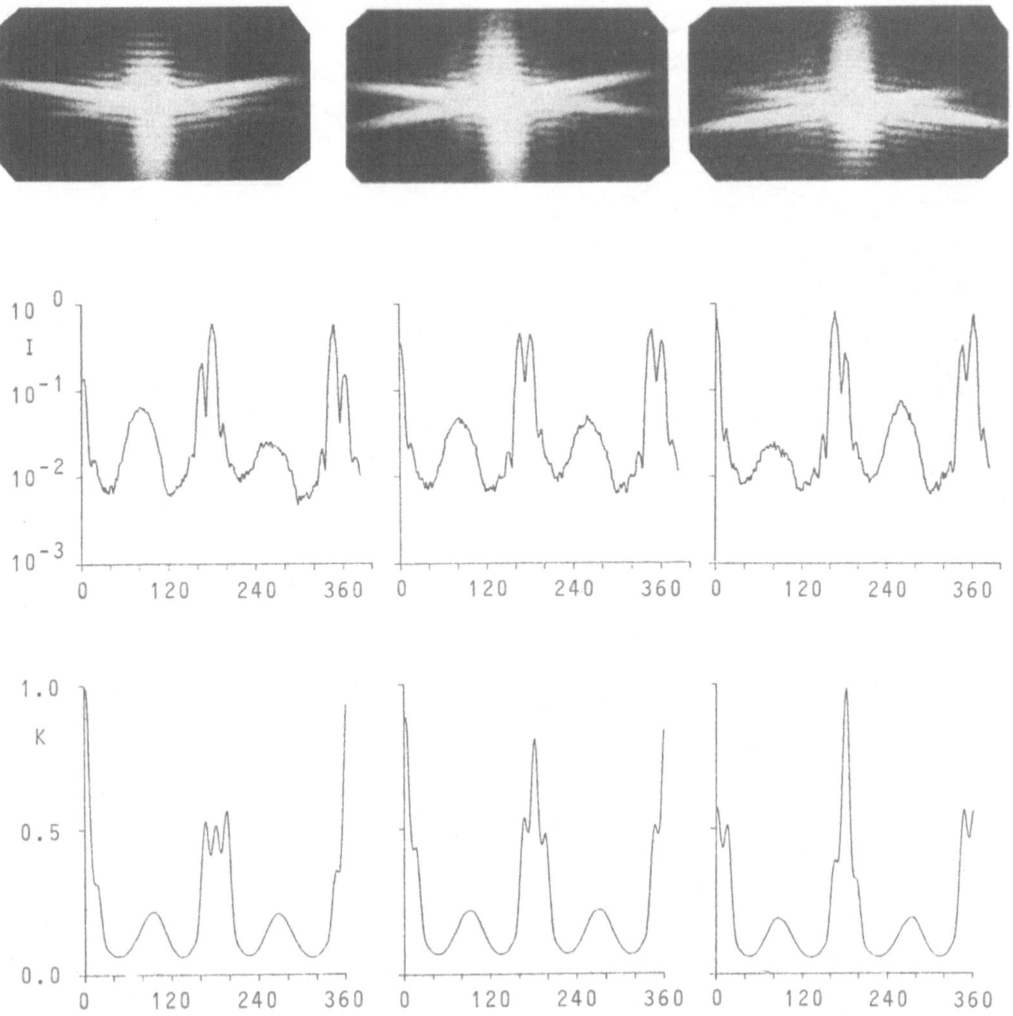

Abb. 4b: Spektren, Intensitätskurven I und Korrelationsfunktionen K
für die Teilbilder 7 (links), 8 (Mitte) und 9 (rechts) aus
Abb. 4a. (0⁰ weist hier in die positive x-Richtung, der Winkel läuft im Uhrzeigersinn um)

dreht sich das Spektrum entsprechend um insgesamt 360°. In Abb. 5b
sind die Spektren von 9 aneinander anschließenden Teilbildern (senkrechte Streifen), die zusammen das ganze Bild überdecken, dargestellt.

Die Spektren aller Teilbilder wurden wieder abgetastet und mit der
bei fester Orientierung gewonnenen Vergleichskurve (Abb. 3) korreliert.
Zwei Beispiele zeigt Abb. 6: Die Meßkurven (a) zeigen wegen der Rich-

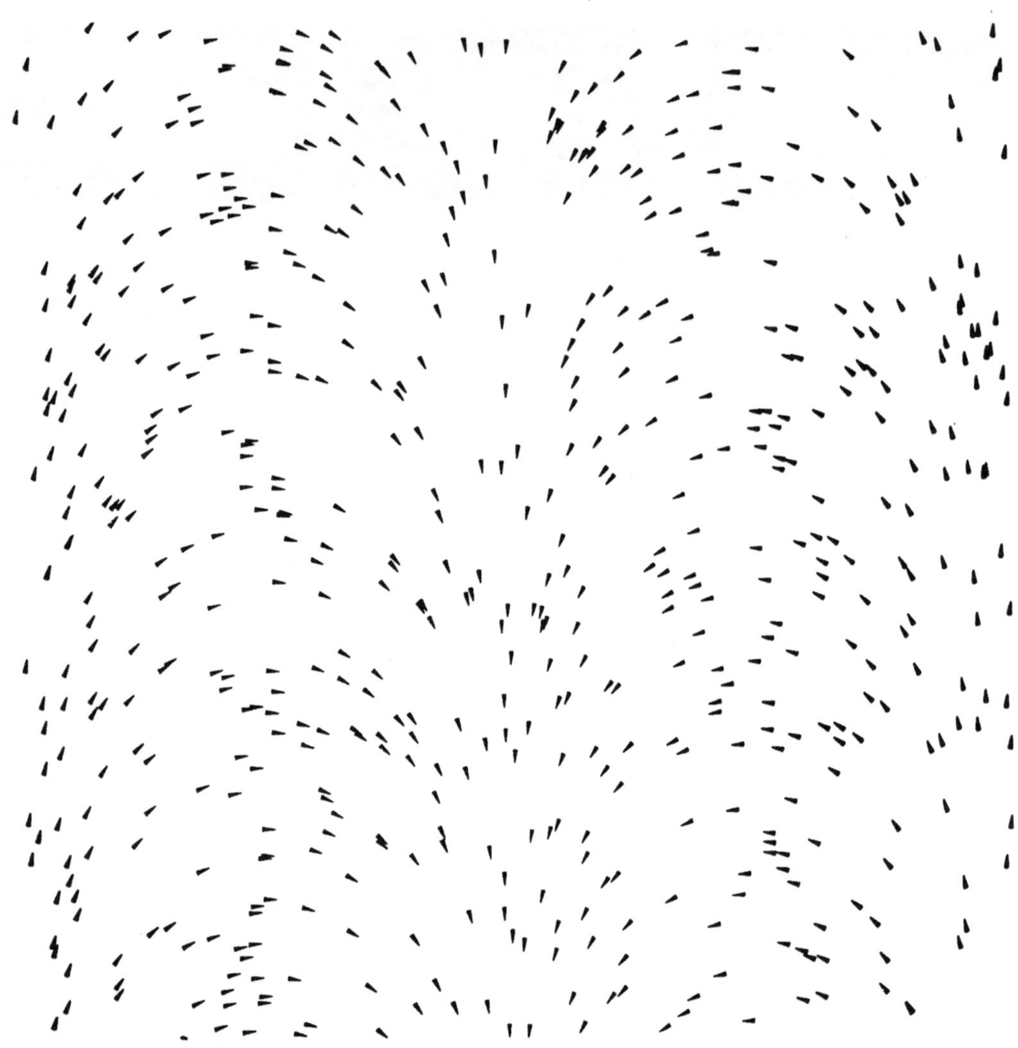

Abb. 5a: Originalbild für eine Vorlage, in der die Orientierungsrichtung der Pfeile linear mit der x-Koordinate von 0⁰ am linken
auf 360⁰ am rechten Bildrand anwächst. Lage der Auswertspal-
te wie in Abb. 4a.

tungsstreuung nicht die ausgeprägten Maxima der Referenzkurve und sind
außerdem wegen der zufälligen Verteilung der relativ wenigen Objekte
im Teilbild (nur ca. 70) stärker verrauscht. Die Korrelation (b) liefert ungefähr die richtigen Mittelwerte für die Richtung der Pfeile;
dadurch, daß die Maxima kleiner werden, fällt die Entscheidung aber
schwerer, wie besonders deutlich beim 6. Teilbild wird, für das zwei
etwa gleich große Spitzen auftreten.

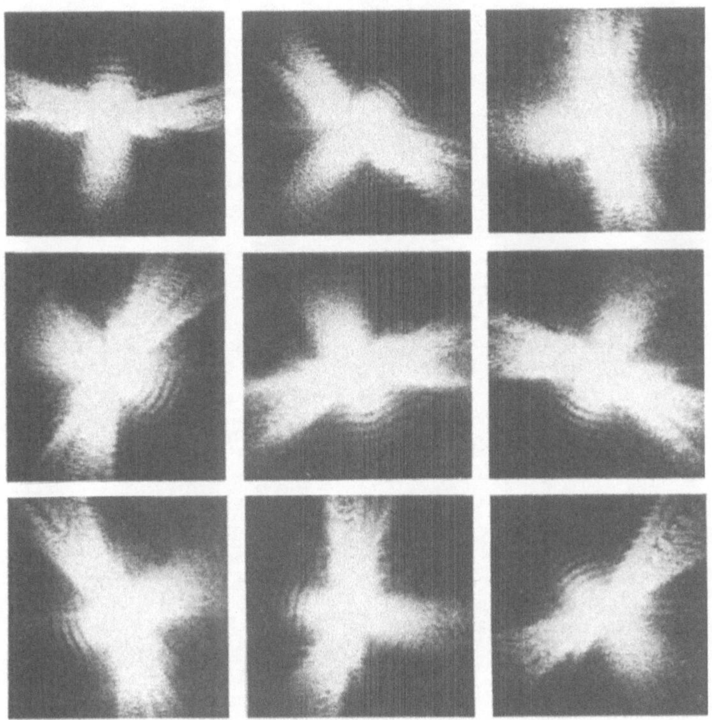

Abb. 5b: Spektren von neun Teilbildern (senkrechte Spalte 1,3 usw. aus
         Abb. 4a) der Vorlage aus Abb. 5a. Es wird jeweils ein Winkel-
         bereich von 40° erfaßt.

Das Spektrum einer Vergleichsvorlage, deren Pfeile nicht exakt ausgerichtet sind, sondern die gleiche Streuung haben, wie in den Teilbildern, sollte eine bessere Referenzkurve liefern und wegen der größeren
Ähnlichkeit mit den Meßkurven besser korrelieren. Dies bestätigen die
Korrelationskurven aus Abb. 6c, in denen wieder eindeutige Spitzen
auftreten, die auch die gesuchten Richtungsmittelwerte genauer wieder-
geben. Die Verwendung einer solchen Referenzkurve setzt aber eine ge-
wisse Kenntnis über die auszuwertende Vorlage voraus, indem die erwar-
tete Richtungsstreuung in den Teilbildern benutzt wird. Ist dies nicht
der Fall, kann eine Serie von Korrelationen mit Referenzkurven von
Bildern mit unterschiedlich großer Streuung eine Aussage über die
Richtungsstreuung im Teilbild liefern.

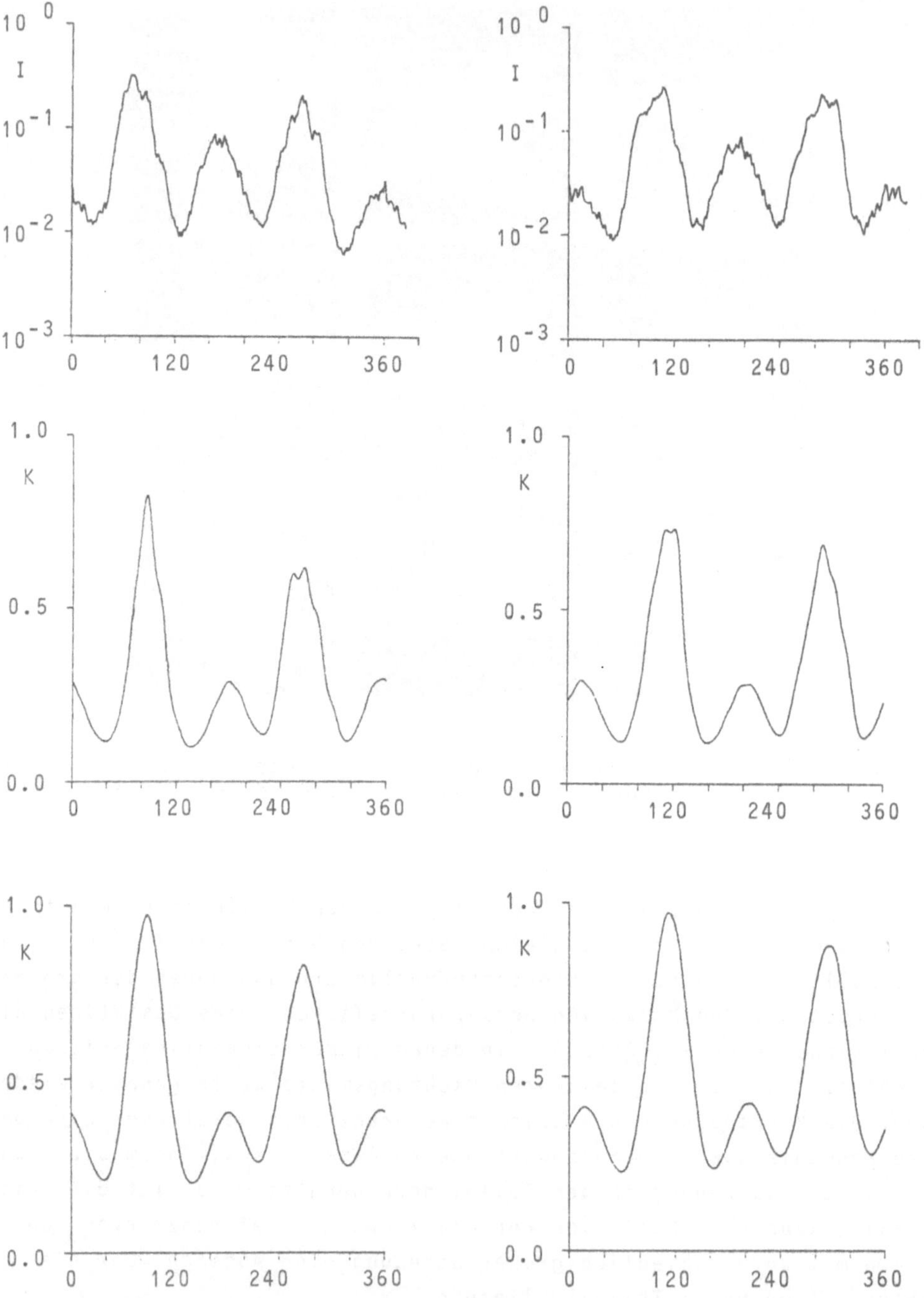

Abb. 6: Meßkurven (oben), Korrelationsfunktionen mit der Referenzkurve von Abb. 3 (Mitte) und Korrelationsfunktionen mit einer
Referenzkurve von 40° Winkelstreuung (unten) für die Teilbilder 5 (links) und 6 (rechts) der Vorlage Abb. 5a.

4. Diskussion

Es wurde an Modellvorlagen gezeigt, daß sich eine Orientierungsanalyse von vielen gleichartigen Objekten mit ortsabhängiger Richtungsverteilung gut im Raumfrequenzbereich durchführen läßt. Durch die optische Implementierung der zweidimensionalen Fouriertransformation entsteht ein Verfahren, bei dem der Aufwand unabhängig von der Anzahl der Objekte ist. Dadurch wird es anderen Analysemethoden überlegen. Ein Test der Methode an realen Objektverteilungen im Zusammenhang mit Untersuchungen zum Schwarmverhalten von Organismen ist in Vorbereitung.

Literatur

1   H. Lipson (Ed.): Optical Transforms, Academic Press, London, 1972.
2   R. Butt, K. Hinsch: Determination of size distributions of small objects by optical Fourier transformation. SPIE Proc. 210, Bellingham, 1980 (erscheint demnächst).

VERLUSTLOSE STRAHLUNGSLEISTUNGSMESSER

G. Busse

Zentrale Wissenschaftliche Einrichtung Physik
Hochschule der Bundeswehr München
8014 Neubiberg, Germany F. R.

Zusammenfassung: Die Ausnutzung des optoakustischen Effekts an optischen Komponenten im Strahlengang einer Lichtquelle mit modulierter Emission ermöglicht eine Überwachung der Strahlungsleistung ohne zusätzliche Komponenten.

Der Einsatz von Lichtquellen z.B. für Spektroskopie oder Abbildungen erfordert eine Überwachung der Strahlungsleistung. Hierzu werden üblicherweise Detektoren verwendet, die die gesamte einfallende Strahlung absorbieren. Ein solcher Detektor wird dann entweder während der Arbeiten z.B. an einem Laser zeitweilig in den Strahl geschwenkt (gestricheltes Rechteck in Abb. 1a), oder es wird mit einem teilreflektierenden Spiegel ein Bruchteil der Leistung ständig abgezweigt und auf einen solchen Detektor D gelenkt, wie ebenfalls in Abb. 1a gezeigt ist. Die erste Möglichkeit hat den Nachteil, daß man entweder mit dem Laserstrahl arbeiten oder seine Leistung messen kann; im zweiten Fall schließen sich diese beiden Vorgänge zwar nicht aus, so daß man ständig die Laserleistung überwachen kann, aber es muß eine zusätzliche Komponente in den Strahl gebracht werden,die seinen Verlauf beeinflußt, prinzipiell einen Leistungsverlust bewirkt und zudem eine Justierung erfordert.

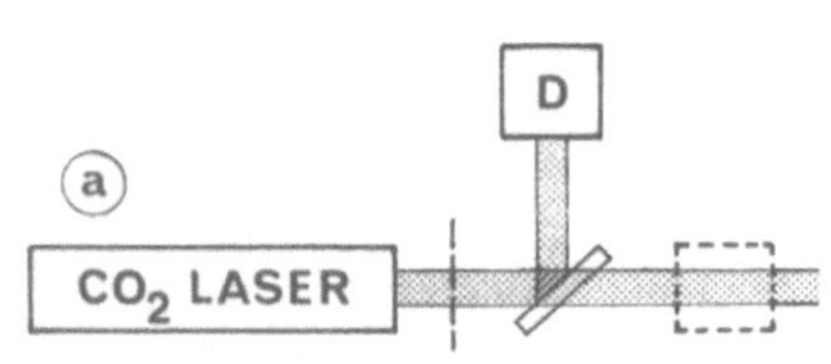

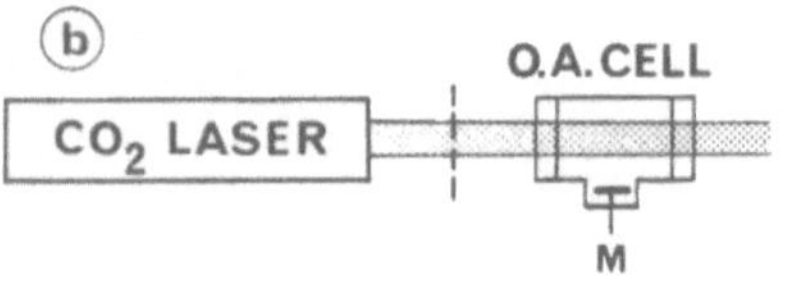

Abb. 1 /3/

1. Leistungsüberwachung mit dem optoakustischen Effekt.

Wünschenswert wäre ein Gerät, das den Strahlverlauf überhaupt nicht
stört und das die einfallende Strahlung zwar anzeigt, sie aber vollständig durchläßt.
Eine optoakustische Zelle - in diesem Fall ein mit einem absorptions-
freien Gas gefüllter Hohlzylinder, der an seinen beiden Stirnseiten mit
transparenten Fenstern dicht abgeschlossen ist - kommt dieser Vorstel-
lung nahe: Ein Laserstrahl durchquert diese Zelle, ohne in seinem Verlauf wesentlich beeinflußt zu werden (Abb. 1b). Die geringen nicht
vermeidbaren Absorptionsverluste in den Fenstern bewirken bei modulierter Strahlung(in Abb. 1 ist der Modulator durch die senkrechte gestrichelte Linie angedeutet) eine periodische Erwärmung des Fenstermateri-
als. Diese läßt sich dann als Druckmodulation des Füllgases mit einem
Mikrofon M nachweisen, das mit dem Hohlzylinder verbunden ist /1,2/.

2. Messbeispiele.

Messungen an einer Anordnung wie in
Abb. 1b /3/ ergaben bei 10 W Laserleistung den in Abb. 2 gezeigten Zusammenhang zwischen Modulationsfrequenz, Mikrofonsignal (a) und Rauschen
(b).Mit zunehmender Frequenz nimmt die
Signalamplitude ab /4/.Das beste Sig-
nal- Rausch- Verhältnis ist etwa
3×10^3 bei 1 Hz Bandbreite und 100 Hz
Modulationsfrequenz.Es wurde ein sehr
einfaches Kondensatormikrofon verwen-
det.Die Signalhöhe im mV- Bereich ist
sogar mit einfachen Geräten meßbar.

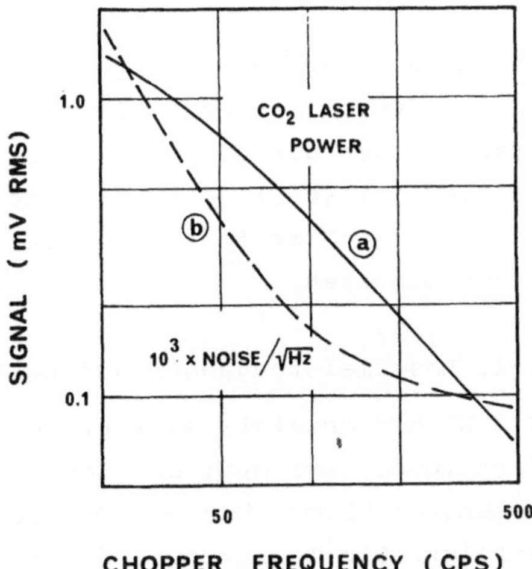

Abb. 2

2.1. Leistungsüberwachung mit integrierter Zelle.

Bei der Anordnung in Abb. 1b muß die Information, die der gut durch-
lässige Detektor liefert, prinzipiell mit einem wenn auch sehr geringen
Leistungsverlust durch die Absorption der Zellenfenster bezahlt werden.
Dieser läßt sich aber vermindern oder sogar ganz eliminieren, wenn Kom-

ponenten, die ohnehin im Strahl vorhanden sind, als Zellenfenster verwendet und die an ihnen auftretenden Verluste zur Leistungsüberwachung ausgenutzt werden können. Das ist in Abb. 3 am Beispiel eines Ferninfrarotlasers gezeigt, dessen Ausgangsleistung moduliert ist: Der beugungsbedingt divergierende Strahl muß von einer Linse gebündelt werden. Verbindet man sie durch ein Rohr mit dem Laser, so erhält man eine optoakustische Zelle, die wegen des Absorptionsverlustes in der Linse ein leistungsproportionales Signal liefert, ohne daß für diese Information zusätzliche Leistung verlorengeht. Die Anordnung ist daher ein verlustloser Strahlungsleistungsmesser /3,5/. In Abb. 3 ist auch eine Anwendung dieses Detektors dargestellt: Bei Absorptionsmessungen können die Leistungen I_o vor der Probe (SPL)

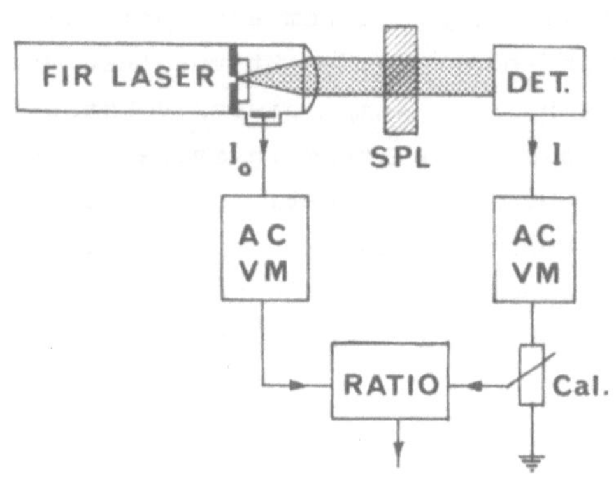

Abb. 3 /3/

und I dahinter zugleich gemessen werden.Ein Quotientenbildner (RATIO) hinter den beiden Wechselspannungsmeßgeräten (ACVM) gibt direkt die Transmission der Probe an. Die Eichung erfolgt dadurch, daß mit dem Potentiometer (CAL) der Quotientenbildnerausgang auf 100% eingestellt wird. - Das Mikrofonsignal läßt sich auch zur Regulierung der Laserleistung benutzen.

2.2. Laserleistungsüberwachung durch modulierte thermische Expansion.

Die bisher gezeigte Ausführungsform des transparenten Detektors erfordert immer zwei optische Komponenten, weil der Nachweis der periodisch erzeugten Wärme über die Druckmodulation im abgeschlossenen Gasvolumen erfolgt. Die Temperaturmodulation der optischen Komponenten läßt sich aber auch über die damit verbundene thermische Ausdehnung nachweisen, etwa durch Dehnungsmeßstreifen oder Piezokeramik /6,7/. In dem Fall kann jede optische Komponente - Fenster, Spiegel, Linse etc - in einem modulierten Lichtstrahl zur verlustlosen Überwachung der Strahlungsleistung verwendet werden.Mit Piezokeramik, die hinter einen Umlenkspiegel geklebt war, wurde das Ergebnis in Abb. 4 erhalten /7/. Bei 10 W Leistung des CO_2 Lasers ist das Signal- Rausch- Verhältnis praktisch konstant etwa 5×10^3 bei 1 Hz Bandbreite zwischen 10 Hz und 1 KHz, die rausch-äquivalente Leistung ist also etwa 1 mW.

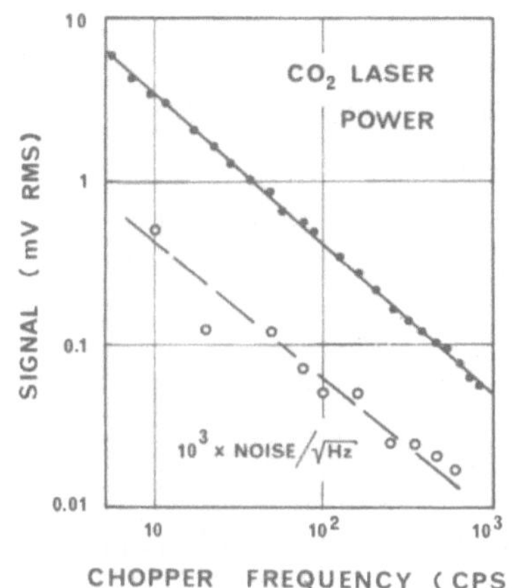

Abb. 4 /7/

Im Vergleich zur Zelle mit dem Mikrofon hat diese Anordnung den Nachteil, daß die Eichung der Anzeige gegen Verschmutzung der Komponenten empfindlich ist, bei der Zelle trägt nämlich nur die an den geschützten Innenseiten der Komponenten erzeugte Temperaturmodulation zum Signal bei. Andererseits liegt ein erheblicher Vorteil darin, daß diese Anordnung nicht nur besonders robust und zuverlässig ist, sondern auch sehr einfach, weil man nur ein Stück Piezokeramik hinter einem Spiegel oder am Rand einer Linse zu befestigen braucht, um an einem üblichen Meßgerät ein leistungsproportionales Signal zu bekommen.

Literatur

/1/ J. G. Parker: Appl. Opt. <u>12</u>, 2974 (1973)

/2/ M. J. Adams, B. C. Beedle, G. F. Kirkbright: Analyst <u>102</u>, 281 (1977)

/3/ G. Busse, H. Schütz: Infrared Physics <u>19</u>, 313 (1979)

/4/ A. Rosencwaig, A. Gersho: J. Appl. Phys. <u>47</u>, 64 (1976)

/5/ Pat. Nr. P 29 08 157.0 angemeldet

/6/ A. Hordvik, H. Schlossberg: Appl. Opt. <u>16</u>, 101 (1977)

/7/ G. Busse, S. Perkowitz: Proc. 4th Internat. Conf. on Infrared and Near-mm Waves, Miami/ USA 1979

Autorenverzeichnis

Aus, H.M.   Institut für Virologie und Immunbiologie der
                                 Universität Würzburg,Versbacher Str. 7, 8700 Würzburg

Bastiaans, M.J.   Technische Hogeschool Eindhoven, Afdeling der
                                 Elektrotechniek, Postbus 513, 5600 MB Eindhoven,
                                 The Netherlands

Becker, H.   Fachbereich 7 der Universität/Gesamthochschule Essen,
                                 Universitätsstr. 5, 4300 Essen1, Postfach6843

Beer, J.   Fachbereich Physik der Universität/Gesamthochschule
                                 Siegen, Postfach 21 02 09, 5900 Siegen

Bley, H.   Lehrstuhl für Informatik 5 der Universität Erlangen-
                                 Nürnberg, Martensstr. 3, 8520 Erlangen

Brennecke, R.   Abteilung für Kinderkardiologie und Biomedizinische
                                 Technik der Universität Kiel, Schwanenweg 20,
                                 2300 Kiel 1

Busse, G.   Zentrale Wissenschaftliche Einrichtung Physik,
                                 Hochschule der Bundeswehr München, 8014 Neubiberg

Butt, R.   Drittes Phys. Institut der Universität Göttingen,
                                 Bürgerstr. 42, 3400 Göttingen

Drechsel, H.   Fachbereich Physik der Universität/Gesamthochschule
                                 Siegen, Postfach 21 02 09, 5900 Siegen

Fercher, A.F.   Fachbereich 7 - Physik der Universität/Gesamthoch-
                                 schule Essen, Postfach 6843, 4300 Essen 1

Hahne, H.J.   Abteilung für Kinderkardiologie und Biomedizinische
                                 Technik der Universität Kiel, Schwanenweg 20,
                                 2300 Kiel 1

Harms, H.J.   Institut für Virologie und Immunbiologie der
                                 Universität Würzburg, Versbacher Str. 7, 8700 Würzburg

Haussmann, G.   Lehrstuhl für Theoretische Nachrichtentechnik und
                                 Informationsverarbeitung der Universität Hannover,
                                 Callinstr. 32, 3000Hannover

Heinrich, W.   Fachbereich Physik der Universität/Gesamthochschule
                                 Siegen, Postfach 21 02 09, 5900 Siegen

Heintzen, P.H.   Abteilung für Kinderkardiologie und Biomedizinische
                                 Technik der Universität Kiel, Schwanenweg 20,
                                 2300 Kiel 1

Herrmann, G.   Institut für Medizinische Informatik und System-
                                 forschung der Gesellschaft für Strahlen- und Umwelt-
                                 forschung mbH, Arabellastr. 4/III, 8000 München 81

Hinsch, K.   Fachbereich IV der Universität Oldenburg
                                 Postfach 2503 , 2900 Oldenburg

Jüptner, W.

Bremer Institut für angewandte Strahlentechnik,
2800 Bremen

Kanstad, S.O.

Central Institute for Industrial Research, P.O. Box
350 Blindern, Oslo 3 - Norway

Kreis, Th.

Institut für Meßtechnik im Maschinenbau der Technisch.
Universität Hannover, Welfengarten 1,
3000 Hannover 1

Kreitlow, H.

Institut für Meßtechnik im Maschinenbau der Technisch.
Universität Hannover, Welfengarten 1,
3000 Hannover 1

Laeri, F.

Institut für Angewandte Physik der Universität Bern,
Sidlerstr. 5, 3012 Bern, Schweiz

Liedtke, C.-E.

Theoretische Nachrichtentechnik und Informationsver-
arbeitung der Technischen Universität Hannover,
Callinstr. 32, 3000 Hannover

Linge, H.

Max-Planck-Institut für experimentelle Medizin,
Hermann-Rein-Str. 3, 3400 Göttingen

Merkle, F.

Institut für Angewandte Physik I der Universität
Heidelberg, Albert-Oberle-Str. 3-5, 6900 Heidelberg

Niemann, W.

Lehrstuhl für Informatik 5 (Mustererkennung)
Universität Erlangen-Nürnberg, Martensstr. 3,
8520 Erlangen

Nordal, P.E.

Central Institute for Industrial Research, P.O. Box
350 Blindern, Oslo 3 - Norway

Parry, G.

Royal Signals and Radar Establishment, Malvern, Worcs
England

Pichler, H.

Institut für Allgemeine Elektrotechnik der
Technischen Universität, Gußhausstr. 27-29,
1040 Wien - Austria

Pipper, J.

Fachbereich Physik der Universität-Gesamthochschule
Siegen, Postfach 21 02 09, 5900 Siegen 21

Pöppl, S.J.

Institut für Medizinische Informatik und Systemforschung der Gesellschaft für Strahlen- und Umweltforschung mbH, Arabellastr. 4/III, 8000 München 81

Prammer, M.

Institut für Allgemeine Elektrotechnik der
Technischen Universität, Gußhausstr. 27-29,
1040 Wien - Austria

Reuter, B.

Gesellschaft für Strahlen- und Umweltforschung mbH,
8042 Neuherberg

Ricker, Th.

AEG-TELEFUNKEN, Forschnungsinstitut Ulm,
Postfach 1730, 7900 Ulm/Donau

Rüter, A.

Institut für Virologie und Immunbiologie der Universität Würzburg, Versbacher Str. 7, 8700 Würzburg

Schedy, H.   Institut für Medizinische Informatik und Systemforschung der Gesellschaft für Strahlen- und Umwelt-
forschung mbH, Arabellastr. 4/III, 8000 München 81

Schedy, M.   Institut für Medizinische Informatik und Systemforschung der Gesellschaft für Strahlen- und Umwelt-
forschung mbH, Arabellastr. 4/III, 8000 München 81

Schneeberger, B.   Institut für Angewandte Physik der Universität Bern,
Sidlerstr. 5, 3012 Bern - Schweiz

Schöfer, B.   Fachbereich Physik der Universität-Gesamthochschule
Siegen, Postfach 21 02 09, 5900 Siegen 21

Schröder, R.   Cambridge Instrument Company GmbH, Postfach 1404,
4600 Dortmund 1

Schucht, R.   Fachbereich Physik der Universität-Gesamthochschule
Siegen, Postfach 21 02 09, 5900 Siegen 21

Tschudi, T.   Institut für Angewandte Physik der Universität Bern,
Sidlerstr. 5, 3012 Bern - Schweiz

Vöhringer, P.   Institut für Medizinische Optik der Universität
München, Barbarastr. 16/IV, 8000 München 40

Wittekind, D.   Anatomisches Institut der Universität Freiburg,
7800 Freiburg

Zarschizky, H.   Drittes Phys. Institut der Universität Göttingen,
Bürgerstr. 42-44, 3400 Göttingen

Zimmer, H.-G.   Max-Planck-Institut für experimentelle Medizin,
Neurochemie, Hermann-Rein-Str. 3, 3400 Göttingen

Lecture Notes in Computer Science

Vol. 22: Formal Aspects of Cognitive Processes. Proceedings 1972. Edited by T. Storer and D. Winter. V, 214 pages. 1975.

Vol. 23: Programming Methodology. 4th Informatik Symposium, IBM Germany Wildbad, September 25–27, 1974. Edited by C. E. Hackl. VI, 501 pages. 1975.

Vol. 24: Parallel Processing. Proceedings 1974. Edited by T. Feng. VI, 433 pages. 1975.

Vol. 25: Category Theory Applied to Computation and Control. Proceedings 1974. Edited by E. G. Manes. X, 245 pages. 1975.

Vol. 26: GI-4. Jahrestagung, Berlin, 9.–12. Oktober 1974. Herausgegeben im Auftrag der GI von D. Siefkes. IX, 748 Seiten. 1975.

Vol. 27: Optimization Techniques. IFIP Technical Conference. Novosibirsk, July 1–7, 1974. (Series: I.F.I.P. TC7 Optimization Conferences.) Edited by G. I. Marchuk. VIII, 507 pages. 1975.

Vol. 28: Mathematical Foundations of Computer Science. 3rd Symposium at Jadwisin near Warsaw. June 17–22, 1974. Edited by A. Blikle. VII, 484 pages. 1975.

Vol. 29: Interval Mathematics. Procedings 1975. Edited by K. Nickel. VI, 331 pages. 1975.

Vol. 30: Software Engineering. An Advanced Course. Edited by F. L. Bauer. (Formerly published 1973 as Lecture Notes in Economics and Mathematical Systems, Vol. 81) XII, 545 pages. 1975.

Vol. 31: S. H. Fuller, Analysis of Drum and Disk Storage Units. IX, 283 pages. 1975.

Vol. 32: Mathematical Foundations of Computer Science 1975. Proceedings 1975. Edited by J. Bečvář. X, 476 pages. 1975.

Vol. 33: Automata Theory and Formal Languages, Kaiserslautern, May 20–23, 1975. Edited by H. Brakhage on behalf of GI. VIII, 292 Seiten. 1975.

Vol. 34: GI – 5. Jahrestagung, Dortmund 8.–10. Oktober 1975. Herausgegeben im Auftrag der GI von J. Mühlbacher. X, 755 Seiten. 1975.

Vol. 35: W. Everling, Exercises in Computer Systems Analysis. (Formerly published 1972 as Lecture Notes in Economics and Mathematical Systems, Vol. 65) VIII, 184 pages. 1975.

Vol. 36: S. A. Greibach, Theory of Program Structures: Schemes, Semantics, Verification. XV, 364 pages. 1975.

Vol. 37: C. Böhm, λ-Calculus and Computer Science Theory. Proceedings 1975. XII, 370 pages. 1975.

Vol. 38: P. Branquart, J.-P. Cardinael, J. Lewi, J.-P. Delescaille, M. Vanbegin. An Optimized Translation Process and Its Application to ALGOL 68. IX, 334 pages. 1976.

Vol. 39: Data Base Systems. Proceedings, 5th Informatik Symposium, IBM Germany, Bad Homburg v. d. H., September 1975. Edited by H. Hasselmeier and W. G. Spruth. VI, 386 pages. 1976.

Vol. 40: Optimization Techniques. Modeling and Optimization in the Service of Man. Part 1. Proceedings, 7th IFIP Conference, Nice, September 1975. Edited by J. Cea. XIV, 854 pages. 1976.

Vol. 41: Optimization Techniques. Modeling and Optimization in the Service of Man. Part 2. Proceedings, 7th IFIP Conference, Nice, September 1975. Edited by J. Cea. XIV, 852 pages. 1976.

Vol. 42: J. E. Donahue: Complementary Definitions of Programming Language Semantics. VIII, 172 pages. 1976

Vol. 43: E. Specker, V. Strassen: Komplexität von Entscheidungsproblemen. Ein Seminar. VI, 217 Seiten. 1976.

Vol. 44: ECI Conference 1976. Proceedings of the 1st Conference of the European Cooperation in Informatics, Amsterdam, August 1976. Edited by K. Samelson. VIII, 322 pages. 1976.

Vol. 45: Mathematical Foundations of Computer Science 1976. Proceedings, 5th Symposium, Gdańsk, September 1976. Edited by A. Mazurkiewicz. XII, 606 pages. 1976.

Vol. 46: Language Hierarchies and Interfaces. International Summer School. Edited by F. L. Bauer and K. Samelson. X, 428 pages. 1976.

Vol. 47: Methods of Algorithmic Language Implementation. Edited by A. Ershov and C. H. A Koster. VIII, 351 pages. 1977.

Vol. 48: Theoretical Computer Science, Darmstadt, March 1977. Edited by H. Tzschach, H. Waldschmidt and H.-G. Walter on behalf of GI. VIII, 418 pages. 1977.

Vol. 49: Interactive Systems. Proceedings 1976. Edited by A. Blaser and C. Hackl. VI, 380 pages. 1976.

Vol. 50: A. C. Hartmann, A Concurrent Pascal Compiler for Minicomputers. VI, 119 pages. 1977.

Vol. 51: B. S. Garbow, Matrix Eigensystem Routines – Eispack Guide Extension. VIII, 343 pages. 1977.

Vol. 52: Automata, Languages and Programming. Fourth Colloquium, University of Turku, July 1977. Edited by A. Salomaa and M. Steinby. X, 569 pages. 1977.

Vol. 53: Mathematical Foundations of Computer Science. Proceedings 1977. Edited by J. Gruska. XII, 608 pages. 1977.

Vol. 54: Design and Implementation of Programming Languages. Proceedings 1976. Edited by J. H. Williams and D. A. Fisher. X, 496 pages. 1977.

Vol. 55: A. Gerbier, Mes premières constructions de programmes. XII, 256 pages. 1977.

Vol. 56: Fundamentals of Computation Theory. Proceedings 1977. Edited by M. Karpiński. XII, 542 pages. 1977.

Vol. 57: Portability of Numerical Software. Proceedings 1976. Edited by W. Cowell. VIII, 539 pages. 1977.

Vol. 58: M. J. O'Donnell, Computing in Systems Described by Equations. XIV, 111 pages. 1977.

Vol. 59: E. Hill, Jr., A Comparative Study of Very Large Data Bases. X. 140 pages. 1978.

Vol. 60: Operating Systems, An Advanced Course. Edited by R. Bayer, R. M. Graham, and G. Seegmüller. X. 593 pages. 1978.

Vol. 61: The Vienna Development Method: The Meta-Language. Edited by D. Bjørner and C. B. Jones. XVIII, 382 pages. 1978.

Vol. 62: Automata, Languages and Programming. Proceedings 1978. Edited by G. Ausiello and C. Böhm. VIII, 508 pages. 1978.

Vol. 63: Natural Language Communication with Computers. Edited by Leonard Bolc. VI, 292 pages. 1978.

Vol. 64: Mathematical Foundations of Computer Science. Proceedings 1978. Edited by J. Winkowski. X, 551 pages. 1978.

Vol. 65: Information Systems Methodology. Proceedings, 1978. Edited by G. Bracchi and P. C. Lockemann. XII, 696 pages. 1978.

Vol. 66: N. D. Jones and S. S. Muchnick, TEMPO: A Unified Treatment of Binding Time and Parameter Passing Concepts in Programming Languages. IX, 118 pages. 1978.

Vol. 67: Theoretical Computer Science, 4th GI Conference. Aachen, March 1979. Edited by K. Weihrauch. VII, 324 pages. 1979.

Vol. 68: D. Harel, First-Order Dynamic Logic. X. 133 pages. 1979.

Vol. 69: Program Construction. International Summer School. Edited by F. L. Bauer and M. Broy. VII. 651 pages. 1979.

Vol. 70: Semantics of Concurrent Computation. Proceedings 1979. Edited by G. Kahn. VI. 368 pages. 1979.

Vol. 71: Automata, Languages and Programming. Proceedings 1979. Edited by H. A. Maurer. IX. 684 pages. 1979.

Vol. 72: Symbolic and Algebraic Computation. Proceedings 1979. Edited by E. W. Ng. XV, 557 pages. 1979.

Vol. 73: Graph-Grammars and Their Application to Computer Science and Biology. Proceedings 1978. Edited by V. Claus, H. Ehrig and G. Rozenberg. VII, 477 pages. 1979.

Vol. 74: Mathematical Foundations of Computer Science. Proceedings 1979. Edited by J. Bečvář. IX, 580 pages. 1979.